TURNING POINTS

Your Career Decision-Making Guide

SECOND EDITION

DIANE DUCAT

LaGuardia Community College

Prentice
Hall

Upper Saddle River, New Jersey
Columbus, Ohio

Library of Congress Cataloging-in-Publication Data

Ducat, Diane Elizabeth
    Turning points : your career decision-making guide / Diane Ducat.—2nd ed.
      p. cm.
    Includes bibliographical references and index.
    ISBN 0-13-042190-1
    1. Vocational guidance—United States.   2. College students—Employment—United
States. I. Title.

HF5382.5.U5 D832 2002
650.14—dc21

2001050020

Vice President and Publisher: Jeffery W. Johnston
Senior Acquisitions Editor: Sande Johnson
Assistant Editor: Cecilia Johnson
Production Editor: Holcomb Hathaway
Design Coordinator: Diane C. Lorenzo
Cover Designer: Ali Mohrman
Cover Art: Linda Bronson/Artville
Production Manager: Pamela D. Bennett
Director of Marketing: Ann Davis
Director of Advertising: Kevin Flanagan
Marketing Manager: Christina Quadhamer
Marketing Assistant: Barbara Koontz

Author's Photo: James A. Whitaker
Illustrations: Adapted from Kenneth B. Smith

This book was set in Sabon by Aerocraft Charter Art Service. It was printed and
bound by Banta Book Group. The cover was printed by Phoenix Color Corp.

Pearson Education Ltd., *London*
Pearson Education Australia Pty. Limited, *Sydney*
Pearson Education Singapore Pte. Ltd.
Pearson Education North Asia Ltd., *Hong Kong*
Pearson Education Canada, Ltd., *Toronto*
Pearson Educación de Mexico, S.A. de C.V.
Pearson Education–Japan, *Tokyo*
Pearson Education Malaysia Pte. Ltd.
Pearson Education, *Upper Saddle River, New Jersey*

10 9 8
ISBN 0-13-042190-1

Contents

CHAPTER 3   Identifying Your Interests and Skills   49

CHAPTER 4   Gathering Information About Careers   73

CHAPTER 8   Finding a Place to Advance Your Career   179

CHAPTER 9   Finding a Job   203

CHAPTER 10   Making a Job Choice   237

PART III   MAKE YOUR EXPERIENCE COUNT   269

CHAPTER 11   How to Take Charge of Your Career   271

CHAPTER 12   How to Learn from Internships, College Jobs, and Extracurricular Activities   293

CHAPTER 13   How to Develop Your Career Network   315

CHAPTER 14   Reflections   333

Preface

Career decisions are among the most important choices you will ever make. Work plays an important part in shaping your lifestyle and contributes significantly to your overall life satisfaction. To engage in career planning is to concentrate on some of life's biggest questions: "What do I want to do?" "Who do I want to become?" "How will I earn my living?"

There are no ready-made, one-size-fits-all answers to these questions. Career planning is a creative endeavor. Each of you has a different set of concerns and a unique life situation, and each of you possesses a distinctive combination of values, interests, personality, and skills. This second edition of *Turning Points* is designed to respond to your individual needs and introduce you to career-planning techniques that will have lifelong advantages.

CAREER DILEMMAS

You want to choose wisely, because your choices will have very important consequences for your life. Yet there are so many issues to consider that it is natural to feel some uncertainty. Read over the list of questions below, and check the ones that are similar to questions you may have.

☐ Which career options really suit me the best?

☐ How can I balance my desire to advance my career with my family needs?

☐ Should I change direction or stay with what I have selected?

☐ Am I too much of a dreamer, never settling on any one direction?

☐ Is it a good idea to continue my education? Now or later? Full-time or part-time? Where can I get the time and money to go on with my education?

☐ What are the best career opportunities in the global marketplace? Which fields hold the most promise in the years ahead?

☐ What kinds of skills do employers want?

Now add any other questions that came to mind.

☐ _____

☐ _____

☐ _____

☐ _____

In this book I call such questions and concerns "career dilemmas" because they often involve difficult and perplexing issues—they are like puzzles. This book will help you define your own personal career dilemmas and provide you with a method for resolving them. You can become more confident about your future. You have made a substantial investment in higher education. Learning practical career-planning techniques helps to ensure that one major benefit of your efforts will be a selection of rewarding career options.

OVERVIEW OF THE CONTENTS

The scope of this book is comprehensive. Its 13 chapters encompass three major topics: (1) searching for information, (2) setting your career direction, and (3) making your experience count. Each of these topics corresponds to one of the three essential tasks—exploration, specification, and implementation—described by Donald Super in his pioneering work on career development.

Part I: Search for Information

This unit, consisting of Chapters 1–5, focuses on exploration tasks. You'll cover the kind of information you need to make good career choices and see whether an advanced degree or additional training is right for you. The purpose of these chapters is to help you conduct a self-assessment, gather information, and identify suitable career and educational options.

Part II: Set Your Direction

In this unit, I introduce a practical model of career decision making. You are encouraged to "Listen to Your Heart" and "Use Your Head." This balanced approach helps you consider your personal dreams, life circumstances, and economic goals. It also highlights the need to ponder external factors, such as workplace opportunities.

This unit, consisting of Chapters 6–10, engages you in setting your career direction. It addresses three important choices: selecting a college major, choosing a work setting, and making a job choice. It also teaches you effective job search tactics and vital job search skills, such as resume writing and interviewing.

Part III: Make Your Experience Count

Chapters 11–13 are devoted to strategies to advance your career while you are still in college. You'll learn how to test your career choices and increase your earning potential through internships, college jobs, and extracurricular activities. You'll become aware of the skills demanded by the workplace of the twenty-first century and the need for networking. This unit gives you a leg up in acquiring valuable career management skills before you graduate.

ACTIVITIES

Throughout the book you will find lots of hands-on activities to help you conduct a thorough self-assessment, conduct a job search, and gather information to make informed choices. Most of the research activities use a handy four-step "ASAP" (Ask–Search–Analyze–Plan) format to structure your information search. You'll be introduced to the best career-planning resources for college students, including Web sites, books, and magazines.

You'll also discover shorter exercises within chapters that will help you understand the major points, clarify your thoughts and ideas, and get you ready for the lengthier research and in-depth appraisal activities found at the ends of the chapters.

BENEFITS

Here is a sampling of some benefits that students have reported as a result of reading this book and completing the activities.

I found out how my career field fits my values and my goals. . . . I also had an opportunity to check if the major I chose was the right decision. I learned how to gather information about further education, . . . scholarships, and job opportunities.

I was able to focus more on my dilemmas and act upon them much more quickly.

I learned new information about myself, my career field and educational opportunities . . . I learned I would like to be my own boss someday. I want to open my own business and earn money for myself.

One dilemma was what to study. I thought of changing my major to accounting or computer science. . . . I found out about the profession of operations research analyst. . . . I can use my knowledge of computers, accounting, and economics all at the same time.

[I learned that] . . . it is very important to establish a network . . . or expand the one you already have. The larger the network, the better your chances of getting a job.

I found the ASAP [Ask–Search–Analyze–Plan] approach to be very useful in solving a dilemma. If I face a dilemma in the future, I will come up with a question, search for information, analyze my findings, and plan my next step. All the assignments . . . made us think about and analyze our *feelings*.

INSTRUCTOR'S MANUAL

An *Instructor's Manual* is available to help instructors and counselors adapt the book's topics and activities to their needs. Suggestions are provided for using the activities in the book in various settings: credit and noncredit courses, seminars, workshops, independent projects, and one-on-one counseling.

THE AUTHOR

Diane Ducat is a psychologist who has worked with college students for more than 25 years. Dr. Ducat is a professor at LaGuardia Community College in New York City, where she was a counselor before joining the faculty of LaGuardia's nationally acclaimed internship program.

Dr. Ducat has taught graduate courses in career counseling and has investigated managerial careers as a member of several interdisciplinary research teams. Her consulting activities center on executive coaching. She holds a master's degree in counselor education from the University of Florida and a Ph.D. in counseling psychology from Columbia University.

Acknowledgments

Throughout the long process of revising this book I have been sustained by the positive feedback from students who found the first edition useful, and by my friends, who have been supportive and understanding. Now that it is finally finished I want to thank the colleagues, friends, and students whose contributions throughout its development have been so significant and valuable.

I received substantial assistance from my colleagues in LaGuardia Community College's Division of Cooperative Education, especially Acting Dean Catherine Farrell and Dean Paul Saladino; my professional peers Karen Anderson, Manny Ayala, Judy Bieber, James Cantwell, Mohammad Fakhari, Michael Frank, Patricia Garrett, Joan Heitner, Patrick James, David Johnson, Doreen Kolomechuk, Paul Levine, Helen Perry, Stacy Perry, Cheryl Powell, Migdalia Reyes, Deborah Robinson, Marie Sacino, Susan Sanchirico, Lucy Sardell, Michele Stewart, Caren Treiser, Theresa Uruburu, Andrew Wainer, Jeffrey Weintraub, Francine White, and John Wolovich; and all the seminar instructors who tested materials—particularly Vincent Banrey, Eleanor DiPalma, Myra Fasner, Patricia Howard, Margo Turkel, and Paula Zimmerman.

I have often discussed the career development of college students with my friend and colleague Pierrina Andritsi of Counseling Services. I tested my ideas on her and sought her advice countless times, relying on her knowledge and experience, intelligence, and intuition.

I also want to thank several other LaGuardia colleagues who provided critical input and support at various times: John Chaffee, Robert Durfey, Irwin Feifer, Judith Gazzola, Ruth Lebovitz, Janet Lieberman, Daniel Lynch, Gilbert Muller, Leo Newball, Jane Schulman, Barry Silverman, and Dorrie Williams.

LaGuardia students are among the most culturally diverse in the nation, and my life has been enriched through my work with them. Many of the book's student profiles are derived from my experiences with them. Other profiles come from interviews with LaGuardia graduates who have gone on to baccalaureate and graduate programs.

I want to thank the following students, who gave their permission to use excerpts from their activities: Michele Bologna, Yanique Best, Jolanta Brzuchnalska, Shannon Choy, Luis Coronell, Carin Diep, Valeria Fernandez, Unkyoung Lee, Liliana Ochoa, Isak Rafailov, Leticia Rodriguez, Jaime Taveras, Joanne Vega, and Tatyana Zlotnikova.

I would also like to thank Jose Apolya, Monica Arboleda, Susan Denninger, George Douramanis, Shahana Koslofsky, and Rafael Molina for their stories.

Since 1985 I have had the good fortune to be associated with the Center for Creative Leadership, a nonprofit organization dedicated to leadership development. The center's groundbreaking studies provided the foundation for the chapter on learning from work experience. My knowledge of career development has grown through my contacts with the center's researchers, trainers, and program participants.

I have had abundant encouragement from friends, colleagues, and family around the country: Judy Aanstad, principal of Aanstad and Associates; Caroline Manuele Adkins, Professor Emerita of Counselor Education at Hunter College; Irene Dombeck, Counselor/Faculty, Anoka Ramsey Community College; Edward Hattauer, Director of Counseling at Northeastern University; teachers and members of the Society for Nanlaoshu; Patricia Imbimbo, Director of the Career Development Center at Baruch College; and Marianne Schubert, Director of the University Counseling Center at Wake Forest University.

I was fortunate to work with Cecilia Gardner during the writing and the revision of the text and Instructor's Manual. She has been patient and supportive. Her editorial suggestions have done wonders to make the text clearer.

I wish to thank Kenneth B. Smith, who conceptualized some of the book's creative illustrations, which serve to enliven the text and reinforce major concepts.

I received able help with the text preparation from Gloria Deschamps, Marzena Jankowski, Lisa Leventer, and Aarkieva Smith.

I want to thank Prentice Hall Senior Editor Sande Johnson and Assistant Editor Cecilia Johnson for their help and support during this revision.

I appreciate the careful attention that the following reviewers gave my proposal and manuscript. I incorporated many of their thoughtful suggestions into the text. They are Kara L. Craig, University of Southern Mississippi; Rita Delude, New Hampshire Community Technical College at Nashua; Susan Ekberg, Webster University; Gary Kramer, Brigham Young University; Patrick Schutz, Mesa State College; Robert C. Spier, Hartnell College; and Nancy P. Thompson, University of Georgia.

This book is dedicated to Roger A. Myers, a wise and perceptive teacher, Richard March Hoe Professor Emeritus, Teachers College, Columbia University.

PART I

Search for Information

CHAPTER 1

Exploring Your Career Options Step by Step

The most powerful way we know for discovering how to solve a hard problem is to find a method that splits it into several smaller ones, each of which can be solved separately.
—Marvin Minsky,
The Society of the Mind

THE NEED TO DECIDE

Y ou could be anywhere—at a family reunion, your niece's birthday party, your cousin's wedding, or just talking with your older sisters in the kitchen—when someone turns to you and asks, "What do you want to do after college?" Answering that question these days isn't easy. Powerful forces such as globalization and technological innovations are changing how work is organized and where jobs are located. You have more options but fewer certainties about the future than your parents had. Even if you have a career direction in mind, doubts often linger. Will I *really* like what I've chosen? Will I succeed at it?

It is easy to avoid thinking about career decisions when you are busy with classes, studying, and tests. But no matter how busy you are, choosing your career direction is a decision that just won't go away.

This book is designed to help you set a career direction with confidence. This first chapter is essential to getting started. It will guide you through a process that gets all your current career concerns on the table. Then, in the following chapters of this book, you will learn how to deal with them one by one.

The best way to get started is to lay the proper groundwork. To make the best use of the chapters in this unit, you need to understand your particular career dilemma. This understanding is vital to your later success.

CAREER DILEMMAS

Your *career dilemma* is a term used in this book to describe the tangled set of interrelated occupational and educational issues that you face. When problems are presented in textbooks, the hard work of describing them has often been done for you. When you first look at your own career dilemma, however, it is often murky and ill defined. Often you are unsure what defining your dilemma entails.

To get you started defining your own career dilemma, let's consider the types of dilemmas that college students who have previously used the material in this book have identified. They fall into two main areas: *career path dilemmas* and *education path dilemmas*.[1] As you read, underline those italicized phrases that reflect elements of your own career dilemma.

Career Path Dilemmas

Career path dilemmas are characterized by some doubts about your career direction. They occur because you are missing some crucial pieces of information. You may need just one piece of additional information or several; each student is different.

One piece that is often missing is how to match your interests to specific occupations or industries. For example, you may say, "I like international relations, but don't know what types of jobs match my interests," or "I want to own my own business someday, but I am unsure what kind of business I want to start." You are uncertain about *which job settings match your interests or goals*.

Many students are concerned about whether they are *being practical*. You want to become an artist or a doctor, for example, but you wonder, "Can I make it as an artist?" or "I don't know if I could get into medical school."

You may be struggling with issues of *balance*. One kind of balance is the focused/open balance—that is, whether to focus on a career goal or to leave the decision open. Some students ask themselves, "Will my current focus close off other options later?" For example, "I want to be a computer programmer, but I don't want to close out other options such as teaching." Others have the opposite concern: "Do I need to focus now?" You may be asking yourself, "Should I eliminate some options from my list and concentrate on just one or two?"

A related concern is the work/life balance. Maybe the work you like will make too many demands and leave too little time for other interests. You want to feel more comfortable about the *fit between your career direction and your other life commitments.*

Frequently students report that they lack *job search skills.* You know that you will be looking for a job after graduation, but you don't know how to generate promising job leads, pick the kind of organization and industry that suits you best, write an effective resume, or interview well.

Education Path Dilemmas

Education path dilemmas often involve difficult choices about *whether to obtain further education* and *what to study.*

Education path dilemmas may also involve addressing such questions as *when to get further education, whether to choose part-time or full-time study,* and *which school or program is best for you.*

ACTIVITY 1.1   YOUR QUESTIONS AND CONCERNS

Look back on the phrases you underlined as you read about the various career path and education path dilemmas. Are your concerns primarily in the career path area or the education path area? Many students find that they have concerns in both areas. List your areas of concern.

_____

_____

_____

_____

_____

_____

Don't become alarmed if you discover you have many questions. This chapter shows you how identifying your dilemma clearly and specifically will enable you to search for the right kinds of information to solve it. And you will learn an easy way to organize any research you need to do.

The real problem arises if you don't take the time to identify all the elements of your career dilemma. This is where many students first encounter difficulties.

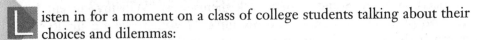

DESCRIBE YOUR DILEMMA CLEARLY AND SPECIFICALLY

Listen in for a moment on a class of college students talking about their choices and dilemmas:

- Christopher is the most confident. "I don't have a dilemma. I want a career in real estate. I believe that I can make a great deal of money in that field."

- Sierra says, "I like to write, so I'm going to be an English teacher. My dilemma is, Can I get a job teaching English?"

- Kevin claims, "I want to own my own company. I have an idea for a successful business. My career dilemma is, How will I pay for my college education?"

- John, Stephan, and Amanda believe they share the same dilemma: They are all questioning whether an engineering career is right for them.

- Kim volunteers, "My uncle said that the health care field is a good career choice. Everyone needs health care, especially senior citizens. My career dilemma is that I find science difficult."

These statements reflect very fundamental forces: the desire to be somebody, to make loved ones proud, and to have a better life—and not to waste time or money getting there. These goals spring from the depths of the students' hearts. We can admire their sincerity and motivation. However, as you will soon see, they are all unaware of what it takes to make an informed career choice. The trouble begins with the way they state their dilemmas. Their statements are too limited and too vague.

To lay the proper foundation for resolving your career dilemma, you must state it clearly and specifically. Many students' ideas about their career dilemmas are in a chaotic state. Bits and pieces surface in their minds, but it is easy to ignore these thoughts and focus on immediate responsibilities. Describing the dilemma aloud or, even better, writing it down is essential to capture its exact elements. However, stating your dilemma clearly and specifically is not always easy.

Common Pitfalls

There are several common pitfalls in describing career dilemmas.

"I don't think I have a dilemma."

Some students don't even realize that they have a dilemma. For example, Christopher has identified real estate as his career goal. He feels completely satisfied because he knows people can make big money in real estate.

Let's dig a bit deeper, though. Is Christopher interested in *commercial* or *residential* real estate? Is he interested in selling private homes in the suburbs or managing commercial rentals in a city? Does he want to invest in real estate? If so, where would he get the money? What kind of education is best? Does he need a license or certification? Is a four-year degree necessary? What personal qualifications are essential for success in this field? These few questions are sufficient to indicate that more information is needed.

Christopher's Career Dilemma	**CASE 1.1**

FIRST VIEW

Christopher doesn't have a career dilemma because he knows what he wants to do:

I want to go into real estate and make a great deal of money.

REVISED VIEW

Christopher's dilemma (stated as clear and specific questions):

I want to go into real estate and make a great deal of money. What are some career options in real estate? What are the educational and licensing requirements? Do I have the personal qualities that lead to success in this field?

"Isn't my real goal out of reach?"

Sometimes students are afraid to state their real dilemma because they believe (or have been told by others) that pursuing what truly interests them is too risky or impractical. Sierra said, "I have decided to become an English teacher." When she was questioned about her interest, she said that she wanted to be an English teacher because it was a clear and secure choice. However, her actual interest is in writing, not teaching.

Sierra's dilemma is that she is afraid to pursue her true interest because she lacks information about how she could build a career based on that interest. She needs to learn more about writing careers.

CASE 1.2   *Sierra's Career Dilemma*

FIRST VIEW

Avoiding the real issue:

What does it take to be an English teacher?

REVISED VIEW

Truthfully stating the situation:

I like to write, but I don't know what occupations would use my interest in writing. It is important for me to have a career in which I can help other people. I have substantial experience in the field of education. However, in my job as an assistant teacher, I notice that I don't like to work with children every day. What I really like is to design programs that improve educational practices. I also like to write poetry and stories.

Now Sierra has a much clearer description of her real career dilemma because she has had the guts to be truthful with herself. She has stopped ignoring her true interest, which is writing, not teaching.

"There is only one obstacle in my way."

Many students focus only on the short-term problems and constraints in their lives and miss the big picture. For example, Kevin has focused on his need for money to stay in college. While this issue is crucial, Kevin is overlooking another part of his dilemma: his need to go beyond having a good idea for a successful business and obtain more information about owning and operating his own company.

Kevin's Career Dilemma

FIRST VIEW

Focusing only on narrow, immediate concerns:

I need money for college.

REVISED VIEW

Taking long-term as well as short-term concerns into consideration:

I want information about how I can pay for a college degree. I also need information about what it takes to own and operate a business. What skills are required? What majors are best? What does it take to succeed as a business owner?

CONSIDER YOUR LIFE SITUATION

A good technique in describing your dilemma is to provide as many details as you can about your personal and family situation.

"Should I become an engineer?"

To illustrate, let's return to Amanda, John, and Stephan. They all had the same initial description of their career dilemmas. Compare that first view with the revised versions to see what a difference personal and family details make in clarifying the individual's situation.

Amanda's, John's, and Stephan's Career Dilemmas

FIRST VIEW

A career dilemma with life situation details missing:

I am interested in engineering, but I don't know whether engineering is the right career for me.

AMANDA'S REVISED VIEW

Details about life situation provided:

I am an 18-year-old single student. I do well academically. My boyfriend and college professors are encouraging me to consider engineering and to apply for scholarships, while my parents and some friends seem surprised at my choice. My dilemma is the need to sort out my personal goals and identify my interests and values. I want to find out if a career in engineering would be right for me.

JOHN'S REVISED VIEW

Details about life situation provided:

I am married and have a full-time union job parking cars at a lot where I get big tips from wealthy customers. My wife works, too, but is thinking about returning to school. We want children, too. Financially, we have a comfortable life, but my work is boring and I know it won't lead anywhere. As a high school student I was unfocused. I joined the Air Force and liked the airplane maintenance training I received. I admired the engineers and feel that engineering will provide more stimulating work and more opportunities. I'm not sure which engineering specialty would be best. My dilemma is selecting the right major and balancing my career goals with my wife's desire to get more education. Should I quit my full-time job to finish faster so we can concentrate on her education? Should she quit her job and start college now while I attend part-time? We would both like to live nearer to a wilderness area. Should we move now or later? Before we move, how can I find out about job availability for engineers in the new location?

STEPHAN'S REVISED VIEW

Details about life situation provided:

I am 33, married, with two children, and I work full-time. Although I was trained as a civil engineer in my country, I had to start all over when I arrived in the United States three years ago. I selected computer repair as my major because the preparation only takes two years. I like computer repair, but I still want to become an engineer. My dilemma, clearly and specifically stated, is that I feel that I am too old to continue to pursue my chosen career. I have too many responsibilities to quit my job. I don't think I can consider a four-year degree because it takes too long to obtain by going to school part-time. My dream is to become an engineer, but can I make this dream come true?

Notice that an interest in engineering unites these three students, yet their dilemmas are different, because their life situations are different. Each of them faces unique issues in deciding whether or not to pursue an engineering career.

Looking closely at your life situation, as the students did in the examples above, provides you with the opportunity to identify personal factors that will influence your career future. It requires you to think about the various life roles you play, and what effect they will have on your decision making. Consider the full range of your commitments: to a spouse or partner, children, parents, and extended family.

You may also feel that your family situation is a less important factor than some other role, such as community member, or a particular leisure activity, sport, hobby, or religious practice. You may want to invest more time in that role or activity and to let your work life take a less central position.

You may also need to take into account other aspects of your life situation. For example, you may be supported by your family emotionally and financially. If so, such support is an important aspect of your career dilemma because it means you have some positive factors working for you. You may face the opposite situation: your family may discourage you, may be unable to provide financial support, or both. Such constraints make your dilemma more difficult.

ACTIVITY 1.2   YOUR LIFE SITUATION

Describe how your commitment to various roles (e.g., parent, caregiver to elderly parents, single father, self-supporting student) and other life goals might influence the upcoming career and educational decisions you are facing. Identify the sources of support and any constraints that you must take into account.

_____

_____

_____
_____
_____
_____
_____
_____

Identify Internal and External Obstacles

Obstacles are hurdles. You can't make much career headway unless you recognize the kinds of hurdles you will face. Once you have identified them, you can begin to devise strategies to get over them so that they don't trip you up. It is helpful to think of obstacles as being of two kinds: internal and external.

Internal obstacles are those aspects of ourselves that get in the way of our success. They include, for example, self-destructive habits and negative attitudes, such as poor time management, procrastination, and lack of confidence. Remember Sierra, our would-be writer? Sierra finally realized she had a big internal obstacle. Here is her description: "My internal obstacle is fear. I am unsure if I have what it takes to succeed as a writer."

Kim, who is interested in health careers, identified shyness as her internal obstacle. It is hard for her to meet new people or to speak up in a public setting. She realizes that this trait is limiting in any career and that she is going to have to overcome her shyness to some extent. Kevin, whose goal is to own his own business, acknowledges that he does not speak up in public either, because he is embarrassed about his accent. He realizes that he is going to have to improve his oral communication skills.

External obstacles are problems related to our life circumstances that have the potential to derail our plans for the future unless we deal with them. Sierra has to surmount some external obstacles. She is going to have to find more reliable child care for her eight-year-old son or she will have to stop school. Kevin, as we already know, identified the need to finance his education as a significant obstacle. Chris, whose goal is a career in real estate, has carpal tunnel syndrome. He has to limit the time he spends at the computer keyboard or his wrists and arms ache. He needs to find out what accommodations are available so that his condition does not worsen.

YOUR INTERNAL AND EXTERNAL OBSTACLES	ACTIVITY 1.3

Identify the internal and external obstacles that you face.

_____
_____
_____
_____
_____

Now that you have examined your life situation and identified your internal and external obstacles, you are ready to make your first statement of your career dilemma. The purpose of this attempt is to get you thinking more deeply about your unique situation.

YOUR CAREER DILEMMA

As you describe your dilemma, write down all the questions, issues, and concerns that you can think of. Let your thoughts flow freely. Your main goal here is to be honest with yourself.

_____

_____

_____

_____

_____

_____

_____

Don't worry if you are unable to capture your career dilemma in full detail on this try. The important point is that you've gotten started. The process of writing it down helps to stimulate your thinking and clarify the important issues. You will have an opportunity to refine your statement of your career dilemma at the beginning of Activity 1.5, Taking Stock of Your Situation.

Once you begin looking at your career dilemma more carefully, your questions naturally increase. You need information. To progress in an orderly fashion, making sure that your information search is comprehensive yet efficient, it is useful to get an overview of the types of information that are vital to making sound career and education decisions.

A HANDY WAY TO ORGANIZE THE KINDS OF INFORMATION YOU NEED

Three different types of information will help you make informed career choices. Think about these types of information as belonging in different databases. This is a handy way to organize the information that is vital to making sound career and education decisions.

Set Up Three Databases

Database #1 consists of information about your personal identity. Database #2 incorporates information about careers. Database #3 covers information about colleges and graduate training. Within each large database you will find three or four smaller sections, each representing some important factor to consider. Table 1.1 provides an overview of the three databases.

Personal Identity	Career	College and Graduate School	TABLE 1.1
Values	Nature of the work	Nature of academic programs	*Overview of the three databases.*
Personality	Entry requirements	Admission requirements	
Interests	Rewards and benefits	School profile and student body characteristics	
Skills	Outlook for the future	Cost and financial aid	

Each database will be briefly described now. You will learn more about the personal identity database in Chapters 2 and 3, the career database in Chapter 4, and the college and graduate school database in Chapter 5.

Database #1: Personal Identity Information

Most people don't realize that a "good job" is like a good article of clothing; it must fit the person who wears it. Something that fits one person perfectly is completely wrong for another. Identifying your values, skills, and interests is an important way to find a career that fits you.

Let's look again at Sierra. An important part of her personal identity is that she likes to write. She is clear about one factor in the personal identity database: her interests. Acknowledging a major interest is a good place to start. However, her interests are just one part of Sierra's personal identity. She also needs to consider what she values and what skills she has. These other aspects of her personal identity database are equally important to consider.

Information about yourself helps you to clarify sources of satisfaction. You come to understand your gifts and dreams. As you obtain information about your personal identity, you will come to form a clearer picture of yourself. You will see who you are and who you want to become.

Database #2: Career Information

Kim is leaning toward a career in health care because she envisions many job openings in this area as the population ages. She is ignoring other equally important sections of the career database: the nature of the work, the entry requirements, and the rewards and benefits. Kim needs information about each of the factors in the career database so that she can compare different options within the health field. How is an occupational therapist different from a physical therapist? What is the role of a physician's assistant? She needs a full and realistic picture of different occupations in the health care field.

Database #3: College and Graduate School Information

Students like Kevin, who wants to have his own business, worry about whether they can afford further education. Cost is indeed an important factor to consider. Often, however, students do not investigate all the ways to pay for an education, and select a college solely on the basis of cost. They overlook other factors that belong in the college and graduate school database, such as the college's entry requirements, the characteristics of its student body, and academic information, such as what majors it offers.

If you are a four-year college student, you may be wondering if you need to consider an advanced degree. You may think that your career direction requires more education than a bachelor's degree, but you may be unsure about the details. Gathering information from the college and graduate school information database will help clarify your next steps.

Whether to transfer to a four-year college is a decision that many community college students face. Even if you do not plan to transfer, examining information about four-year colleges will help you understand the key factors to consider when investing in further education. You may think about on-the-job training programs, distance-learning courses, or continuing education in the same way that you might consider a transfer to a four-year college.

Use All the Factors in All the Databases

You typically need to search more than one database. Kim, who focused on the career database, was ignoring the personal identity database. She finds science difficult and boring, which is a statement about her interests and skills. This is important information, because the preparation for most health careers requires many science courses. Kim runs the risk of making an unwise choice based on partial information.

Sierra made the opposite mistake. She focused on her writing interests (which is information about her personal identity), but ignored information about careers. Similarly, Kevin focused only on the college and graduate school database and ignored the need to understand more about his career options and about his personal identity.

Information-poor decisions frequently lead to failure, blind alleys, and the surrender of dreams. It is hard to keep putting your heart into a job once you have discovered, too late, that you find it unfulfilling. It is heartbreaking to train for a certain type of work only to discover that it will soon become obsolete. Using information from all three databases is a way to be thorough, not superficial. Using all three databases allows you to look inward at yourself and simultaneously to look outward at your career and educational options.

TAKING STOCK OF YOUR INFORMATION NEEDS

The process of clearly and specifically describing your dilemma inevitably reveals that you need more information. You probably know some kinds of information that would be helpful, but you may be overlooking the fact that you need other types of information as well. You need to take stock of your dilemma in order to make a thorough appraisal of the types of information you lack.

At the end of this chapter you will find Activity 1.5, Taking Stock of Your Situation. This activity lets you pinpoint the exact kinds of information you need to solve your career dilemma. Take a few minutes to complete it, either now or after you finish reading the chapter. This is an extremely valuable use of a few minutes of your time. It will raise your personal awareness, and you will begin to understand your own information needs.

The process of describing your dilemma and taking stock of your situation is significant because it provides the groundwork for solving every career problem. You understand that you have a dilemma. You have the courage to be honest with yourself and have made the effort to be clear and specific in describing your dilemma. Taking stock means taking a thorough look at the kinds of information searches that will be helpful in solving your dilemma. The next major section of the chapter introduces a way to make your search efficient and effective.

ASK, SEARCH, ANALYZE, PLAN (ASAP): A POWERFUL WAY TO CONDUCT YOUR INFORMATION SEARCHES

Some people place so much faith in information that they believe it can actually tell them what to do. They decide, "I'll go to the library," or "I'll ask my uncle." This approach is like going to the grocery store and hoping that you will get a good meal by picking items blindfolded off the shelves.

In reality, you survey the grocery shelves and select the items that meet your particular needs and then transform them into a meal. In the same way, you have to select the best information from an abundant supply and transform it into a meaningful array of knowledge that will help you solve your career dilemma.

This search process can loom as a difficult job if you lack a systematic approach. You will learn a simple way to break down your search into four steps: ask, search, analyze, and plan (see Figure 1.1). This systematic, sequential process allows you to extract the meaning of the information for your personal situation. First, you *ask* the right questions. Subsequent chapters will guide you in identifying the important questions for each of the three databases. Second, you *search* for the information, recording its sources. Third, you *analyze* your findings, digesting what you have discovered and using it to solve your dilemma. In this step you will compare options and list

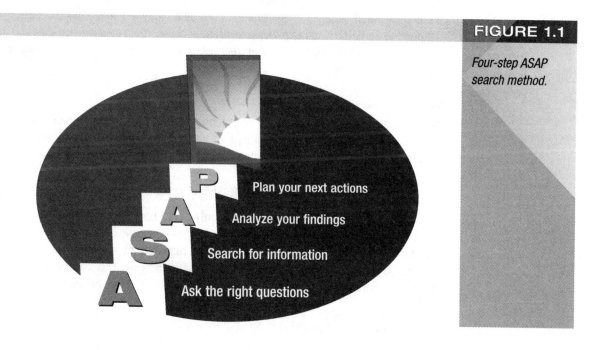

FIGURE 1.1

Four-step ASAP search method.

P — Plan your next actions

A — Analyze your findings

S — Search for information

A — Ask the right questions

their advantages and disadvantages. Fourth, you *plan* your next actions. You summarize your learning and identify next steps. Many times this means identifying new options to explore and additional sources of information to consult. The case below offers an example of this four-step method.

| CASE 1.5 | *The ASAP Approach to Solving a Career Dilemma* |

STEP 1. ASK THE RIGHT QUESTIONS

The specific purpose of this research is to find out if everyday people like me can be entrepreneurs and whether they need a lot of money to start a business. I elected to do this particular kind of research because one day I want to be an entrepreneur. . . . Is there a chance for me to be successful? My research began with *Black Enterprise*. The title of the article [I selected] is "Small Starts in Big Malls," by Tania Padgett.

STEP 2. SEARCH FOR INFORMATION

The first question I asked was, Do I need a lot of money to start up a business? According to the article, the answer to that question is no. The article explores how people can start their own business with $3,000–$8,000. "On average, it costs $150,000 in seed money to open a small retail store, plus an extra $7,000 a month for rent. But a pushcart costs only $3,000–$8,000 in start-up capital and an extra $1,000 a month for rent" (Padgett, p. 74). My next question was, Can anyone do this? Yes, was the response I received from this article. Even though it wasn't said in so many words, the article did describe people who didn't have a lot of money but were determined to make their dreams come true by becoming entrepreneurs. "Smith didn't let go of her dream. On the day the doors of the 225,000-square-foot underground Atlanta Mall opened, Smith was open for business, not as an owner of a retail store, but as a proprietor of a 6 ft. x 3 ft. pushcart selling Georgia nuts and pecans" (Padgett, p. 72).

STEP 3. ANALYZE YOUR FINDINGS

After doing some research, I learned that more and more people are opening their own businesses and are becoming successful entrepreneurs. What is so great about this research is that it shows you don't need . . . to be an intellectual to start a business. You just need to be determined to make your dreams come true. I also learned that you don't need to be a millionaire to be an entrepreneur, but you can be an entrepreneur and become a millionaire.

STEP 4. PLAN YOUR NEXT ACTIONS

My next actions would be to decide what kind of business I want and to develop a business plan. A business plan is an outline of what steps are needed in order for me to achieve my goals. . . . It also will allow me time to gather pertinent information . . . to become a successful business owner.

In a later assignment the student Yanique B. reflected:

I will approach any future dilemmas differently than I have in the past. By breaking the problem down into a question-and-answer form, I can develop questions designed to help me focus on my dilemma. By doing so, I can research the answers and make a decision based on the information and what's best for me. The career advancement technique I would employ would definitely be the ASAP information search.

—Yanique B.

AVOIDING THE HAZARDS
OF INTERNET SEARCHES

The Internet is now the first stop for most students in their quest for career-planning information. There are more than 10,000 career-related sites to choose from.[2] You can research career fields, occupations, and companies. The Internet is also a place to get information about colleges and universities, majors, and graduate programs. Other career-related uses of the Internet include searching for jobs, posting your resume, getting advice, and networking. Unlike a library, the Internet never closes. It provides access to a remarkable fund of information day and night, seven days a week.

Internet searches do have their challenges. They can be overwhelming, misleading, frustrating, or all three.

So that you won't be overwhelmed, this book provides you with activities that let you practice using the Internet to search for career information. In addition, you will find references to Web sites in almost every chapter. These sites have been chosen because of their usefulness for college students. The sites selected for inclusion are well established and include such reliable sources as the U.S. Department of Labor's *Occupational Outlook Handbook,* **stats.bls.gov/oco home.htm.** As you use this book, keep track of the sites you use. If you have your own computer, create a folder marked "Career" or "Turning Points." Whenever you come across a useful site, add it your folder. If you are using the school's computer, list your favorite sites in a separate log and keep it with this book.

Feeling frustrated during a search is common. Web sites continually move, change addresses, are acquired or merged, and go out of business. This book is as up-to-date as possible, but it is impossible to guarantee that the sites mentioned here will still be available when you go online.

To avoid frustration, you may find it easier to use a search engine such as Yahoo!, Dogpile, or Alta Vista and type in the site name—for example, "Riley Guide," rather than its URL, **www.dbm.com/careers**. The search engine will provide a list of possibilities to match "The Riley Guide." Read the site descriptions and choose the best match from the list of options the search engine provides. Once you link to the home page, examine the headers or check out the site map to find more specific information. You may have to drill down into the site to find what you want. As a safeguard against total frustration in completing those activities in this book that involve Web searches, you are always provided with several possibilities, so that if one site leads you unexpectedly to a dead end, another will be an information gold mine.

If you have not used the Internet for research, check your college library or computer lab; they usually give orientation workshops. A friend may help you get started. In this book we assume you have had some experience using the Internet, but you don't have to be a Web whiz.

When you find a Web site on your own, here are some questions to keep in mind as you evaluate the site:

■ Who sponsors the site and what is its purpose? Is there a contact person whom I can e-mail with questions? What indications do I have of the quality of the contact (e.g., excellent reputation, background, and credentials of author or organization). Good bets are professional associations, links provided by a college career-services site, and well-known brand names with reputations to protect such as the *Wall Street Journal, U.S. News & World Report,* or the College Board.

■ When was the site last updated? This is particularly important for sites with job listings, because you don't want to waste time applying for jobs that are already filled.

■ What are the privacy safeguards? Before you give personal information such as your Social Security or credit card number, check with your counselor, instructor, or advisor. Web fraud is real.

■ Is there a cost? Before you pay for a service, check to see if you can get that service for free at your college. Most colleges offer resume workshops and provide current job listings. They also offer self-assessment inventories so that you can get a better understanding of your interests and personality. You have the added benefit of being able to review your results with a counselor.

The Internet provides so much information so fast that it can breed "Internet laziness." If you fall prey to this syndrome, you pile up massive printouts from a Web site and believe that you are finished with your career information search. Sierra, who was fearful that an interest in writing would not match any occupation except novelist, went to the *U. S. News & World Report* Careers site with the question, "What are some careers for people who like to write?" She found a listing of the top 10 jobs for writers. In terms of the ASAP four-step method, she has completed the "A" (ask the right questions) and "S" (search for information) steps. In terms of the second "A" (analyze your findings), she needs to identify the pros and cons of each option. Finally, "P" (plan the next action) would probably include new searches to find out more detailed information about the options she is most attracted to.

Perhaps one of the most useful sites that Sierra could consult is her own college's career or cooperative education Web page. These pages will acquaint her with the career services offered by her college. Career services or cooperative education home pages often have Internet links that have been selected for their particular usefulness to college and graduate students. Activity 1.6, Accessing College Career Services on the Internet, helps you practice getting career-planning information using the Internet. It lists six colleges with extensive links to career-related sites on the Web. They will supplement your college's own Web listings.

Finally, don't rely on the Internet alone. Use people and media sources. Interview people: counselors, professors, alumni, internship contacts. Consult books, magazines, and newspapers, and view videos. Using different sources of information will usually give you a more well-rounded picture. Some of the same caveats apply: Check for information bias, that is, overly favorable or unfavorable reports. Remember too, all information must be current.

WHERE STUDENTS GET STUCK, AND WHAT TO DO IF IT HAPPENS TO YOU

Getting Practical Too Soon

Let's examine one of the most frequent ways students get stuck once they have described their career dilemma and life situation. Ellen entered college with the intention of becoming a lawyer. When she looked at her life situation, she found that her many commitments—worker, single parent to a little girl, granddaughter taking care of her aging grandfather, and student—

all demanded a great deal of time. Once she began to describe her dilemma and see her many commitments, she felt so discouraged that she wanted her counselor to suggest some quick, practical training. She asked her counselor, "Isn't my law-school goal unrealistic and impractical?"

Her counselor gave her some good advice. While she was in the search stage, gathering information from all three databases, he advised her to widen her search to look at many possibilities. It was sensible to explore a range of career options, from those involving lengthy preparation, such as becoming a lawyer, to those with fewer educational requirements.

Ellen's search for information would be her chance to open doors and identify different career and educational prospects. Her counselor suggested that she begin with the personal identity database—information about herself—for two reasons. First, this information would enable her to recognize occupations where she would experience personal satisfaction. Second, this information would enable her to recognize personal qualities and skills that are prized by others in the workplace. This tactic offers Ellen a way to discover an array of suitable possibilities. She won't dismiss her dreams as unrealistic and impractical before she has even begun to uncover the opportunities to make them come true.

After the search, when she comes to the task of setting her direction, then it will be time to come to terms with how her career and educational choices could be integrated with her commitments.

Ellen's counselor gave good advice that can help you too, even if you are not feeling overwhelmed by your life commitments. A good place to start your information search, regardless of whether you already have a career possibility in mind, is the personal identity database. It is the best way to uncover a variety of options that fit your personality, values, interests, and skills. The next two chapters explore the personal identity database in detail.

SUMMARY

Getting started on setting your career direction is a three-part process. Begin by describing your career path and educational path dilemmas completely and specifically. Next, take stock of your information needs, using the three databases: personal identity, career, and college and graduate school. Then, search for information using the four-step Ask–Search–Analyze–Plan (ASAP) approach.

KEY POINTS

1. *Career dilemma* is the term used in this book to describe the tangled set of interrelated career issues that you face. Two major categories of dilemmas are:
   a. career path dilemmas
   b. education path dilemmas

2. Describe your career dilemma clearly and specifically.
   a. Write it down and talk it over with others.
   b. Be truthful.
   c. Be specific about your life situation.

3. A complete description of your career dilemma includes the relevant aspects of your life situation and a list of the internal and external obstacles you face.

4. The kinds of information you need to solve your dilemmas will fit into three databases:

   a. The *personal identity database* includes information about your personality, values, interests, and skills.

   b. The *career database* contains information about the nature of the work, the entry requirements, the rewards and benefits, and the outlook for the future.

   c. The *college and graduate school database* contains information about academic offerings, entry requirements, the school profile and student body, and costs and financial aid.

5. In taking stock of your situation, you identify which databases to search and what factors to consider.

6. Use the four-step ASAP method to structure your search for information:

   a. *Ask* the right questions.

   b. *Search* for the information.

   c. *Analyze* your findings.

   d. *Plan* your next move.

7. Although the Internet is a rich source of information about career and educational options, an Internet search can be overwhelming, mislead-

---

EXAMPLES: STUDENTS' CAREER PATH AND EDUCATION PATH DILEMMAS

Here are some ways students began to formulate their dilemmas. Use these as examples as you begin to formulate your own dilemmas.

Business is a broad field. How can I narrow it down? Do I want management, accounting, advertising, or marketing?

I did not think I had a dilemma. After doing the first assignment, I realized time is a major dilemma for me. I am going to school part-time, and at this rate it will take me another five to six years to complete my education and earn my B.A. I realized that I want to finish school in a more timely fashion.

The dilemma that I'm faced with is sticking to one career choice. It seems that every time I decide to go after one career option, I always decide to do something else. I think this happens because I have so many ideas that it is difficult to stick to just one.

I dislike my current major very much, but I'm not sure what my ideal career would be. The career I choose not only has to be ideal for me, but also for my family as well. It is one of the hardest decisions I've had to make.

Should I go to a four-year college right away or get experience in my field first?

Which is better? To start working in a firm where people who speak my native language are around, or go to an American firm where I can improve my English skills faster?

I am about 75 percent decided on becoming a physician's assistant. Which school should I go to?

The only major I am interested in is women's studies, but I am not sure what I want to do with it.

When should I pursue my graduate degree? I want to spend time with my children, ages four and nine.

ing, and frustrating. Stay with reputable site sponsors who update the content frequently and safeguard your privacy. Don't pay for services that you can get for free at your college.

8. You may want a short, easy answer to your career dilemma. However, at the beginning of your search, your best approach is to explore many options. This tactic offers the best hope that you won't dismiss your dreams as unrealistic and impractical before you have begun to uncover opportunities to make them come true.

TAKING STOCK OF YOUR SITUATION   ACTIVITY **1.5**

NAME _____

OVERVIEW

In this activity you will lay the groundwork for solving your career dilemma. You will discover the amount of information that you need, identify which of the three databases to consult, and select some factors that require your initial attention. There are four tasks in this assessment.

TASK 1 DESCRIBE YOUR CAREER DILEMMA

- Make your description as specific as possible. Use additional pages if necessary.

- Provide details about your life situation. Life situation factors include your family situation and your life roles, where you want to work and live, your current economic situation, and your dreams.

- Identify internal and external obstacles.

_____

_____

_____

_____

_____

_____

_____

_____

_____

_____

TASK 2 COMPLETE YOUR ASSESSMENT

Consider your career dilemma carefully. In order to solve it, you may want to get to know yourself better. You may want to get a better idea of your interests, values, and skills. You may require information about several career fields, job opportunities, or the current job market. You may want to get a better idea of possibilities for transfer to four-year college or graduate training, or of other ways to further your education. You will probably want to obtain more information in several areas.

INSTRUCTIONS

Keeping your career dilemma in mind, circle the best response to each item.

T = True   F = False   ? = Uncertain

PERSONAL IDENTITY DATABASE

1. In order to solve this dilemma, I need to know more about my personality.   T F ?

2. In order to solve this dilemma, I need to know more about my values.   T F ?

3. In order to solve this dilemma, I need to know more about my career interests.   T F ?

4. In order to solve this dilemma, I need to know more about my skills.   T F ?

5. In order to solve this dilemma, I need to know more about the kind of life that I want and the kind of person that I would like to be in the future.   T F ?

6. In order to solve this dilemma, I need to know more about career management skills, such as how to set priorities, avoid procrastination, and take action.   T F ?

CAREER INFORMATION DATABASE

7. In order to solve this dilemma, I need more information about my career field.   T F ?

8. In order to solve this dilemma, I need more information about several career fields.   T F ?

9. In order to solve this dilemma, I need more information about the nature of work in certain careers.   T F ?

10. In order to solve this dilemma, I need more information about the entry requirements in certain careers.   T F ?

11. In order to solve this dilemma, I need more information about the rewards and benefits in certain careers.   T F ?

12. In order to solve this dilemma, I need more information about the job market and outlook for the future in certain careers.   T F ?

FOUR-YEAR COLLEGE AND GRADUATE SCHOOL INFORMATION DATABASE

13. In order to solve this dilemma, I need more information about transfer to a four-year college.   T F ?

14. In order to solve this dilemma, I need more information about graduate programs.   T F ?

15. In order to solve this dilemma, I need more information about which majors are appropriate for my goals.   T F ?

16. In order to solve this dilemma, I need more information about which academic programs are offered in the colleges or graduate schools that I am considering.   T F ?

17. In order to solve this dilemma, I need more information about the schools' admission requirements.   T F ?

18. In order to solve this dilemma, I need more information about the types of students who attend these schools.   T F ?

19. In order to solve this dilemma, I need more information about the cost of further education and possibilities for financial aid.   T F ?

20. In order to solve this dilemma, I need more information about other ways to further my education.   T F ?

TASK 3 IDENTIFY THE INFORMATION THAT YOU NEED

To assess your need for information, review the preceding survey.

1. Get a general idea about the amount of information you need.
2. Identify the types of information that will be most useful to you. What databases are important to search?
3. Identify the most important pieces of information to search for first.

A. GENERAL OVERVIEW OF THE AMOUNT OF INFORMATION THAT YOU NEED

How many items did you check as "True" or "Uncertain"?

I checked _____ items out of the 20 items as "True" or "Uncertain."

Are you surprised by the number of items that you checked as "True" or "Uncertain"? It is not uncommon to check more than 10 items. Most students realize that to solve their career dilemmas they will need a lot of information.

B. TYPES OF INFORMATION ORGANIZED BY DATABASE

Now examine the survey in terms of each of the three databases.

Personal Identity Database

If you circled items 1, 2, 3, 4, 5, or 6 as "True" or "Uncertain," you need more information about you. You need to conduct a self-assessment of your values, personality, interests, and skills.

    If so, check the following box.

☐ *I need more information about myself.*

Career Information Database

If you circled items 7, 8, 9, 10, 11, or 12 as "True" or "Uncertain," you need more information about careers.

    If so, check the following box.

☐ *I need more information about careers.*

Four-Year College and Graduate School Information Database

If you circled items 13, 14, 15, 16, 17, 18, 19, or 20 as "True" or "Uncertain," you need more information about colleges, graduate schools, or other types of further education.

    If so, check the following box.

☐ *I need more information about further education.*

TASK 4 PLAN YOUR FIRST INFORMATION SEARCH

Congratulations! Taking stock of your situation requires you to be honest with yourself. This process is not always easy. It is tempting to find excuses and avoid looking at our career dilemmas. Reaching this point means that you have made important career progress.

However, some students feel a little discouraged at this point. Why? It is not uncommon for students to check the need for information in all or most of the areas. So they feel lost. It is important to realize that if you stop the process here you will remain confused about your career dilemma.

What do you need to do next? Search for information. The next two activities, Accessing College Career Services on the Internet and the Career Browser, will help you do just that. You will get an overview of the various kinds of information that will help you solve your career dilemma. They will acquaint you with various Internet sites that you will want to use again and again.

After you complete Activities 1.6 and 1.7, proceed to the following two chapters. They will guide you in looking at your personal identity database.

ACTIVITY 1.6 | **INTERNET SEARCH:** ACCESSING COLLEGE CAREER SERVICES ON THE INTERNET

OVERVIEW

The purpose of this activity is to help you find career services using college Web pages.

Visit three college Web sites, including your own college's, and survey their career services. Typical services for students include career counseling, placement, on-site recruitment, career fairs, job fairs, workshops on resume writing and interviewing, internships, career courses, career testing, and computerized guidance systems.

If you are unsure about which other colleges to include in your survey, try TWO of the following colleges:

College of William and Mary (Career Services): **www.wm.edu**

Purdue University (Center for Career Opportunities): **www.purdue.edu**

Rensselaer Polytechnic Institute (Career Development Center): **www.rpi.edu**

University of California at Los Angeles (Career Center): **www.ucla.edu**

University of Florida (The Career Resource Center): **www.ufl.edu**

University of North Carolina at Chapel Hill (University Career Services): www.unc.edu

TASK 1

For each of the three sites you selected, give the college's name and URL (Internet address) and summarize the types of career services it offers.

TASK 2

One typical service is a list of Internet links that you can use to gather information and aid in your job search. Which of the three sites that you surveyed provided the most useful links to the Internet?

TASK 3

Which site(s) will you use again? Why?

Note: Web sites are frequently reorganized, so you may experience some difficulties during your search. Once you get to the college home page (e.g., University of Florida), you may find it helpful to drill down into the site using the key words in parentheses.

INTERNET SEARCH: CAREER BROWSER   ACTIVITY **1.7**

OVERVIEW

The purpose of this activity is to sample some of the Web sites that provide information about careers and further education. You will browse Internet sites that provide the following kinds of help: (1) career information, (2) resume and interview preparation, (3) job search leads and advice, (4) salary information, and (5) college and graduate school programs. For each of these five categories, you will be provided with a choice of sites to explore.

To provide some focus for your research and learning, there are seven questions to answer. Do not hand in copies of the Web page, but summarize the information asked for in the question on separate paper. Always provide the site reference.

CAREER INFORMATION

1. Using one of the sites below, describe the "outlook for the future" for your preferred occupation. If you are not sure what occupation to select, choose one of the following: accountants, reporters and correspondents, urban and regional planners, or university and college professors.

   The Occupational Outlook Handbook: stats.bls.gov/ocohome.htm

   Career Exploration Links: UC Berkeley (Career Exploration Links): www.berkeley.edu

RESUME AND INTERVIEW PREPARATION

2. Describe one resume-writing or interviewing tip from one of the following sites:

   The Riley Guide: www.dbm.com/jobguide

   The Job Hunter's Bible: www.jobhuntersbible.com

JOB SEARCH

3. Describe ONE job of interest from one of the sites. Give the job title and a brief description of the skills and responsibilities the job involves.

   Monster.com (business and general): www.monster.com

   Dice.com (technical): www.dice.com

   Cool Works.com (adventure jobs, travel & tourism): www.coolworks.com

   National Teachers Recruitment Clearinghouse (teachers): www.recruitingteachers.org

SALARY

4. Select an occupation and provide salary information.

   Job Star (salary information): **www.jobstar.org**

   The Riley Guide (salary guides & guidance): **www.dbm.com/jobguide/**

COLLEGE AND GRADUATE SCHOOL INFORMATION

5. List one highly ranked private college and one public college.

   U. S. News & World Report (Education): **www.usnews.com**

6. List all the local colleges or graduate schools that offer opportunities for continuing your education in your preferred major or program.

   Yahoo!: dir.yahoo.com/Education/Higher_Education/Colleges_and_Universities/

   Google: directory.google.com/Top/Reference/Education/Colleges_and_Universities

   Mindedge (College & Universities): **www.Mindedge.com**

   OnlineLearning.net: www.onlinelearning.net

DISCOVERY

7. Search for one additional career or school site. List the name and URL and briefly describe the contents. Would you recommend this site to others? Why or why not?

REFLECTIONS

8. What is the most interesting discovery you made during this career browser activity?

   Note: Web sites are frequently reorganized. Locate the site (e.g., University of California, Berkeley, *U. S. News & World Report*) and then drill down into the site using the key words in parentheses.

CHAPTER 2

Identifying Your Values and Personality Type

Tell me who you walk with and I'll tell you who you are.
—Spanish saying

REASONS FOR CREATING YOUR PERSONAL IDENTITY DATABASE

This chapter and the next are all about you. Their purpose is to teach you to describe yourself in ways that will enable you to make good career choices. You will consider in turn four dimensions of yourself. We have grouped these dimensions and called them the *personal identity database*. They are:

- Values
- Personality type
- Interests
- Skills

The time you spend in creating a picture of yourself on these four dimensions will help you to achieve three desired outcomes of choosing a career: career satisfaction, continued personal development, and workplace success.

Career Satisfaction

Career researchers have shown that you will be most satisfied when you choose work that fits your personal identity. Suppose you say, "I want to become a marine biologist." This choice is likely to be satisfying if you **value** ocean life, if you see your **personality type** as liking to acquire new scientific knowledge, if you have an **interest** in understanding the habits of living creatures, and if you acquire scientific **skill** in biology and chemistry lab classes. In other words, your **values, personality type, interests,** and **skills** will ideally match those of a marine biologist.

If you **value** saving the whales, but are **uninterested** in studying biology or are relatively **unskilled** in science-related areas, the match between your personal identity and a typical marine biologist is incomplete. Would you be happy as a marine biologist if you lacked an interest in the study of biology? And how satisfying would your work be if you were called on to use skills that were poorly developed?

Your career satisfaction depends in part on a good match between who you are as a person and the requirements of an occupation. If you have examined and described your values, personality type, interests, and skills, you are more likely to determine whether your choices are congruent with who you are.

Continued Personal Development

When you select your work, you join a work family of your own choosing. The developmental process by which your family formed and molded your personal identity as you grew up continues in adult life. When you join a work group, you begin to be influenced by that group's values. Certain aspects of your personality are reinforced, and some interests and skills are nurtured while others are not. The work group that you join will shape your personal identity during your working years.

Let's look at Joe, who likes computers. He studied the characteristics of systems analysts and other people who worked in the computer industry. Did he want these people to influence his future development? Would he feel a sense of belonging if he joined these groups?

Some students, like Erin, find it difficult to accept that we are shaped by the groups we join. She went to a high school where many students did not graduate and few went on to college. She felt that she was strong enough to escape the negative influences around her. She wondered why she should bother with looking at the characteristics of the group. With an effort of will, you can shield yourself to some extent from group influence, but often the price you pay is loneliness and alienation from your surroundings. Groups satisfy our basic need for connection to other people. This sense of belonging provides the support that enhances your ongoing development.

Associating with people who have developed themselves in ways that you would like to develop yourself is only sensible. Consider Eric and Charles, who were looking at choices in the military. Charles wanted to join the Air Force, because he thought that being a pilot would be exciting. However, when he considered the effect of membership in the military on his future development, he decided against it. He realized that he would not feel comfortable in a group where so much behavior was regulated. He felt that learning the techniques of war would reinforce his own tendency to solve problems by force or threats—a tendency he was trying to change. Eric felt differently; he thought that the discipline of the military life would make him a stronger person. He would value joining a group that defended freedom and a democratic way of life. Eric would be proud to feel connected to the military, while Charles believed that it would not support the development that he wanted for himself as an adult. In Case 2.1 Vanessa and Karen also come to different conclusions about which groups they want to join.

CASE 2.1   *Where Do I Belong?*

Vanessa and Karen are considering two occupations, elementary school teacher and social worker, because both want to help children. When Vanessa looked at each occupational group more closely, she concluded that she would be happier as a teacher. By becoming a teacher, she would enhance her own development because she would acquire instructional skills. Moreover, she has enjoyed helping her younger brothers and sisters to learn. She sees educators as a group devoted to helping large numbers of children in our society, and she wants to be a part of that group.

Upon reflection, Karen came to a different conclusion. She feels that her best personal quality is empathy. She likes solving problems. She feels that if she trained to become a social worker she would be surrounded by people who care about children with psychological problems. She would be proud to be a part of a group that helps to rescue children who have been abused or neglected.

Both Vanessa and Karen are wise in thinking through the effect of group membership on their personal development. This understanding enables them to make choices that are in line with the ways they want to develop in the future.

Workplace Success

Another compelling reason to seek information from the personal identity database is that doing so will teach you to appraise your worth in the job market. This hardheaded approach to self-appraisal will increase your chances for success because it will point to skills and qualities that are essential for workplace success. Information from the personal identity database enables you to determine what skills and personal qualities you have to offer that will be important to an employer. It will also enable you to answer this question: What qualities and habits must I cultivate to become successful?

Suppose you say, "I want to be an interior designer," because you love to look at home-decorating magazines and fantasize about living in a spectacular home. A look at yourself from an employer's viewpoint will help you to assess whether you have the imagination and perseverance that employers want. You will seek more evidence that you are creative, with an eye for detail and a sense of balance and proportion. When you have the skills and qualities that employers want, you will be more confident about your chances for workplace success.

So you begin by gathering information from your personal identity database that will enable you to get a picture of yourself. With this picture you can judge whether you have (or are willing to develop) what employers want in a given kind of work. Moreover, your self-portrait will help you discover what kinds of work are likely to be satisfying and to promote your personal development.

CAREER DREAMS: LOOK AT YOUR IDEAL LIFE 10 YEARS FROM NOW

One way to understand better who you are and the kind of person you want to become is to look at the career dreams you have for yourself. Your career dreams represent an aspect of your ideal life as you want it to be several years from now.

These dreams can be very specific, such as *I want to be a nurse, a stockbroker, or a Navy SEAL.* You may dream about playing a certain kind of role: leader, wise one, mentor, competitor, protector, glamour queen, or creative force, to name a few. Dreams can also be more general, representing a lifestyle choice, such as owning your own home, living in a large city, or traveling around the world.

YOUR CAREER DREAMS	ACTIVITY 2.1

The purpose of this activity is to let your imagination soar. Take a few moments and paint a picture of your life as you would like it to be 10 years from now. In particular, focus on the kind of work you see yourself doing. What is your role (e.g., the technical expert, the adventurer, or the examiner)? What is the setting? Who are the people around you? What kinds of rewards will you be receiving? Use additional paper if necessary.

Don't hold back or censor yourself as you write. When you are done, read it over and give your dreams a title.

Title: _____

_____

_____

_____

_____

_____

_____

_____

_____

_____

Reading over what you have written, what do your dreams say about you as a person?

_____

_____

_____

_____

_____

Looking at your dreams is just one way to deepen your awareness of who you are as a person. The remainder of this chapter is devoted to two aspects of your personal identity database: your values and your personality type. In the next chapter, you will consider the other two dimensions: your interests and your skills.

WORK VALUES

The sense that life is worth living is based in part on using one's life energy to pursue meaningful goals. The Dalai Lama, Bill Gates, Stephen King, and Tiger Woods spent or are spending their life energy pursuing different goals: respectively, helping the poor, building a corporate computer empire, writing best-selling novels, and honing physical gifts to win golf championships. All are highly successful in the ways that they use their life energy, but their choices reflect different value orientations.

You could say that the Dalai Lama values spirituality; Gates values leadership; King, verbal creativity; and Woods, physical skill. Just as their choices reflect their values, your choice of work is a statement to the world about how you have decided to spend a significant portion of your life energy. You will feel better about your work (and about yourself) when you spend your life energy on something that you consider important and meaningful.

In Activity 2.2 you will find a list of work values. Some of these values reflect our striving for development through our work, such as having the opportunity for variety, self-improvement, or autonomy. Other values reflect the importance of different kinds of rewards that work offers, such as money, providing for family, or having balance in our lives. Take a moment to complete Activity 2.2. It will provide you with an opportunity to assess the values that are central to your life and work.

ACTIVITY 2.2   WORK VALUES SURVEY[1]

Draw an arrow to indicate how important you consider each of the following work values to be in your life.

Example: Achievement

| NOT IMPORTANT | SOMEWHAT IMPORTANT | QUITE IMPORTANT | EXTREMELY IMPORTANT |

Example: Aesthetics

| NOT IMPORTANT | SOMEWHAT IMPORTANT | QUITE IMPORTANT | EXTREMELY IMPORTANT |

1. **Self-improvement:** Having continued opportunity and resources for enhancing personal abilities and interests.

| NOT IMPORTANT | SOMEWHAT IMPORTANT | QUITE IMPORTANT | EXTREMELY IMPORTANT |

2. **Achievement:** Being successful, reaching desired goals.

| NOT IMPORTANT | SOMEWHAT IMPORTANT | QUITE IMPORTANT | EXTREMELY IMPORTANT |

3. **Creativity:** Being free to try original and new things, procedures, ideas, or to express yourself in any of the creative media, such as the performing arts, art/design, writing, fashion, culinary arts.

| NOT IMPORTANT | SOMEWHAT IMPORTANT | QUITE IMPORTANT | EXTREMELY IMPORTANT |

4. **Use of Skills:** Having the opportunity to make full use of your most highly developed talents.

NOT IMPORTANT   SOMEWHAT IMPORTANT   QUITE IMPORTANT   EXTREMELY IMPORTANT

5. **Variety:** Performing varied tasks that are not amenable to routine solutions.

NOT IMPORTANT   SOMEWHAT IMPORTANT   QUITE IMPORTANT   EXTREMELY IMPORTANT

6. **Supervisory Relations (Autonomy):** Having considerable freedom to decide how to execute your responsibilities.

NOT IMPORTANT   SOMEWHAT IMPORTANT   QUITE IMPORTANT   EXTREMELY IMPORTANT

7. **Adventure, Risk, Excitement:** Participating in activities that have above-average risk.

NOT IMPORTANT   SOMEWHAT IMPORTANT   QUITE IMPORTANT   EXTREMELY IMPORTANT

8. **Physical Activity:** Engaging in activities that require the active use of your body.

NOT IMPORTANT   SOMEWHAT IMPORTANT   QUITE IMPORTANT   EXTREMELY IMPORTANT

9. **Leadership:** Having a recognized influence over others, either formally or informally.

NOT IMPORTANT   SOMEWHAT IMPORTANT   QUITE IMPORTANT   EXTREMELY IMPORTANT

10. **Helping Others:** Contributing directly and obviously to the welfare of other individuals.

NOT IMPORTANT   SOMEWHAT IMPORTANT   QUITE IMPORTANT   EXTREMELY IMPORTANT

11. **Prestige:** Being accorded honor and esteem by significant persons.

NOT IMPORTANT   SOMEWHAT IMPORTANT   QUITE IMPORTANT   EXTREMELY IMPORTANT

12. **Aesthetics:** Having an appreciation for beautiful things and surroundings.

NOT IMPORTANT   SOMEWHAT IMPORTANT   QUITE IMPORTANT   EXTREMELY IMPORTANT

13. **Associates:** Having frequent contact with colleagues who share your goals and outlook.

NOT IMPORTANT   SOMEWHAT IMPORTANT   QUITE IMPORTANT   EXTREMELY IMPORTANT

14. **Security:** Being free of uncertainty (physically, economically, personally).

NOT IMPORTANT   SOMEWHAT IMPORTANT   QUITE IMPORTANT   EXTREMELY IMPORTANT

15. **Money:** Having or accumulating sizable financial resources.

NOT IMPORTANT   SOMEWHAT IMPORTANT   QUITE IMPORTANT   EXTREMELY IMPORTANT

16. **Balance:** Having time to pursue personal, family, and community activities.

NOT IMPORTANT   SOMEWHAT IMPORTANT   QUITE IMPORTANT   EXTREMELY IMPORTANT

17. **Family:** Providing for the needs and desires of your dependents.

NOT IMPORTANT   SOMEWHAT IMPORTANT   QUITE IMPORTANT   EXTREMELY IMPORTANT

18. **Spirituality:** Having the opportunity to practice freely all aspects of your religious and spiritual beliefs.

NOT IMPORTANT   SOMEWHAT IMPORTANT   QUITE IMPORTANT   EXTREMELY IMPORTANT

List your top three values as identified in your survey.

_____

_____

_____

ACTIVITY 2.3 — WORK VALUES AND OCCUPATIONAL CHOICES

The following five occupations call for different uses of one's life energy and reflect different value orientations. Identify the values that you feel would be expressed by selecting each of these occupations.

1. Minister _____

2. Athletic coach _____

3. College professor _____

4. Tax lawyer _____

5. Broadcast journalist _____

Taking time to reflect on what you care about or what you truly value helps you to choose work that makes you feel rewarded for your expenditure of life energy. Do you believe it is important to have the opportunity to exercise autonomy? To strive for high achievement? To use a well-developed skill? Do you value the rewards of associates? Surroundings? Prestige? Occupations offer different combinations of opportunity for development and reward. For example, although the Nobel Prize winner in physics and the Navy helicopter pilot are accorded prestige for their work, the Nobel Prize winner is more likely to value a life of high achievement, and the Navy helicopter pilot is more likely to value a life of adventure, risk, and excitement.

ACTIVITY 2.4 — VALUES, FAMILY, AND CULTURE

Our values often reflect what our family of origin valued. Toni Morrison is the author of *Sula, Jazz, The Bluest Eye, The Song of Solomon,* and the Pulitzer Prize–winning novel *Beloved.*

> On certain childhood days Toni Morrison's father would tell her matter-of-factly, "Today I welded the straightest seam on any ship about to sail on any sea anywhere. Before a slab of metal was welded over it, I signed my name on the seam." Each time Toni reminded him that no one would ever see his signature, her father answered, "But I saw it."
>
> Toni's mother always wanted to sing. To sing everything, Opera, Gospels, Spirituals, Blues. And she sang every day and anywhere. She said, "No one in this town has ever been born, married or been buried without me singing at the ceremony. That is, not if I could help it."
>
> —Maya Angelou, "The Divining Ms. Morrison"[2]

What values were instilled in Toni Morrison by her parents?

_____

_____

_____

_____

_____

Our values are also molded by our culture, religion, ethnic identity, and gender identities. These can be a source of strength. For example, in the Greek culture, the most respected members of society are those with a good education. Someone who has earned advanced degrees is more respected than an athlete or king. Greek children learn from their parents to value education. They want to excel in school to earn the respect of others.

We often take in our values without examining whether they fit us. Sometimes they may restrict which careers we consider. For example, in the U. S. culture, boys often are taught that competition is good, while girls are taught that caring for others is an important life activity. As a result, men may avoid nurturing activities and women may avoid competition on the job. Examining these influences on your values increases your awareness of their impact on your choices.

Identifying your work values helps you evaluate whether your choices are harmonious with how you want to spend your life energy. Work that is congruent with your values is essential for career satisfaction and continued personal development.

Now we will turn to the personality dimension of the personal identity database. You will be provided with two methods for describing your personality. Both these methods will make it easier to identify career options that fit your personality characteristics.

HOLLAND'S PERSONALITY TYPES

Selecting an occupation that fits your personality type has proved to be an effective way to increase your chances of career satisfaction. You may have heard the saying "Birds of a feather flock together." Simply stated, eagles inhabit a territory that is favorable for eagles and avoid the environments of sparrows or robins. Likewise, when you are surrounded by people who like the same activities, enjoy using the same types of skills, and hold the same values, you feel at home.

John Holland, a distinguished psychologist, has developed a system that will help you identify specific occupations that will be compatible with your personality type.[3] Once you identify your personality type using the Holland system, you can select occupations in which your type will thrive.

If eagles and sparrows don't need help in identifying the kinds of environments that will satisfy their particular needs, why do people need career experts to help them? Think about Michael: Michael was being pressured to be an engineer by his parents, and he thought that was a good choice when he entered college. Now he is not so sure, because he finds his courses hard. Is he trying to please his parents? Is his personality type similar to that of other engineers? Should he find another career or study harder so that he can pass his engineering courses? Knowing your Holland type helps you confirm that your career choice fits your personality.

Determining your personality type also provides great ideas for exploration. Denzel thought about being a news director, an environmental analyst, and a dean of students. All these careers seemed very different. Was there any common theme that united these three types of work? If Denzel could see a pattern, he could expand the number of career options that would be a good fit for him.

Unlike birds, we are not genetically programmed to pick our work environments. Using a career family system such as Holland's helps you to identify which work environments are likely to feel comfortable for someone of your personality type.

The system developed by John Holland includes six personality types:

- Realistic (R)
- Investigative (I)
- Artistic (A)
- Social (S)
- Enterprising (E)
- Conventional (C)

Table 2.1 lists the attributes of each type. Study each type's preferences for activities and occupations. Compare the differences in their values. Notice that each type's self-descriptions are unlike another type's and that other people see each type in distinct ways. Finally, note that each type tends to avoid certain activities.

The type you resemble most is your *primary* type, yet typically you may share the characteristics of a second and a third type. Usually, you use a three-letter code like ISA (Investigative, Social, and Artistic) or RCE (Realistic, Conventional, and Enterprising) to describe your personality type, starting with the most important letter.

Resources for an accurate assessment of your Holland type include *The Self-Directed Search*® (SDS®), the *Vocational Preference Inventory*™ (VPI), the *Strong Interest Inventory*, and the *Career Assessment Inventory*™.

Michael took the *Self-Directed Search*® and found that his Holland type is SEC (Social, Enterprising, and Conventional). He realized that he had "people" skills and that he liked to help others. He avoided mechanical and technical activities that were common in the engineering field. He decided to explore Social occupations because they would provide environments where he would feel most at home. When Denzel reviewed the Holland typology, he realized that he was an Enterprising personality type. At his college career center, he looked up the Holland codes for the occupations that interested him in the *Dictionary of Holland Occupational Codes* (DHOC). He found that each had an Enterprising component: news director, ESA; environmental analyst, ESR; dean of students, SEA. Denzel now realized that he should explore Enterprising occupations.

You can use your Holland personality type to generate a sensible list of occupations to explore further or to confirm that a particular occupation is compatible with your personality. In Chapter 4, you will learn how to conduct occupational research. You will find that many career information resources use the Holland typology, so knowledge of your Holland personality type will make your exploration more efficient and fruitful.

Holland's system of six career personalities and six corresponding work environments is not the only one that will help you understand your personality preferences. Carl Jung, a pioneering Swiss psychiatrist, studied the behavior of different personality types. Looking at your personality from a Jungian perspective can increase your understanding about the potential for work satisfaction in various work environments. The Myers–Briggs Type Indicator® will help you do that.

TABLE 2.1   *Holland's personality types.*

Personality Type

Attribute	Realistic (R)	Investigative (I)	Artistic (A)	Social (S)	Enterprising (E)	Conventional (C)
Preferences for activities and occupation:	Manipulation of machines, tools, and things	Exploration, understanding, and prediction or control of natural and social phenomena	Literary, musical, or artistic activities	Helping, teaching, treating, counseling, or serving others through personal interaction	Persuading, manipulating, or directing others	Establishing or maintaining orderly routines, application of standards
Values:	Material rewards for tangible accomplishments	Development or acquisition of knowledge	Creative expression of ideas, emotions, or sentiments	Fostering the welfare of others, social service	Material accomplishment and social status	Material or financial accomplishment and power in social, business, or political arenas
Sees self as:	Practical, conservative, and having manual and mechanical skills—lacking social skills	Analytical, intelligent, skeptical, and having academic talent—lacking interpersonal skills	Open to experience, innovative, intellectual—lacking clerical or office skills	Empathic, patient, and having interpersonal skills—lacking mechanical ability	Having sales and persuasive ability—lacking scientific ability	Having technical skills in business or production—lacking artistic competencies
Others see as:	Normal, frank	Asocial, intellectual	Unconventional, disorderly, creative	Nurturing, agreeable, extroverted	Energetic, gregarious	Careful, conforming
Avoids:	Interaction with people	Persuasion or sales activities	Routines and conformity to established rules	Mechanical and technical activity	Scientific, intellectual, or abstruse topics	Ambitious or unstructured undertakings

Source: Adapted and reproduced by special permission of the publisher, Psychological Assessment Resources, Inc., from the *Dictionary of Holland Occupational Codes*, Third Edition by Gary D. Gottfredson, Ph.D., and John L. Holland, Ph.D., Copyright © 1982, 1989, 1996.

THE MYERS-BRIGGS TYPE INDICATOR®

Jackie and Alexandra are high-performing airline customer service reps, helping passengers check in and issuing tickets at a busy airport. Jackie is good at greeting people, likes to have people around at work, and usually enjoys talking on the telephone. Her preference is for extroversion. Alexandra has trouble remembering customers' names and faces, is content to work alone, and dislikes telephone interruptions because she loses her concentration. Her preference is for introversion. Can you guess which one loves her job? Which one often feels uncomfortable at work, like a fish out of water, and drained of energy after a day's work?

Jackie prefers to direct her energy outward toward people and things, whereas Alexandra prefers to direct her energy inward and to focus on ideas. Both women have developed their people skills and perform well on the job. The big difference between them is not in their job performance, but in their job satisfaction. The lesson here is that when your work environment matches your personality preferences, you are more likely to be happy at work.

The Myers–Briggs Type Indicator® (MBTI) is an inventory that sorts people according to their preferences on four key dimensions that have relevance to workplace happiness:

- Extraversion–Introversion
- Sensing–Intuition
- Thinking–Feeling
- Judging–Perceiving

Katharine Cook Briggs and Isabel Briggs Myers, a mother–daughter team, worked for years to design this inventory, which is based on Jung's insights about the human personality. It has become widely popular, in part because it helps people to understand themselves and use their preferences in a positive way.

These preferences do not reflect your intelligence, maturity, or skills. Alexandra had the people skills to succeed at the airport job, but the job did not suit one of her basic personality preferences.

A brief overview of the MBTI's four dimensions is given next. You may want to see if a professional who is trained to administer and interpret the Myers–Briggs Type Indicator® is available to help you understand your preferences. Check with your campus counseling center.

Extraversion–Introversion

Jackie and Alexandra illustrate the difference between the preference for extraversion and introversion. *Extraverts* are energized through their contact with others, like to think out loud, and tend to be more action-oriented. *Introverts* reflect on ideas silently and want to know the ideas behind a project. They like to think things over before they talk with others about their ideas. Crowds drain their energy, and they usually prefer one-on-one and small-group contact with other people.

Alexandra has found a new job as a writer of travel brochures. She still gets to indulge her love of travel, just as Jackie does, but now she works by herself or with small groups of people whom she knows well. This job fits her preference for introversion.

Sensing–Intuition

Dan has a preference for *sensing*. When he takes in information, he relies on his five senses, gets all the details right, and likes practical, immediately useful information. He is the sensible realist. Beth Anne has a preference for *intuition*. When she takes in information from the world around her, she searches for possibilities, always imagining the future, speculating on what is possible. She is the inspired dreamer.

Dan's strength is the step-by-step, steady way he works, with a realistic idea of how long a task will take. He is careful with facts and good at precise work. These strengths are useful in his work as assistant to a plant manager, where he is responsible for keeping the production line operating.

Beth Anne follows her hunches, sometimes leaping to a conclusion quickly. She dislikes precise work and is impatient with detail. Her strength is in improving things, seeing new relationships between things. These strengths are useful in her work as a paraprofessional, where she helps people create better lives.

Thinking–Feeling

Thinking and Feeling are two different approaches to decisions. People with a *thinking* preference use logic and analysis to make decisions. They look at problems objectively, weighing facts and evidence. They want decisions to be fair and rational. People with a *feeling* preference are influenced by how others will feel and consider the effects of their decisions on other people and on relationships. They emphasize harmony and empathy.

Judging–Perceiving

People who prefer *judging* live in an orderly way, planning ahead, organizing, following through. They respect deadlines and do their best to meet them. They tend to like schedules and lists. People who prefer *perceiving* live in a more flexible, spontaneous way, adapting to new circumstances as they arise. They like to keep things open, gather more information, and have many options. While those who prefer judging may decide too quickly, overlooking new information, those who prefer perceiving resist deadlines and feel time pressures too late.

Knowledge of your Myers–Briggs type can give you clues about the kinds of work environments that you might like. It can also help you to understand why you are uncomfortable in some work environments, when they don't match your preferred way of operating in the world. You can use your understanding of your preferences to find more congenial working and learning environments and to improve your relationships with different types of people.

| *What Careers Suit Me?* | **CASE 2.2** |

My biggest dilemma was not knowing what my interests and values are. What occupational field can I choose that satisfies my personality? . . . I took a self-assessment test called the Myers–Briggs Type Indicator® (MBTI). It indicated that my type is ISFJ. The letter *I* stands for *Introvert,* meaning that my energy flows inward. The letter *S* stands for *Sensing.* My learning style is sensing because I tend to focus on the present and concrete information gained from the senses. [*F* stands for *Feeling,* and feeling types are sympathetic, compassionate, and accepting.] The letter *J* stands for *Judging.* My lifestyle is judging [planned, orderly].

My [Holland] Self-Directed Search indicated that my code is CSI. The letter C stands for *Conventional.* I like to examine, record, and gather information. I am able to follow procedures. . . . [*S* stands for *Social,* and *I* for *Investigative*]. I like helping people in need. . . . It's amazing how my [Holland] code, CSI, helped me see how many different occupations are right for me. One of the occupations was medical record technician, and [there were] many others.

—Liliana O.

WHERE STUDENTS GET STUCK,   AND
WHAT TO DO IF IT HAPPENS TO YOU

"I want to take a 'test' that will tell me what to do."

Pat loves animals and children. Should she try to become a veterinarian? A pediatrician? She signed up for career counseling, and her first question was, "Can you give me a test that will tell me what to do?" Many students are like Pat, hoping that there is a simple way to solve their career dilemma. They hear about career tests and believe that taking such a test will solve all their problems. Career inventories can be of tremendous value, since they help to identify promising areas and provide an organized picture of interests or personality; but they cannot replace your search for information. Your best bet is to define your dilemma clearly and specifically and then to search the three databases for information. A test is not a substitute for this search process.

Your career direction in life is unique and personal. In reading this chapter and in completing the activities, you have launched your search for information. The next chapter completes the search of the personal identity database by looking at your interests and skills. Let your search continue to unfold, and build a solid base for sound career and educational decisions.

KEY POINTS

1. Information from your personal identity database is essential to making career and educational decisions that hold the potential for personal satisfaction, continued development, and workplace success.

2. To increase the potential for personal satisfaction, select an occupation that is congruent with an identity that will make you proud and that will enable you to be a part of groups in which you feel valued and supported.

3. Looking at your career dreams is one way to deepen your awareness of who you are as a person.

4. Taking time to reflect on what you care about, what you truly value, helps you to choose a type of work in which you feel rewarded for the expenditure of your life energy.

5. Selecting a career that matches your personality type has proved to be a useful method.

6. Use the six Holland personality types—Realistic, Conventional, Enterprising, Social, Artistic, Investigative—to identify which occupational families fit your personality.

7. The Myers–Briggs Type Indicator® enables you to understand your preferences on four basic dimensions:

   a. Extraversion–Introversion

   b. Sensing–Intuition

   c. Thinking–Feeling

   d. Judging–Perceiving

8. Students can get stuck when they believe erroneously that a "career test" will magically tell them what career they should pursue.

WHERE ARE YOU?

Your third grade teacher said you had a problem with math. You gave up on math, and you forever eliminated two-thirds of the jobs available in this world.

Somebody decided the Navy needed a cook. After your hitch, you opened a restaurant. Mother was a nurse. Now you are. Why are you where you are?

Because *you* want to be there? Think about it. Maybe you ought to be somewhere else. Maybe it's not too late to figure out where, and how to get there.

© 1984 United Technologies Corporation. Used with permission.

YOUR WORK VALUES AND SUCCESS

ACTIVITY 2.5

NAME _____

OVERVIEW

In this activity you will have the opportunity to identify your work values.

TASK 1 A SUCCESSFUL PERSON

Out of all the people you know personally, who would you say has done especially well for herself or himself in terms of a career?

Name _____

Relationship to you _____

Career _____

What makes you say that this person is successful?

_____

_____

_____

_____

_____

Using the list of work values in Activity 2.2 (pp. 32–33), identify the three top values that you believe have guided your successful person's career, and write them in the spaces below.

1. _____
2. _____
3. _____

TASK 2   YOUR CAREER CHOICE

Now look at your own tentative career choice and your values. If you are unsure of your career choice, identify an interesting career possibility.

What is your career area?

_____

Think of people who are successful in your chosen career area. What values are important to this group of people?

1. _____
2. _____
3. _____

Now list the top three values that guide your life.

1. _____
2. _____
3. _____

One reason to choose a particular occupation is that it will provide you with the opportunity to use your life energy in ways that you find worthwhile.

In what ways does your career choice allow you to spend your energy in ways that you find worthwhile?

_____

_____

_____

_____

_____

Do you anticipate any conflict between what you value and your career choice (e.g., you value creativity in the arts and have selected a career area that typically offers limited opportunities for such creative expression)?

_____

_____

_____

_____

_____

_____

_____

_____

TASK 3   WORK VALUES AND CULTURAL INFLUENCES

Power, money, and fame are indicators of career success in U. S. culture. You may share this view or you may have other indicators of career success.

Discuss the importance of attaining power, money, and fame through your career.

_____

_____

_____

_____

_____

Identify how much money you would like to make annually in your peak earning years. Will your career choice allow you to reach this goal?

_____

_____

_____

_____

_____

TASK 4   Reflect on Your Learning

What did you learn from this activity about yourself and your values?

_____

_____

_____

_____

_____

ACTIVITY 2.6   WHO AM I?[4]

NAME _____

OVERVIEW

In this activity you will gather information from your personal identity database. Your purpose is to increase your understanding of your values, personality, interests, and skills.

Some students have a pretty good sense of who they are. Others may find the question "Who am I?" more difficult to answer. Regardless of how easy or difficult you find it, you will increase your understanding of your personal identity database by spending time thinking carefully about the question "Who am I?"

After engaging in this activity, you may find some things about yourself that you want to change or improve. This kind of awareness is valuable. With this understanding, you can set some personal goals to change your behavior in ways that will enhance your chances of success. However, you must not be too critical of yourself. It is equally important to become aware of your strengths—the things about you that have contributed to your success so far and will continue to be career assets. Your goal is an honest, balanced self-picture.

Looking at yourself is not always easy. If possible, find a quiet spot where you can spend some time working on your self-appraisal without interruption.

TASK 1 SEE YOURSELF FROM DIFFERENT PERSPECTIVES

A good way to start a self-appraisal is simply to identify adjectives that seem to describe you as a person. In this section you will describe yourself and consider how others see you.

Description by Friends

Using three short phrases, indicate how your friends might describe you.

_____

_____

_____

Self-Description

Now describe yourself, using three short phrases.

_____

_____

_____

Description by Your Boss

If your bosses (a current one and/or past bosses) were talking about you to a stranger, how would they describe you as a worker?

_____

_____

_____

_____

TASK 2 DESCRIBE YOURSELF USING SYMBOLS

In this section you will describe yourself by choosing symbols to represent important aspects of your personal identity.

What animal or car represents an important aspect of your personality? Provide a rationale for your selection.

Example: An ant represents the part of my personality that is hardworking and does my part in any teamwork situation.

Example: A Volvo represents the part of my personality that likes to create practical and functional things.

_____

_____

_____

_____

_____

What animal, car, or color will describe your life as you hope it will be ten years from now? Why?

Example: I hope my life is like the color blue. I selected blue because blue represents calm and serenity.

_____

_____

_____

_____

_____

What is one thing that you would like to improve or change about yourself?

_____

_____

_____

_____

_____

What did you learn from this self-appraisal that will be helpful to you in the future?

_____

_____

_____

_____

_____

Our deepest fear is not that we are inadequate. Our deepest fear is that we are powerful beyond measure. It is our light, not our darkness, that most frightens us. We ask ourselves, who am I to be brilliant, gorgeous, talented and fabulous? Actually who are you not to be? . . . Your playing small doesn't serve the world. There is nothing enlightened about shrinking, so that other people won't feel insecure around you. As we let our light shine, we unconsciously give other people permission to do the same.

—Nelson Mandela

ACTIVITY 2.7   HOW DO OTHERS SEE ME?[5]

OVERVIEW

In completing this activity, you will interview at least five people to obtain positive feedback. You will learn what traits or qualities they admire in you and hear their ideas on how these strengths might be helpful in your career. Your main purpose will be to *gather information* that will (1) help you understand your positive qualities, (2) help you set your career direction, and (3) allow you to practice obtaining positive feedback.

Although a thorough assessment always includes positive and negative qualities, in this activity the accent is on the positive. When positive and negative feedback are mixed together, many times the positive feedback is overlooked. In this activity you will focus exclusively on your strengths.

If you need more room, or if you are instructed to do so, type your answers separately.

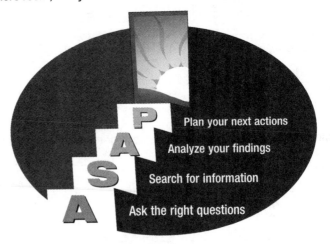

P Plan your next actions
A Analyze your findings
S Search for information
A Ask the right questions

STEP 1 ASK THE RIGHT QUESTIONS

Identification of Potential Feedback Givers

Select seven people who could provide you with positive feedback on your strengths and skills. Select people from different parts of your life: your family, friends, classmates, coworkers, or boss. This wide selection allows you to get a picture of yourself from a variety of perspectives.

_____

_____

_____

_____

Avoid asking your parents or children for feedback. Typically, those closest to you find it difficult to single out just one or two of your traits.

For each person you select, give the person's name, describe his or her relationship to you, and list the reasons why you selected the person to give you feedback.

STEP 2 SEARCH FOR INFORMATION

Obtaining Feedback from Each Person

Ask each of the seven people for a few minutes of uninterrupted time. You may use the following paragraph to introduce the task:

> *I am being asked to obtain some positive feedback about my qualities and skills as part of a career development assignment. I believe that your feedback would be valuable, and I welcome your views. Please identify a quality or trait that you like or admire in me. I would be interested to hear your perspective on how this trait or quality might be an advantage or disadvantage in my career.*

Take notes on each person's response. You may want to copy the following Positive Feedback Data Sheet and use it to record each person's feedback. Ask questions so that the feedback is as specific as possible. When the person has finished, thank the person for her time and the feedback. Repeat the process with each person you selected until you have received feedback from at least five people.

POSITIVE FEEDBACK DATA SHEET

Name _____

Relationship _____

My reasons for selecting this person

_____

_____

_____

The quality or trait that this person admires in me

_____

_____

_____

Does this person believe that this trait is an advantage or disadvantage in my career? Why?

_____

_____

_____

_____

_____

_____

STEP 3 ANALYZE YOUR FINDINGS

Step 3.1 Themes and Patterns

Your first task is to understand the themes and patterns in the feedback that you received. Look for skills and qualities that several people mentioned. Comment on any surprises.

In analyzing this feedback, what conclusions did you reach?

_____

_____

_____

_____

Step 3.2 Overlooked Qualities and Skills

What is one talent you have that you feel no one else really knows about?

_____

STEP 4 PLAN YOUR NEXT ACTIONS

Step 4.1 Learning Summary

What did you learn about yourself?

_____

_____

_____

_____

Step 4.2 Plan for Additional Feedback

Periodic feedback is important to update how you are perceived by others as you advance in your education and career. You need to think about *when* you will seek more feedback and *whom* you might ask.

What is your plan to obtain from others additional feedback about your strengths?

_____

_____

_____

_____

Why do I work in the theatre? I've often asked myself why. And up to the present, the only answer I've been able to make will strike you discouragingly trivial: simply because the theatre is one of the places in the world in which I am happy.

—Albert Camus, *"Why I Work in the Theatre"*

CHAPTER 3

Identifying Your Interests and Skills

When love and skill work together, expect a masterpiece.
—John Ruskin

3

WHAT YOU LIKE, AND WHAT YOU ARE GOOD AT

In Chapter 2 you reflected on your values and got a picture of your personality type—two of the dimensions of your personal identity database. In this chapter we turn to the other two dimensions: your interests and skills. You will get to know Campbell's work orientations, a neat way to look at both these dimensions together. This will help you to appraise your current skills and to see which ones will lead to workplace success. When you conclude your work on your personal identity database, you will have the confidence to list the educational and career options that hold the most promise for bringing you satisfaction, continuing personal development, and workplace success.

YOUR INTERESTS AND CAMPBELL'S WORK ORIENTATIONS

Your career interests are the kinds of work activities you are attracted to, what you like to do. These interests become stable in early adulthood.[1] As a result, the same kinds of activities that you like at the beginning of your career will still be enjoyable many years later. Your interests play a central role in determining your career satisfaction.

To help you identify and understand your career interests, David Campbell, an expert on careers and work, has arranged the different ways to make a living into seven work orientations.[2] As you can see in Table 3.1, each orientation rep-

Influencing

Influencing activities involve taking charge and being responsible for results through positions of leadership, politics, public speaking, and marketing.

People who like Influencing activities typically work in organizations. Although they may not necessarily be at the top, they still tend to find their way into positions heading specific functions that interest them.

Organizing

Organizing activities bring orderliness to the work environment by structuring the work of others, managing, and monitoring financial performance.

People who are inclined toward Organizing activities are good at planning procedures, managing projects, and directly supervising the work of others. They emphasize efficiency and productivity, are good with details, and usually enjoy solving the day-to-day problems that inevitably crop up in organizations.

Helping

Helping activities provide personal services, such as teaching, healing, and counseling.

People who like Helping activities are deeply concerned with the well-being of others. They enjoy having personal contact with the people they are working with and are genuinely concerned with helping their students, clients, or patients live full, satisfying lives.

Creating

Creating activities involve undertaking different kinds of imaginative pursuits, such as creating artistic, literary, or musical productions, or designing products or environments.

People drawn to Creating activities select a creative medium such as writing, art, music, or invention. They have the ability to create new products and concepts.

aNalyzing

Analyzing activities involve evaluating data, conducting scientific experiments, and working with mathematics.

People who are attracted to Analyzing activities are comfortable with numbers and intellectual concepts; they have a strong need to understand the world in a scientific sense.

Producing

Producing covers practical, "productive," hands-on activities, such as farming, construction, and mechanical crafts.

People who favor Producing activities generally like to work with their hands and see the results of their labors. They are generally good with tools and enjoy taking on new construction projects or repairing mechanical breakdowns.

Adventuring

Adventuring activities involve risk taking, tests of endurance, and a degree of physical danger through, say, police and military work or athletics.

People who like Adventuring activities frequently seek out excitement. They often like working in teams.

TABLE 3.1

Campbell work orientations.

Source: Adapted from *Manual for the Campbell™ Interest and Skill Survey (CISS™).* Copyright © 1992 by David Campbell, Ph.D. Published and distributed exclusively by NCS Pearson, Inc., PO Box 1416, Minneapolis, MN 55440. Reproduced with permission by NCS Pearson, Inc.

"CISS" is a registered trademark and "Campbell" is a trademark of David P. Campbell, Ph.D.

resents a different kind of activity. For example, if you like creating, it is logical that occupations involving creativity would hold your interest. The Creating orientation encompasses occupations in the arts, the performing arts, writing, fashion, and the culinary arts. Perhaps you are interested in finding adventure and enjoy taking risks: the Adventuring orientation encompasses occupations in police and military work and in athletics. Identifying your predominant orientation helps to summarize the kinds of activities that you find attractive, and points you to a family of occupations that would allow you to engage in those activities.

ACTIVITY 3.1 **SELF-ASSESSMENT OF YOUR INTERESTS USING THE CAMPBELL WORK ORIENTATIONS[3]**

Use the descriptions of the seven Campbell work orientations in Table 3.1 to answer the following questions.

1. If you attended a large social event where people from the seven types gathered in seven different areas, which group would you join first?

_____

2. After leaving the first group, which would you join next?

_____

3. Which of the seven would you especially avoid?

_____

Once you identify which Campbell work orientations you lean toward, you can consider career "families" that match them. Table 3.2, Sixty Occupations and Their Campbell Work Orientation Codes, will help you understand which families of occupations might correspond to your interests. As you study this table, underline the occupations that you are attracted to. Let yourself be open to new possibilities, as Jennifer did. Once Jennifer realized that she had Organizing interests, she moved from a narrow focus (accounting) to considering a broader range of business careers involving Organizing interests. She began to look at many business-related majors, especially those in health care administration. This possibility was especially attractive because she has a Helping orientation.

Consider the match between your interest orientation and the orientation of a particular occupation. For example, attorney is an Influencing occupation. If you have an Influencing orientation and are interested in the legal field, there is a good match between your occupational interests and your work orientation. If you have a Producing orientation, however, know that most attorneys likely do not share your primary interest.

Consider both your primary and secondary likes and dislikes. Specialties within the legal field utilize secondary interests. For instance, an attorney specializing in patents, copyrights, and intellectual property cases is likely to have both Influencing and Analyzing tendencies, while an attorney specializing in senior law is more likely to have Influencing and Helping interests.

Now go back briefly to Activity 3.1 and identify your favorite primary and secondary Campbell work orientations. Ideally, these work orientations will be the same in those occupations that you found appealing in Table 3.2. For example, if you identified your interests as Adventuring and Influencing in Activity 3.1 and you underlined Police Officer in Table 3.2, there is a good match between your interests and the kinds of occupations you like. If your favorite work orientations do not match the families of occupations you were

TABLE 3.2
Sixty occupations and their Campbell work orientation codes.

Influencing

I	Attorney
IO	Financial Planner
IO	Hotel Manager
IO	Manufacturer's Representative
IO	Marketing Director
IO	Realtor
IOA	CEO/President
IOH	Human Resources Director
IOH	School Superintendent
IC	Advertising Account Executive
IC	Media Executive
IC	Public Relations Director
ICH	Corporate Trainer

Organizing

O	Secretary
OI	Bank Manager
OI	Insurance Agent
OI	Retail Store Manager
OIH	Hospital Administrator
ON	Accountant (CPA)
ON	Bookkeeper

Helping

H	Child Care Worker
H	Guidance Counselor
H	Religious Leader
H	Teacher K-12
HC	Social Worker
HNC	Psychologist
HN	Nurse (RN)
HIO	Nursing Administrator

Creating

C	Commercial Artist
C	Fashion Designer
C	Liberal Arts Professor
C	Librarian
C	Musician
C	Translator/Interpreter
C	Writer/Editor
CO	Restaurant Manager
CP	Chef

aNalyzing

N	Physician
NP	Chemist
NP	Medical Researcher
NPH	Math/Science Teacher
NO	Computer Programmer
NO	Statistician
NOP	Systems Analyst
NP	Engineer

Producing

P	Carpenter
PN	Electrician
PN	Veterinarian
PNA	Airline Mechanic
PO	Agribusiness Manager
PNC	Landscape Architect
PC	Architect

Adventuring

AI	Police Officer
AIO	Military Officer
AP	Ski Instructor
APN	Test Pilot
AH	Athletic Coach
AH	Athletic Trainer
AH	Emergency Medical Technician
AH	Fitness Instructor

Source: Manual for the Campbell™ Interest and Skill Survey (CISS™). Copyright © 1992 by David Campbell, Ph.D. Published and distributed exclusively by NCS Pearson, Inc., PO Box 1416, Minneapolis, MN 55440. Reproduced with permission by NCS Pearson, Inc.

attracted to, talk to a counselor or your instructor, who can help you clarify your interests.

Once you have identified your interests, one more dimension remains to be tackled: your skills. Let's turn to this dimension now.

THE SKILL DIMENSION OF YOUR PERSONAL IDENTITY DATABASE

Unlike values, personality, and interests, which are relatively stable dimensions of your personal identity database, the skill dimension changes continually as you add to your inventory of competencies. Although, strictly speaking, your career skills are what you can do right now, you can increase your skills with training, practice, and experience.

Because your skill base has the potential for sizable expansion, your skill appraisal has two goals. The first goal is to identify what skills you have already acquired. The second goal is to learn what additional skills would be advantageous for you to master. With this knowledge you can direct your college and work experience to build skills for success.

You will examine your skills from several viewpoints. First, you will identify the skills that are associated with your interests. Then you will identify the skills that are the best all-around bets for today's workplace. Finally, you will learn to describe your skills in the language that employers understand.

Develop Skills Related to Your Interests

If you are like most people, you would find it satisfying to be paid for activities you enjoy. That is why we start by looking at the kinds of skills that are related to your career interests. For example, if you are attracted to the Helping orientation, it is important to assess your "people skills," such as those employed in counseling and teaching. Do your friends find you to be a good listener? Have you taken the time to tutor a friend for an exam? If you answered yes, you have already begun to acquire counseling and teaching skills. Your interests and some confirmation of aptitude provide you with the confidence to work on your helping skills.

Campbell has conveniently arranged a skills list to correspond to his seven interest orientations (Table 3.3). When you analyze your skills using the Campbell work orientations, you can simultaneously identify activities you like and the corresponding skills that it would take to be successful.

ACTIVITY **3.2**	**SELF-ASSESSMENT OF YOUR SKILLS USING THE CAMPBELL WORK ORIENTATIONS**

1. Review the skills list in Table 3.3 and specify your top three skills and their Campbell work orientation.

SKILL	CAMPBELL WORK ORIENTATION
Example: Sales	Influencing

SKILL	CAMPBELL WORK ORIENTATION
A. _____	_____
B. _____	_____
C. _____	_____

2. How well do your top skills match your top interests? If your skills do not match your interests, identify some ways to develop skills in the areas you like.

_____

_____

The Campbell™ Interest and Skill Survey (CISS™) is a systematic and comprehensive inventory of your interests and skills. For a moderate fee, you can take the CISS™ on the Internet. You can find it on the *U. S. News & World Report* (**www.usnews.com**) site by clicking on "Education" then "Career" and selecting the "Career Self-Assessment" interactive tool. After you complete the survey, you will receive an eleven-page report of your interests and skills.

TABLE 3.3

Campbell's seven skill orientations.

Influencing

Leadership
Law/politics
Public speaking
Sales
Advertising/marketing

Organizing

Supervision
Financial services
Office practices

Helping

Adult development
Counseling
Child development
Religious activities
Medical practice

Creating

Art/design skill
Performing arts
Writing
International activities
Fashion
Culinary arts (cooking)

aNalyzing

Mathematics
Science

Producing

Mechanical crafts
Woodworking crafts
Farming/forestry
Plants/gardens
Animal care

Adventuring

Athletics/physical fitness
Military/law enforcement
Taking risks/adventure

Source: Manual for the Campbell™ Interest and Skill Survey (CISS™). Copyright © 1992 by David Campbell, Ph.D. Published and distributed exclusively by NCS Pearson, Inc., PO Box 1416, Minneapolis, MN 55440. Reproduced with permission by NCS Pearson, Inc.

Many college counseling services provide this inventory for free as part of their career planning services. Reviewing the results of the CISS™ with a trained counselor will increase its value and is strongly recommended for a thorough and accurate understanding of the results.

There are other ways to describe skills that will enable you to identify competencies important to workplace success. Let's begin with identifying the ten basic skills that form the foundation for much of today's knowledge work.

The O*NET Basic Skills

The U. S. Department of Labor has developed the O*NET, a database system that describes the skill requirements of different occupations.[4] The foundation of the O*NET skills system is a list of ten basic skills. These are defined in Table 3.4.

TABLE 3.4	Content Skills	
*Definitions of O*NET basic content and process skills.*	Content skills provide the foundation that is needed to work with and acquire more specific skills in a variety of domains.	
	Reading Comprehension	Understanding written sentences and paragraphs in work-related documents
	Active Listening	Listening to what other people are saying and asking questions as appropriate
	Writing	Communicating effectively with others in writing as indicated by the needs of the audience
	Speaking	Talking to others to effectively convey information
	Mathematics	Using mathematics to solve problems
	Science	Using scientific methods to solve problems
	Process Skills	
	Process skills contribute to more rapid acquisition of knowledge and skills across a variety of domains.	
	Active Learning	Working with new material or information to grasp its implications
	Learning Strategies	Using multiple approaches when learning or teaching new things
	Critical Thinking	Using logic and analysis to identify the strengths and weaknesses of different approaches
	Monitoring	Assessing how well one is doing when learning or doing something

Source: Matthew Mariani, "Replace with a Database: O*NET Replaces the *Dictionary of Occupational Titles*," *Occupational Outlook Quarterly,* 43, No. 1 (Spring 1999): 2–9;

O*NET Online (online.onetcenter.org); U. S. Department of Labor, Employment & Training Administration, www.doleta.gov/programs/onet/. O*NET Online provides the quickest and easiest way to learn about the latest O*NET developments. You can also use this site to identify careers suited to your skills. O*NET™ 3.0 is a trademark of the U. S. Department of Labor, Employment and Training Administration.

You may be surprised to see that the list of basic skills is no longer confined to the "3 R's," reading, writing, and arithmetic. They make the list, of course, but notice what is added: the *process skills*, such as critical thinking and active learning, that allow you to acquire knowledge and solve new problems.

Much of your college coursework is helping you elevate your basic skills so that you are ready to perform more complex jobs in the workplace. Your assignments do more than acquaint you with new information. You are improving your basic skills when you make a class presentation (i.e., speaking), when you tackle a new subject area (i.e., active learning and learning strategies), or when you perform a lab experiment (i.e., critical thinking).

Portable Skills

Although many students can identify the skills that correspond to their interests, they are sometimes confused and misinformed about what employers want. Like many students who major in the liberal arts, Leslie began her job search thinking, "I'm a history major; I can't *do* anything." This kind of statement reveals a lack of familiarity with different skill types. Students often believe that unless they have specific job-content knowledge (e.g., how to write advertising copy, argue a case in court, plan a highway, or market a new product), they can't do anything that an employer would value.

To help you understand your potential career skills, we will divide them into two categories: job-content skills and portable skills. *Job-content skills* are those skills that require specialized knowledge and know-how related to a particular job or occupation. For example, it takes special knowledge and know-how to be a sports marketing specialist or public relations writer. However, students usually overemphasize the importance of job-content skills, believing that these kinds of skills are all they really need to succeed.

Portable skills, which are grouped into six "clusters" in Table 3.5, are not linked to one occupation; they are useful in many kinds of work. With technology eliminating, transforming, and creating occupations, portable skills are your best all-around bets; they offer the flexibility that will allow you to take advantage of evolving opportunities. For example, once you master the skill of commanding the attention and respect of others when speaking in a group, you can use it in many different kinds of work.

Activity 3.4, Your Portable Skills Profile, found at the end of this chapter, is a list of 88 portable skills arranged in the six clusters given in Table 3.5. Performing the activity will help you to use the language of the workplace to describe the assets you developed in college. As a result, you won't overlook valuable skills or underrate your college achievements and their relevance to workplace success. These abilities are important not only in the business world, but also in the professional world of doctors, dentists, pharmacists, lawyers, engineers, teachers, psychologists, and so on.

TABLE 3.5

Six portable skill clusters.

Interpersonal skills	Problem-solving skills
Communication skills	Change-management skills
Computer skills	Self-management skills

In reviewing the six clusters, you may notice the heavy emphasis on "people" skills. The complexity of modern work requires more information sharing, more cooperation, more teamwork, and more work across disciplines. In fact, according to a recent survey by the National Association of Colleges and Employers, on the top of employers' list of "must-have" skills is communication and teamwork.[5]

Technological competence is another must. Most employers today assume you can use popular word-processing programs. Knowledge of other common software applications, such as spreadsheets and presentation packages, is often required too, even for nontechnical jobs. Problem solving is also vital. You need to be an expert problem solver, meeting problems head-on and working with others to find solutions.

The most recent cluster to be added to the portable skills profile is change-management skills. New research shows that employers see the ability to deal with change as an essential skill.[6] Change-management skills include flexibility and adaptability, multitasking or handling a number of projects simultaneously, and working effectively with diverse groups of people.

In the self-management cluster are a number of skills that pertain to acting in an ethical, responsible manner, following through on commitments, and managing your time. If you are like many students who are juggling work, family, and student life, you know you must be organized and plan ahead. These same skills are important in the workplace.

In later chapters, you will find out more about the challenges of today's workplace. Right now, focus on describing your competencies in the language employers understand.

Remember Leslie, the history major? She believed that all she had to offer to an employer was some knowledge of a few historical facts. When she filled out her portable skills profile, however, Leslie realized that she was developing important portable skills in college: researching unknown topics and issues; gathering information from databases and libraries; analyzing problems carefully; and viewing problems and situations from different perspectives. In the business world, product planning, market research, and purchasing are just some of the job categories that need Leslie's skills. She might investigate the publishing industry, journalism, law, or even work as a CIA agent. Leslie knew that she had to do some research on occupations, but now she felt a lot more confident because she knew how to describe her skills in practical, real-world language.

Estimating Your Skill Level

When you appraise your skills, estimate the level of your proficiency. It is natural not to have the same level of proficiency in all your skills. Our mastery of some skills is so great that we can call ourselves "expert." When we compare ourselves to other people, we are confident that our skills in these areas are excellent. However, when it comes to other skills, we realize that our skill level is lower than other people's. We may know how to perform these skills, but we could certainly improve our proficiency.

When you do Activity 3.4, you have six choices to describe your level of skill on each of the 88 items. These six choices range from "Expert" to "None." It is not enough to evaluate whether you have a particular skill; you must also figure out how well you can perform that skill compared to other people. Using a scale with six levels will help you practice judging your degree of skill. When you rate yourself, it is important to be neither too harsh nor too generous.

WHERE STUDENTS GET STUCK, AND WHAT TO DO IF IT HAPPENS TO YOU

Expanding Your Experience Base

An accurate assessment of your personal identity database depends on having a number of rich experiences. Don grew up on a farm and planned to take it over from his father. When the farm had to be sold, he started at the local community college. His self-appraisal was difficult because he had such limited experience and knowledge of options. He needed to explore many subject areas and try new things. Tami was a teenage mother who had dropped out of high school and worked in a few retail jobs. After obtaining her GED, she decided to try college. It was an awakening for her. She was curious and stimulated by the experience. Like Don, she has limited knowledge of her possible interests and has not developed an array of skills. And like Don, she needs to try many different things so that she can develop her personal identity database. While anxious to choose a career, both Don and Tami now realize that they have to explore and sample many different courses first.

Don't Overlook Career Stallers

It is just as important for you to identify what might block your career as it is to know your assets. No matter what your assets are, you may not be able to advance as far and as fast as you wish if you lack crucial skills that employers require. Such areas of weakness are called "career stallers," and they require fixing before you can become successful in the workplace.

Ian, a computer science major, didn't think he had to learn how to write well. He neglected this area because it made him uncomfortable. When he started looking for jobs, he found that he was not able to compete with other computer science majors who could write letters and memos. His job search took longer, and he wasn't pleased with the pay or level of challenge that accompanied the one offer he did receive. After speaking with his placement counselor about his disappointment, he decided to take some continuing education courses to improve his business writing skills.

An honest self-appraisal will help you to start thinking about how to overcome potential obstacles through additional coursework, tutoring, or help from fellow students.

MAKING SENSE OF THE INFORMATION IN YOUR PERSONAL IDENTITY DATABASE

Now that you have explored each of the four dimensions of the personal identity database in Chapters 2 and 3, it is time to check whether you have a good picture of yourself.

Typically, when you look at the personal identity database, you use introspection. You look inside and ask yourself about your past, your present, and your vision of the future. It is a way of holding a mirror to yourself. The "Who Am I?" activity in Chapter 2 guides you through an introspective self-appraisal.

You may feel uncomfortable using introspection because you have not worked with this method before. Unfortunately, the task of assessing our interests, skills, personality, and values is typically neglected in our schools until it is time to set our career direction. The result is that we lack experience using introspection to get a picture of ourselves.

Moreover, we all have the capacity to fool ourselves. Sometimes our self-appraisal is distorted because we deceive ourselves into thinking we are either better or worse than we really are.

To build a more complete and accurate self-picture, ask for help from others and use a variety of appraisal tools. It is important to engage people you trust to help you with your appraisal. Many students turn to professionals. Counselors can help you avoid the risks of self-appraisal, ask pertinent questions, and structure helpful activities. Other professionals who might help in appraisal are advisers, placement officers, and professors. None of these people can do the self-appraisal for you or tell you what kind of work to select, but their assistance will enrich your understanding of this complex database.

And don't overlook the help you can get from friends and family. Their feedback can help you clarify your strengths and areas where you might improve. Activity 2.7 (How Do Others See Me?) is a tool for getting feedback from them.

Career inventories are also important appraisal tools. Although you should not rely too heavily on these "tests," they are an important source of information. Check with your counseling services office to see if they are available. Popular inventories include the Campbell Interest and Skill Survey™ (CISS™), the Holland Self-directed Search®, the Strong Interest Inventory®, and the Myers–Briggs Type Indicator®.

The National Association of Colleges and Employers' CareerPlanit site (**www.careerplanit.com/resource/assessment.htm**) provides links to a variety of Web self-assessment tools, including two of the most popular, The Career Key and the Keirsey Temperament Sorter. The College Board (**www. collegeboard.com**) and Princeton Review (**www.review.com**) are two other sites that offer self-assessment tools. Use Web instruments as a fun way to stimulate your thinking. Be cautious about the results, however. They may not be accurate or trustworthy because many Web-based assessments do not meet rigorous psychological testing standards for validity and reliability.

Sometimes you can get expert career help by using specially designed computer programs that permit a self-directed, systematic exploration of your personal identity database. They can also provide help with your career and educational searches. Some of the most popular programs are DISCOVER, SIGI PLUS, and FOCUS.

Using all these methods of data collection—introspection, help from experts, feedback from others, career inventories, and computer-aided searches—provides a richer, more balanced view. The result is a more trustworthy and precise understanding of your personal identity database.

THE VALUE OF PERSONAL IDENTITY INFORMATION: THEMES AND PATTERNS EMERGE

btaining accurate information from the personal identity database is central to making sound decisions. Yet at this point in the process, many students begin to doubt that this is so. For example, Keisha had to declare a major the next semester and was feeling some pressure. She completed the activities in Chapters 2 and 3 and began to get a picture of herself. Her first reaction was that these activities had been a waste of time, since she still wasn't sure which major to choose. She felt impatient and confused. Her counselor helped her to gain a new perspective by explaining that the information she had gathered from her personal identity database would help her focus her search for a college major. The selection process would be more efficient and more effective.

With her counselor's help, Keisha summarized some key points of information as follows: "I am extroverted and like to interact with others. My interests are organizing and influencing, and my skills are analyzing and adventuring. I also have good communication skills." This summary suggests that Keisha would do well to explore careers in business involving contact with people.

Keisha narrowed her search from seven orientations to four, with two, organizing and influencing careers, showing the most promise. This reduced her frustration because she felt that she now had some manageable targets. It confirmed that she should research business majors, since they lead to organizing and influencing careers. And because she identified analyzing and adventuring skills, just to be sure, she added careers in computers, the military, and police work to her list of career options to research. Keisha had no interest and few skills in the helping, creating, and producing career families, so she eliminated them from her search possibilities.

Keisha felt good about knowing how to direct her search of career options. She was confident that she had a strategy that guarded against overlooking some good possibilities until she had had a chance to study them thoroughly.

Her friend Emily summarized the key points of her own information search as follows: "My Holland personality type is conventional. I am introverted and value security. I have organizing interests and skills in the computer cluster." This summary suggests that Emily look at business careers involving administration, record keeping, and accounting. She might like the banking or insurance industries. Similarly, your ability to describe yourself in career-relevant terms will help you identify possible career options.

After you formulate your summary, look for several pieces of information that point in the same direction. For example, Belinda, one of Keisha's classmates, began to think about the common threads in her list: (1) I am involved in my children's PTA; (2) I volunteer to teach crafts in a church summer camp; (3) I take child development electives in college; (4) I admire my oldest daughter's teacher. What pattern do you see in these statements? What fields might Belinda consider? What roles might Belinda consider?

Getting to the outcome of an appraisal is like chiseling to make a sculpture. An outline or form emerges over time, gradually becoming more defined and specific. For instance, knowing your Holland personality type or your Campbell work orientations will help you to become more specific about your personality, interests, and skills. This awareness will increase your efficiency and effectiveness in conducting your research on career families. Using the Campbell and Holland systems makes your search more purposeful and systematic. You can focus on those career families that offer you the most potential for satisfaction and association with a valued group.

At the same time, increasing your awareness of your interests and skills also makes your search broader. You can take a more open-minded approach. Using the Holland and Campbell systems, you can identify a family of options to explore. This increases your options and makes you richer in possibilities. This is important, because college is a period of intense development of your personal identity database. Your skills are evolving, you are introduced to new subjects, and you may discover new interests. Chapter 6, Making Choices, will help you to narrow your options and set your career direction. But for now, before you conduct your research, don't close any doors too soon.

ACTIVITY 3.3   YOUR PERSONAL IDENTITY DATABASE SUMMARY

Using the four dimensions of your personal identity database—your values, personality, interests, and skills—how would you describe yourself? Based on your description, what are the career fields and occupations you will explore further? What are the career fields and occupations that you will avoid? Make some preliminary notes below and then use separate paper to complete your summary.

_____

_____

_____

_____

_____

_____

_____

KEY POINTS

1. Your career interests are the kinds of work activities you are attracted to, what you like doing.

2. One effective way to identify your work interests is to use Campbell's work orientations.

3. Each of the seven Campbell orientations represents the primary activity of a family of occupations: Influencing, Organizing, Helping, Creating, Analyzing, Producing, and Adventuring.

4. Your career skills are what you are able to do right now, but you can increase your skills with training, practice, and experience.

5. The two goals in skill appraisal are (a) to identify what skills you have already acquired, and (b) to discover what additional skills would be advantageous for you to master.

6. When you analyze your interests and skills using the Campbell work orientations, you can simultaneously identify activities you like and the corresponding skills that it would take to be successful.

7. In the O*NET system there are six basic content skills: reading comprehension, active listening, writing, speaking, mathematics, and science. Four important process skills are now considered basic skills, too: active learning, learning strategies, monitoring, and critical thinking. This change reflects how important it has become for you to be able to learn continually in the workplace.

8. Skills can be classified into two types. Job-content skills are those skills that require specialized knowledge and know-how related to a particular job or occupation. Portable skills are not linked to one occupation; they are useful in many kinds of work.

9. Skills that are essential in any occupation or workplace are organized into six "clusters":

   a. Interpersonal skills
   b. Communication skills
   c. Problem-solving skills
   d. Change-management skills
   e. Computer skills
   f. Self-management skills

10. The Portable Skills Profile is an assessment tool that helps you appraise the level of your skill in each of these six clusters.

11. Students can get stuck by having limited personal experiences and by overlooking "career stallers."

12. Several methods can help you collect information from your personal identity database:

   a. look within yourself
   b. take career inventories
   c. consult with others
   d. use computer guidance systems

13. Information from the personal identity database enables you to organize your career search around those options that promise satisfaction, development, and success. As you explore the career information and college and graduate school databases, keep all your options open.

YOUR PORTABLE SKILLS PROFILE[7]   ACTIVITY 3.4

NAME   *Brian*

OVERVIEW

In this activity you will conduct a comprehensive skill appraisal. You will rate your current level of skill on 88 items, which have been grouped into six clusters. The six clusters consist of portable skills; that is, they would be useful in any job, occupation, industry, or company. These clusters are

1. Interpersonal skills
2. Communication skills
3. Problem-solving skills
4. Change-management skills
5. Computer skills
6. Self-management skills

No one can be expected to perform all 88 skills at the highest level. It is natural that you would be stronger in some clusters than in others. Your first goal is to identify the skills you have already acquired. These are your skill assets. However, since all the skills are important, your second goal is to learn what additional skills would be advantageous for you to master. Once these skills are identified, you can plan ways to improve them in the future.

For each item, you will be asked to rate your skill on a six-point scale that ranges from *Expert* to *None*. It is not enough to evaluate whether you have a particular skill; you must figure out how well you can perform it relative to other people. This activity will give you some practice making these comparisons. When you rate yourself, be honest. It is important not to be either too hard on yourself or too generous!

SAMPLE

Review the following Portable Skills Profile sample to see how to complete your profile:

Lauren Anderson wants to be a teacher someday. Currently, she works as a sales associate in a large department store.

| *Scale* | E = EXPERT | sa = slightly above average | P = Poor |
| | G = Good | sb = slightly below average | N = NONE |

COMPETENCY	RATING
1. Convince others about the value of a product, service, or idea	E (G) sa sb P N
2. Manage my time well	E G sa sb (P) N
3. Understand and work with information presented in statistical or numerical forms	E G (sa) sb P N

1. Lauren rated her ability to "Convince others about the value of a product, service, or idea" as "Good." When a customer is uncertain, she is often able to persuade him or her to make the purchase. Since teachers need to persuade students to do their homework and tackle difficult subjects, she is pleased with this rating.

2. Lauren rated "Manage my time well" as "Poor." Since she started working more hours, she has had a hard time organizing enough study time. She still goes out too much and forgets important deadlines. Her grades have dropped, and this semester she has several difficult courses. She is concerned with this rating because teachers have a big workload preparing lessons and grading homework. If she can't manage her time well, she will not succeed.

3. Lauren rated "Understand and work with information presented in statistical or numerical forms" as "sa." She gets average grades in math, and she has to work hard to understand statistics. She knows that as a teacher she must understand test scores and interpret graphs and tables that show different rates of student progress.

TASK 1   COMPLETE THE PORTABLE SKILLS PROFILE

For each item, circle the rating that best describes your level of skill right now.

Scale   E = EXPERT   sa = slightly above average   P = Poor
      G = Good   sb = slightly below average   N = NONE

Interpersonal Skills

Interpersonal skills are your "people skills." You must be able to establish good working relationships with all types of people. Interpersonal skills also include the ability to inform, persuade, negotiate, motivate, teach, advise, advocate, lead, and deal with conflict.

COMPETENCY	RATING
1. Relate to people in a friendly, accepting manner	E **(G)** sa sb P N
2. Work comfortably and effectively with people in authority over me (e.g., boss and other higher-ups)	E **(G)** sa sb P N
3. Cooperate with my coworkers	E **(G)** sa sb P N
4. Work comfortably and effectively with direct reports or anyone for whom I am responsible (e.g., students, clients)	E G sa **(sb)** P N
5. Work comfortably and effectively with the public (e.g., customers, clients, or patients)	E G sa **(sb)** P N
6. Keep my boss informed about my work; bring any problems to her attention in a timely way	E G **(sa)** sb P N
7. Build and utilize a strong network at work—people I count on to provide me with relevant information, instruction, and support	E G **(sa)** sb P N
8. Build trust with others by following through on commitments	E **(G)** sa sb P N
9. Show respect for all people regardless of background, culture, ethnicity, religion, age, gender, disability, or lifestyle	E **(G)** sa sb P N
10. Convince others about the value of a product, service, or idea	E G sa **(sb)** P N
11. Motivate others (e.g., work team members, students, clients, direct reports). Encourage them to take action, achieve, and excel	E G **(sa)** sb P N
12. Teach or train others (e.g., new employees, coworkers, students, clients)	E G **(sa)** sb P N
13. Coach others	E G sa **(sb)** P N
14. Advise others	E G **(sa)** sb P N
15. Supervise others	E G sa **(sb)** P N
16. Lead others	E G **(sa)** sb P N
17. Advocate for others (e.g., clients, patients, students)	E G **(sa)** sb P N
18. Cope with conflict constructively	E G sa **(sb)** P N
19. Maintain good working relationships even if I disagree on an issue	E G **(sa)** sb P N

Communication Skills

People who are expert communicators are at ease when they talk or listen. They are effective in one-on-one encounters, over the telephone, on-line, or in a group. Their oral and written communication skills are excellent.

20. Pay attention to the ideas, opinions, and questions of others — E **(G)** sa sb P N

21. Listen without interrupting — **(E)** G sa sb P N

22. Consider others' ideas thoughtfully even when they are different from my own — E **(G)** sa sb P N

23. Explain my point of view. Give my opinion — E G sa **(sb)** P N

24. Make "small talk"; be sociable — E G sa sb **(P)** N

25. Express myself well in one-on-one conversations — E G sa **(sb)** P N

26. Use excellent vocabulary in spoken communication — E **(G)** sa sb P N

27. Use standard English — E **(G)** sa sb P N

28. Answer the telephone professionally and respond appropriately to the caller — E **(G)** sa sb P N

29. Provide accurate information over the telephone — E G **(sa)** sb P N

30. Take accurate and detailed messages — E G **(sa)** sb P N

31. Give clear and concise paper or electronic documents — E G, **(sa)** sb P N

32. Use correct grammar in written and electronic communications — **(E)** G sa sb P N

33. Listen well in a group — E **(G)** sa sb P N

34. Command attention and respect of others when speaking in a group — E G **(sa)** sb P N

35. Am an effective team member; contribute whenever possible — E **(G)** sa sb P N

36. Lead a team; take charge when appropriate — E G **(sa)** sb P N

37. Prepare and deliver effective presentations in front of a group — E G **(sa)** sb P N

Problem-solving Skills

Constructive problem solving entails defining a problem adequately, seeking information about possible solutions, weighing the alternatives, making decisions, and implementing the solution.

38. Take the initiative in solving problems; don't wait for others or avoid problem areas — E G **(sa)** sb P N

39. Keep an open mind about possible solutions — E **(G)** sa sb P N

40. Dig deeply; don't just stay on the surface — E G **(sa)** sb P N

41. Analyze problems carefully; view problems and situations from different perspectives — E **(G)** sa sb P N

42. Research unknown topics and issues; gather information from databases and libraries — E **(G)** sa sb P N

43. Demonstrate effective study techniques for solving problems using books and manuals — E G **(sa)** sb P N

44. Actively seek others' ideas about a problem   E   G   sa   (sb)   P   N

45. Ask appropriate questions; try to learn as much about the problem as I can   E   G   (sa)   sb   P   N

46. Don't give up or accept a marginal solution   E   G   (sa)   sb   P   N

47. Experiment; try anything to find solutions to problems   E   G   (sa)   sb   P   N

48. Understand and work with information presented in statistical or numerical form   E   G   (sa)   sb   P   N

49. Read and use information presented in graphs, charts, and tables   E   G   (sa)   sb   P   N

50. Weigh the advantages and disadvantages of each course of action before making a decision   E   G·   (sa)   sb   P   N

51. Make decisions; take action when required   E   G   sa   (sb)   P   N

52. Plan and implement a solution   E   G   (sa)   sb   P   N

53. Set milestones to see if solution is working   E   G   sa   sb   (P)   N

Change-management Skills

The ability to adapt quickly and positively to rapid change in the workplace is an important skill to cultivate. Coping with changes in technology, organizational structures, project assignments, and team members requires you to be flexible and adaptable.

54. Multitask; work on a number of projects simultaneously   E   G   (sa)   sb   P   N

55. Adapt quickly to changes in plans, project goals, and team members   E   (G)   sa   sb   P   N

56. Meet deadlines in a fast-paced work environment   E   (G)   sa   sb   P   N

57. Learn from coworkers who come from different cultures and have different world views   E   G   (sa)   sb   P   N

58. Face the challenge of dealing with new problems with determination   E   G   (sa)   sb   P   N

59. Respond coolly to emergency or crisis situations   E   G   (sa)   sb   P   N

60. Have healthy outlets to handle stress effectively   E   G   (sa)   sb   P   N

61. Read and attend conferences regularly so that I can be aware of technological and global forces that are affecting my field, my industry, and my organization   E   G   sa   sb   (P)   N

62. Manage my career rather than leaving it to others   E   G   (sa)   sb   P   N

63. Continue to build my portfolio of marketable skills   E   G   sa   sb   (P)   N

Computer Skills

Computer-related skills help you obtain information, share information with others, and perform a number of work tasks, such as communication using E-mail, research using electronic databases and the Internet, and use of common computer software packages.

64. Correspond professionally via E-mail   E   (G)   sa   sb   P   N

65. Use search engines and electronic databases to answer specific questions   E   (G)   sa   sb   P   N

66. Use word processing software, such as Microsoft Word or WordPerfect, to prepare documents   E   (G)   sa   sb   P   N

67. Use spreadsheet software, such as Excel and Lotus   E   G   sa   (sb)   P   N

68. Create an effective multimedia presentation on a   E   G   (sa)   sb   P   N
    given topic

69. Use the Internet to aid in my career management   E   G   (sa)   sb   P   N
    (gathering information about careers and further
    education, searching for jobs, networking)

70. Keep up with legal and ethical issues in technology   E   G   (sa)   sb   P   N
    (e.g., privacy, intellectual property rights, hacking)

71. Seek out and learn new technologies as they emerge   E   (G)   sa   sb   P   N

Self-management Skills

Self-management skills include managing your time, taking care of your own needs, acting
in an ethical, responsible manner toward others, and following through on commitments.

72. Manage my time well   E   G   sa   (sb)   P   N

73. Set goals; prepare to-do lists   E   (G)   sa   sb   P   N

74. Set priorities; deal with most important tasks first   E   (G)   sa   sb   P   N

75. Plan ahead realistically to get my work done and meet   E   G   (sa)   sb   P   N
    my goals

76. Refrain from putting things off; don't procrastinate   E   G   sa   (sb)   P   N

77. Get to meetings and appointments on time, or even   E   (G)   sa   sb   P   N
    arrive a little early

78. Act responsibly; do my part of the job   E   (G)   sa   sb   P   N

79. Am dependable; get the job done   E   (G)   sa   sb   P   N

80. Am assertive; don't let others take advantage of me   E   G   sa   (sb)   P   N
    at work

81. Show initiative; ask for challenging assignments   E   G   (sa)   sb   P   N

82. Persist despite obstacles   E   G   (sa)   sb   P   N

83. Have self-confidence   E   G   sa   (sb)   P   N

84. Act with integrity; am honest; don't lie or cheat   E   (G)   sa   sb   P   N

85. Demonstrate high ethical standards at work   E   (G)   sa   sb   P   N

86. Dress appropriately for my work setting; maintain a   E   (G)   sa   sb   P   N
    neat, clean, professional appearance

87. Strike a balance between home, work, and student life   E   (G)   sa   sb   P   N

88. Take good care of myself (e.g., diet, exercise, sleep) E   (G)   (sa)   sb   P   N

TASK 2 ANALYZE YOUR PORTABLE SKILLS PROFILE

1. Identify your career goal or a field that might be a possibility for you.

   My career goal is to be a   professional   pilot

2. Review the six skill clusters. Identify your strongest cluster and your weakest cluster.

   (1) Interpersonal skills   (4) Change-management skills

   (2) Communication skills   (5) Computer skills

   (3) Problem-solving skills   (6) Self-management skills

My strongest cluster is Self management

My weakest cluster is Change management

3. Describe your career assets.

Go back over the Portable Skills Profile and list ten items on which you rated your-self as "Expert," "Good," or "slightly above average." Select your best assets by listing the highest-rated, most important items for your career area.

(1) Work well w/ others
(2) build trust
(3) listener
(4) good grammar
(5) Ask questions
(6) problem solving
(7) research
(8) set goals
(9) learn new tech
(10) integrity

From this asset list, select one of your best competencies. Provide evidence that you have developed this skill. Use examples from your school or work experience (e.g., course grades, praise from a customer or boss). Be specific and provide details. Use additional sheets if necessary.

Integrity - core Army belief. Always honest, even when not advantageous, even overseas

4. Identify four skills that you want to improve.

Go back over the Portable Skills Profile and look for skills in need of improvement. These are usually skills that you rated "slightly below average," "Poor," or "None." You may also want to include in this list skills that you rated "slightly above average," because there is room for improvement.

(1) Assertive
(2) Procrastination
(3) Social skills w/ strangers
(4) Keeping up w/ job outlooks

Which of the above skills are career stallers? Go back over the list of items to improve. Place a star (*) next to those items that would interfere with your career success.

5. Describe ways to improve these skills. List coursework or work experience that would help you.

In what ways can you improve some of these skills, especially the career stallers?

_____
_____
_____
_____
_____
_____
_____
_____

TASK 3 REFLECT ON YOUR LEARNING

What did you learn from this activity?

_____
_____
_____
_____
_____
_____
_____
_____
_____

ACTIVITY 3.5   LIFE ACCOMPLISHMENTS[8]

OVERVIEW

In this activity you will select two life accomplishments to describe in depth. After you complete each description, you will identify the skills and personal qualities that were important in producing a successful outcome. The purpose of this activity is to increase your awareness of your strengths.

TASK 1 LIST FIVE LIFE ACCOMPLISHMENTS

Life accomplishments are events that are personally meaningful, ones in which you have a sense of a job well done. For the purposes of this exercise, it doesn't matter how big or small this event might have been in the eyes of the world.

You may find it easier to identify your life accomplishments if you think about your life in ten-year intervals. List your accomplishments, decade by decade. For example, during the first decade (ages 0–10), one person might list "mastering a two-wheel bicycle," while another might list "winning a prize in grammar school." During adolescence one person might describe "overcoming shyness at a party," while another names "being selected for a sports team." Life accomplishments may reflect important personal victories, such as "quitting smoking," or they may have been widely praised, such as "saving a stranger from drowning."

Review the events in your life and list at least five life accomplishments.

_____

_____

_____

_____

_____

_____

_____

_____

_____

_____

_____

TASK 2   SELECT TWO LIFE ACCOMPLISHMENTS

From your list of accomplishments, select two to describe in depth on separate paper. Complete a one- to two-page essay on each event, following these instructions:

- Give the essay a title.
- Explain the challenge or problem that you had to overcome.
- Describe specifically what you did. What were your actions in the situation?
- What skills and strategies did you use to meet the challenge?

TASK 3   ANALYSIS OF SKILLS AND PERSONAL QUALITIES

What did you learn about yourself from this experience? Mention discoveries about values, interests, and personal qualities. Take notes here and complete on separate paper.

_____

_____

_____

_____

_____

_____

_____

_____

_____

_____

CHAPTER 4

Gathering Information About Careers

Nearly three-fourths of working adults surveyed said if they could start over again, they would try to get more information about their career options.
—*Occupational Outlook Quarterly*

THE VALUE OF CAREER INFORMATION

In Chapters 2 and 3 we saw that getting to know yourself requires you to look inward and to ask yourself what kind of person you are and who you would like to become. In this chapter we will see that getting to know a career requires you to look outward and discover a variety of career options that will give you more freedom of choice.

Just as a travel brochure acquaints you with a place you have never been, or a novel acquaints you with an experience you have never had, career information introduces you to new career possibilities. Career information allows you to try out a possible option *mentally* before you invest your time and money actually preparing to pursue it. Getting to know careers is like shining a light into the dark: you are less likely to stumble. Your path will be clearer.

The goal of a search for career information is to identify or confirm career possibilities. This will enable you to pick your courses, your major, and your internships with greater confidence. Even if you have already selected a career option, your search will confirm that you have a complete and accurate picture of that career. Also, knowing how to search for career possibilities is in itself a valuable skill.

As your career unfolds, your own development and career advancement, as well as changes in occupations and industries, will mean new, unforeseen career possibilities and threats. Getting to know careers will help you avoid problems and take advantage of opportunities as they arise.

Using the Career Information Database and the ASAP Four-Step Search Method

To make your searches easier and more effective, this chapter shows you what kinds of information to gather and how to conduct your search. Just as you spent the past two chapters using the personal identity database to get to know yourself, in this chapter you will use the *career information database* to get to know careers. The career information database, outlined in Table 4.1, is a way of organizing the essential kinds of information to search for. You will see that using the career information database is important, because doing so will keep you on track by identifying the kinds of information that are worth gathering.

To organize the search process, you will employ the four-step ASAP search method introduced in Chapter 1. Take a moment to look at Figure 4.1 to review these four steps.

		TABLE 4.1
Nature of the Work	Rewards and Benefits	*The career infor-*
Entry Requirements	Outlook for the Future	*mation database.*

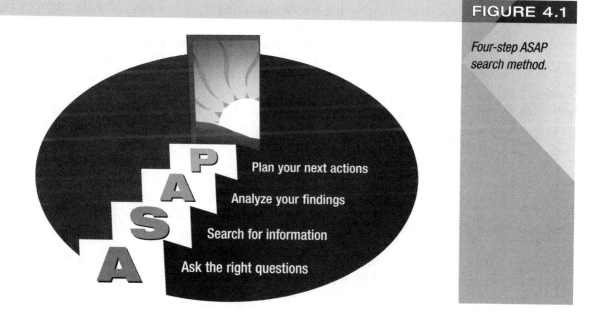

FIGURE 4.1

Four-step ASAP search method.

P — Plan your next actions
A — Analyze your findings
S — Search for information
A — Ask the right questions

This chapter will provide you with details and examples that will show you how the ASAP search method will keep you on track as you conduct your search. You will learn to recognize when you have searched long enough and what to do if you get stuck. Activity 4.2, the Career Comparison, provides you with an opportunity to use the ASAP approach to gather information about two career options that interest you.

Identify the Start Point of Your Search

The start point of your search depends on *how specific* and *how certain* your choice of occupation is right now. Before you plunge into your search, it is necessary to describe your personal start point.

To understand why this is necessary, consider the different situations of Angela and Michelle. They both are accounting majors. Angela does well in her accounting courses and has enjoyed working part-time in the accounting office of a small magazine publisher. Since she is both *specific* in her occupational choice and *certain* that it is a good one for her, Angela's career search is focused. She knows she wants to go into accounting, and she only wants her search to help identify the setting or industry. Michelle, in contrast, has also made a *specific* occupational choice, but she is *uncertain* that it suits her. She finds her accounting courses boring, which makes it hard to keep up. She is very outgoing and likes to talk with people, but she doesn't find her classmates very interesting. Michelle needs to look at career options that take advantage of the skills she has developed in accounting, but that also fit her personal qualities.

Most students who search for career information can identify a *general* career area, but it is too broad to be useful for selecting a major or courses. They wish they could be more *specific*. For example, Matt wants a career in the legal field. He is not sure what his occupational options are. Another student, Jeff, is good at helping customers in his part-time job at McDonald's. He wants to know how he can use his skills in specific occupations with good advancement possibilities. Tamara has secretly dreamed about a career in the television industry, but wants to know if such a career is practical. Kyoko wanted to be a nurse and was a prenursing major, but she didn't do well in the science courses and was not admitted to the nursing program. She wants to know what her alternatives are now. David has many interests, some of them conflicting. He likes photography and computers. He has thought of engineering. He also realizes that he is a deal maker, good at bringing people together, and he wonders about sales and marketing careers. He wants to know how, with so many interests, he can ever find an occupation. Michelle, Matt, Jeff, Tamara, Kyoko, and David all need to become *more specific* and want to feel *more certain* about their career direction. At first, their career search will produce more, not fewer, options. Then they can begin to narrow them down to more specific choices.

ACTIVITY 4.1   WHAT IS THE START POINT OF YOUR SEARCH?

1. Write down your career interests. Put down as many interests as you have. Do not hold back now. List all the career options you are interested in.

I am interested in

_____

_____

_____

_____

2. *How specific are you regarding a career option?*
   (Circle the one response that best describes your current situation.)

   a. I am very specific about my chosen occupation. My career interests are well defined.

      Like Angela, your interests are well defined and you are specific about your occupational choice.

   b. I am headed toward a career field (e.g., law, business, health care), but need more information about all my options.

      Like Matt, Jeff, and Kyoko, you are able to identify a broad area of interest.

   c. I have an interest in a particular setting (e.g., TV).

      Like Tamara, you have dreamed about a particular setting, but have not focused on skills or occupations in that industry.

   d. My interests are conflicting, include many unrelated options, or both.

      Like David, you have many interests. You may have discovered new interests since you started college.

3. How certain are you about your choices?
   Now think about how certain you are that you have chosen a good career path for yourself.

   a. I am certain that I have chosen a good career path.

      Again, like Angela, you are certain that you have chosen the best career path for yourself.

   b. Sometimes I have doubts that I have chosen a good career path.

      Like Matt, Jeff, and Kyoko, you sometimes have doubts that you have chosen a good career path.

   c. I am very uncertain that I have chosen a good career for me.

      Like Michelle and David, you feel uncertain. You may feel you are not in the right major, or you are uncertain because many options seem appealing.

   Now you know what type of search to conduct. If you are both specific and certain [you selected answer (a) to both questions 2 and 3 in the exercise], you need to do a focused search about a particular occupation. If you are not specific and feel any uncertainty, you need to conduct a broad search of several career options before you can become more specific. Then, once you have specified an option, you can do a focused search to make certain that it is right for you. Searches, both focused and broad ones, depend on the quality of the questions you ask.

STEP 1: ASK THE RIGHT QUESTIONS

The career information database in Table 4.1 is composed of basic types of information that you must gather to get a good picture of a career possibility: (1) the nature of the work, (2) the entry requirements, (3) the rewards and benefits, and (4) the outlook for the future.

We will examine each of these types of information more closely and explain why you would want this kind of information. You will end up with specific questions that will provide a full picture of a career option. You will have an opportunity to use these questions at the end of the chapter in Activity 4.2, the Career Comparison, as well as in Activity 13.3, the Career Information Interview. Become familiar with these questions and use them whenever you have an opportunity to increase your knowledge of career options.

What Is the Nature of the Work?

The first type of information to search for concerns the nature of the work. You want a picture of what the work in a particular field is like: the tasks, the working conditions, the major employers, and the places in the country where this kind of work is found. Ask yourself if you would like to engage in these activities as described on a daily, weekly, monthly, and annual basis.

Here is a list of questions to ask regarding the nature of a given field of work.

1. What kind of work is done in this field (types of tasks, responsibilities, assignments, projects)?
2. What kinds of people would I work with? Try to get an idea of their work values, interests, and skills.
3. How much of the work is with data, with people, and with things?
4. Would I work indoors? Sitting? Standing? Would I work outdoors? Would I travel?
5. What kinds of pressures are felt by a person working in this field?
6. What are the working conditions? Could they affect my health and safety?
7. How flexible are the work hours in this field? Does it involve long hours, shift work, overtime, or weekends?
8. Who are the major employers?
9. What are the areas of concentration in this field?
10. What are the related occupations?

What Are the Entry Requirements?

Questions about entry requirements provide a picture of the level of education that you will need before you enter an occupation, the kinds of skills that are required, and the personal qualities suited to the occupation. Careful investigation of entry requirements helps you select the most appropriate major for your career goal.

You need to see how difficult it is to be admitted to a training program. You may like the work, feel good about its rewards and benefits, and see a bright job outlook, but discover that it is very difficult to get admitted to a training program. In this case you will want to explore some other career options as alternatives. For example, physical therapy is a growing occupation. However, space in physical therapy programs is limited and competition for entry is very stiff. Fortunately, there are many career options in health care and in other helping professions.

Examine a particular career option with an eye to your personal qualities. An insurance sales representative should generally be outgoing and optimistic. An emergency room technician must be able to work quickly under pressure. For an accountant, accuracy is important.

Here is a list of questions that you need to ask about educational requirements and qualifications.

1. What education is required for someone who is entering this field (associate's, bachelor's, master's, or other advanced degrees)?

2. What college majors are suggested as the best route to enter this field?

3. How competitive are the entrance requirements to the educational programs in this field? Are such programs available in my area?

4. Which courses typically are the most difficult in the training program? What special actions (e.g., obtaining tutoring, joining a study group, or meeting with the professor during office hours) could I take to improve my chances of success in these courses?

5. What kinds of people tend to do well in this field? What skills and qualities are important (e.g., attention to detail, ability to work under pressure, or ability to negotiate)?

What Are the Rewards and Benefits?

Figuring out what you would gain in a particular occupation means looking at two things: your monetary earnings and your psychological rewards. A typical compensation package is a good way to examine the monetary rewards of a particular career option. Compensation is a broad term that covers your salary, bonuses and commissions (if applicable), and benefits. While looking at a career, you will want to find out about salary, but you will also want to learn about any commissions, bonuses, and benefits that will supplement the salary.

For example, an FBI agent's starting salary was about $46,000 in 2001.[1] The agent's compensation package would be a higher total than this because it would include the monetary value of the medical and life insurance, paid vacation, and retirement benefits. In contrast, a business owner may earn more than $46,000, but must buy health insurance, set aside money for retirement, and cover days lost to illness or vacation. So in looking at the financial rewards of a career, remember to consider the total compensation package.

When examining the monetary rewards of an occupation, most people focus on the salary (and other compensation) they would receive when they *enter* the occupation. That's important information, but don't forget to follow up by determining how high your salary is likely to go *with experience.* An experienced FBI agent can earn a base salary of $73,000—considerably more than a beginning agent does. However, senior sales and marketing executives in large corporations typically earn six-figure salaries—much more than a senior FBI agent. Find out about the range of salary and compensation at the highest level of the occupation you are considering.

Another important type of career reward is psychological. Psychological rewards include having power, authority, status, or autonomy. For instance, as a manager you have the power to make the decisions, and people look up to you. As a teacher, you work free from daily, direct supervision. As a paralegal, you might work in a plush corporate law office. What types of psychological rewards do you seek?

Here is a list of questions to ask about the monetary and psychological rewards of an occupation.

1. What does a typical worker earn in this field?
2. What is the salary range of people in this field after they have acquired some job experience?
3. Are such employee benefits as paid vacation, sick leave, pension, and health insurance typical in this occupation?
4. Is there an opportunity to learn new skills?
5. Will my work be recognized by my coworkers?
6. Will I work independently? Be closely supervised? Work in teams?

What Is the Outlook for the Future?

Since occupations are changing rapidly, questions concerning the impact of technology, the future job market, the opportunities for advancement—in short, the occupation's long-term potential—are more important than ever before. You will want to know the best predictions about the future of the occupation. You will want to know if this occupation fosters the development of portable skills, that is, skills that would be important in other lines of work if you wanted or needed to make a switch. This set of questions looks at the potential for advancement and personal development and at the probability that this occupation will survive well into the twenty-first century.

Here are some questions to ask about the job outlook:

1. How is technology changing this field?
2. What is the job market in this area?
3. Are job opportunities increasing or decreasing in this area? What are the reasons for predicting an increase or decrease?
4. Is there much competition in this area for jobs in this field? What are the reasons for this?
5. What factors influence advancement in this field?
6. Can you describe a possible sequence of jobs that will lead to increased responsibility and earning power in this field?
7. Will I be able to develop skills that I can transfer to another field?

There are several factors to consider when you assess the future job market. One factor is how fast an occupation is growing (e.g., slower than average, average, faster than average). According to U. S. Department of Labor projections through 2008, 16 of the 20 fastest-growing occupations are associated with health services or computer technology. Some other rapidly growing occupations are desktop publishing specialists, paralegals, and social- and human-services assistants.

Don't overgeneralize. Check specific occupations carefully. For example, two computer-related occupations, systems analysts and computer engineers, are projected to have fast growth and high earnings. However, computer operators are among the occupations projected to have the largest decline in employment.[2]

Also consider the size of the occupation (number of people with that job) to get a picture of the job outlook. For example, elementary school teacher is one of the occupations that provides many jobs for college graduates because of its large size. Although the projected growth rate for elementary school teachers is expected to be slightly slower than the average rate of 14 percent through 2008, the sheer size of the occupation means that there will be many openings.[3]

A look ahead to the future possibilities for employment in a specific occupation completes the areas that you need to investigate to make an informed choice. Now you have a good understanding of the career information database and know what questions to ask. Answers to the 28 questions in the four areas of the career information database can provide a well-rounded picture of a career option.

What Are Some Good Sources of Information?

Two excellent sources of career information are provided by the U. S. Department of Labor: the *Occupational Outlook Handbook* and its companion guide, *The Career Guide to Industries*. These reference books are updated every two years and are available in print form and on the Internet. These sources are often a good place to begin your search.

You can find many sites on the Internet that provide career and industry information. To help you, Table 4.2 provides a listing and brief description of 12 such sites.

Some publishing groups (e.g., VGM, Facts on File, JIST) specialize in career information. Some examples of print sources are given in Table 4.3. Career information centers, placement offices, libraries, and bookstores stock these kinds of books.

Don't overlook magazines. Magazines such as *Black Enterprise* and *Hispanic Business* are gold mines of information for the potential business owner. *Working Woman* has many career-related articles of interest to women.

Find out if your school has a computerized guidance system. You can use such a system for either a broad or a focused search. Four frequently used systems nationwide are FOCUS, DISCOVER, SIGI PLUS, and GIS. Your college may also subscribe to a computer system that provides career information tailored to your geographical area.

To find all these sources, start with your library. Many colleges have set up a special location for career material, such as a career resource center, an area of the library, the counseling center, or the placement office. A good bookstore may have a section for books about various careers. After a careful look, you may decide to buy one or two books for your personal library.

TABLE 4.2

Web sites that provide career and industry information.

America's Career Infonet: www.acinet.org

This comprehensive site has a Career Resource Library section that allows you to explore occupational groups by broad subject categories, such as business and financial operations, legal occupations, or farming, fishing, and forestry occupations.

Career Guide to Industries: www.bls.gov/cghome.htm

This U. S. Department of Labor guide is a companion guide to the *Occupational Outlook Handbook*. It provides overviews of 42 major industries, accounting for over 7 out of every 10 wage and salary jobs.

Hoover's Online (Industry Snapshot): **www.hoovers.com**

Use the Industry Snapshot section to get an industry overview.

JobHuntersBible.com: www.jobhuntersbible.com

Richard Bolles's well-known mega-site offers updated links to career information in a section called "Research." He also lets you know which sites he thinks are best.

JobStar California: http://jobstar.org

This extensive site, maintained by the California library system, contains a section called Career Guides.

Military Career Guide Online: www.militarycareers.com

This site provides details about 152 enlisted and officer occupations in the Army, Navy, Air Force, Marine Corps, and Coast Guard.

Occupational Outlook Handbook: http://stats.bls.gov/ocohome.htm

This U. S. Government site profiles approximately 87 percent of all the jobs in the nation—250 occupations. For each occupation you will find a description of the nature of the work, entry requirements, rewards and benefits, and outlook for the future.

The Princeton Review: www.review.com

This site provides a section that allows you to research careers.

The Riley Guide: www.dbm.com/jobguide/careers.html or www.rileyguide.com

This excellent mega-site contains updated links to many career information sources.

University of California, Berkeley, University Health Services Career Exploration Links: www.uhs.berkeley.edu/Students/CareerLibrary/Links/careerme.htm

This university site provides links to more than 800 career information sites.

University of Manitoba, Counseling Service: www.umanitoba.ca/counselling/careers.html

This Canadian university's site provides links to a wide variety of occupational information sources.

Wetfeet.com: www.wetfeet.com

This site provides industry information and features a "real people" section. Its career information is more limited and focuses on business careers.

Note: Web sites are frequently reorganized. If you experience difficulties, try a key word search (e.g., JobStar) and drill down until you find the occupational or industry information section of the Web site.

You can get free information from professional organizations. These organizations and their addresses are always listed in every entry of the *Occupational Outlook Handbook*. Drop them a postcard. All you need to write is, "Please send information on (name the occupation) to (your name and your home address). Thank you." Another option is to check the organization's Web site.

Standard reference books, such as the *Occupational Outlook Handbook*, provide a general overview of many occupations. Other valuable resources, such as magazines, newspapers, experts, and friends, may focus on only one or two types of information, such as salary or outlook for the future. They highlight one aspect and ignore others. Make it a habit to use multiple sources of information so that your information about various career options is both comprehensive and detailed.

Career Families	TABLE 4.3
Occupational Outlook Handbook (U. S. Government Printing Office)	*Some print sources of career information.*
Careers in Child Care (VGM)	
Careers in Social and Rehabilitation Services (VGM)	
Career Opportunities in Education (Checkmark Books)	
Guide to Careers in Community Development (Island Press)	
How to Get Into Advertising: A Guide to Careers in Advertising, Media, and Marketing Communications (Cassell Academic)	
Careers in Focus: Business (Ferguson Publishing)	
Paralegal Careers (Delmar Publishing)	
The Harvard Business School Guide to Careers in Marketing (Harvard Business School Press)	
Careers in Art and Graphic Design (Barron's Educational Series)	
Careers in Communications and Entertainment (Kaplan)	
Opportunities in Performing Arts (VGM)	
Opportunities in Visual Arts (VGM)	
Is There an Engineer Inside You? (Bonamy Publishing)	
Opportunities in Occupational Therapy Careers (VGM)	
Opportunities in Biotechnology Careers (VGM)	
Opportunities in Dental Care Careers (VGM)	
Guide to Careers in the Health Professions (Princeton Review)	
Opportunities in Home Economics (NTC/Contemporary Publishing)	
Internet Jobs for the Rest of Us (Berkeley Publishing)	
Careers in the Environment (VGM)	
Opportunities in Electronics Careers (VGM)	
Opportunities in Sports and Fitness Careers (NTC/Contemporary Publishing)	
Careers in Criminology (Lowell House)	

(continued)

TABLE 4.3	**Interests**
Some print sources of career information, continued.	*Careers for Animal Lovers & Other Zoological Types* (VGM)
	Careers for Aquatic Types and Others Who Want to Make a Splash (VGM)
	Careers for Nature Lovers and Other Outdoor Types (NTC/Contemporary Publishing)
	Careers for Computer Buffs & Other Technological Types (VGM)
	Great Jobs for Anthropology Majors, . . . for Biology Majors, . . . for English Majors, . . . for History Majors, . . . for Psychology Majors, etc. (VGM)

Industry

Career Guide to Industries (U. S. Government Printing Office)

Opportunities in Banking . . . in Hotel and Motel Management Careers . . . in Publishing Careers (VGM)

Career Opportunities in Television, Cable, Video, and Multimedia (Facts on File)

100 Careers in the Music Business (Barron's Educational Series)

Opportunities in Government Careers (NTC/Contemporary Publishing)

The Harvard Business School Guide to Careers in the Nonprofit Sector (Harvard Business School Press)

America's Top Military Careers: The Official Guide to Occupations in the Armed Forces (JIST Works)

Special Factors

Learning a Living: A Guide to Planning Your Career and Finding a Job for People with Learning Disabilities, Attention Deficit Disorder, and Dyslexia (Woodbine House)

The Work-At-Home Mom's Guide to Home Business (Hazen Publications)

The Shoestring Entrepreneur's Guide to the Best Home-Based Franchises (Griffen Trade)

Best Home Businesses for the 21st Century (Career Press)

Home-Based Business for Dummies (Hungry Minds)

The Military Advantage: Your Path to an Education and a Great Civilian Career (Learning Express)

Work Worldwide: International Career Strategies for the Adventurous Job Seeker (Avalon Travel)

Career Solutions for Creative People: How to Balance Artistic Goals with Career Security (Allworth Press)

Pathways to Career Success for Women: A Resource Guide to College, Financial Aid, and Work (Ferguson)

Best Careers for Bilingual Latinos (VGM)

Geographic Location

If you want to (or must) live in one of our large cities or a particular state or region listed below, the Adams Job Bank Series suggests both jobs and companies (use the volumes that fit your plans): *Atlanta, Austin/San Antonio, Boston, Chicago, Dallas–Fort Worth, Denver, Detroit, Houston, Las Vegas, Los Angeles, Minneapolis–St. Paul, Metro New York, Philadelphia, Phoenix, Pittsburgh, Portland, San Francisco, Seattle, Washington D. C.; Carolina, Connecticut, Florida, Indiana, Missouri, New Jersey, Ohio, Tennessee, Virginia*

STEP 2: SEARCH FOR INFORMATION

To search for career information efficiently, you need to know how it is organized. There are three major ways in which career information is organized:

- By occupation
- By industry
- By career family

The most specific way that career information is organized is by occupation. This approach can be used if you know specifically what kind of work you want to do.

Information about industries focuses on the setting where the work is performed (such as the television industry or the travel and tourism industry) and is particularly useful if you know *where* you want to work, but not the kind of work you want.

Information on career families covers groups of occupations that are related. Information on career families is most useful if you know generally what kind of work you want or what kind of skill you want to use in your work. For example, if you learned in Chapter 3 that your Campbell work orientation was primarily "influencing" and you didn't like "creating," you could look at Campbell's "influencing" career family, which includes attorney, human resource director, CEO or president, school superintendent, and media executive; and avoid looking at career families in "creating," such as the performing arts.

To collect information efficiently, you search for career possibilities according to the three ways in which the information about them is organized: by occupation, industry, and career family. We will examine these three kinds of searches by following the career information searches of the students you met earlier: Angela, Michelle, Matt, Jeff, Kyoko, Tamara, and David.

Search by Occupation

An occupation is defined by the nature of the work. For example, the nature of engineering work is to use theories and principles of science and math to solve practical, technical problems. Within any occupation there are subspecialties. For example, civil engineering, electrical engineering, and mechanical engineering are subspecialties of engineering. The links between subspecialties are like blood ties between brothers or sisters. They are related by the similar type of work. But, like all siblings, they are also different in important ways. For instance, a civil engineer designs and supervises the construction of bridges, roads, tunnels, and buildings and may be employed by the state. An electrical engineer designs, tests, and supervises the manufacture of electrical and electronic equipment and may be employed in the aviation industry. A mechanical engineer is involved with the production and use of mechanical power and heat and may be employed in the automobile industry. These engineering jobs are rather different, yet all use *math* and *science* to solve practical, technical problems. When David, who found so many options attractive, looked at engineering as an occupation, he became aware of the nature of the work and its many subspecialties.

Angela, the happy accounting major, focused on occupational information almost exclusively, looking at subspecialties in accounting. She identified an interest in accounting careers in federal, state, and local government. She learned that the government uses accountants to deal with tax revenues, make expenditures according to regulations, and administer budgets. Of all the subspecialties she investigated, she was most attracted to doing accounting work for the government.

Search by Industry

A second way that career information is organized is by the *setting* where the work is performed. The television, cable, and video industry is a setting in which different occupations are found. It offers career opportunities for performing artists, producers, programmers, advertisers, and broadcasting administrators. Tamara, who had only dreamed of a TV career, began to look at possibilities in administration, programming, news, and video marketing.

Search by Career Family

Much of the career information developed to help college students has been grouped into related occupations so that you can search efficiently. Kyoko wants a career in the health care field, but was not admitted to the nursing program. In addition to her skills in helping people, she sees herself as an organizer. She likes planning and managing. In her college career center, Kyoko found a file that contained health care careers organized as you see in Table 4.4.

Just looking at how the health care career family is organized helped Kyoko decide where to search further. She identified three potential areas for exploration that seemed to combine her interest in the medical setting and her skills as an organizer:

TABLE 4.4	Health Care Cluster
A career family.	Mental Health and Mental Health Services
	Medical and Biological Science Services
	Dentistry and Dental Science Services
	General Hospital and Medical Office–Related Occupations
	Medical Emergency Services
	Administration of Health Services
	Personal and Community Health Services
	Pharmaceutical Science and Services
	Professional Medical Supportive Personnel
	Medical Professions

Source: Ronald Fredrickson, *Career Information* (Upper Saddle River, N.J.: Prentice Hall, 1982). Adapted with permission.

- General Hospital and Medical Office–Related Occupations
- Administration of Health Services
- Personal and Community Health Services

After identifying these three areas from the health care cluster, she turned to the *Occupational Outlook Handbook*, where she browsed through many occupations, but especially that of health service manager. She wrote the American College of Health Care Administrators and the Association of University Programs in Health Administration to get more information about health service management. She read selected sections of *Guide to Careers in the Health Professions*. She read about the growing occupations of managed health care manager and home health care specialist in *Working Woman* magazine. She got a computer printout on the career of medical records technician.

After summarizing what she had learned, she decided to select a major in business administration with a specialty in health care. She is attracted to the public health area and has decided to do volunteer work in the admitting office of a hospital near her home to learn firsthand about the work of health services administrators.

Matt thought he wanted to be in the legal field. He began his search for information by looking in the table of contents of the *Occupational Outlook Handbook* for careers in law. He found occupations in professional specialties (lawyer and judge), in administrative support (paralegal, legal secretary, and court reporter), and in the protective services (police, corrections officers, and special agents). He noticed that people in the legal field work in a number of settings: law firms, government courts, and state prisons, to name a few. Careers in corrections, specifically those involving rehabilitation programs, appealed to him the most. He knew that some of his high school classmates had trouble with drugs and the law. He wanted to help teenagers to get a second chance. And since he was interested in rehabilitation, he began to look at social work and counseling as well.

Jeff, who liked to help customers, looked at marketing and sales careers on the *Occupational Outlook Handbook* Web site and in books on sales and marketing. In searching for information about selling, he began to understand the difference between wholesale and retail trade. He learned about types of compensation packages (e.g., commission, fixed salary, and bonuses). He learned about sales promotion and marketing service agencies that design the contests and movie tie-in promotions like the ones he had seen at McDonald's. It had never occurred to him that people were employed to think up the sweepstakes or toy giveaways. He learned about a new area called services marketing, whose long-term job outlook was excellent because of the growth of service industries. He realized that there were many ways he could use his skills in selling. Many opportunities offered high growth and long-term potential.

You might be interested in using a career family search system organized by personality type. In Chapter 2 you identified your personality type using the system of six types created by John Holland. He organized career environments into the same six categories. The search is conducted by identifying your personality type and then examining the careers listed for that type.

Michelle worked with her counselor and realized that she fit the "enterprising" personality type—someone who is people-oriented and likes to lead.

She realized that one of her skills lay in speaking and convincing others to share her point of view. She began to look at careers in the enterprising area, such as retail manager and real estate agent. Accountants, she discovered, are a different personality type, called "conventional." Conventional types like to follow through on instructions and keep detailed records and are often skilled at clerical tasks. No wonder she felt she was different from her accounting classmates! Michelle used the computer system DISCOVER to explore career families associated with her personality type. You, too, might enjoy a computer guidance program.

Since David couldn't focus his interests, he was determined to look at all career options that were of interest and value. He searched for career information by looking at various occupations and industries. He went first to the *Occupational Outlook Handbook*, but preferred books describing career families, such as *Opportunities in Biotechnology Careers, Is There an Engineer Inside You?* and *The Harvard Business School Guide to Careers in Marketing*. He mulled over the options in computers and engineering. Then he followed up by using some of the Web sites from Table 4.2. The major difference between David and his classmates Matt, Kyoko, Jeff, and Michelle is the greater number of career families he decided to explore. Because of his many interests, he used many more sources of information.

Now you should understand the different ways to conduct focused and broad searches for career information by looking at occupations, industries, and career families. Although it seems confusing at first to have so many ways to look at career options, before long you see how useful it is to look at your career options from all these different angles. If you are very specific and certain, it is useful to search by occupation. However, most students are relieved to find that career experts have grouped similar careers into families. The grouping allows students to expand their thinking by seeing related but previously unidentified options that might be of interest. This is what happened when Kyoko, Matt, and Jeff conducted their searches.

STEP 3: ANALYZE YOUR FINDINGS

By asking the right questions and using them to guide your search, you obtain a full picture of a career option. Then it is time to examine this picture from your personal perspective. Step 3 will help you digest the information you gathered and see what it means from a personal vantage point. In Step 3, you weigh an option's advantages and disadvantages. You examine what effects becoming a member of this occupation would have on your life. You see if your self-image corresponds to the image of people in this occupation.

Compare the Advantages and Disadvantages of Career Options

Begin by making a list of each option's advantages and disadvantages. The primary way to identify whether something is an advantage or a disadvantage is to consider how the career option fits with your personality, values, interests, and skills. For instance, Angela is attracted to accounting in government settings. She is not a big risk taker, so she wants something safe. She likes to know precisely what is expected of her, and she describes herself as dependable. For her, the advantages of this option are the rewards and benefits of government positions, including good health care, pension benefits, and a measure of job security through the civil service system. Accounting work requires dependability. As you see, when the nature of the work and the rewards and benefits fit with important aspects of your personal identity, as in Angela's case, then they are advantages.

For Michelle, who dislikes her accounting courses, her search has confirmed these disadvantages: (1) she does not like the nature of accounting work—the tasks that she would have to do every day; (2) she is not detail oriented and she does not enjoy analyzing facts and figures—activities that form a major part of accounting work. When there is a lack of fit with one's personality, as in Michelle's case, the nature of the work is a disadvantage.

Your list is unlikely to have exclusively advantages or disadvantages. Angela learned that an accounting degree requires many specialized courses and that she won't have much time for some electives that she hoped to take. Michelle was attracted to the prestige of working for a big, well-known accounting firm and saw that as an advantage. Be sure to consider both advantages and disadvantages.

Consider the Effects of Group Membership

Another way to look at an occupation is to imagine yourself as a member of that group. Remember that when Michelle consulted with her counselor she found that her personality was an "enterprising" type. Like other enterprising personality types, she is energetic and self-confident and likes leadership. She enjoys persuading others to her point of view. She began to realize that if she pursued a career as a real estate agent or went into retail management she would feel a sense of belonging. In these fields she could see that the people were more like herself: ambitious and liking power, status, and the opportunity to make a lot of money.

Matt, who was considering a career in criminal justice or counseling, began to imagine his life as a drug enforcement agent and as a counselor working in rehabilitation programs. Both careers could have a positive effect on the community, but in different ways. As he looked at the nature of police work, he saw that it often involved shift work and working on weekends, holidays, and nights. The injury rate is higher than in other occupations. He would be exposed to danger. While some of his classmates found this kind of life appealing, he wasn't sure that he wanted to belong to a group with this lifestyle. He and his fiancée put a high value on a shared family life. Furthermore, Matt had a strong interest in helping others. He felt that he would be proud to be a part of a profession such as counseling, which dedicates itself to helping others.

Take a Practical Look at Your Career Options

The costs of pursuing a particular career option are also essential to consider. The costs include the money it takes to pay for the required education and the time that you would need to devote to study. For example, Matt has several education choices in the counseling field. These include obtaining an associate's degree to become a paraprofessional, a bachelor's degree in special education, a master's degree in social work or counseling to become a certified social worker or counselor, a doctorate to become a psychologist, or a medical degree and specialty training to become a psychiatrist. Each of these educational options differs in duration and expense. Moreover, many advanced degree programs are highly selective and entry is competitive. However, greater economic rewards often go to those with the advanced degrees. As Matt looks at the various programs and their approaches to counseling, he will also have to take a hard look at his chances to gain entry into competitive programs, and consider how he would pay for his schooling. A discussion with his fiancée will help him to sort out the impact of each option on their plans to start a family.

Jeff, who is attracted to marketing and sales careers, has health concerns. As he looks at sales positions in different industries, he will gather information about the need to perform product demonstrations, the amount of time spent away from the home office, and the access to health care in sales territories. These practical concerns will be important factors as he considers various options. He must look at the feasibility of meeting specific job requirements, the need for reasonable accommodation, and his special needs for medical care.

As you look at a career option, you must think about whether you can get the training and education required to pursue it. Your career choice must mesh with your life situation, including any health concerns and family obligations. Whether making a lot of money is relatively important, as it is to Jeff, or unimportant, as it is to Matt, a look at the typical compensation in the field will help you determine whether it holds the promise to provide the economic support you dream about for the future.

STEP 4: PLAN YOUR NEXT ACTIONS

Summarize Your Learning

Sometimes, by the end of a search, an occupation that you have considered turns out to have more disadvantages than advantages. You don't see yourself as a member of that group. Yet the search itself has produced much valuable learning. Take the time to summarize this learning. For example, a search for information may help you to identify the kinds of skills you want to learn. You may see more clearly that you want to increase your skills with computers, writing, or graphic design. Your knowledge about the kinds of skills that you want lets you select your major or courses.

When David completed his broad search, he carefully summarized his learning: "(1) Keep the doors open to careers in engineering and computer science by taking high-level math courses, and (2) explore business careers because they offer many more career opportunities than I initially realized." As a result of his summary, he saw the usefulness of selecting courses that would be acceptable in both an engineering and a computer science degree. In addition, he decided to take an "introduction to business" course to explore the business field. This planned sampling of courses would provide more information, while at the same time giving David six months to continue his research before declaring a major.

Tamara learned about careers in the media, and her learning summary noted several new options in programming and production. Tamara was satisfied to have a sharper focus, even though many decisions lay ahead. She was excited that her search had provided some realistic ideas for a career possibility that had been only a daydream.

All the students we have been considering are planning to continue their search for information to help them advance their careers. Angela, Matt, Kyoko, and David have started their searches for information on four-year colleges and graduate programs. Jeff wants to investigate fast-growing industries in his area, since such industries need salespeople and are more likely to give opportunities to inexperienced workers. Tamara has selected an internship in a small cable TV station. Michelle plans to speak to family friends in the real estate and retail businesses during her school break. Both students will use Activity 13.3, the Career Information Interview, to structure their next information searches.

You can see by looking at the career situations of Angela, Michelle, Kyoko, Tamara, Matt, Jeff, and David that the search for information is ongoing. They need information for decisions such as what courses to register for or what kind of summer job to search for, as well as for general career information to set their long-term direction. All career professionals recommend that the search for career information be considered an ongoing, open-ended process.

TIPS FOR HANDLING THE EMOTIONAL UPS AND DOWNS OF A CAREER INFORMATION SEARCH

You are familiar with information searches because you have written research papers or completed course projects that require them. Yet the search for career information can be a more challenging task psychologically, because it touches central concerns in your life and thus stirs more emotions. For example, you may see many possible career paths and feel excited, or you may feel overwhelmed by discovering more options and possibilities than you had known existed. You may be turned off to searching, because occupational information is often written up in scientific, dry language with few concrete examples. In looking at a particular option, you may feel attracted to the nature of the work and discouraged if you find that the entry requirements are more difficult than you expected. You may feel reassured if you see that the outlook for the future is excellent, and at the same time disappointed about its rewards and benefits. Searching can lead to a sense of confusion, an uncomfortable state that you may be tempted to avoid by stopping your search.

David's search was characterized by ups and downs. He became excited when he read about biomedical engineers and biophotographers. Then he remembered he hated studying anatomy. His initial high excitement turned to discouragement when he realized that he really had to eliminate those options. Next he came up with database marketing manager, a business option that combined computers and marketing. What about software engineer? Would that be a better choice? He was confused. While David wanted to have the comfort of saying to friends, "I'm going to be a software engineer," he knew it was more important to keep his options open. He can explain this to his parents truthfully by saying, "Right now college is giving me the skills to pursue a variety of high-tech careers. I'll have plenty of opportunity because I know that I am developing important skills in math and computers."

Michelle's search led to more options than she had known existed. While she no longer felt trapped, her career path was not as neat and clear as she had hoped it would be. Now, however, when her friends ask what she is going to be, she says with the confidence that comes from having conducted a search, "I am looking at hotel management, real estate, and retail management because those fields offer good opportunities for a person of my skills and personality type." And she has a plan to continue her research in those three areas.

Once you begin searching, you may experience confusion as you find more options than you expected, barriers to a career possibility that you hadn't known existed, or new opportunities that seem more attractive than your original dreams. It may feel as if you are more in the dark than ever before. These results are emotionally draining. How can you handle these emotions?

To keep your feelings from overwhelming you, here are some ways to handle your emotions:

- Follow a structured process for your search that mirrors the suggestions given in this chapter. Activity 4.2, the Career Comparison, uses the ASAP steps and allows you to weigh the advantages and disadvantages of two career options.

- Collect information in several short sessions rather than in one long one. Many students try to do too much at once. It is better to return to the library several times for shorter periods. Photocopy materials and get computer printouts to read at home. Shorter sessions give you time to digest the information.

- Start a file. Michelle recorded the results of her search in an unused portion of an old notebook, Angela chose five-by-eight-inch cards, while David put everything in three big envelopes that he labeled "My Future." You may want to create a file on your computer.

- Remember the advantages of both the broad and the focused search strategies. If, for instance, you find out that a possible career option is not for you, go back to a broad search in the same career family.

- Check your information for completeness and accuracy. Review the list of questions from the career information database given in Step 1 earlier in this chapter. Remember to consult multiple sources of information.

Most people end up more uncertain because they stop at the point of collecting information. The most important way to handle the increase in the number of options and the emotional factor is to use Step 3: Analyze Your Findings. You list the advantages and disadvantages of particular options. You begin to imagine whether you would be proud to be identified as a member of this occupation. Matt's comparison of drug enforcement agent and counselor helped him to see which occupation was a better fit with his values and with the kind of family life he wanted to lead. Don't overlook practical issues either. What will be the economic rewards if you pursue this option? Can you acquire the necessary training given your life situation? After collecting information, you need to take the time to analyze your findings rather than hope that merely collecting the information will make the perfect occupation appear.

WHERE STUDENTS GET STUCK, AND WHAT TO DO IF IT HAPPENS TO YOU

ven when students overcome these emotional factors, some can still get stuck. The cases described here may help you when you feel stuck.

You Have Made No Space in Your Life for the Career Information Search

Sara finds searching for information to be too time-consuming. She works and is taking a full course load. She is determined to keep her grade-point average up. She feels that this is the best way to make sure that she gets a good job when she graduates. "Extra" trips to the library to search for career information seem hard to fit in. Career experts, however, would characterize her well-meaning approach to career advancement as backward: "Fire, ready, aim." Although she is willing to work hard because she wants a good future, she doesn't take any time to get ready by searching for career information.

The Start Point Is Too Vague

Perhaps you know a student like Ashley. She says, "I am interested in working with children." She has identified a particular group of people (children) that she would like to work with. However, it is not enough just to decide to "work with children." Ashley needs to be more specific about the kinds of skills that she wants to use in working with children. Table 4.5 identifies some ways in which she might do so. You will notice immediately that, once she identifies the kinds of skills to use, she can begin her search using career families of various kinds.

You can see that the search for career options requires you to express your career interests in a way that matches how career information is organized. If you, like Ashley, are having trouble beginning your search, review Chapter 3, in which you identified your interests and skills. Also, ask your college's counselors or co-op advisors to help you become more specific about the skills that you would like to use.

Kind of Skill	Career Search Options	TABLE 4.5
I would like to **teach** children.	Teaching careers	*Skills to use in working with children.*
I would like to **heal** children.	Health care careers	
I would like to **nurture** children **emotionally.**	Mental health careers Social service careers	
I would like to **understand how children develop.**	Developmental psychology Medical research	
I would like to **entertain** children.	Careers in media Careers in writing Careers in art	

You Wrongly Believe that Information Alone Will Make Your Path Clear

Anthony is impatient about getting his future settled. He is considering newscaster and actor as possible career paths. He has investigated both career options. When he analyzes his findings, he sees that they share the same disadvantage from his viewpoint; that is, competition for jobs is keen. He is annoyed that his information search has not clearly pointed out which path he should take.

While your search for information can sometimes clarify that a path is unacceptable and can be eliminated, as you saw earlier, most career options have both advantages and disadvantages. Information doesn't make decisions—you do. A framework to help you with your career decision-making tasks is provided in Chapter 6, Making Choices. Don't be too impatient; before you can make good decisions, you must explore your options and become information rich. Anthony needs to gather information about additional options.

If you feel stuck for any reason, get help from professionals, including counselors, librarians, placement staff, internship coordinators, and professors. They will help you identify your interests and skills, suggest sources of information and ways to search, and help you clarify what you have learned.

KEY POINTS

1. Information about career possibilities allows you to try out an occupation mentally before you commit to it.

2. Your start point determines what kind of search is appropriate for you now. If you are specific in your interests and certain of your direction, you can conduct a focused search, looking at specific occupations or industries. If you are less specific or have many or conflicting interests, you need to conduct a broad search, looking at career families.

3. The career information database is a way of organizing the types of information that are important to gather:
   a. Nature of the work
   b. Entry requirements
   c. Rewards and benefits
   d. Outlook for the future

4. Career material is organized by occupation (similar kinds of work), industry or setting (similar places of work), and career families (similar occupational groups).

5. During the search, you may feel confused and find that the number of career options that you are considering increases. You can meet the challenge of a career information search by using the ASAP system.

   Step 1: **Ask the right questions.** Use the questions provided in the text to get a mental picture of a particular career option.

   Step 2: **Search for the information.** Collect your information in several short sessions. Start a file where you keep your notes.

Step 3: **Analyze your findings.** List the advantages and disadvantages, imagine yourself as a member of the occupational group, and address practical issues.

Step 4: **Plan your next actions.** Summarize your learning. Identify what kinds of action to take next. Keep your search ongoing and open-ended.

6. Here are some ways that you may get stuck.
   a. You make no space in your life for an information search.
   b. Your start point is too vague.
   c. You wrongly believe that information alone will make your path clear.

7. If you get stuck for any reason, get help from professionals, including counselors, librarians, placement staff, internship advisors, and professors. They will help you identify your interests and skills, suggest sources of information and ways to search, and help you clarify what you have learned.

Great scientists and artists have one trait in common: they both tend to be single-mindedly devoted to their work. Renoir painted every day of his life, and when old age had made his fingers too arthritic to hold a brush, he got someone to tie the brush to his hand. Haydn rose early each morning to compose; if ideas failed him, he clasped his rosary and prayed until Heaven sent him fresh inspiration. . . When Newton was asked how he had arrived at his insights, he answered, "By keeping the problem constantly before my mind."

—Max Perutz, *Is Science Necessary? Essays on Science and Scientists*

CAREER COMPARISON | ACTIVITY 4.2

NAME _____

OVERVIEW

In this activity you will compare the characteristics of two career options. Your main purpose is to describe the advantages and disadvantages of each option.

The value of comparing two career options is that you might see something in one that you might not find in the other. This will encourage you to evaluate how important the presence or absence of this factor is to you. Also, comparing two options will give you the confidence that you have made your decision rationally, using good information.

If you need more room, or if you are instructed to do so, type your answers separately.

STEP 1 ASK THE RIGHT QUESTIONS

Step 1.1 Selection of Questions

Review the list of questions in Step 1 of the chapter. Select at least one question from each of the four types of questions that you need to consider in selecting a career option.

Nature of the work

_____

_____

_____

Entry requirements

_____

_____

_____

Rewards and benefits

_____

_____

_____

Outlook for the future

_____

_____

_____

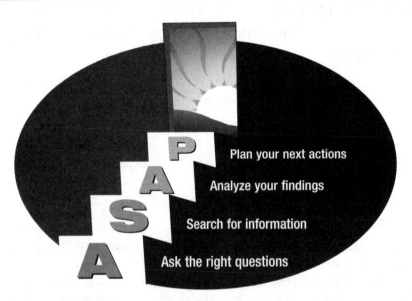

Step 1.2   Selection of Two Career Options

Write in your selections.

CAREER OPTION 1

_____

CAREER OPTION 2

_____

STEP 2 SEARCH FOR INFORMATION

Use one of the standard reference books, such as the *Occupational Outlook Handbook,* or a computer program such as Discover, Focus, or Sigi Plus. You may wish to use a Web site from Table 4.2.

Search for information from the sources that you selected and answer the questions from Step 1. Take notes. Use additional paper if necessary.

CAREER OPTION 1

_____

_____

_____

_____

_____

_____

_____

_____

_____

CAREER OPTION 2

_____

_____

_____

_____

_____

_____

_____

_____

_____

STEP 3 ANALYZE YOUR FINDINGS

Step 3.1 Comparison of Advantages and Disadvantages

List the advantages and disadvantages of each career option.

Option 1 _____

Advantages +	Disadvantages −

Option 2

Advantages +	Disadvantages −

Hints and Reminders

A comprehensive list of pluses and minuses covers several issues. Examine how well a career option fits (or does not fit) you as a person—your values, personality type, interests, and skills. For instance, if your Holland or Campbell type is similar to people in the field, it is a good sign, because you are more likely to be satisfied with your choice. Think about the skills that you would learn if you went into this field. Skills that you value acquiring would be listed on the advantage side.

Look into the future and imagine how you would like working with the people in this field. List those values and life priorities that you share on the advantage side; those that you don't, on the disadvantage side.

Costs and rewards are practical issues. Look carefully at the costs of pursuing the education required to enter each option that you researched, and the economic rewards associated with working there. If your financial goals would be met, that's an advantage. Finally, list any internal or external obstacles that must be overcome on the disadvantage side.

Only a complete list of advantages and disadvantages is a truly useful tool for deciding whether a particular option is right for you.

Step 3.2 Select the Better of These Two Options

Review your analysis. Typically, every possibility has both good points and drawbacks.

Which career option is more appealing based on your research so far?

Career option

The reasons that I selected this option are

STEP 4 PLAN YOUR NEXT ACTIONS

Step 4.1 Learning Summary

What did you learn that will be useful to you in the future? How is the information that you gathered useful in solving your career dilemma?

_____

_____

_____

_____

_____

Step 4.2 Sources of Information

What additional sources will you consult to get more information about the more appealing career option?

1. Print and media resources

_____

_____

_____

2. People

_____

_____

_____

Step 4.3 Two Additional Career Options

List two additional career options to look at as you continue to explore your career options.

_____

_____

The whole secret of a successful life is to find out what it is one's destiny to do, and then do it.

—Henry Ford

CHAPTER 5

Gathering Information About Four-Year Colleges and Graduate Schools

Learning is like
rowing upstream:
not to advance is to
drop back.
—Chinese proverb

5

THE VALUE OF FOUR-YEAR COLLEGE AND GRADUATE SCHOOL INFORMATION

Educational path dilemmas often involve difficult choices about whether to obtain further education and, if so, which program to select. You may wonder, "Is an advanced degree beneficial? Practical? Should I make it an important priority in my life?"

Students, confused and uncertain, frequently listen to half-truths and hearsay. They conclude, "It's too expensive"; "I'll go part-time"; "I'll apply later"; "I will only go to a private college"; "I can only afford a state school." These hasty, ill-informed decisions can close doors, waste their time and money, and lead them in the wrong direction.

This chapter will help you make sound decisions with confidence, because it provides a good system for answering your questions about going on for an advanced degree. Community college students are usually most concerned with going on to a four-year college. Four-year college students are typically concerned with graduate education (e.g., obtaining a master's, doctorate, or professional specialty degree in an area such as law or medicine). The *four-year college and graduate school information database* helps you understand what factors to consider as you decide, and the four-step ASAP (Ask–Search–Analyze–Plan) approach will guide your search.

It's best to begin the search early. For competitive colleges and programs, financial aid, and scholarships, you must apply by mid-February in order to be accepted for the following September. With tightening budgets, even state-supported schools have a first-come, first-served policy that makes early application essential.

WHAT IS THE START POINT OF YOUR SEARCH?　　ACTIVITY 5.1

Education path dilemmas typically start out as a tangled assortment of issues. To clarify your dilemma, circle all the questions that apply to your situation.

*I wonder **whether** I should go on for a more advanced degree.*

1. Is an advanced degree necessary to reach my career and life goals?
2. Will an additional credential be seen favorably by an employer?
3. Am I really interested in further education?

*I wonder **where** I should go for a more advanced degree.*

4. What options are available?
5. What factors should I consider?
6. Which schools have the kind of program and major I want?
7. Which are better: private or public colleges?

*I wonder **what** the application process involves.*

8. What are the deadlines?
9. What grades do I need?
10. Will I have to take any tests?
11. Will I need letters of recommendation?
12. Will I have to write an essay?

*I wonder **how** to overcome the external obstacles in continuing my education.*

13. What will an advanced degree cost?
14. Is there a college within a convenient commuting distance?
15. Can I afford to go away to school?
16. (For transfer students) How many of my credits will transfer?

*I wonder **how** to overcome the internal obstacles in continuing my education.*

17. What major is best for me?

18. Will I be able to succeed?

19. How long will it take to finish?

*I am unsure **what** priority to place on obtaining an advanced degree.*

20. Should I go on for my degree now or later?

21. Should I go part-time or full-time?

22. How will going on fit with my life situation?

Summarize your thinking about going on for a more advanced degree. What are the key issues? What personal and family considerations are relevant?

_____

_____

_____

_____

_____

_____

STEP 1: ASK THE RIGHT QUESTIONS

The four-year college and graduate school information database, pictured in Table 5.1, is a way of organizing the essential kinds of information to research. Whether your dilemma concerns undergraduate or graduate education, you gather information along these same four dimensions.

We are going to examine each of these types of information and explain why they are important. You will end up with specific questions that you can use to get a detailed picture of a college and its programs. Become familiar with these questions. Use them whenever you can to increase your general

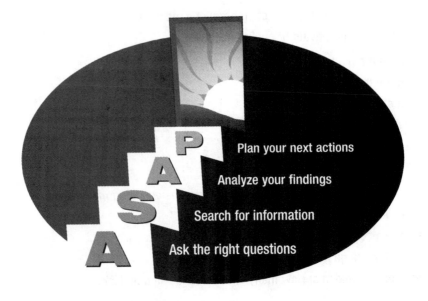

P Plan your next actions

A Analyze your findings

S Search for information

A Ask the right questions

TABLE 5.1

The four-year college and graduate school information database.

Nature of Academic Programs

Admission Requirements

School Profile and Student Body Characteristics

Cost and Financial Aid

fund of knowledge about educational options. Circle the questions that are particularly relevant to solving your current dilemma.

What Is the Nature of the Academic Programs?

The first dimension of the database concerns program offerings and ways to judge their quality. Here is a list of questions that you will want answered:

1. What is the academic reputation of the college? How is it ranked?
2. Does the college have an outstanding reputation in certain majors or programs? Which ones?
3. Describe the quality of the faculty. Are they known as good teachers? Known for their research and publications? Are they concerned about undergraduates? graduate students? Are they available to students outside class hours? Are most introductory classes taught by full-time faculty?
4. How large are the classes? How competitive are the students?

What Will It Take to Get Admitted?

Colleges vary in their entry requirements. Some require just a simple application form and proof of a C average at your prior school. Others have many entry requirements, including essays and letters of recommendation, and admit only a few students, with very high grades. Sometimes transfer students must follow a different application procedure from that used by high school students.
Here are some good questions to ask:

1. What are the admission requirements (e.g., grade-point average, letters of recommendation, a personal statement, tests)?
2. For transfer to a four-year college: What kinds of credits from the community college are likely to be accepted toward the bachelor's degree? Are there any special procedures and requirements for transfer students?
3. For graduate school: Is my background appropriate? Are my grades high enough? Will I need additional coursework prior to acceptance?

How Would You Describe the College and Its Students?

This section of the database concerns the characteristics of a college and the students who go there. It includes the physical description of the college, the academic facilities, and the student services. The makeup of the student body—their average age, gender, ethnic background, academic achievement, and so forth—indicates the kind of group that you would be joining.

1. Describe the physical qualities of the college: location, setting (rural or urban), the campus, and the surrounding area.

2. Describe the classrooms, libraries, labs, computer facilities, sports and arts complexes, and dormitories.

3. Describe the student services and special programs: counseling, tutoring, cooperative education, placement office, study abroad, and the like.

4. Describe the students: How many students are enrolled? What is the ratio of men to women? Where are the students from (e.g., one state, many countries, mostly urban, mostly rural)? What is the ethnic make-up? How many international students attend?

5. Describe the interpersonal atmosphere of the college: friendly, competitive, social, religious, and so on.

What Does It Cost, and Is Financial Aid Available?

Usually, college cost is a big worry. Financial assistance (including grants, scholarships, work–study opportunities, internships, and loans) is a crucial factor in evaluating whether you can afford to go on.

When they learn that private colleges can cost over $30,000 per year, many students eliminate them from consideration without investigating the availability of financial aid. Even though you may not qualify for aid at a public institution, you may at a private one. And don't overlook possible tuition reimbursement from your company. Some employers will pay for job-related courses whether you go to a public or a private school.

1. What does it cost to attend per year: tuition, room and board, commuting costs, books, and so on?

2. What scholarships and financial aid are available?

STEP 2: SEARCH FOR INFORMATION

Before you begin your search, you need to create a list of possibilities. There are more than 3,500 institutions of higher learning and thousands of graduate programs. What you'll want is a manageable list to research.

You may already be aware of some options, but it is easy to make a comprehensive list using Web sites and reference books especially designed for this purpose. They ask you a series of questions about your academic record and selection criteria. You can select any criteria that you believe are important, such as location, major, size, and religious affiliation. The sources recommend specific colleges and programs based on your answers. You may need to experiment a bit with different criteria to get a workable list.

Search Guidelines

Once you prepare a list of possibilities, you have three avenues of investigation:

- Consult print and Internet sources
- Talk with people
- Visit prospective colleges

Consult Print and Media Sources

Use reference guides first. Reference sources (see Table 5.2 and Table 5.3) are the most impartial and fair, seeking to provide objective facts. Begin your search with them and then study the materials produced by the college.

There are many excellent reference sources that provide comprehensive facts, updated annually. The standard references describe colleges in a uniform format so that you can make comparisons easily. You can find them in college libraries, counseling centers, and bookstores.

For example, you can create a picture of a college's student body just by studying the demographic profile. Take two colleges: the first one has 3,000 students: 50 percent female, 3 percent minorities, from 46 states. The second has 32,000 students: 60 percent female, 24 percent minorities, and 93 percent from one state. The first college is small and geographically diverse, with a small minority population. The second is a much larger college and is more diverse in terms of ethnicity, but less so geographically.

TABLE 5.2

Some sources of print information.

General References—Colleges

The College Handbook (College Board)

The Fiske Guide to Colleges (Times Books)

Profiles of American Colleges (Barron's)

General References—Graduate School

America's Best Graduate Schools (U. S. News & World Report)

The Best Medical Schools (Princeton Review)

Business Week Guide to the Best Business Schools (McGraw-Hill)

Graduate Study in Psychology (American Psychological Association)

How to Get into the Right Law School, . . . Medical School, . . . Business School (VGM)

Graduate Programs in the Humanities, Arts & Social Sciences, . . . Biological Sciences, . . . Engineering and Computer Science, . . . Physical Sciences, Mathematics, Agricultural Sciences, the Environment & Natural Resources (Peterson's)

Specific Guides

The College Board International Student Handbook (Henry Holt)

Bear's Guide to Earning Degrees by Distance Learning (Ten Speed Press)

The Hillel Guide to Jewish Life on Campus (Princeton Review)

America's Black & Tribal Colleges (Sandcastle Publishing)

Peterson's Colleges with Programs for Students with Learning Disabilities or Attention Deficit Disorders (Peterson's)

The Complete Book of Catholic Colleges (Princeton Review)

Traditional Degrees for Nontraditional Students: How to Earn a Top Diploma from America's Great Colleges at Any Age (Farrar, Straus & Giroux)

Cool Colleges: For the Hyper-Intelligent, Self-directed, Late Blooming and Just Plain Different (Ten Speed Press)

(continued)

TABLE 5.2	Cost Guides
Some sources of print information, continued.	*The 2000 Hispanic Scholarship Directory* (National Association of Hispanic Publishers)
	The Scholarship Book 2001: The Complete Guide to Private-Sector Scholarships, Fellowships, Grants, and Loans for the Undergraduate (Prentice Hall Press)
	Don't Miss Out: The Ambitious Student's Guide to Financial Aid (Octameron Associates)
	The College Board College Cost & Financial Aid Handbook (Henry Holt)
	Athletic Scholarships, 4th Ed. (Checkmark Books)
	The Black Student's Guide to Scholarships: 700+ Private Money Sources for Black and Minority Students (Madison Books)
	Free College and Training Money for Women (InfoUSA)
	How to Go to College Almost for Free (Waggle Dancer)
	Dollars for College Series: The Quick Guide to Financial Aid for: Art, Music and Drama, . . . Business and Related Fields, . . . Education, . . . Liberal Arts (Humanities and Social Science), . . . Science, . . . Women in All Fields (Garrett Park Press)
	Tips
	Graduate Admissions Essays: Write Your Way into the Graduate School of Your Choice (Ten Speed Press)
	Master the ACT Assessment, . . . GRE Cat, . . . GMAT (Arco)
	Panic Plan for the SAT (Peterson's)
	Kaplan GRE, . . . GMAT, . . . LSAT (Simon & Schuster)
	Real SAT II: Subject Tests (College Board)
	Information on Particular Colleges
	College catalogs
	Admission brochures
	Web sites
	Videos

Some reference guides address specific issues. For example, a guide might cover graduate programs in one discipline, such as *The Official Guide to U. S. Law Schools* (Law School Admission Council). Others help specific types of students. For instance, *Free College and Training Money for Women* (Info USA) concentrates on the financial needs of women. Still others give advice on how to get admitted, such as *Game Plan for Getting into Medical School* (Peterson's).

Print and Media Sources from a College

To get a picture of a college and its distinctive culture, use the material that it produces. Write, call, or send E-mail requesting that such information be sent to your home. The University of Texas Web site (**www.utexas.edu/world/univ**) is a good place to begin an Internet search. It has links to many other college and university sites.

The most partial print and media sources are college videos, admission brochures, and Web sites. These sources are a kind of infomercial. They mix advertisement and information. A video or home page is designed to project the image that the particular college wants to show the world—its most attractive face. It will tell you a lot about the culture of the college. Notice the types of students it highlights. Often this information is very helpful, but keep in mind that its purpose is to persuade you to apply.

TABLE 5.3

Web sites that provide information about further education.

Review.com: www.review.com

Peterson's: www.petersons.com

The College Board: www.collegeboard.org

USNews.com: www.usnews.com/usnews/edu/edu.home

These four sites offer information about colleges and graduate schools, test preparation, and financial aid. All have search features that help you identify suitable schools according to the criteria you specify.

CollegeSource Online: www.cfa.org

Check with your librarian to see if your college subscribes to CollegeSource Online. Using this Web site, you can read relevant sections of your prospective colleges' catalogs. This site is very helpful when you need specific information about programs, course offerings, and professors.

The Willner Guide: www.alx.org

The Willner Guide is a part of America's Learning Exchange that allows you to search a wide variety of education and training resources on the Internet. You will find links to sources on adult continuing education, federal and state government-sponsored training opportunities, distance learning options, and so on.

Mindedge.com: www.mindedge.com

Degree.Net: www.degree.net

These sites specialize in distance learning.

FinAid! The SmartStudent™ Guide to Financial Aid: www.finaid.org

This is an excellent resource for learning about all forms of financial aid, including loans, scholarships, and grants.

The Student Guide: Financial Aid from the U. S. Department of Education: www.ed.gov/prog_info/SFA/StudentGuide/

This federal government document is available in English and Spanish. Updated annually, it describes the three major programs of student financial aid offered by the U. S. government and explains how to apply for these grants, loans, and work–study programs.

The Riley Guide: www.dbm.com/jobguide/

The Education & Training Options section of this career mega-site is devoted to training and education links. Helpful annotations about each link save you search time.

Note: Web sites are frequently reorganized. If you experience difficulties, try a key word search (e.g., The Willner Guide) and drill down until you find the information related to your needs.

The most comprehensive print source is the college catalog. It takes some effort to understand the information in the typical catalog, but a catalog is invaluable for the details that it provides.

Talk with People

Other people are a rich source of information, advice, and feedback. Check your school's counseling services office first. The professionals there have experience helping students with college selection issues.

One caveat about talking with others: Don't rely on just one person. All people have biases. For instance, some people believe that small colleges are best, and they emphasize the personal attention that you would receive there. If your source favors State U, she will highlight that university's strong points while overlooking its possible weaknesses. Talking with more than one person is a good idea because you will get a variety of views.

In Table 5.4 you will find a list of people to consult. There is one special source you should not overlook: a current student or recent graduate.

Interview a Current Student or Recent Grad

Talking to a current student or recent graduate of a particular college allows you to tap the firsthand experience of someone who has been there. You can find out the strengths and weaknesses of the college as seen by a student. Even

TABLE 5.4 *People resources.*	Recruiters
	Recruiters usually stress the best points that a particular college has to offer. These people are often found at college fairs.
	Counselors
	Counselors focus on your personal situation. They help you consider how your needs might be satisfied at a particular college. They have helped other students to transfer. See a counselor by appointment. Attend workshops if your college offers them.
	Faculty and Internship Advisors
	Advisors and faculty provide important advice and information. They are often the people who write letters of recommendation for you. They may know important information about the academic reputation of a college. Ask to speak with them during their office hours.
	Alumni
	Graduates provide information from the student's perspective—information about their experience at a particular college.
	Coworkers
	Your coworkers at your current and former workplaces and internship sites are often excellent sources of information. It is often valuable to obtain your boss's perspective as well.

if the college or program is not of particular interest, you may pick up several important tips during your discussion.

Here is a list of questions to ask:

1. How did you go about selecting this college? If you had to do it over, what would you do differently?
2. What is the best thing about college life? What is the worst thing?
3. What is the biggest adjustment that you had to make in attending this college? What surprised you most about this college?
4. How much time do you spend studying? In what ways have your study habits changed since you have attended this college?

Visit Prospective Campuses

A visit allows you to observe the college's life firsthand. Most colleges regularly offer campus tours and open-house events. All you need to do is call the admissions office for a schedule.

A tour of the campus will include all the important facilities: the library, classrooms, and labs; the student union; sports, music, dance, and art facilities; and, if the college is residential, the dormitories.

A typical visit lasts two hours. The tour is often led by a student. It is an opportunity to ask the questions outlined above. In addition, you might want to ask about food services, off-campus housing, campus security, transportation, and parking.

If you are contemplating entering a competitive college, arrange this visit carefully. It might involve an admissions interview, which will help the school to decide whether to admit you and/or to award you scholarship aid. Consult a college guide for more detailed information on how to prepare for this kind of visit.

If you can't visit, you may take a virtual tour of the college at its Web site. Remember that a virtual tour will emphasize the positive qualities of the college. Still, it will allow you to form impressions about the culture and atmosphere.

The Campus Visit   CASE 5.1

Both Tracy and Sherell wanted to be teachers. Together they made two campus visits to decide where to transfer.

The first college was an urban campus, downtown in the middle of a large city. The classes were held in five large towers within walking distance of each other. Tracy didn't like this atmosphere. She felt it was cold and officelike. The students seemed rushed and unfriendly. Sherell had the opposite reaction. She relished the fast tempo. Furthermore, she found it was an easy commute from her job.

The second college that they visited had a traditional landscaped campus in the suburbs. The buildings on this campus were spread out over several lovely acres. Tracy felt that she had space to breathe and think; she felt at home. Sherell wondered how she could manage taking courses at this college at night without a car. She didn't like the distance between buildings.

Both colleges provided a major in education and were affordable. However, Tracy and Sherell have different personal factors to consider and different personal reactions to the two colleges. Their experiences illustrate why the college visit is an important source of information.

ACTIVITY 5.2   **NICK'S AND JENNA'S SEARCHES: HOW ARE THEY DOING?**

Jenna is considering a small private college about two hours from her home. She talked with a friend who goes there, saw their neat video, and asked questions of the admissions officer during a campus tour.

Jenna's cousin, Nick, is leaning toward a state university about 45 minutes from his home. He began his search by checking a standard reference guide. He found two higher-ranked, but more expensive, private colleges about the same distance away. He discussed these three alternatives with a counselor, checked their catalogs, and looked at their Web sites. Last week he talked to a recent graduate from one of the private colleges and a coworker who attends the state school.

1. Whose search seems more complete? Why?

2. What suggestions do you have for Jenna? for Nick?

STEP 3: ANALYZE YOUR FINDINGS

Asking the right questions and using them to guide your search provides you with a picture of several possible options. Step 3 is about analysis. It's time to evaluate each option carefully. Your goal is to understand which one would be best for you.

Your approach is the same one you took when you analyzed information about various career options. You compare the advantages and disadvantages of each option and examine the far-reaching consequences of your choice.

Compare the Advantages and Disadvantages

Where to go for further education depends on how you weigh various factors in the selection process. Everyone wants to find a high-quality, affordable program. The relative weight of various factors—the academic offerings, the cost, the college's characteristics—depends on your life situation and your priorities.

Your academic record will define the range of your options. If your record is excellent, you have more choices. Be honest with yourself and find the best programs you can get into.

Your life situation will eliminate certain colleges from consideration. For instance, if you must live at home because of your family situation, your choices are limited to schools within commuting distance.

Your subjective preferences will place additional limits on your options. For example, some students enjoy the peace of a rural campus, and others thrive in a city. Some students like big schools and find them exciting; others prefer small schools because they find them more personal.

Every college has advantages and disadvantages depending on your academic background, your personal situation, and your subjective preferences. After you identify the relative importance of various factors, you can compare the advantages and disadvantages of various college options. Activity 5.3, The College Comparison, is structured so that you can look at the advantages and disadvantages of several options at the same time.

Consider the Far-Reaching Implications of Your Choice

College is a place where intellectual development is cultivated. You expect to increase your knowledge and improve your skills. But the potential impact of the college experience is not limited to this one aspect.

All facets of your development—your social, emotional, physical, and spiritual life—can undergo substantial changes during your college career. When you become a student at a particular college, you are subjected to the influence of its members. Your fellow students' level of intellectual, social, and emotional development will affect how your own development unfolds.

A group that will help your development the most is one that provides a combination of challenge and support.[1] When the people around you are tackling difficult tasks, you are encouraged to set up challenging goals. When you aim high, you are likely to accomplish more.

Support from a group keeps you going, motivating you by celebrating your success and encouraging you to make your dreams come true. When you hit a rough patch—a difficult course, a personal crisis—you may be tempted to give up, to drop out. Your college friends' understanding and help can get you through.

It is also important to note that groups do not always have a good effect. Your classmates can hinder your development. If they are not intellectually capable, socially competent, or emotionally mature, the pace of their development will act as a drag on yours. For example, at a "party school" you may be influenced to become a "party animal." While your social skills may improve, what about your cognitive and emotional development? They'll probably be neglected.

The power that your fellow students have to promote or hinder your development is widely recognized by all schools that have competitive entrance criteria. Colleges of all-female or all-male student bodies, schools with strong religious orientations, and historically black universities (HBUs) take this awareness a step further. They hope to remove significant obstacles to development, such as racism or sexism. The idea is that a student will feel more comfortable and find more support in a group whose members are alike in some important way.

As you examine various educational options, consider two additional consequences of your choice. The college and program you select will affect how you see yourself, and the initial view that others have of you.

All individuals use groups as an important source of data about themselves. Thus, a group's characteristics can powerfully affect how you see yourself. If the college is composed of "smart people," it is easier to see yourself as smart. If the students are "going places," it is easier to see yourself as going places.

Prospective employers will consider the schools that you have attended as they evaluate you. Your educational background is a permanent part of your resume. A school's prestige and academic standing color an employer's initial judgment of your knowledge, skills, and abilities. If you attend a highly selective school, you belong to an elite club. Membership can open doors to interviews and opportunities.

To obtain the numerous benefits of the college experience—challenge and support for all facets of your development, enhanced self-esteem, and favorable first impressions by employers—follow these guidelines when selecting a school.

- Look for fellow students whose character, values, and attributes are those that you admire and want to cultivate in yourself.

- Look for a group that makes you feel as though you belong: one that encourages you to take on new and difficult challenges; one that will support you if you falter; one that will give shelter if there is a storm in your life.

- Look for a college whose faculty members have a reputation for excellence, so that you will be viewed favorably by employers.

- If you are limited in your choice of school and don't care for the overall environment of the one that you must attend, don't try to do without the benefits of group support and challenge. Find a group of friends within the school who come closest to meeting the guidelines given above.

STEP 4: PLAN YOUR NEXT ACTIONS

Reflect on Your Learning

After your analysis, summarize your learning. This summary will allow you to capture your insights. For example, one student wrote, *"I have discovered many new educational opportunities and options."*

Gather Additional Information

When you reflect on your learning, a typical outcome is the realization that you want more information. List the questions you have. These questions may guide a more in-depth examination of a particular college or help you come up with additional options. List potential sources of information—what you will read, whom you will talk with, where you will visit.

If you decide to go on for an advanced degree, the application process requires a plan that includes sending in application and financial aid forms, having transcripts sent, taking entry tests and having the scores forwarded, asking for letters of recommendation, and writing essays. Key elements of your plan should be making a list of requirements and starting well in advance of the deadlines.

Transfer Shock

Transfer shock is the term given to the initial adjustment period in a new college. Here is how Monica, who transferred from a community college to a top engineering school, described her experience:

CASE 5.2   *Coping with Transfer Shock*

I went through a period of doubt the first year. They give you more work than you can handle, on purpose. The students come from the top of their class. It was called "home sweet hell."

I put on weight, cried; I thought of changing to everything but engineering. There is a saying there: "Get acquainted with the letter C."

I studied with friends. It was the only way to survive, at least for me. We worked together, gave each other moral support. Each one learned a section, made photocopies, and taught it to everyone else. It lowered the amount to learn. You could do it alone if you didn't eat or sleep. I graduated with a 3.3.

—Monica A.

To ease your adjustment, make a plan that incorporates the following suggestions: Attend the orientation programs of your new college. Learn everything you can about your new school. Take more initiative in seeking the services you need. Meet with an academic advisor before you register. Take a relatively light course load the first semester and avoid taking any very difficult courses until after you have made your adjustment. Spend more time with the books, and take study skills workshops to learn more effective ways to learn. Form a study group and seek tutoring the first semester. After you adjust, your grades, like Monica's, will probably begin to climb again.

MAKE SACRIFICES NOW TO GAIN BENEFITS LATER

When you go on for an advanced degree, you make sacrifices. School costs you money and uses up your time. After you pay for tuition and books, little is left over for clothes, a car, or a place of your own, much less for any luxuries. You don't have much leisure time for friends and relaxation. Your world is textbooks, exams, and research papers. Life and fun seem to be passing you by. "Will I be in school forever?" It can feel that way, especially if you haven't paused since kindergarten or you go to school part-time on top of a full work and family life. You wonder if you have the motivation to sign up for several more years of this kind of life.

There is a bright side to your big sacrifices. First, people who are more highly educated gain substantial career advantages: increased knowledge and skills, more career opportunities, and greater earning potential. These are not trivial rewards, and can have lifelong consequences for you and your family. Second, in making sacrifices, you cultivate your *emotional intelligence*. Daniel Goleman, author of *Emotional Intelligence—Why It Can Matter More Than IQ*, cites research that shows that people who possess greater emotional intelligence tend to achieve more and to be more interpersonally effective and self-confident.[2]

People who possess emotional intelligence can resist the impulse for immediate gratification. Goleman found that such people are able to motivate themselves to achieve, training long hours with enthusiasm and persistence. For instance, Olympic athletes, chess champions, and world-class musicians practiced longer hours than others who had started out with roughly equal ability. In one music academy, for example, the top students had 10,000 lifetime hours of practice; second-tier students averaged around 7,500 hours.

You cultivate your emotional intelligence when you delay the impulse for immediate gratification—when you put off getting the material things you want until you finish school, when you study long hours in the library instead of sitting in front of the TV. And, according to evidence cited by Goleman, emotional intelligence is a big factor in success.

WHEN YOU HAVE MORE EDUCATION THAN YOUR FAMILY

When you surpass your parents' or your spouse's education level, you must cope with the reactions—theirs and yours. Although many families are thrilled at their loved ones' educational achievements, it is not universally the case. Although pride may be part of the picture, family members may also see you as "getting uppity" or "putting on airs." They may feel envy because they never had the opportunity that you have. They may be ashamed of their own lack of education and wonder whether you look down at them now. In a few extreme cases, there is anger at your newfound ability to become economically independent.

The disapproval of those we love is difficult to bear, but your awareness of this possibility will help you to cope. Sometimes your family needs to be reassured that you still care for them. It is important to remember that your education will make you better equipped to help your family make their way in the world. Your educational resources can benefit everyone in the family, especially the next generation. You are a model for others to look up to and follow. You show the way and provide the guidance.

Meanwhile, you have to cope with your own reactions to surpassing your parents or spouse. At an unconscious level you may feel as if you are abandoning them, leaving them behind. This can lead to guilt. Another feeling is sadness. You no longer feel as if you belong to them in the same way you did before. You are somehow apart from them now. You may feel confused about your own identity. Do you belong to the neighborhood or to some other group? Do you fit in either group?

Allow some time to adjust. You are going through an important transition. You will need some time to form a new self-definition. Talking with others who are going through or have gone through the same transition will help you cope with your feelings.

WHERE STUDENTS GET STUCK, AND WHAT TO DO IF IT HAPPENS TO YOU

Applying to Highly Selective Colleges or Programs

You may want to get into a popular college or program that has limited space. These programs require superior grades, and competition to get in is keen. Sometimes test scores, interviews, and letters of recommendation determine who is chosen.

When you apply to a highly selective college or program, map out a strategy as if it were a military campaign. Never apply without a lot of advice and background information. Know the type of student that the program wants, and assess whether you fit that profile. Formulate strategies to overcome any weaknesses. For example, if you are not good at standardized tests, take a review course. If you need a good grade in a key course, pour your energy into this endeavor; don't overload yourself with other hard courses at the same time.

In programs that have more qualified applicants than seats, you may be rejected despite your excellent qualifications. When applying to highly selective programs, you need to define some alternatives for yourself so that you do not just drift if you are not accepted.

Some students redouble their efforts and try again. Other students choose different career paths. One strategy is to review the career options that you found attractive in Chapter 4, ones with less demanding entrance requirements. Since there is more than one career option that will fit your values, personality, interests, and skills, there are usually good alternatives.

| *Information about Career Families Opens Doors and Reduces Anxiety* | **CASE 5.3** |

My career dilemma consisted of what college to choose and my fear of being rejected by a physical therapy program. To overcome these dilemmas, my first step was to engage in research about physical therapy as a career. I became very interested, since my interest lies with helping disabled children. Then I did research on schools that offered physical therapy. I called the schools and asked for information about the physical therapy program.

I also did research on careers related to physical therapy. One career that sparked my interest was speech pathology and audiology. I became interested because I would be working with the same population. By looking into related careers, I have reduced my fear of being rejected by a physical therapy program.

—Valeria F.

Not Wanting to Get Out into the Real World

Many students, like Amy, get comfortable in college and are reluctant to leave. So Amy's confession to her advisor is not unusual. She admits that she has been filling out grad-school applications because school has become a familiar lifestyle. She is uncertain of her career direction and is afraid of a job search.

In this case, going on is a waste of resources because its real purpose is to run away. Amy's commitment to graduate school is halfhearted, so she risks failing or giving up. And then she would be left with the same dilemma that she is seeking to avoid.

If you suspect that you are falling into this trap, confront yourself honestly. State in a positive fashion what you hope to accomplish by obtaining an advanced degree.

Needing the Credential but Not Liking School

Some students are hands-on, action-oriented learners. As a result, they often feel uncomfortable in formal academic settings, where theory is emphasized over practical application.

Sean was a successful local bank manager who was passed over for promotion because he didn't have an advanced degree. Sean is typical of many people—especially those in business, sales, and marketing—who are successful in the workplace and learn better on the job than in the classroom.

The Campbell™ Interest and Skill Survey (CISS™) has a scale that shows your comfort level in academic settings. When Sean's counselor went over this scale, Sean came to understand his discomfort in formal academic settings. He realized that, unlike most of his classmates and professors, he preferred practice to theory. This new self-understanding about his lack of comfort in formal academic settings reassured Sean. With a better understanding of his discomfort, he enrolled in an advanced degree program. He was determined to stick it out so that he could get his promotion.

AN EFFICIENT AND EFFECTIVE SEARCH

A search of the four-year college and graduate school information database provides you with the information that you need to make a sound choice. It ensures that you have explored all the options thoroughly. The ASAP approach guides the sequence of your search. Instead of ending up confused, with a jumbled mess of facts, you have an organized and systematic way to proceed. The information that you gather will help solve your specific educational dilemma. Your search process is both efficient and effective.

Even if you decide not to go on to a four-year college or graduate school right now, you can always change your mind later. When new circumstances permit you to reconsider your decision, you will know what questions to ask and what sources to consult.

KEY POINTS

1. One dilemma that college students face is whether to go on for a more advanced degree. You want to make sure that your decision is information rich, in line with your preferred career direction, and based on your personal situation.

2. The four-year college and graduate school information database is a way of organizing the types of information that you'll want:

    a. Nature of academic programs

    b. Admission requirements

    c. School profile and student body characteristics

    d. Cost and financial aid

3. To begin, create a list of possibilities to research. Be aware of the difference between sources of information that are intended to be factual and objective, such as reference books, and those that are intended to promote a favorable image of the school, such as videos and home pages.

4. Use the four-step ASAP approach to solve your educational dilemma:

    Step 1: **Ask the right questions.** Use the questions provided in the text to get a mental picture of particular educational options.

    Step 2: **Search for information.** Search by consulting reference books and Web sites, talking with people, and visiting prospective campuses.

    Step 3: **Analyze your findings.** List the advantages and disadvantages and consider the far-reaching implications of your choice.

Gathering Information About Four-Year Colleges and Graduate Schools

Step 4: **Plan your next actions.** Summarize your learning. If you need to gather more in-depth information about a particular option, or find new options, plan your search. If you must meet deadlines for applications, transcripts, scholarships, and financial aid, the key element of your plan should be to make a list of requirements and start well in advance of the deadlines. Plan to diminish the effects of transfer shock.

5. There may be two potential internal obstacles to overcome:

   a. Learning to make the sacrifices that college demands

   b. Coping with the emotional reactions—yours and your family members'—of surpassing your parents' (or your spouse's) educational level

6. Typical points where students get stuck include the following:

   a. Applying to highly selective colleges and programs

   b. Not wanting to get out into the real world

   c. Needing the credential, but not liking school

A School Paraprofessional Rearranges Her Priorities and Makes New Trade-offs | CASE 5.4

I am going to school part time, and at this rate it will take me another five or six years to complete my education and earn my B.A. . . . The more I thought about the number of years it is going to take me to get my B.A., the more crazed I became. I decided I needed to make this happen faster. This meant taking more credits each semester and going to school more. I realized it was something I needed to talk to my husband about. He couldn't understand why I was so upset. He agreed that the only solution to this dilemma was to take more credits each semester and that we would find a way for this to work itself out.

[I found out about] an intensive program for adults in which you could earn your degree in two years. I have made an appointment . . . to learn more about the program.

My major concern is my children. I feel it is important for us to be there if they need help with homework or any other problem that might come up. We decided that it will probably be best if I attend classes in the evening, so I will be there in the afternoon when they get home from school and my husband will be there in the evening. We will be able to eat dinner as a family and I can go off to school.

—Michele B.

COLLEGE COMPARISON | ACTIVITY 5.3

NAME _____

OVERVIEW

In this activity you will make comparisons between two educational options. Your main purpose is to identify the advantages and disadvantages of each option so that you can choose the better one.

The value of making comparisons is that you might see something in one that you do not find in the other. This will encourage you to evaluate how important the presence or absence of this factor is to you. Also, making comparisons will give you the confidence that you made your decision rationally, using good information.

If you are at a community college, you might want to compare two four-year colleges. If you are about to obtain a baccalaureate, you might want to compare two graduate programs.

If you need more room, or if you are instructed to do so, type your answers separately.

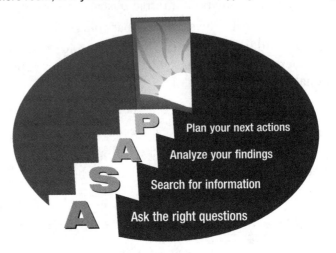

Plan your next actions

Analyze your findings

Search for information

Ask the right questions

STEP 1 ASK THE RIGHT QUESTIONS

Step 1.1 Selection of Important Factors

Determine three factors (e.g., size, cost, convenience, location, curriculum, male/female ratio, reputation) that you will weigh most heavily in making your choice.

Factor 1 _____

_____

_____

Factor 2 _____

_____

_____

Factor 3 _____

_____

_____

Step 1.2 Selection of Colleges or Graduate Programs

Select two colleges or graduate programs to compare.

College/Program 1 _____

_____

College/Program 2 _____

_____

STEP 2 SEARCH FOR INFORMATION

Consult the standard reference books such as *Peterson's Guides, Barron's Profiles,* and *The College Board Handbooks.* They are usually found in the reference section of the library or your college's career services center. Or, use the Web sites found in Table 5.3.

On separate paper, take notes that relate to the important factors that will influence your choice.

You can summarize your two profiles in one of two ways. You can identify the factors that you considered and the information that you found for each, or you may prefer to summarize the main points. Put your summary in writing.

STEP 3 ANALYZE YOUR FINDINGS

Step 3.1 Comparing Advantages and Disadvantages

List the advantages and disadvantages of attending each college. Remember that the advantages and disadvantages are selected in light of the important factors that you identified in Step 1.

Option 1

Advantages +	Disadvantages −

Option 2

Advantages +	Disadvantages −

Step 3.2 Considering the Far-Reaching Implications

Identify which college provides a more favorable environment of challenge and support.

_____

_____

_____

_____

Would one college or the other be looked upon more favorably by employers?

_____

_____

_____

_____

Step 3.3 Selecting the Better of These Two Options

Review your analysis. Typically, every possibility has both good points and drawbacks.

Which option is more appealing based on your research so far?

College/Program _____

The reasons that I selected this option are:

_____

_____

_____

_____

STEP 4 PLAN YOUR NEXT ACTIONS

Step 4.1 Learning Summary

What did you learn that will help you solve your educational dilemma?

_____

_____

_____

_____

Step 4.2 Next Steps

What's next? Who can help? What sources of information will be useful?

_____

_____

_____

_____

COLLEGE INFORMATION INTERVIEW

OVERVIEW

In this activity you will interview a four-year college or graduate student. Your main purpose is to *gather information* from someone enrolled in that college about going on for an advanced degree. This interview will (1) give you a student's perspective, (2) supplement the kinds of information found in reference sources, and (3) allow you to practice holding effective college interviews.

P Plan your next actions

A Analyze your findings

S Search for information

A Ask the right questions

If you need more room or are instructed to do so, type your answers separately.

STEP 1 ASK THE RIGHT QUESTIONS

Step 1.1 Selection of Questions

To conduct a college information interview, you will need to prepare a list of questions. You were introduced to these questions in Chapter 5. They are repeated here for your convenience.

Check the types of information that are particularly important to you.

☐ Nature of course offerings and academic programs

☐ Admissions requirements

☐ College profile and student body characteristics

☐ Cost/financial aid

☐ Firsthand knowledge about the college from the person being interviewed

Eighteen questions are grouped according to these five types of information. Be sure that you cover each type of college information by asking at least one question in each area.
 Circle at least ten questions that you want to ask during your college information interview.

College Interview Questions

NATURE OF ACADEMIC PROGRAMS

1. What is the academic reputation of the college? How is it ranked?

2. Does the college have an outstanding reputation in certain majors? Which ones?

3. Describe the quality of the faculty: Are they good teachers? Are they concerned about undergraduates? Graduate students? Are they available for appointments outside class hours? Are most introductory classes taught by full-time faculty?

4. How large are the classes? How competitive are the students?

ADMISSIONS REQUIREMENTS

5. What are the admission requirements (e.g., grade-point average, letters of recommendation, a personal statement)?

6. Transfer students: Are there any special procedures and requirements for transfer students? What kinds of credits are likely to be accepted toward the bachelor's degree?

7. For graduate school: Is my background appropriate? Are my grades high enough? Will I need additional coursework prior to acceptance?

COLLEGE PROFILE AND STUDENT BODY CHARACTERISTICS

8. Describe the physical qualities of the college: location, setting (rural or urban), the campus, and the surrounding area.

9. Describe the classrooms, libraries, labs, computer facilities, sports and arts complexes, and dormitories.

10. Describe the student services and special programs: counseling, tutoring, cooperative education, placement office, study abroad, and the like.

11. Describe the students: How many students are enrolled? What is the ratio of men to women? Where are the students from (e.g., one state, many countries, mostly urban, mostly rural)? What is the ethnic makeup? How many international students attend?

12. Describe the interpersonal atmosphere of the college: friendly, competitive, social, religious, and so on.

COST/FINANCIAL AID

13. What does it cost to attend per year: tuition, room and board or commuting costs, books, and so on?

14. What scholarships and financial aid are available?

FIRSTHAND KNOWLEDGE ABOUT THE COLLEGE FROM THE PERSON BEING INTERVIEWED

15. How did you go about selecting a college? If you had to do it over, what would you do differently?

16. What is the best thing about college life? What is the worst thing?

17. What is the biggest adjustment that you had to make in attending this college? What surprised you most about this college?

18. How much time do you spend studying? In what ways have your study habits changed since you began attending this college?

Step 1.2 Your Personal Concerns

In order to address your specific educational or career dilemma, write down any additional questions that you want to research.

_____

_____

_____

_____

Step 1.3 Identification of Possible Interviewees

List three four-year college or graduate school students (or recent graduates) whom you might like to interview either over the telephone or in person. What are the reasons for each selection?

_____

_____

_____

Step 1.4 Interview Appointment

Contact one of the people you listed above. Most people enjoy talking about their experiences. However, you may feel shy about asking them to talk with you, especially if you don't know them. Here are a few tips to help you out:

- Organize your request. Many students feel more comfortable after they write out a short script.
- Role-play your request with a friend and practice the interview questions beforehand.
- If you don't know the person, introduce yourself and state how you got his or her name.
- State your purpose in terms that are complimentary to the person whom you would like to interview.
- Be ready to suggest several different time slots that are convenient for you to talk. Arrange to spend enough time with the student to get through all your questions.

SAMPLE SCRIPTS:

Melanie Johnson gave me your name because I was looking for someone who could provide balanced and fair information about _____ college. Is this a convenient time for you to talk, or would Wednesday night or Thursday morning be better?

As part of a course assignment, I am researching graduate study in _____. I would welcome the opportunity to talk with you because of your firsthand knowledge and experience. Is late afternoon a good time for us to speak?

Provide the name of the college. Record the interviewee's name, major, and most recent date of enrollment. Note the date and time of the interview.

_____

_____

_____

STEP 2 SEARCH FOR INFORMATION

Ask each question on your list and take notes on separate paper.

You can summarize your interview in one of two ways. You can list each question that you asked and the interviewee's response, or you may prefer to summarize the main points of the interview. If you quote from the college catalog or other material that the interviewee brought to the interview or sent to you, be sure to cite the source and page number. Do not copy long sections from a catalog. Summarize.

STEP 3 ANALYZE YOUR FINDINGS

Step 3.1 Comparison of Advantages and Disadvantages

Every college has some attractive features. However, in order for you to select the best college, you must decide which top three factors are most important to you.

In selecting a college, what are the top three factors (e.g., size, cost, convenience, range of curriculum, male-to-female ratio, reputation) that you would consider?

In light of these factors, list the advantages and disadvantages of this college.

Hints and Reminders

In assessing the advantages and disadvantages of a particular option, remember to assess the far-reaching implications of your choice as well as the more immediate issues.

Imagine what your everyday life would be like if you enrolled in this particular institution. Do you sense that there would be an environment of challenge and support? Consider the students in the college. Do you believe that your fellow students would welcome you?

No matter how many advantages a college or graduate program may have, a crucial aspect of your analysis is to determine your chances for admission and whether you can afford to go. List any internal or external obstacles that must be overcome on the disadvantage side.

Advantages +	*Disadvantages −*

Step 3.2 Tentative Decision

In view of your list of advantages and disadvantages, are you considering this college seriously? Identify the advantage(s) or disadvantage(s) that most heavily influenced your decision.

Assuming a 40-year worklife after graduation, the median earning of college graduates will be $640,000 more than that of high school graduates. Even subtracting the cost of a college education—average tuition, room, and board of about $40,000, and forgone earnings of about $84,000—college graduates still come out ahead by more than half a million dollars.

—Kristina Shelly, *Occupational Outlook Quarterly*

STEP 4   PLAN YOUR NEXT ACTIONS

Step 4.1   Learning Summary

How is the interview information useful to you in terms of solving your educational dilemma? Sometimes, even if you decide that a particular college is not right for you, the interview provides important information.

What did you learn from this interview that will be useful to you in the future?

_____

_____

_____

_____

Step 4.2   Additional Information

What are your plans for obtaining additional information?

_____

_____

_____

_____

Hints and Reminders

Possible ways to get additional information include interviewing additional students, consulting college and graduate school reference guides, checking the college Web pages, viewing college videos, reading college catalogs, and visiting college campuses.

ASSESSING YOUR NEED FOR FURTHER EDUCATION   ACTIVITY 5.5

OVERVIEW

In this activity you will assess your need for further education and examine various options. You will outline a plan for obtaining additional information.

TASK 1   EDUCATIONAL ASSESSMENT QUESTIONS

Answer the following questions on a separate sheet of paper. Use them to guide your analysis and planning.

1. What are the primary reasons that you would seek further education?

2. What factors must you consider? List your strengths and any internal or external obstacles.

3. What alternatives are you considering? Some typical options are as follows:

   a. Immediate transfer, full-time

   b. Immediate transfer, part-time

   c. Transfer later, after I gain some work experience, my children are older, or I pursue other goals, and so forth.

   d. Investigate corporate training opportunities.

    e. Keep up with my field by reading or by joining professional organizations and by going to meetings and conferences.

    f. Enroll in on-line or distance learning programs.

4. What are the advantages and disadvantages of each alternative that you are considering?

TASK 2   YOUR PLAN

Describe your plan for obtaining additional information and help.

PART II

Set Your Direction

CHAPTER 6

Making Choices

It is no longer possible to follow the paths of previous generations. Our lives not only take new directions; they are subject to repeated redirection. . . .
—Mary Catherine Bateson, *Composing a Life*

6

SETTING A CAREER DIRECTION IS A PROCESS

While many people erroneously believe that choosing a career is a one-time event, in reality, you will make a series of decisions. Psychologists use the word *specification* to describe this process of setting your career direction.[1] You move from a general goal to a more specific implementation of it. For example, you start by wanting to become a doctor. This first decision, to become a doctor, requires at least four additional decisions over a period of several years to turn your general goal into a specific reality. You must select

(1) an undergraduate major, (2) a medical school, (3) a specialty, and (4) a place to practice.

The number of career direction–setting decisions and their timing differ from student to student. It may be that right now you don't even feel any urgency about making a decision. If you have decided on an educational path that is related to a specific occupation, such as elementary education or engineering, you may wonder what decisions are left to make. Or you may have found that your information searches have helped you to identify the best of several alternatives: what advanced degree you want, or whether accounting is more attractive than finance.

You feel satisfied that you have solved your career dilemma. Even if you are not under immediate pressure to make a choice, a grounding in career decision making will serve you well, because career specification is a *process.*

First, recognize that you have already built a solid foundation for setting your career direction. You are information rich, thanks to your systematic research using the four-step ASAP approach. You have cultivated an internal readiness by getting to know yourself—an awareness that you reached through searching the personal identity database. You have identified some alternatives through your searches of the career information database and the four-year college and graduate school information database. Now you are ready to look at the larger picture of career decision making.

As you know, your career decisions have far-reaching consequences. To bring this point into sharper focus, we will review the impact that your choice of work has on your life, by bringing together ideas presented in earlier chapters. Frankly, your career decisions would be easier if it weren't for one important fact. Career decisions are not isolated events, but part of the larger process of living in the twenty-first century. In this chapter you will see that setting your career direction takes place in the context of your life situation and the opportunities in the job market.

WHAT'S AT STAKE: THE SIGNIFICANCE OF CAREER DECISIONS

When you set your career direction, a lot is at stake. Your choices will form an important part of your identity in society, nurture or starve your subsequent personal development, affect the rhythm of your life, and influence the lifestyle that you can afford.

As we examine the significance of career decisions, we'll refer to Lisa's choices as she describes them in the following case.

Lisa's Choices	**CASE 6.1**

After high school, I obtained a clerical position and earned a good salary in a stock brokerage company. After two years, I was promoted to administrative assistant and worked for a vice president. Over time I realized that I didn't like the people I worked with every day. We didn't seem to share the same values.

My success at work did give me the confidence to enroll in a community college as a liberal arts major. Despite my parents' lack of financial or emotional support for a college education, I had my eye on a law career.

In a career development workshop I was taught the ASAP approach. Inspired by my professor, I began to research elementary school teaching. I found, for example, that this occupation fit with my "Who Am I?" descriptions of "caring, sensitive, and dependable." Although I felt that lawyers could earn more income, I believed that a career as a teacher would make an important contribution to society. I wanted to transfer to a private university for my bachelor's, if I could get financial aid.

Three months after my graduation, my life situation changed with the birth of my daughter. I decided to continue my part-time job as a research assistant for a nonprofit organization that specialized in historical preservation projects. Although I earned less than when I was with the stockbrokers, the job had a variety of interesting duties. For example, I got to participate in designing history projects for elementary school children—something I found exciting. The job also had health benefits, something I needed since my husband was an independent construction contractor.

When my baby was nine months old, I enrolled in a state university branch, taking two courses, but I didn't like them. The classes were large and the professors impersonal. The private university, which I liked better, did not offer aid for part-time students, so I enrolled at night, taking one course at my own expense. I loved the private university with its peaceful, beautiful campus. I did notice that I was one of the few students who had a child, and there was very little accommodation to my needs as a mother. In addition, they only took half my credits in transfer. After obtaining just six credits in one year (at great expense), I am now at a decision point. To stay at the private university is a financial burden. It would take me years to finish.

My husband will support any decision I make and is thinking of going to college when I finish. My parents and the rest of the family still feel that I should think about my daughter, quit school, and go back to full-time at the stock brokerage firm. They believe that with a better-paying job and no class or homework commitments in the evenings or weekends, I would have more time for my daughter and more money in my pocket.

Your Work Gives You an Identity

In this society, people are defined in large part by the work they choose. A person's work is a major source of status and respect in the eyes of others. To learn more about someone we have just met, we ask about their work: "What do you do?" In large measure because of the importance that society places on work, we also come to think about our own identity in terms of the work we do. It becomes a central part of how we see ourselves. Thus, working on projects for elementary schoolchildren at work made Lisa feel respected. She liked telling her friends what she did for a living.

Your Work Influences Your Personal Development

As you will recall from the activities on values in Chapter 2, your career decisions are about how you will use a substantial portion of your life energy. Your task is to specify—to make commitments to what you value. Take Lisa. Her parents and friends urge her to spend her life energy in the business world. She believes that a commitment to elementary education would be more meaningful.

She also believes that her continued personal development is best served by becoming a teacher. Having values and interests similar to those of your coworkers promotes a sense of belonging. Their support facilitates your continued personal development. Lisa believes that she will be happier in this regard if she has teachers as coworkers.

Your Work Affects the Rhythm of Your Life

Your choice of work affects how a large portion of your waking hours is spent over the course of a day, a week, and a year. It determines how you will spend your time and how long you have to work, when you will be busiest, and how much time will be left over for other activities.

The alternatives that Lisa has considered have very different life rhythms. A lawyer may have to work long hours to meet a court deadline. An administrative assistant in the business world usually has regular nine-to-five hours, but little flexibility about when to begin or end a workday. A teacher is in the classroom from eight to three, prepares lesson plans, and corrects homework in the evenings, but has summers and holidays free.

Your Work Provides You with Money, Which Affects the Lifestyle that You Can Afford

Let's consider the bottom line: how much money you want or need to make. If you are determined to own your own home, send your children to college, or have a fancy car, your choice of work determines how easy or difficult it will be to acquire these things. One reason that Lisa was attracted to a career in law was because she knew that in all probability she would earn more money as an attorney than as a teacher or administrative assistant. You have to consider whether your choices will permit you to have the lifestyle that you want.

COMPLICATING FACTORS: YOUR EVOLVING IDENTITY, YOUR OTHER LIFE COMMITMENTS, AND THE CHANGING JOB MARKET

As you make your choices, you must take into account your evolving identity, your other life commitments, and the changing job market. These three factors complicate your career decision making.

Your Evolving Identity

Your career decisions, like Lisa's, arise from your ideas about who you are as a person. These ideas about yourself are not fixed, but are continually evolving.

Typically, by the time you are a college student you have started to clarify your values, but college itself often enlarges your view of what is important or causes you to question previously held notions. Increased self-confidence gained in college often gives you the courage to consider new options. For example, where once you dreamed of studying to become a manager, now you wonder if you should go into business for yourself. Or, where once you liked science, now you are more interested in sociology.

This internal process of change often means that the decisions that you made last year are no longer acceptable to you. That's why Lisa moved away from her original goal. Being a lawyer did not fit her changed and refined view of herself. As you make career decisions, your identity emerges and evolves.

Your Other Life Commitments

Forging a career direction takes place in the context of your family and community life. Whenever you face a career decision, you must take into consideration its implications for other commitments in your life, both those that you have now and those that you are thinking about making in the future. You are deciding about the amount of life space to devote to work. Is work central? How much of your time and energy do you want to reserve for your family and community life?

One aspect of the conflict between Lisa and her parents is about the time and energy to allocate to various commitments in her life structure. Her parents favor more of a commitment of time and energy to her family. She favors devoting some of her time and energy to getting her bachelor's degree.

If you are just moving out of your parents' home, you are beginning to shape your own life structure. You are deciding what commitments to make, if any, in the marriage–family–community arenas. If you already have marriage–family–community commitments, you will want your choice of work to harmonize with these commitments.

The Job Market

An equally important aspect of the larger context in which your career decisions are made is the job market. You want to consider the demand that exists for the kind of work you want to do. Ideally, you want work that is in high demand and in which opportunities are expanding. In the popular press these are called "hot jobs."

The predictions about hot jobs are based on studies by the U. S. Department of Labor, which tries to identify areas of job growth. When you gathered information about the outlook for the future in the career information database, you were getting a picture of the job market.

Deciding in the Context of Change

You are a person who is changing every day within a life structure that is evolving as you grow older. Around you, technological, political, and economic forces are transforming your world. With such changing conditions, it is tempting to give up any attempt to control your future through effective choices—to ride the current of life and see where it takes you. Yet as a college student, you have started to take your destiny into your own hands. What kind of guidelines will help you decide which path to take next?

LISTEN TO YOUR HEART AND USE YOUR HEAD

You need an approach that tests whether your career alternatives will provide satisfaction and success. This approach must address issues of identity formation, personal development, and lifestyle; it must also help you

FIGURE 6.1

Listen to your heart and use your head.

to take into account your other life commitments, the job market, and the changing condition of the world. Does this seem to be a complex process? It is. The good news is that two simple guidelines encompass all the pertinent questions that you need to raise about any specific alternative. When facing a choice, your best bet is to listen to your heart and to use your head.

Decide with Your Heart

When you decide something with your heart, you are paying attention to what you like. Look inside your heart and ask yourself, "Does this career fit my values, the things that are important to me? Does it fit my interests? Does it lead me toward a life that I consider worthwhile? Does it fulfill a dream?" Contemplate whether the particular career would encourage or stifle your personal development. Would your coworkers be compatible and supportive and provide a sense of belonging? Ponder whether it would give your life the rhythm that you desire and the space that you want for other life commitments. For work satisfaction and personal development, listen to what your heart tells you.

Decide with Your Head

When you use your head to make a decision, you take a practical point of view. In choosing among career alternatives, one important practical consideration is the money you will earn, both now and in the future. Using your head is a way of looking out for your economic prospects and future lifestyle.

The second practical consideration is a down-to-earth assessment of your chances of reaching your goal. Are your skills and motivation sufficient to pursue this career? Is your life structure favorable when it comes to having the time and money to pursue your dreams?

This self-assessment is especially important when you face highly competitive work or work that requires a lengthy educational preparation. For instance, to win a spot at one of the top ten law schools, such as Stanford, requires excellent grades and LSAT scores. The tuition is high. Can you get accepted, and can you afford to go there?

In general, when you face greater competition and longer educational preparation, you will need more resources to reach your goal: higher-level skills, greater motivation, more space and flexibility in your life structure, and a substantial amount of money (e.g., earnings, loans, or scholarships).

A Balanced Style

Listening to your heart increases the probability that you will like your work. Using your head increases the probability that the alternative is a practical one. Lisa, who chose a private college, earned only 12 credits in $2\frac{1}{2}$ years. She needs 50 more. Is she being practical? Not very, but if she follows her parents' suggestion of administrative work, will she like it? Like Lisa, you should strive to make a decision that takes into account both your heart and your head.

THE DECISION STYLE WINDOW[2]

The *decision style window* is a technique for checking the style you use in making decisions. Table 6.1 presents four decision styles in different windows: window 1 is the *balanced style;* window 2 is the *sacrifice style;* window 3 is the *daydreaming style;* and window 4 is the *haphazard style.* You will see the advantages of window 1, the balanced style. You will be shown how the other three styles are flawed and can lead to an unwelcome career outcome. You will also see how to turn a flawed decision style into the balanced style.

Window 1: The Balanced Style (Like ♥ / Practical ♀)

This is the ideal decision style because it involves both listening to your heart and using your head. You can say that you are headed in a direction you *like.* Your choice fits your personal identity and fosters your development. It is also *practical.* You considered its economic rewards. After an assessment, you believe that you have the resources to make this choice a reality. This is the decision style that you want to use for your career choices.

TABLE 6.1		♥ Like	♥ Dislike
Decision style window.	Practical ♀	1. Balanced style ♀ ♥	2. Sacrifice style ♀ ♥
	Impractical ♀	3. Daydreaming style ♀ ♥	4. Haphazard style ♀ ♥

Window 2: The Sacrifice Style (Dislike ♠ / Practical 💡)

When you make this kind of choice, you decide with your head only. Your style is *practical*, which is good, but it neglects your psychological needs, and that can lead to work that you *dislike*.

Reading the following case will help you understand the dangers of a sacrifice decision style.

Greg's Obstacles

CASE 6.2

Greg is a psychology major who wants to become a clinical psychologist. He is a bright, articulate student who has an A-minus average, but he is putting off taking a required statistics course because he doesn't like math.

To help pay for college, Greg obtained a part-time job as a sorter with a parcel delivery service, and within a year he moved up to the position of supervisor. Greg is becoming increasingly self-confident and independent. He has just moved into his own apartment, too.

Recently, Greg met his academic advisor, who asked when he was going to take statistics and get moving on his applications to graduate school. Greg admitted that he was afraid of this course. He wasn't sure about graduate school either. Although he didn't like his job, he liked the money. With his own apartment and the related expenses, he wasn't sure if he could afford to pursue an advanced degree.

Greg is sliding toward unsatisfying work because he won't confront the two obstacles in his path: his fear of math, and his apartment costs. His decision style is practical. He can pay his bills. His economic prospects are good at his job because he could get promoted to manager. Now he feels stuck, believing that he must be practical and sacrifice a career direction that he would like to take.

You can take steps to turn a sacrifice style (practical only) into a balanced style. To do this, you must figure out how to overcome the obstacles that are preventing you from choosing work you like. Greg realizes that to overcome his obstacles he must increase his resources: his skills, motivation, and financial assets. One by one he has begun to face these issues. He has registered for statistics and hired a tutor. He has gotten a roommate so that he can decrease his living costs, and he has started to save for graduate school. He has met with his advisor, and they have worked out a plan. He will work for a year to save some money. In addition, he will volunteer to be a "big brother" in a group home for troubled teens so that he will build some experience, stay motivated, and learn more about the field of clinical psychology.

Greg is once again headed toward work he likes, while making practical adjustments to his situation. His decision style is now balanced (like ♥ / practical 💡).

Window 3: The Daydreaming Style (Like ♥ / Impractical 🌢)

When you make a choice that leads you in a direction that you *like*, but is *impractical*, you are really daydreaming. You are unlikely to reach your goal.

Reading the following case will help you understand the dangers of a daydreaming decision style.

CASE 6.3   *"I Want It All"*

Willa is in her second year at community college. She is studying accounting, but has decided that she would like to broaden her business knowledge. Therefore, she has decided to attend a four-year college part-time and major in marketing.

She would also like to earn more money, because she has two children, ages 2 and 10. The 10-year-old attends a private religious school, and it is important to Willa that he has this education preparation. Therefore, she has decided to work full-time rather than part-time. Full-time work would also allow her to stop taking out student loans.

Aware that she needs to examine the consequences of these two decisions, she has discussed her situation with her cousin, who already has her bachelor's degree. Willa wonders how long it would take her to graduate from a four-year college if she attends part-time. She had planned to take two courses at night, but was very much against going to summer school. Her cousin estimates that Willa has to take about 75 credits at the four-year college. Earning 12 credits per year while attending part-time, it would take almost 7 years to finish.

Willa is shocked. Seven years is too long. She reviews several other possibilities, including staying in accounting, attending the hated summer school, and giving up her dream of a bachelor's degree. To decrease her financial burden, she could apply for financial aid for her son's school. Each option that she discusses with her cousin has some advantages, but some unwelcome disadvantages. Willa finally looks at her cousin and wails, "But I want it *all!*"

Thanks to her cousin, Willa realizes that she has been daydreaming. Studying for an additional seven years is unrealistic for her. She feels that she could not juggle work, parenting, and school responsibilities for such a long period. It is painful for Willa to discover that she has to make trade-offs. To get something that she wants, she is going to have to give up other things that she also wants.

You can take steps to turn a daydream into a balanced choice. To do this, you must become more practical. Willa is now attending a four-year college full-time for 2 years to obtain 55 of the 75 credits she needs. After that she will work, attending school part-time. This new plan will allow her to earn her degree in three and a half years. Attending school full-time has an additional advantage: it gives her more time for her two-year-old. She doesn't like the idea of two more years of struggling to make ends meet, but that is the trade-off she has to make if she is to reach her most important goal of a bachelor's degree.

Now Willa is headed toward a baccalaureate, a direction she likes, while making practical adjustments to her situation. Her decision style is now balanced (like 🖤 / practical 💡).

Window 4: The Haphazard Style (Dislike ♠ / Impractical 🕯)

When you make a choice that leads you in a direction that you *dislike* and is *impractical*, you are really floundering. Your decision style is haphazard. You drift. No career identity is formed. You spend your life energy, but you fail to move toward what you value, or to discover what is important to you and make progress toward it.

Scott's situation will help you understand the dangers of a haphazard decision style.

Scott's Floundering

CASE 6.4

Scott has been floundering. His parents are pressuring him to achieve in school and select a high-status, high-paying career, but his strength is not academics. He likes to help people.

He has been participating in the college internship program. Every time he has spoken to his internship advisor he has had a new career goal: paralegal, business, criminal justice, computers. All have been impractical given his skills and motivation. Furthermore, they would not lead to careers he would enjoy. He has chosen internships that involved helping others: one in a nursing home, another in a nonprofit international aid agency, and a third in a home for foster children.

Scott is grasping at straws trying to please his parents. He has made decisions about his career goals impulsively, and he changes his mind frequently. He and his parents cannot come to terms with his weaknesses or use his real strengths in helping people.

Without listening to his heart and using his head, Scott would continue to flounder. His internship advisor advised him to see a counselor to sort out his confused feelings, which were at the root of his haphazard style. In counseling, Scott has come to terms with his strengths. With the counselor's help he has learned how to deal with other people's expectations about his career path. He is now headed toward a career in the helping professions. He has obtained a job in the patient advocacy program of a prestigious hospital, helping patients to communicate with health care professionals. His parents are somewhat satisfied by being able to say that their son works at a world-class hospital, and he is happy helping others.

TRADE-OFFS AND UNKNOWNS

With so many variables to take into account in any career decision, you rarely find perfect alternatives. It is unusual to have an option that satisfies you in every way. Both Greg and Willa did not face perfect choices. Like them, we have to make trade-offs, giving up some things to obtain others that are more important to us.

Finally, no decision style can guarantee your success. Even after extensive exploration and planning, every choice involves unknowns. We cannot predict the future with complete accuracy. Remember, though, luck and chance are unreliable friends when it comes to decision making. Using the power of your heart and mind to set your direction offers you the best chance to get on the road to success.

SETTING YOUR CAREER DIRECTION TAKES TIME

Many of our early career and educational decisions are tentative. For example, Lisa could not have predicted that she would shift from law to teaching. We try out various paths; we make false starts; and our career identity is modified, refined, even reformed. Psychologists tell us that this process takes five to seven years.[3]

One reason it takes time to forge your career direction is that you have to test your skills. Just when Willa transferred, she was promoted to supervisor at her part-time job. Encouraged by her boss's support, she began to take management courses and did well in them. She switched from marketing to management because she realized this major fit her interests and skills better.

Another reason why setting a career direction takes so long is that you need to sort out your priorities and try out various goals in light of your other life commitments. If you take on family commitments as you are forging your career direction, you may rethink earlier decisions in the light of these new responsibilities. We've already noted that a new self-picture may make earlier career decisions unacceptable. You may find yourself abandoning a career direction that was based on an identity you have outgrown.

When it comes to the amount of time and energy you want to give to your career, you must consider your priorities. Some students select a career goal that will fit into their established life structure. Other students will move across the country and totally alter their living situation to pursue a dream. Your choice depends on your values and the importance of this dream to your life.

No one can set priorities for you. You must be comfortable with your choices and aware of the trade-offs you are making. It is wise to seek advice and talk things over with other people in order to get new perspectives. Remember Willa's cousin, whose listening ear, sharp questions, and knowledge of the road ahead really helped Willa to understand the consequences of her initial decision. With her cousin's help, Willa clarified her priorities.

Uncertainty and doubt are common feelings. Lisa often felt confused about her priorities. After a long talk with her parents on Thanksgiving, she began to feel that they were right—that she should concentrate on her daughter and give up a four-year college. She began to scan the want ads for administrative assistant positions. Then she discussed her options with her husband. He reminded her of the things that she disliked about those positions. They reviewed the household budget and talked about their child's needs once again. He reminded her how much she was attracted to teaching. Once again she felt uncertain about what trade-offs to make.

The path you forge seldom proceeds in a straight line, with each decision leading in a single clear, consistent direction. Most people have false starts and trials, many twists and bends. Don't be too hard on yourself if you feel confused at times.

WHERE STUDENTS GET STUCK, AND WHAT TO DO IF IT HAPPENS TO YOU

Make a Plan to Implement Your Decision

When you announce a career decision, you are making a statement about how you want your life to unfold. For example, if you say that you will get a four-year college degree, you want at some future time to have the knowledge and skills of someone who holds a bachelor's degree. If you tell others that you have decided to invent video games, you are making a statement about an occupation you wish to pursue after college.

Some students are proud to declare their vision of the future, but they overlook an important tool that will help them make their career dreams come true. They fail to make a plan.

A plan helps you plot out a series of actions that you will have to perform to reach the situation you desire. For example, if you decide to transfer to New York University, a list of the actions for implementing your plan would include obtaining an application, writing the application essay, giving the proper forms to the people who have agreed to be your references, and applying for financial aid—all by the admissions deadline. Without a plan, you might omit one of these crucial actions or fail to leave enough time to complete them. Making a plan is a way to increase the chances that you will know what to do and when to do it to make your dream come true.

Write down your plan. The act of writing helps you think through each part of the plan, and the written plan provides a visual reminder of the actions you need to take. A plan consists of several components:

- A clear statement of your career decision
- The date when you will begin implementing your plan, and the date when you hope to complete it
- A list of potential internal and external obstacles and the strategies you might use to overcome them
- A list of possible resources: people, publications, Internet resources
- A list of actions you will need to take, along with targeted completion dates for each one

Notice that a good plan even helps you identify strategies to triumph over any internal and external barriers. A plan also encourages you to identify the resources that will help you succeed. Activity 6.2, Making a Plan, explains each component of a plan in greater detail, while leading you through the process of creating one. Use it to map out what you need to do to achieve your goal.

A HERO'S JOURNEY

Forging your career direction is your own personal quest. Your challenge is to listen to your heart and set a path that nourishes your inner development. You can expect to face obstacles on the road to reaching your career goals. Difficulties in reaching your dream are so common that this theme is found in stories of the hero's quest in cultures the world over. From the Greek classic Homer's *Odyssey*, to the contemporary *Lord of the Rings* trilogy by J. R. R. Tolkien, many stories detail the terrors and hardships involved in confronting seemingly insurmountable obstacles to reach a goal. These stories inspire us to have the courage to undergo the psychic transformations involved in moving from dependence and a childish state to self-responsibility and personal ownership of our lives.

The tales about heroes warn us that every dream has its tests and trials. Everyone struggles with temptations that derail growth, such as selling out or laziness. Greg was avoiding statistics, a difficult course that would take a great deal of his time and energy. Still, when he faces that challenge, he not only puts himself in a better position for graduate school, but he nourishes his inner development. He will learn more about confronting a difficult task and getting the proper help. His fear of math will no longer drive his career search. We may not think of Greg as facing a hero's quest, but his personal trials involve deciding whether to go on for an advanced degree and whether to take statistics. If he shirks these tasks, he may set a course that will leave him dissatisfied.

Setting a career direction may mean becoming different from those around us. We may have to leave home, at least psychologically, to live the kind of life we value. This is Lisa's situation. Although she is married and has her own family, her parents' messages have lived on in her thinking.

Your career decisions open some doors and close others. One difficulty that we often have in making choices is not in selecting one option, but in letting the others go. Opening doors is exciting, but closing others involves the loss of unlimited possibility.

A notable part of the hero's journey is that it is a voyage you make alone. While professors, family, and friends can point the way, give clues, and provide help, you must take responsibility for deciding which doors to open and which to close.

KEY POINTS

1. Setting your career direction requires several decisions. You move from a general goal to a more specific implementation of it. Psychologists tell us that the specification process takes five to seven years.

2. When you set your career direction, a lot is at stake. Your choices will form an important part of your identity in society, nurture or starve your subsequent personal development, affect the rhythm of your life, and have a substantial impact on the lifestyle that you will be able to afford.

3. As you make your choices, you must take into account your evolving identity, your other life commitments, and the job market. These three factors complicate your career decision making.

4. Using the power of your heart and mind to set your career direction increases your chances of satisfaction and success.

5. Listening to your heart means that the option gives you what you want in terms of personal identity, inner development, and lifestyle.

6. Using your head means that you take a practical approach, looking at the economic prospects of an alternative and determining whether you can reach your goal.

7. The decision styles window is a technique for checking the style that you use in making career decisions. You strive for a balanced style, one that is practical and leads to work you like. You want to avoid using a sacrifice, daydreaming, or haphazard style.

8. Usually an option does not fit your needs perfectly. You make trade-offs, giving up some things you want because other things are more important to you.

9. Forging a career direction takes time. You must test your skills, determine your own priorities, and structure your life space to meet your

work–family–community commitments. The path you forge seldom advances in a straight line, with each decision leading in a single clear, consistent direction.

10. A common mistake that students make is to neglect making a plan to implement their career decisions.

11. A good plan has several components:

    - a clear statement of the decision
    - the start date and the completion date for implementing the plan
    - a list of potential internal and external obstacles and ways to overcome them
    - a list of possible resources: people, publications, and the Internet
    - a list of actions with a projected completion date for each one

12. Forging your career direction is your hero's quest. You must take responsibility for the paths you select and overcome the obstacles to reaching your goal.

Listening to Your Heart and Using Your Head to Make Career Decisions

CASE 6.5

One of my biggest career dilemmas was the position I have as an entry-level data entry clerk. Although the position has taught me new things about using a computer, the salary is not great. It does not cover all the expenses that my wife and I incur in a month due to the new house and baby. I also feel that the job does not satisfy me. . . . I am a smart man with many talents and an active imagination. I have an eagerness to earn and make money in many creative ways. The job is very monotonous. It does not vary from day to day. This monotony bores me. I am afraid that this monotony will make me lazy. I need to do something that will keep me on my toes. I need excitement on the job to make the job seem worthwhile.

After doing some self-assessment and conducting information searches, I have made some decisions. . . . First, I learned I would like to be my own boss someday. I want to open my own business and earn money for myself. This will allow me to use my imagination to the fullest to benefit me. Second, I learned that I enjoy working with computers. . . . [As a data entry clerk] there is nowhere I can go in this company. But there are different types of jobs that one can do. . . . I can become an information systems manager. This combines the principles of business and computers into one. . . . I have discovered many new educational opportunities and options. . . . Many schools offer information systems management as a major. I plan on approaching my future dilemmas differently. . . . There are many aspects that affect one's decisions. There are certain things that one has to look at in order to make a good decision. First, I have to look at myself and the changes that occur in my life. For example, I have realized that my decisions affect not only me, but also my family. Second, I have to look at how the world has changed. I need to be aware of the economic, social, and political situations around me. I need to be informed of all the new technological advances being made in the field of study that I am interested in.

—Jaime T.

ACTIVITY 6.1   MAKING A BALANCED DECISION

OVERVIEW

In this activity you will describe a career or educational decision and test the reasons for your choice. You'll want to make sure that you listened to your heart and used your head. In this way you can be more confident that your decision will meet your psychological and economic needs by using a balanced decision style.

Often a decision will mean making trade-offs and overcoming obstacles before you can reach your goal. This activity also asks you to consider these trade-offs and to outline your plans for overcoming any anticipated difficulties.

On a separate sheet of paper, complete the following five tasks.

TASK 1 DESCRIBE A CAREER DECISION

Describe a career decision that you have recently made or one that you are about to make.

TASK 2 LISTEN TO YOUR HEART

How does this career decision fit with your values and interests?

In what ways does this choice nourish your development as a person?

TASK 3 USE YOUR HEAD

If your decision was related to your career path, use the following questions.

1. Describe in what ways your skills and personal qualities match or do not match those required by this career option. What additional education will allow you to overcome any skill deficits?

2. What is your idea of financial success? Looking at the entry-level salary as well as the salaries for experienced workers, will you meet your financial goals?

If your decision was related to your educational path, use the following questions.

3. How competitive is the admissions process? What can you do to increase your chances of being accepted?

4. What plans do you have to finance your education?

TASK 4 TRADE-OFFS

Most decisions require trade-offs. We have to give up some things that we like in order to get something that is more important to us.

What trade-offs are connected with this decision (e.g., giving up some things that I want, such as a better car, in order to get a degree, or taking less money for the right job)?

TASK 5 NEXT STEPS

Do you foresee any external or internal obstacles that might interfere with the pursuit of the option that you have chosen? What might you do about them?

What's next (e.g., get more information, take some action to implement the decision, rethink the decision)?

Life is like playing a violin solo in public and learning the instrument as one goes on.

—Samuel Butler

MAKING A PLAN

OVERVIEW

The purpose of this activity is to construct a plan for implementing a career decision that you have made. This decision may be to enter a specific occupation or industry, search for a particular type of job after graduation, or apply to graduate school or a four-year college.

If you need more room or are instructed to do so, type your answers separately.

TASK 1 DESCRIBE YOUR DECISION

Examples:

- I have decided to become a lawyer.
- I have decided to transfer to the University of South Florida.
- I have decided to major in a computer-related field.
- I have decided to enter the movie business.
- I have decided to look for a job in sports marketing.
- I have decided to own my own travel agency in 10 years.
- I have decided to apply for scholarships to private colleges.

Describe a career decision that you have recently made.

_____

_____

TASK 2 SET DATES

Indicate when you will begin to implement this decision and when you want to complete it.

Start Date _____

Completion Date _____

TASK 3 IDENTIFY STRATEGIES

Identify strategies to overcome any internal and external obstacles that would interfere with your success. A good planning tip is to outline the possible internal and external obstacles that might prevent you from putting a plan into action. Be honest with yourself. If you tend to procrastinate, list this as a possible internal obstacle. If paying for your education is a problem, record it as an external obstacle.

For each obstacle you list, describe some strategies that you might use to overcome it. Enlist help and support. Use the ASAP information search method to gather information. Refer to Chapters 4 and 5 for some good ideas.

List any internal obstacles that would interfere with implementing your plan, and identify what you might do to overcome each one.

_____

_____

_____

_____

_____

_____

_____

_____

List any external obstacles that would interfere with implementing your plan, and identify what you might do to overcome each one. Enlist help and support. Use the ASAP information search method to gather information.

_____

_____

_____

_____

_____

_____

_____

_____

TASK 4 PLAN ACTIONS

List the actions you will take to implement your plan. For each action, indicate a completion date. A plan consists of a set of actions that must be completed in a specific sequence. For example, if you want to work for a specific company such as Goldman Sachs, 3M, Abbott Labs, Southwest Airlines, Cisco Systems, or Sony Pictures, a list of actions would include going to the Web site, identifying suitable positions, and completing an application following the company's stated procedures. You must also check with the placement office of your college to determine if the company sends recruiters to your college or is represented at an area job fair. Other actions might include applying for internships, taking additional coursework to build your qualifications, or talking to someone who works for the company. By listing these actions separately, each with its own completion date, you will be better able to estimate when you need to take action, and to set a realistic timetable to implement your decision. Sometimes these completion dates are called *milestones* because they mark your progress toward your goal.

A partial list of action steps for applying to graduate school in business is as follows:

- Investigate three schools that offer a master's in business by 11/01.
- Identify three professors who agree to provide reference letters by 11/15.
- Get an application and find out due dates by 11/28.
- Apply for MCAT examination by 12/01.
- Prepare for MCAT examination during holiday break.
- Prepare a draft of application essay by 12/28.

- Apply for financial aid by 1/15.
- Send in completed application(s) by 2/01.

Break the actions into small steps. For example, the action step "Have three people review essay draft and revise by 1/15" can be broken into several more specific steps, each with its own completion date.

- Give Professor Levine, Counselor Alan Myers, and friend Kelly Adams my draft essay by 1/05.
- Schedule appointments with each person, and review essay by 1/10.
- Revise essay by 1/25.

An action such as obtaining reference letters also requires many small steps, including identifying potential references, checking on their willingness to complete the required forms, giving them the materials and background information about your qualifications and achievements, and following up before the due date to make sure the documents were completed and mailed.

Action #1
_____
_____

Action #2
_____
_____

Action #3
_____
_____

Action #4
_____
_____

Action #5
_____
_____

Action #6
_____
_____

Action #7
_____
_____

Action #8
_____
_____

TASK 5   REVIEW YOUR PLAN WITH ANOTHER PERSON

Identify someone whose opinion you respect, and discuss your plan with him or her. Choose someone whose judgment you respect. Ideally, this person has knowledge about and/or experience in implementing a similar decision. However, even talking with a classmate who's facing a similar decision is a good way to review your plan. He or she may raise questions you have not thought of, or suggest ways to implement your plan that would increase its chances of succeeding.

After your discussion, add to your plan or revise it if necessary.

I will discuss my plan with

_____

I have chosen this person because

_____

_____

_____

TASK 6   KEEP YOUR PLAN VISIBLE

Place the dates by which you want to complete each action step in your calendar. Post the list of actions you need to take in a prominent place—your refrigerator door, your bedroom mirror, your closet door—where it is always visible to you. Then cross off each action as you complete it. The process of realizing your career dreams is underway.

I will keep my plan visible by

_____

_____

_____

CHAPTER 7

Selecting a Major

If your train is
on the wrong
track, every station
you come to is the
wrong station.
—Bernard Malamud

MAJOR CHOICE AND CHANGE DURING COLLEGE

Choosing a major field of study is an important step in the process of setting your career direction. Your choice of major shapes your personal development. It anchors your college study in one field so that you graduate knowing more about that one field than all the rest.

Your choice of major affects your future earnings, too. Average starting salaries after graduation vary dramatically from one field to another. In one study, choice of major was found to be a more important factor in determining earning power than whether a student went to an Ivy League school or a state college.[1]

THE TRUTH ABOUT COLLEGE MAJORS

Before we go further, test your knowledge about college majors. Mark each of the following statements about college majors either true (T) or false (F).

_____ 1. Students rarely change their majors.

_____ 2. Your major will make you an expert in your field.

_____ 3. The purpose of a college major is to prepare you for a specific career.

_____ 4. There is one best major for every occupation.

_____ 5. Your major always determines the type of job that you'll get upon graduation.

_____ 6. Majors associated with the highest earnings either include substantial coursework in mathematics or rely on mathematical techniques.

_____ 7. Liberal arts majors don't really acquire any skills useful in the workplace.

_____ 8. Majors with strong links to well-paying jobs are chosen less frequently by women than by men.

_____ 9. A good major and a college degree guarantee a good income.

_____ 10. I can sign up for any major I want.

_____ 11. The only value of a major is to prepare you to earn a good living.

You will find the answers to all these questions as your read the chapter. Some of them may surprise you.

1. STUDENTS RARELY CHANGE THEIR MAJORS.

False. Researchers estimate that three out of four students will change their major at least once during their undergraduate years.[2]

Most entering students don't believe that they are likely to change their major. Over 92 percent come to college with a major in mind, and fewer than 15 percent believe that they will change their major.[3]

Yet most students will change their major. In one university study, 10 percent changed four or more times.[4] Rafael, whose college career we will look at later, summarizes what students go through in settling on a major: "There is a lot of frustration and anxiety." For many students, like George, a change of major can turn out to be the best course of action. Frequent changes of mind can be costly, though. A study of Illinois graduates found that students who change majors two or more times take at least an additional year to graduate.[5]

There is no such thing as failing. Life is just telling you to try something else.

CASE 7.1

I got to talking with George about colleges at a friend's house one summer night. "What is your major?"

George replied, "Biomedical engineering."

"Wow," I said, "How did you choose it?"

He looked embarrassed and said, "Well, a pretty girl I was seeing suggested it."

"Did you ever consider anything else?"

He seemed surprised by my question, but said, "Yes, I started in architecture."

Naturally I asked, "Why did you change?"

"Oh, I didn't like the professor. Maybe that isn't a good reason."

George had taken a special accelerated course in high school geared toward architecture. In his first semester of college he took an introductory architecture class with the new, young rising star of the faculty, the dean of the architecture school.

As George told me, the dean had divided the class into two sections: one section had "potential"; the other didn't. George was in the less favored group. His half of the class received just a few comments on their work each week, mostly negative, and then were ignored as the dean spent most of his time with the other half.

In addition, George had a few personal problems that semester and didn't work as hard as he should have. However, he thought he would get a C and was stung when he got an F.

Probing deeper into these events, George admitted that in this introductory college course some students were very talented, and perhaps he was not in the first rank of this extremely competitive field, as he had believed he would be in high school. His loss of interest, disruptive personal problems, and focus on the dean allowed him to avoid looking at his skills objectively.

"Although his method of 'teaching' seems to be arrogant and disdainful of all but a select few, maybe that dean did you a favor," I suggested.

"Why do you say that?"

"He forced you to find out what you are really good at."

We puzzled over why, of all the suggestions he got, he followed up on the one from the "pretty girl." He noted that he was so intrigued by her recommendation that he went to the college library and did some research, since he wasn't sure what biomedical engineers do.

After some discussion, he volunteered, "When I was very young, I wanted to be a doctor."

His choice of biomedical engineering now made sense. He could work in the medical field, as he had once dreamed of doing. He could even continue in design, changing his focus from designing houses to designing artificial limbs. Later, he could decide to go to medical school because his new major gives him the right foundation.

—George D.

This chapter is devoted to giving you a broad understanding of the relationship between college majors and careers. It also outlines a process for ensuring that you have chosen (or are choosing) wisely.

Community college and four-year college majors are discussed, and special topics of immediate interest both to two- and four-year students are addressed. Skim the special topics that don't apply to you.

The good news is that you have so many choices. The bad news is that we cannot discuss every possibility or permutation here. We'll focus on the most typical majors and the preferred level of training for the most popular occupations.[6] After reading the chapter, you can work with your counselor or advisor to identify the best choice for you.

2. YOUR MAJOR WILL MAKE YOU AN EXPERT IN YOUR FIELD.

False. "[A] major of a minimum of 24 credits cannot provide mastery of a field; it is actually little more than an introduction to it." *Undergraduate Bulletin 1998/00, Baruch College*[7]

MAJORS AND DEGREE REQUIREMENTS

Will You Become an Expert?

Why would the catalog of a college that has an acclaimed national reputation for training business students sound this cautionary note? You'll understand better when you have a clear picture of the credit requirements for majors, and their importance in the credits that you earn toward your degree.

A major is a set of courses concentrated in one field or, in the case of interdisciplinary areas, concentrated on one theme. There are hundreds of possibilities, ranging from Agriculture, African–American Studies, Archaeology, and Art History to Visual Arts, Women and Gender Studies, and Zoology.

A major is usually the equivalent of 8 to 15 three-credit courses (or about one and a half years' worth of study). That's not enough to make you an expert in any field.

Occupationally oriented majors in two-year colleges (A.A.S. degrees) tend to have the highest concentration of coursework in their major, maybe up to 70 percent. Liberal arts students in two- and four-year colleges tend to have the lowest percentage of coursework in their major, ranging generally from 25 to 40 percent.

Degree Requirements Overview

A college degree is much more than a major. To summarize briefly, the three components of a college degree are as follows:

- General education courses (also known by other names, such as core courses and distribution requirements)
- Major requirements
- Elective courses

General education and electives make up a substantial portion of your degree. Table 7.1 shows typical proportions of these three degree components in various two- and four-year degree programs.

Whereas a major allows you to pursue a subject in some depth, the general education courses guarantee that your education has breadth. Since most of these required courses are taken early in your college program, they provide an additional benefit. Course sampling is one of the best ways to select a major. It introduces you to a variety of possibilities, some of which you never had in high school. Once you get a taste of a subject, you may decide that you want to go back for more.

TABLE 7.1		2-Year Degree[a]			4-Year Degree[a]	
Components of two-year and four-year degree programs.		AAS	AS	AA	BA	BS
Components						
A.	General Education	20	30	45	60	48
	Communications[b]					
	Humanities[c]					
	Social studies[d]					
	Mathematics[e]					
	Science/computer science					
	General education electives					
B.	Major	40	31	13	40	60
	Major core					
	Major					
	Major electives					
C.	Free Electives	4	3	6	28	20
	Total for Degree	64	64	64	128	128

[a]AA (Associate in Arts), AS (Associate in Science), and AAS (Associate in Applied Science) degrees vary from 60 to 70 credits.

BA (Bachelor of Arts) and BS (Bachelor of Science) degrees vary from 120 to 132 total credits.

Some special degrees (e.g., Architecture or Engineering) may require more credits due to studio, internship, or other specialized courses.

[b]Communications may include skill and placement tests.

[c]Humanities include special topics or courses at some colleges.

[d]Social science requirements at some colleges may consist of some special sequence of courses.

[e]Math and science may be specific curriculum-related courses.

Source: Dr. Kenneth Maugle, Middlesex County College, NJ. Adapted with permission.

3. THE PURPOSE OF A COLLEGE MAJOR IS TO PREPARE YOU FOR A SPECIFIC CAREER.

False. Four of the most common four-year college majors in recent years—business, engineering, health sciences, and teaching—ready you for particular career fields. Yet three others, also hugely popular—psychology, English, and the social sciences—do not prepare you for specific occupations. Even in community colleges, which are traditionally seen as more occupationally oriented, a third of the students graduate without preparation for a specific career.[8]

DIFFERENCES IN STUDENT GOALS

College is so attractive, in part because it promises such beneficial career outcomes: most reliably, higher earnings and lower unemployment.[9] You may think that you can get a better job because you obtain occupational training. However, research shows that the cognitive skills that you develop in the process of acquiring and using knowledge are more important.[10] College graduates are more inclined to keep learning, too.[11] That's why, even if you don't opt for specific occupational preparation, you are likely to achieve more career success than if you had not gone beyond high school.

Specific career preparation is not the thrust of all majors, because students want to follow different paths. Students have three broad alternatives in college: (1) to prepare for occupational entry into a specific field; (2) to prepare for entry into a specific graduate school program; and (3) to keep their options open, either to go on for further education or to work. It can be helpful to think about majors in terms of these three alternative paths, and so we will discuss the following:

- Occupationally oriented majors
- Graduate school readiness majors
- Multipotential majors

Occupationally Oriented Majors

We've coined the term *occupationally oriented majors* to refer to programs that are designed primarily for students who plan on working immediately after graduation. Graphic design, nursing, and accounting are examples of occupationally oriented majors. Majors associated with particular industries, such as hotel management, textiles and clothing, and automotive technology, are also included in this category.

Students who choose this type of major decide to devote a portion of their college work to specific occupational preparation. Table 7.2 provides an overview of different types of occupationally oriented majors.

If you choose an occupationally oriented major, you have made a tentative commitment to a particular career path by seeking knowledge and skills related to entering a specific occupation or industry upon graduation. The transition from school to work is likely to be smoother because your job objective is related to the training you received in college.

If you discover that you don't like the field you've chosen, however, you may feel stuck because of all the effort that you've already put into learning specific occupational skills. We'll see a case a little later of a student who realized after a while that he didn't like his major (computer science), but kept on going. He knew he was wasting time and money, but it was more than a year before he had the courage to make a change. Counselors will attest that this happens more often than you might guess. Avoid committing too soon, and make sure that you don't overspecialize by taking all your electives in one area.

To overinvest in occupationally oriented courses poses another danger: You could spend all your time developing a knowledge base that technological change soon will render obsolete.

TABLE 7.2	
Popular types of occupationally and industry-oriented majors.	**Health care majors,** such as X-ray technician, nurse, occupational therapy assistant, medical record technician, dietitian
	Technical majors in such fields as engineering and computer science
	Industry specialties, such as paralegal, journalism, radio and TV broadcasting, travel and tourism
	Education majors, including preparation for teaching in elementary and secondary schools and special subjects such as special education, physical education, and music education
	Business majors, including business administration, human resources, management, marketing, operations research, and computer information systems
	Visual and performing arts majors, such as dance, commercial art, and cinematography

Graduate School Readiness Majors

The second type of major we call *graduate school readiness majors.* This type of major signals a commitment to a specific type of work that requires advanced education beyond the baccalaureate.

These advanced degrees are (1) the master's, (2) the doctorate, and (3) the first professional degree. Table 7.3 outlines the types of graduate degrees and the preferred level of graduate training for various occupations and professions.[12]

Note that the educational requirements are described in a general fashion, focusing on the minimum amount of full-time study beyond the bachelor's degree. Often much more study is required. Check for more specific information, including whether licensing or certification is necessary to practice in a given field.

A graduate school readiness major is an excellent choice when you have to compete for a spot in graduate school. It ensures that you have taken the proper prerequisites and have built the appropriate skills. For instance, lawyers need to write well, and a major such as political science or English that builds writing skills will help them to succeed.

Students headed for graduate school often choose their major by working backward from their long-term career goal. They consult the appropriate publications and advisors about which majors and courses will best prepare them for admission to the graduate program of their choice.

If you believe that a graduate degree is part of your future, you need to look carefully at the ease with which you could enter your preferred graduate program with your undergraduate major.

About 60 percent of students who enter college aspire to get a graduate degree.[13] A year after graduation, however, only about 18 percent of students are in graduate school, and 6 percent of them are part time.[14] Obviously, many students change their plans. They plunge into the work world right after they complete their undergraduate degree, though eventually they may go on to grad school. Given this reality, it makes sense to take some courses that would also make you marketable immediately. It is likely that you will find yourself working right after graduation, at least for a while.

First Professional Degree				TABLE 7.3

The first professional degree is the minimum preparation for entry into law, medicine, dentistry, the clergy, and the other professions listed here. This degree requires at least two years of full-time academic study beyond a bachelor's degree, and usually more.

Overview of graduate degree types and preferred training for many popular occupations.

J.D.	Lawyer	D.V.M.	Veterinarian
M.D.	Physician	D.C.	Chiropractor
B.D. or M.Div.	Member of Clergy	O.D.	Optometrist
D.D.S. or D.M.D.	Dentist	D.P.M.	Podiatrist

Master's Degree

The Master of Arts (M.A.), Master of Science (M.S.), and Master of Education (M.Ed.) require one or two years of full-time study beyond the bachelor's degree.

Other well-known master's degrees are the M.B.A. (Master of Business Administration), the M.S.W. (Master of Social Work), and the M.L.S. (Master of Library Science).

The master's degree is preferred for counselors, librarians, speech-language pathologists and audiologists, urban and regional planners, management analysts, and many teaching positions.

Doctorate

The Doctor of Philosophy (Ph.D.) and the Doctor of Education (Ed.D.) require at least three years of full-time academic work beyond the bachelor's degree. Independent research culminating in a dissertation is often an additional requirement.

The doctorate is preferred for college and university faculty, biological and medical scientists, physicists, astronomers, mathematicians, and psychologists.

Source: Adapted from Darrel Patrick Wash, "A New Way to Classify Occupations by Education and Training," *Occupational Outlook Quarterly,* 39, No. 4 (Winter 1995–96): 28–40.

Multipotential Majors

The third type of major we call *multipotential.* Liberal arts and sciences majors, such as history, sociology, and comparative literature, are multipotential. This type of major fosters your intellectual growth while giving you a great deal of flexibility.

As an example, the Emory University catalog lists some career directions that anthropology majors pursue: "Anthropology majors go on to careers as professional anthropologists, physicians, attorneys, librarians, social workers, environmental specialists, teachers, translators, and laboratory researchers."[15] This description stimulates you to think about the many possibilities open to you if you major in anthropology. Of course, many of them require graduate work.

The multipotential major allows you to delay setting your career direction until you have done more exploration. It is also a pragmatic choice for some. Part-time and evening students often cannot follow complicated course sequences or are working when required courses are offered. They are forced to be practical and select a multipotential major that has relatively few restrictions.

The multipotential major often leads to graduate school. The earlier you know what specific graduate program you want, the better. To gain admission to some programs, you may need to add certain courses not required in your major.

Multipotential majors qualify you to respond to the many job openings that specify only "associate's required" or "bachelor's preferred." These job postings underscore the fact that all majors develop your mental powers and communication skills.

The transition from school to work can be rocky if you choose a multipotential major. Since you lack occupational focus, formulating a job search objective can be more difficult. Chapter 8, Finding a Place to Advance Your Career, is especially helpful to read before you begin your job search.

CASE 7.2   *The Savvy Idealist*

Rafael is a man of many interests who just earned an M.B.A. Talking with his former college counselor during a break from his high-level job at the Federal Reserve Bank, he reflected on the twists and turns of his career path:

"I began college wanting to work at saving the natural environment," Rafael recalled. "My plan was to major in biology, get a Ph.D., become a research scientist, and save the planet. But I just didn't like the labs, so I switched to philosophy, which was challenging." Finally, he chose international affairs. "I liked the mix of political science, history, and economics, and I also had room to take computer science and calculus." He found a major that had elements of many different subjects that interested him. Then he added courses such as computer science and calculus, which gave him a tremendous edge in his later career.

"There was a lot of anxiety and frustration going through this process," he said. "It fell into place a bit at a time."

Along the way he worked on a public health project in Nicaragua, stopped out for a while to work in a law firm, and completed a senior thesis on the environmental legislation of the United Nations.

He thought his major in international affairs helped him to develop the necessary verbal skills to get accepted to law school when he graduated, but at that time he concluded law school was too expensive and went to work instead.

His major also helped him to get an interview for his current job. His counselor observed, "I'm sure they liked the combination of his quantitative skills, coursework in economics, and the international perspective developed during college." Rafael was attracted to the job because it was an opportunity to learn about public policy and legislation.

Later his major proved to be excellent preparation for a joint master's in business administration/master's in international affairs. He chose business school to deepen his understanding of the workings of the global marketplace. Graduate work in international affairs furthered his understanding of the global environment, policy formulation, and public health issues.

Rafael's career direction remains tied to his original respect and love for the natural world. His emphasis has shifted, though, spurred by the kind of background that he acquired through his college major. He is involved in economic development issues and the effect of business and governmental policies on the environment. He credits his multipotential major with giving him the background to see environmental issues in a broader context.

He is a fervent believer in creating many possible future avenues by selecting a multipotential major, especially with interdisciplinary themes. To his mind, specialization is "just not worth it anymore." He believes interdisciplinary majors are "the wave of the future."

By the way, do you find it surprising that Rafael and his new bride chose a nature preserve off the coast of Brazil for their honeymoon?

—Rafael M.

---

4. THERE IS ONE BEST MAJOR FOR EVERY OCCUPATION.

False. There are many exceptions to this sweeping statement.

COLLEGE MAJORS AND CAREER OUTCOMES

Many students overgeneralize and assume that there is always a relationship between one's college major and future occupation. They are thinking primarily about such occupations as nurse, dental assistant, and elementary school teacher. For many occupations, especially those requiring graduate education or on-the-job experience, you will discover that the link between your major and your future occupation is a weak one.

For example, there is no one "best" major that prepares you for admission to law school. In *How to Get into the Right Law School*[16] Paul Lermack cites a survey of the entering class at Valparaiso University Law School. These students had 48 different majors. Admission to medical school does not depend on your major, either. Certain subjects are required, such as biology and chemistry,[17] and declaring a major in science is often a convenient way to meet these requirements. Still, many English, humanities, and social science majors with science coursework have gone on to become physicians. Understanding how the commercial world operates may get you off to a running start in business careers, but there are also plenty of company executives who were liberal arts majors in college.

5. YOUR MAJOR ALWAYS DETERMINES THE TYPE OF JOB THAT YOU'LL GET UPON GRADUATION.

False. Statistics show that working in a field different from one's major is very common.

According to a National Center for Education Statistics study, about 75 percent of students one year after graduation reported that their job was related to their degree.[18] Studies that track graduates for longer periods show that many people migrate to unrelated career fields over time.[19]

Those men and women who stay in career fields related to their major are concentrated in occupationally oriented fields, as you can see in Table 7.4. In

TABLE 7.4	
Strong relationships between college major and subsequent career field.	In a survey* of over 200 thousand individuals having a bachelor's degree or higher, over half the graduates in these seven fields of study were in occupations directly related to their major. Pharmacy (87%) Nursing (82%) Physical therapy and other rehabilitative and therapeutic services (80%) Health and medicine technologies (67%) Computer and information sciences (65%) Engineering (56%) Accounting (56%)

Source: Adapted from Daniel Hecker, "Earnings of College Graduates 1993," *Monthly Labor Review,* 118, No. 12 (December 1995), Table 5. *Survey by National Science Foundation with analysis by Bureau of Labor Statistics.

addition, although exact matches are more difficult to make, analysis showed that a majority of those with various business majors were found in managerial or business-related occupations. Looking just at women graduates, we should add that more than half the women who studied education were in jobs related to their major.

Career fields with a weak link or no link to subsequent occupations include history, political science, government, economics, psychology, and sociology. This means that very few history majors, for example, go on to become historians, and very few economics majors become economists.[20]

As you may have observed, liberal arts graduates are the least likely to have jobs related to their field of study. Liberal arts graduates are generalists, and they pursue many career routes after graduation.

Many parents, especially if they did not attend college themselves, are chagrined when their college-educated children study one thing in college but end up in unrelated careers. Some graduates themselves appear to be embarrassed to admit that they are not in a career related to their major.

That many students end up in fields unrelated to their majors does not mean that your choice of major and your coursework won't influence your career (and your life). Let's examine some data on the relationship between choice of major and earnings.

> **6. MAJORS ASSOCIATED WITH THE HIGHEST EARNINGS EITHER INCLUDE SUBSTANTIAL COURSEWORK IN MATHEMATICS OR RELY ON MATHEMATICAL TECHNIQUES.[21]**
>
> *True.*

MAJORS AND EARNINGS

Seventy-four percent of first-year college students, no matter the type of school—public, private, two-year, four-year, religiously affiliated, or minority-dominated—cite "make more money" as a very important reason that they are in school.[22] Given this goal, it is surprising that most students are unaware of the key role that mathematics and quantitative reasoning skills play in high-income occupations.

Both men and women who majored in economics, engineering, physics, and pharmacy earn more than the average college graduate. So do women who majored in health and medical technology occupations.[23] Other fields of study associated with higher incomes are mathematics and computer and information sciences.[24]

Many students develop an image of themselves as "bad at math." They see remedial work and required mathematics courses as a special plague visited upon them to ruin their college years. If you have this self-image, your options are constricted. A lack of math skills closes the door to many interesting and lucrative careers. Knowing this, you might reexamine your attitude and reconsider some of your choices about courses, even your major. As you learned in Rafael's case, his quantitative skills not only helped him to get his job, but also helped him to get admitted and succeed in business school.

7. LIBERAL ARTS MAJORS DON'T REALLY ACQUIRE ANY SKILLS USEFUL IN THE WORKPLACE.

False. Researchers have found that in college you gain skills in abstract reasoning, critical thinking, and reflective judgment. You increase your ability to deal with conceptual complexity.[25] These thinking skills are cultivated through the study of liberal arts and are essential for success in high-level occupations.

Liberal arts subjects help you increase your intellectual skills, which are highly valued in today's workplace. Much of the factual information gained in college is quickly forgotten or becomes obsolete, whereas your cognitive skills enable you to adapt quickly to new situations.

In the words of Pascarella and Terenzini, who have studied how college affects students, college fosters the capacity to:

- Communicate more effectively
- Draw objective conclusions from various types of data
- Use reason and evidence in addressing ill-structured problems
- Evaluate new ideas and techniques efficiently
- Examine arguments and claims critically
- Make reasonable decisions in the face of imperfect information[26]

Study this list for a moment. Wouldn't these skills be valuable for your career, whatever it may be?

8. MAJORS WITH STRONG LINKS TO WELL-PAYING JOBS ARE CHOSEN LESS FREQUENTLY BY WOMEN THAN BY MEN.[27]

True.

On average, women earn less than men in all age groups and in nearly all fields. Discrimination exists, yes; however, it is not the whole story.

A crucial reason that college-educated women earn less than men is their choice of major. Women tend to major in fields associated with lower pay, such as teaching. Nearly a quarter of all women major in education. Only 6.4 percent of college men are education majors. Engineering, a major that is associated with higher earnings, is chosen by fewer women (1.5 percent) than men (13.3 percent). When women do choose a high-paying field, their earnings are very close to men's.[28]

---

9. A GOOD MAJOR AND A COLLEGE DEGREE GUARANTEE A GOOD INCOME.

False. Bear these two facts in mind:

- No major (or degree) guarantees either high or low pay.
- Not all differences in earnings are attributable to your college major.

Your major is no guarantee of future earnings. *Every* major has some people who end up in the highest-earning group and others who are in the lowest-earning group. For example, majoring in a lucrative career field such as engineering does not guarantee a high income. In 1998, the top 10 percent of civil engineers earned more than $87,000. However, the lowest 10 percent earned less than $35,000.[29]

Your personal characteristics, general skills, subsequent jobs, and (if you go on) graduate degree can put you in a top earning group, no matter what your major. For example, the entrepreneurial head of a leading software company majored in classics.[30] His leadership skills, not the facts that he learned in his undergraduate major, have figured in his later success.

KEY ACTIONS IN CHOOSING A MAJOR

When Yun Jong Moh first came to this country from Seoul, Korea, at the age of 20, he chose a major based on a common stereotype of success. *"My goal was to become a computer programmer and make a lot of money. I thought that to be happy in America you had to have money, a good education, friends with titles after their names, cars, a good house, a wife, kids—social status."* Even after he realized that computer science was not the appropriate major for him, he continued *"because it was what I knew."*[31] He spent several years pursuing a goal that did not fit his values. Eventually, he switched to political science, a field of study more in line with his own interests.

Self-Assessment

Self-assessment, as you discovered in Chapters 2 and 3, involves examining your personality, interests, and skills, as well as your values. When you try to live out someone else's vision of success, you may find yourself, like Yun Jong Moh, majoring in a subject that does not fit who you are as a person.

Conducting Research on Majors and Careers

Looking at yourself is not your only task in choosing a major. It is helpful to understand the relationship that your choice has to possible career paths.

LOOKING AT MAJORS: PRELIMINARY RESEARCH	ACTIVITY 7.2

There are two ways to examine the relationship between majors and career fields. The first route is to survey the array of possibilities that your college offers, and answer some basic questions.

1. *What is the primary purpose of the major?* As you read the catalog's overview sections for various majors, look for key words that suggest the purpose of a major. Then ask yourself, "How does the purpose of the major correspond with my goals after I graduate?"

2. *What kinds of skills does it emphasize?*
   a. Take a highlighter and mark the relevant skill descriptions from the college catalog.
   b. Classify the skills according to the Holland types described in Chapter 2 (Realistic, Investigative, Artistic, Social, Enterprising, and Conventional) or the Campbell Work Orientations described in Chapter 3 (Influencing, Organizing, Helping, Creating, Analyzing, Producing, Adventuring). Once you know the major's Holland or Campbell type, you can more easily identify relevant career families.

3. *What careers might this major lead to?* Several colleges have prepared resource kits for various majors. These kits provide descriptions of occupations, sample job titles, and links to relevant professional associations. Check your own college's Web site or use the sites in Table 7.5 to learn more about career paths associated with specific majors.

Remember that many majors have a great deal of elasticity, which means that you have not limited yourself to only one path. If George, our biomedical engineer, decides to go to medical school instead of working as an engineer, he will have most of the prerequisites. However, if you make a radical change of career plans, say, from a French undergraduate major to counseling and psychology graduate work (as the author did), you will probably have to take additional courses to prepare for your new career field.

Another way to find an appropriate major is to work backward from your occupational choice. In this method of choosing a major, you begin by identifying an occupation. Then you research its entry requirements using the four-step ASAP approach.

MAKING A BALANCED DECISION

Your choice of major shapes how you see yourself and how others will see you. You'll want to choose something that is congruent with who you are and who you want to become. Your choice is a way of announcing to the world, "Among all the possibilities, I want to be a person who is a scientist (businessperson, actor, journalist, and so forth)."

TABLE 7.5

What can I do with a major in . . . ?: College Web sites that can help you.

College of Mount St. Joseph www.msj.edu

The Kaleidoscope of Careers is found on the home page of the Career Development and Graduate Services.

Kansas State University www.ksu.edu

What Can I Do with a Major In . . . ? is found on the home page of the Academic and Career Information Center.

St. Lawrence University www.stlawu.edu

What Can I Do with a Major In . . . ? is found on the home page of Career Services and Leadership Education Planning.

University of Delaware www.udel.edu

The Major Resource Kits are found on the home page of the Career Services Center.

University of Missouri/Columbia www.missouri.edu

Career Maps are found on the Career Center home page.

University of North Carolina at Wilmington www.uncwil.edu

What Can I Do with a Major In . . . ? is found on the Career Services home page.

University of Tennessee, Knoxville www.utk.edu

What Can I Do with This Major? is found on the Career Services home page.

University of Texas at Austin www.utexas.edu

Majors to Careers is found in the Career Ideas section of the Career Exploration Center home page.

Note: The best strategy for locating major and career information is to go to a college's main home page (e.g., www.utexas.edu). Then, do a site search using the locator tips that are provided for the particular college (e.g., Career Exploration Center home page, Career Ideas section).

With your choice, you single out a specific body of knowledge and emphasize certain skills to learn. For example, human services majors work on learning interpersonal skills, biology majors emphasize learning to conduct research using the scientific method, and German majors stress the learning of a foreign language. Your decision reflects your belief that this subject is worthy of your intensive study.

Your choice will open some doors and close others. For example, a major in Islamic studies takes you into the international arena and enriches your knowledge of other societies. However, you won't have much time to explore the physical world. In contrast, oceanography takes you to the depths of the sea, but leaves you with little time to learn about rich cultural and religious traditions. Sometimes choosing is difficult because you realize that there are many interesting possibilities that you won't have time to pursue.

Listening to Your Heart

As you mentally try out various possible majors, listen to your heart. Ask yourself, would choosing this major fit with who I am as a person? In what ways will majoring in this subject be harmonious with the dreams I have for my life? As one student put it, "Why waste time and money doing something that in the long run will not satisfy you? Find something with which you can be happy."[32]

Using Your Head

Using your head in choosing a major means taking into account such practical variables as the job market and your skills. If you have in mind an occupationally specific major or one that will ready you for graduate education, you need to be clear about the nature of the career that you are preparing for. What skills does this major provide that will be useful in the workplace?

Before you make a commitment to the field, information about the job market is a basic practical consideration. However, experts caution against using labor market projections as the sole basis for choosing your major, thinking you have guaranteed yourself plenty of job opportunities. Sometimes students flock to an area because the field is touted in the press as a "hot career." By the time that they finish their preparations, there is an oversupply.

Suppose you have decided that graduate school is in your future. Have you checked the relevant graduate school guides to make sure that your major will give you the necessary background? Do you have a fallback plan in case you don't go on to grad school right after graduation?

If you choose a multipotential major, what steps are you taking to set your career direction (in addition to the kind of research and self-assessment encouraged in this book)? Remember, internships and fieldwork can be very helpful.

Most important, in using your head you are evaluating whether you have the skills to succeed in this major. If your honest self-assessment yields some weaknesses, you need a strategy to develop the skills you need. Using your head helps you formulate a realistic plan for success.

---

10. I CAN SIGN UP FOR ANY MAJOR I WANT.

False. Some majors are highly selective, and not every student who applies is accepted.

SEEKING ADVICE WHILE REMAINING INDEPENDENT

Sometimes your admission to a particular college will not guarantee your acceptance into your preferred field of study. For example, a college may offer a degree in occupational therapy, but you find there is a separate admission process to this program. Be sure to read the catalog carefully regarding the required procedure for acceptance in the major you want.

Meredith wants to be a physician's assistant; Grace wants to transfer to a prestigious music school. Both programs are competitive. There are fewer spots than interested students. Although both students had top grades, they didn't understand how the admission process works. As a result, despite their strong motivation, they failed to gain admission the first time they tried.

Top grades are often necessary for admission to competitive programs, but grades alone may be insufficient to win you a spot. A well-written application essay, high standardized test scores, glowing letters of recommendation, and, for artistic fields, a portfolio or an audition count heavily toward admission. Finding out about such considerations requires doing your homework.

Consulting with a counselor or adviser is important. He or she can provide information about the ingredients that give your candidacy a competitive edge, and provide you with assistance during the application process.

Timing is key, too. Meredith did seek out a counselor, but only a week before her application was due. There wasn't much the counselor could do to help her at that point.

The second time around, both Meredith and Grace began the application process early. Meredith worked closely with her counselor, and Grace with her adviser in the music department. They became better informed and strengthened their chances for success.

Actually, all students can benefit from early advisement, yet many avoid advisers, often in creative ways, because they see counselors and advisers as a threat to their independence. They are tired of having educators tell them what they can and cannot do. Every student has a horror story about a counselor who gave bad advice. In their view, college is the place where they are finally on their own.

Some counsel is frequently misinterpreted. When counselors suggest that you slow down, it may not signal a lack of faith in your ability. Rather, from experience, counselors know that demanding courses are better spaced out over time. When you consult counselors, the doubts that they create can be troubling. No one likes to change course without a good reason.

The psychological challenge here is to withstand the experience of having an expert review your goals and plans. Perhaps the adviser will fail to understand you or your situation fully, but he just might alert you to potentially fatal flaws in your planning.

By consulting with advisers and counselors, you gain experience in judging whether a particular piece of advice is appropriate and worth taking. You also cultivate your capacity to accept input from others, while at the same time taking responsibility for your own actions.

11. THE ONLY VALUE OF A MAJOR IS TO PREPARE YOU TO EARN A GOOD LIVING.

False. Students have a variety of life goals. Making money is only one possibility.

WHERE STUDENTS GET STUCK, AND WHAT TO DO IF IT HAPPENS TO YOU

Students Have a Variety of Life Goals

When the relationship between majors and earnings was presented earlier in the chapter, its purpose was to draw your attention to pertinent research and break down some common misconceptions. That discussion was not to suggest that you should choose your major solely on the basis of what you might earn in the workplace.

Other factors besides future earnings drive the choice of a major: spiritual fulfillment, a career dedicated to helping others, or the desire to lead an artistic life, for example.

You probably won't be surprised to learn that theology, philosophy, and religion majors have lower earnings when compared to people in other majors. Nor do most students who gravitate toward these majors identify "making a lot of money" as their principal life goal.

Social work and education are other majors that typically lead to lower earnings. Again, students selecting these majors are typically motivated by humanistic concerns.

Many who major in the visual and performing arts struggle to make ends meet. For example, although a few stars earn fabulous incomes, most actors do not earn enough from acting to support themselves.[33] Yet, for creative types, the artist's life exerts a stronger pull than money.

Some research on the question, Can money buy happiness? indicates that making money can be overemphasized. Consider these survey results. While 95 percent of those making over $75,000 per year report being "very happy" or "pretty happy," so do 92 percent of those making between $30,000 and $50,000, and 90 percent of those making $20,000 to $30,000.[34] Other studies show similar results. In the United States, Canada, and much of Europe, higher incomes have not been found to be related to greater personal happiness.[35] Obviously, other factors contribute to happiness, including challenging work, family and friends, and good health.

Whatever major you choose, make sure that you have an accurate notion of its likely consequences for your future earnings. How much weight you give to making money in selecting your major depends ultimately on your personal values.

If I Fail a Crucial Course, Do I Quit?

It is not uncommon to stumble and struggle on the road to success. One of the most difficult challenges you face is deciding whether to give up a career option if you fail a crucial course. For example, after failing Accounting 1 the first time, can I still learn the accounting necessary to complete my business degree, or should I look into another major? Many doctors and nurses did not particularly like organic chemistry, for example, but they decided that their overall interest in a medical career made it worthwhile to persist until they had passed that course. Others, however, take organic chemistry, are overwhelmed by it, and change their career fields. What is and is not too difficult depends on many factors, including your motivation, knowledge preparation, ability to concentrate, and current life situation. If you find yourself attracted to a career area that requires skills you lack, get advice on how to master this area before you give it up.

Sometimes an area can be so difficult that it is better to build a career on skills that are easier for you to acquire. If you decide to change majors, reassess your interests and skills to find another career field. A counselor can help you sort through new options.

CHOOSE YOUR MAJOR WITH CARE

This chapter has touched on many different points related to choosing a major. It seeks to help you choose your major by showing you that majors are designed to accommodate differences in student goals.

It is possible to use your major to set your career direction. Occupationally oriented majors and graduate school readiness majors are strongly associated with specific career goals. Yet you have another option. You can select a multipotential major to explore a variety of possibilities, and decide on your career direction later. Both courses of action have advantages and disadvantages. You'll have to make trade-offs.

All majors have some elasticity. No matter what you choose, you have not locked yourself into one path and you are always developing your cognitive skills. In the long run, your major is not the sole determinant of your career direction or your future earnings. Other factors play a role, and you will face many career choices during your working life.

Still, the choice of major influences the ease of entering the job market and of getting admitted to graduate school. It will determine how much leeway you have to explore different subject areas while in college.

Your choice of a major affects your personal and intellectual development, another reason to exercise care. You train your mind to look at the world through the lenses of one discipline. In turn, this discipline will influence how you approach problems and understand the world.

The only sound approach to choosing a major is a combination of self-assessment and research. Then you can make a balanced decision.

KEY POINTS

1. Researchers estimate that three out of four students will change their major at least once during their undergraduate years.

2. A major is a set of courses concentrated in one field or, in the case of interdisciplinary areas, concentrated along one theme. There are hundreds of possibilities, ranging from Agriculture, African–American Studies, Archaeology, and Art History to Visual Arts, Women and Gender Studies, and Zoology.

3. A college degree has three components: general education requirements, major coursework, and elective courses.

4. There are different types of majors, corresponding to differences in students' goals.

   a. *Occupationally oriented majors* are designed for students who plan to go to work immediately after graduation.

b. *Graduate school readiness majors* are designed for students who know early on that graduate work is necessary to achieve their career goals.

c. *Multipotential majors* are liberal arts and science fields that permit students to engage in a great deal of career exploration.

5. Many students overgeneralize and assume that there is always a relationship between one's major and one's future occupation. For many occupations, especially those requiring graduate education or on-the-job experience, you will discover that the link between what you study and your subsequent career field is a weak one.

6. Statistics show that working in a field different from the one in which a degree was obtained is very common.

7. Majors associated with the highest earnings include substantial coursework in mathematics, or rely on mathematical techniques.

8. Liberal arts courses in English, humanities, mathematics, and social sciences cultivate intellectual skills, which are crucial for success in high-level occupations.

9. Majors having strong links to well-paying jobs are chosen less frequently by women than by men.

10. Two facts to bear in mind:

a. No major (or degree) guarantees either high or low pay.

b. Not all differences in earnings are attributable to one's college major.

11. When selecting a major, an essential ingredient is self-assessment.

12. Two research strategies are useful to identify links between majors and careers:

a. Research a major and discover what careers it leads to.

b. Research an occupation and find out what majors are suggested as the proper educational background.

13. When choosing a major, listen to your heart and choose something you like. Your major is a choice that will shape your adult identity.

14. When choosing a major, use your head and be practical. Don't overlook such factors as the job market and your skill level.

15. Some majors are highly selective. Do your homework and consult an advisor about how to gain admission.

16. Students have a variety of life goals and select their majors accordingly.

COLLEGE MAJOR PROFILE   ACTIVITY **7.3**

OVERVIEW

In this activity, your main purpose is to *gather information* about one or more college majors from college catalogs, major handbooks, and knowledgeable people. Use this research to help you to select or confirm your choice of a college major.

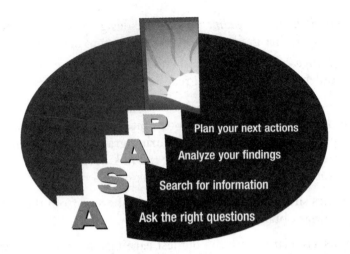

If you need more room, or if you are instructed to do so, type your answers separately.

STEP 1 ASK THE RIGHT QUESTIONS

Step 1.1 Major Overview

You may wish to research one of the majors that your college offers. If so, select one from your college catalog. If you are transferring to a four-year college or are unsure that you will stay at your present college, scan the following list of majors and check (✓) all the majors that you are curious about.

150 Popular Majors

AGRICULTURE
Agribusiness
Agricultural education
Agronomy
Animal sciences
Entomology
Fisheries and wildlife
Food sciences
Forestry
Horticultural science
Soil sciences

ARCHITECTURE AND DESIGN
Architecture
City, community, and regional planning
Interior design
Landscape architecture

THE ARTS
Art education
Art history
Arts management
Dance
Dramatic arts/theater

Film arts
Fine arts
Graphic design
Music
Music business management
Music performance
Music therapy
Photography
Religious music
Studio art

BIOLOGICAL AND LIFE SCIENCES
Biochemistry
Biology
Biophysics
Biotechnology
Botany
Marine biology
Microbiology
Molecular and cell biology
Science education
Wildlife management
Zoology

BUSINESS AND MANAGEMENT
Accounting
Business administration
Finance
Human resources management
Insurance and risk management
International business management
Labor/industrial relations
Management
Management information systems
Management science
Marketing
Real estate

COMMUNICATIONS
Advertising
Communications
Journalism
Public relations
Radio/television broadcasting
Speech

COMPUTER/INFORMATION SCIENCES
Computer science
Information sciences and systems

EDUCATION
Early childhood education
Elementary education
Parks and recreation management
Physical education
Secondary education
Special education
Technology (industrial arts) education

ENGINEERING
Aerospace/aeronautical engineering
Agricultural engineering
Chemical engineering
Civil engineering
Computer engineering
Electrical engineering
Industrial engineering
Materials/metallurgical engineering
Mechanical engineering
Petroleum engineering

HEALTH SCIENCES AND SERVICES
Athletic training
Clinical laboratory science
Dental hygiene
Health services management
Medical record administration
Nuclear medical technology
Nursing
Occupational therapy
Pharmacy
Physical therapy
Speech pathology/audiology

HOME ECONOMICS
Day care administration
Family/consumer resource
    management
Fashion merchandising
Food sciences and nutrition
Home economics
Home economics education
Hotel/motel and restaurant
    management
Housing and human development
Individual and family development
Textiles and clothing

HUMANITIES
American literature
Chinese
Classics
Comparative literature
Creative writing
English
English education
French
German
History
Italian
Japanese
Linguistics
Philosophy
Religion
Russian
Spanish

(continued)

INTERDISCIPLINARY, AREA,
AND ETHNIC STUDIES
African studies
Afro-American studies
American studies
Asian studies
Environmental studies
European studies
International relations
Jewish studies
Latin American studies
Middle Eastern studies
Urban studies
Women's studies

MATHEMATICS
Mathematics
Mathematics education
Statistics

PHYSICAL SCIENCES
Astronomy
Atmospheric sciences and meteorology

Chemistry
Geology
Geophysics
Oceanography
Physics

SOCIAL AND BEHAVIORAL SCIENCES
Anthropology
Criminal justice studies
Economics
Geography
Gerontology
Political science and government
Psychology
Public administration
Social studies education
Social work
Sociology

THEOLOGY
Bible studies
Theological studies

Source: Reproduced with permission from *The College Board Guide to 150 Popular College Majors.*
Copyright © 1992 by College Entrance Examination Board. All rights reserved.

Step 1.2 Selection of a Major

What major(s) are you researching? What are the reasons for your selection?

_____

_____

_____

Step 1.3 Selection of Questions

There are 17 questions arranged in three categories:

A. Nature of the major

B. Career information

C. Firsthand knowledge about the college major from a student

The first 10 questions are essential to get a good picture of the major. If you have the opportunity to interview a student who is majoring in this area, seven additional questions are provided. Some questions have background explanations to clarify their significance.

College Major Questions

A. NATURE OF THE MAJOR

1. How many credits are required in this major?

2. What are some key courses in this subject area?

3. What are the prerequisite courses for the introductory course in this major?

4. How much time will it take to earn a degree in this major?

5. Describe the competition (if any) to enter this major.

   Some majors have their own admission requirements, and students compete to be accepted. Other majors are open to anyone who completes the general prerequisites. What is the situation for the major that you are considering? Describe the required GPA, any special requirements (e.g., interview, essay, or volunteer work), and the personal qualities of someone who is admitted into this major.

6. What are the skills and qualities of students who succeed in this major?

7. If applicable:

   a. What community college major best prepares you to enter this major?

   b. What courses are important to take to prepare for this major?

   c. What colleges in your area offer this major?

B. CAREER INFORMATION

8. What are the goals of this major? Is it occupation specific (e.g., accounting or engineering)? Does it prepare you for professional training at the graduate school level (e.g., law or medicine)? Is it a multipotential major that provides a general educational background (e.g., English or sociology)?

9. What careers might this major lead to?

10. What skills do you gain in studying this major (e.g., speaking, writing, scientific experimentation, or helping people)?

C. FIRSTHAND KNOWLEDGE ABOUT THE COLLEGE MAJOR FROM A STUDENT

If you are interviewing a student who is majoring in this area, add the following questions:

11. How did you go about selecting this major?

12. Have you changed your mind about your major? When? What factors led to the change?

13. In what ways is your career goal (if you have one) related to your choice of major?

14. What is the best thing about your major? What is the worst thing?

15. What surprised you about your major?

16. What advice would you give me about selecting a major?

17. If applicable:

    a. What could you have done differently at your community college to increase the number of credits that transferred?

    b. What courses were most—and least—helpful in preparing you for transfer?

Step 1.4 Add Questions to Reflect Your Personal Concerns

Write down additional questions related to your specific educational dilemma or career concerns.

_____

_____

_____

Step 1.5 Sources of Information

There are many sources of information about a college major:

- Books
    - A. College catalogs
    - B. Books on majors, such as *150 Popular College Majors*

- Web sites
    - A. Specific college
    - B. General information. See Table 7.5.

- Knowledgeable people
    - A. Transfer coordinators and counselors
    - B. College students who study this major, and alumni
    - C. Professors in the subject area

Cite the books and catalogs that you consult. Give the names (and, if appropriate, titles) of the people with whom you talked. Use at least two sources of information.

_____

_____

_____

_____

STEP 2 SEARCH FOR INFORMATION

Information Summary

Search for information from the sources that you selected, and answer the questions from Step 1. Take notes on separate paper.

You can summarize your profile of a major in one of two ways. You can list each question that you researched and the information found, or you may prefer to summarize the main points.

STEP 3 ANALYZE YOUR FINDINGS

Step 3.1 Comparison of Advantages and Disadvantages

List the advantages and disadvantages of selecting this major.

Hints and Reminders

These hints and reminders will help you think about the possible advantages and disadvantages of selecting this major. Remember to use a balanced approach.

Listen to your heart.

- Assess which interests and values might be good matches and poor matches with this major. In the "Advantages" column, it will be helpful to list specific required courses that you are attracted to. In the "Disadvantages" column, identify specific required courses that you believe would be uninteresting.
- Consider your dreams and preferred lifestyle. Does this major put you on a path that will help you fulfill your life goals?

Also remember to use your head.

- Assess how practical it is to pursue this major (e.g., chances of being admitted, course availability, level of difficulty).

- Describe the skills and personal qualities that would be assets (advantages) or underutilized in this major (disadvantages).

Advantages +	Disadvantages −

Step 3.2 Tentative Decision

In view of your list of advantages and disadvantages, are you seriously considering this major? Identify the advantage(s) and disadvantage(s) that most heavily influenced your decision.

STEP 4 PLAN YOUR NEXT ACTIONS

Step 4.1 Learning Summary

What did you learn that will be helpful to you in the future? How is the information that you gathered useful in solving your dilemma?

Step 4.2 Next Steps

What's next?

CHAPTER 8

Finding a Place to Advance Your Career

A journey of a thousand miles begins with a single step.
—Lao Tzu

JOB SEEKERS: DIRECTIONS AND DECISIONS

No matter what your college major, as a job seeker you have important decisions ahead. These choices will affect your day-to-day job responsibilities and future career path. Many students (like those we will follow throughout this chapter) feel uncertain, sometimes even a bit panicky, because they don't know where to start.

At the root of their confusion is a lack of understanding about the decisions that they need to make, and a lack of familiarity with the various ways in which the workplace is organized. They are unable to match their needs, interests, and skills with specific jobs.

The secret to making good career choices for yourself is to learn about a variety of work settings. Armed with this understanding, you can make some preliminary decisions about where to focus your job search efforts.

This chapter provides a guide to four different settings. You will examine industry choices in business, self-employment, government, and nonprofit work. You will also see how choosing an organizational specialty, such as human resources or marketing, may be another useful way to set your career direction.

We will follow six students' quest to define their career directions. Get acquainted with them now as you begin this chapter.

In terms of the job world, Courtney, Robert, Naomi, and Jason are generalists. They do not have occupationally specific knowledge or skills.

Courtney has majored in sociology. Although she thought she was going to be a sociologist, she has realized that an academic career is not for her. Now she wants a job with "potential," but doesn't know exactly where to look or even how to define the kinds of things that she might like to do. She is eager to move to New Orleans with a sorority sister, repay her debts, and earn some money.

Robert is getting married soon. When he entered college, he wanted to be a doctor. He switched majors from biology to history and put off any decisions about a career direction. He wants a job that makes a contribution to the community.

Naomi, an English major, likes to write, but has recently abandoned the idea of becoming a journalist. She wants to live near her aging parents, in a small city that has several chemical plants. She believes that she would be happy working with people.

Jason, an avid amateur photographer, had wanted to go to law school. He finds that he must work, at least until he pays off part of his undergraduate loan and saves some money.

Chen Zhang majored in accounting (an occupationally oriented major). Brittany majored in travel and tourism (an industry-related major). Both have a false sense of security about their career paths and job searches. They believe that all that they need are a few job search tips. However, all of these six students, Chen Zhang and Brittany included, have some important career decision making to do.

FOUR WORK SETTINGS

One way to set your initial career direction after graduation is to choose between profit-oriented and not-for-profit work settings. The business world is profit oriented. Your choice here can be subdivided into working for a business firm or owning your own business. So whether you work for a profit-oriented company, such as Cargill, U. S. Robotics, Aetna, or Mastercard, or you have your own KFC franchise or interior design firm, the underlying goal of your efforts would be to make a profit for the organization.

Not-for-profit work settings can be subdivided into government agencies and nonprofit organizations. The government is the largest not-for-profit employer, providing such public services as defense, law enforcement, and education. In addition, over a million nonprofit organizations provide services such as cultural enrichment, political advocacy, spiritual guidance, and charitable help for the needy.[1]

Figure 8.1 shows the approximate percentage of the workforce employed in the four work settings described above.

FINDING A PLACE IN BUSINESS

Profit-oriented enterprises have the greatest number of workers. Most people, about 80 percent, work in businesses whose goal is to make money for their owners. This includes the 8 percent who are self-employed.

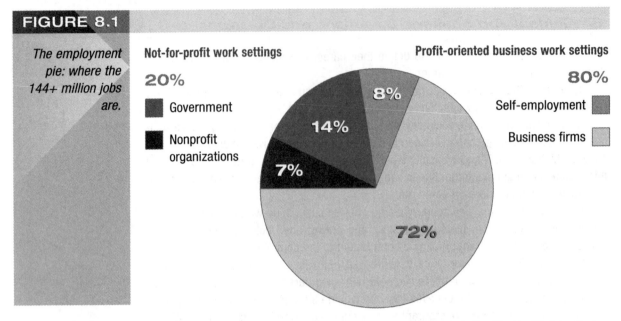

FIGURE 8.1

The employment pie: where the 144+ million jobs are.

Not-for-profit work settings

20%

■ Government

■ Nonprofit organizations

8%

14%

7%

72%

Profit-oriented business work settings

80%

Self-employment ■

Business firms □

Sources: These figures are the result of studying a variety of U.S. Bureau of Labor Statistics sources, including *The Monthly Labor Review Online,* (November 1999), Vol. 122, No. 11 (revised March 2000 projections); the *Occupational Outlook Quarterly, Special Issue: Charting the Projections 1998–2008* (Winter 1999–2000), Vol. 43, No. 4, and other reference material cited in this chapter.

There are over 100 million jobs in profit-oriented enterprises. They range from large, well-known companies such as BankAmerica, Wal-Mart, Procter & Gamble, and Motorola to your neighborhood dry cleaner or copy shop.

You will find a wide range of salaries and benefit packages in the business world. High-level executives can earn pay and stock worth millions. When you are self-employed, your compensation is tied to the success of your business. If it prospers, you prosper.

Choosing an Industry

The profit-oriented world is so large that this setting is divided into industries. Industries comprise groups of companies that are engaged in producing similar products or services. For example, Snapple, Pepsi, and Coca-Cola belong to the soft drink industry, while NBC, CNN, and ABC belong to the television industry. Career opportunities are better evaluated by looking at a specific industry rather than at the profit-oriented setting as a whole.

Some industries, such as those in manufacturing, mining, and agriculture, provide products, or *goods.* Other industries provide *services,* such as telecommunications (e.g., telephone service) or entertainment (e.g., movies and music). Unlike the services provided by government and nonprofit organizations, these services are marketed and sold to make money.

Industries that provide services, especially health and business services, are the fastest growing.[2] A good example of a business service is tax preparation. H&R Block, for example, will prepare your income taxes for a fee. The health services industry includes employment in hospitals, offices of physicians, nursing homes, home health care, and medical labs.

Your career thrives when you work in an industry rich in opportunity. A simple analogy underscores this point. A gardener who has some good seed and wants to cultivate a flourishing garden will try to plant the seeds in rich soil. Of course, the gardener also needs to consider the particular kind of plant and its need for sunlight, water, and so forth. Similarly, you'll want to "plant" your work efforts in an expanding industry, taking into consideration your interests, skills, and values. Of course, just as some hardy plants do well in poor soil, there are people who have successful careers in industries that are in decline. Usually, however, a healthy, growing industry offers you the best chances of career success.

Investigate the industries that you find appealing, focusing on their outlook for the future. Be especially aware of the impact of technology and the forces that will influence an industry's future. For example, one reason the health care industry is growing is that the aging baby boom generation is beginning to need more health-related services.

Government agencies are excellent sources of industry data. The U.S. Department of Labor's *Career Guide to Industries* (**www.bls.gov/cghome. htm**), for example, provides an overview of 42 major industries. Also helpful are electronic databases, such as Lexus–Nexus, publications of industry trade associations, such as *Industry Week, Beverage World,* and *Women's Wear Daily,* Web sites, such as Wetfeet.com, and business periodicals, such as the *Forbes* "Annual Report on American Industry."

Since industry information is used for so many purposes, it is not as user-friendly for the career explorer as the occupational literature you looked at in earlier chapters. When you begin, you may be overwhelmed by facts and figures. But if you know which questions you want answered, you can skim until you find the information you want. Activity 8.1, the Industry Profile, will guide your research.

Naomi, who planned to move to the city dominated by the chemical plants, realized that she had to find out more about the chemical industry. It didn't sound very appealing to her, but she really didn't know very much about it. Courtney, who wanted to move to New Orleans, realized that she needed to find out about the major industries located there. Jason, because of his interest in becoming a lawyer, thought that he needed to find out more about the legal services industry. Work experience in that industry could help him decide whether to hold on to his dream of becoming a lawyer. His interest in photography also led him to decide that he should get more information about the photographic equipment and supply industry.

Owning Your Own Business

Overview

Growing numbers of people, including many women and minorities, are choosing to go into business for themselves. Women own or control over 6.5 million enterprises in the United States.[3] Women own about 40 percent of small businesses.[4] Start-ups of businesses owned by African Americans, Hispanics, and Asian Americans increased dramatically in the past few decades.

Using Self-Employment to Create "The Good Life"   **CASE 8.2**

Several years ago a financial planner known to the author moved to a small college town to be close to major ski resorts. He established a very successful business there. Only a few of his clients reside in that town; most are scattered around the state. He communicates with them by phone, fax, and computer and travels occasionally for face-to-face meetings. He and his family enjoy the lifestyle of a small community, while he enjoys the earnings usually associated with working in the big city.

Terms used to describe people who are self-employed include small business owner, entrepreneur, consultant, and freelancer. Of course, your business does not have to remain small. Many companies, including Microsoft, started with one or two people working in a garage or basement and grew to employ thousands and dominate their market.

There are many advantages to being self-employed. These include the following:

- *You are the boss.* You have authority to make important decisions.
- *You can try out your ideas.* Many businesses began with someone's bright idea. Such innovations as power steering, the helicopter, and air conditioning are products of small companies and individual inventors.[5]
- *You can work with your family members.* You can build a business for and with your family.
- *You often establish personal relationships.* Small business owners depend on close relationships with their customers. Many also value the less formal relationships that they have with employees.
- *Your lifestyle is more independent.* You are free from a work structure imposed by others. Although you are constrained by the demands of your business, you may have the freedom to work at home or to decide when to take time off.

The disadvantages to being self-employed include the following:

- *High failure rate.* Sixty percent of new businesses fail within six years. Failures can be attributed to poor planning, neglect, lack of capital, and poor management skills.[6]
- *Potential loss of job challenge.* If you do not expand your business, over time your day-to-day responsibilities could become repetitive. The stimulation and growth that come from new job challenges are lacking.
- *Difficulty in obtaining resources.* It can be difficult to get the money to expand your business or keep it going in hard times.

Licensing, franchising, and distributorship arrangements can lower the personal and financial risks of owning your own business. For example, you might operate a fast-food restaurant as a franchise operator. Or you might run a car dealership or a gasoline station and agree to pay a percentage of the profits to the parent corporation. Popular franchises include Subway, Mail Boxes Etc., and Choice Hotels International.[7]

Another way to lower your personal risk is to buy an established business or go into business with partners. Some people even start businesses within the companies they work for. Called *intrapreneurs*, these employees launch a new product or service and may arrange to take part of the profits if they succeed.[8]

For Brittany, the idea of owning her own business is a new one. It is both appealing and scary. She is particularly attracted to a growing segment of the

Services (37.9%)	**TABLE 8.1**
Personal and business services are among the fastest-growing and most popular. Examples include travel agencies, catering, and child day-care centers. Business services include graphic design, publicity, clipping services, and desktop publishing. Nursing services for the elderly is just one example of the many health care businesses.	*Popular types of small business.*

Real estate, insurance, and finance (8.3%)

These businesses include buying and selling homes and commercial property; investment counseling; selling auto, medical, and life insurance policies; and providing accounting and billing services.

Retail (21.9%) and wholesale (7.4%) establishments

While a retail business owner sells products directly to the consumer, a wholesale business owner buys in bulk and then resells smaller amounts to various retail establishments. Small retail stores often are specialty boutiques because the owners wish to avoid competition with larger department and grocery stores. They specialize in selling items such as maternity clothes or Native American pottery and sculpture, or food products such as coffee, bagels, or frozen yogurt. Wholesale businesses may specialize in any product that retail stores need, from fish and meat to pet supplies and pool and garden products.

Source: Percentages from William Pride, Robert Hughes, and Jack Kapoor, *Business,* 5th ed. (Boston: Houghton Mifflin, 1996), p. 138.

tourism market: walking tours and adventure vacations. She believes that work experience in a company that specializes in this market would be good preparation for opening her own business.

Popular business areas are personal, business, and health services; real estate, insurance, and finance; and wholesale and retail establishments. These make up about 75 percent of U. S. small businesses. They are described in Table 8.1. Agriculture, manufacturing, construction, and transportation are other favorites for small business ownership.

Tips to Get Started

There are many ways to prepare yourself to be a business owner and to decrease the risks associated with starting your own business.

- *Get industry-related job experience.* Working in a similar business, especially a small or mid-sized company, will provide you with invaluable experience. You gain expertise in the product or service and develop business skills. Experience in finance and marketing is especially worthwhile.[9]

- *Moonlight.* In this arrangement you keep your full-time job and start a business during nonworking hours. A teacher might run a summer camp. A corporate accountant might invest money in the stock market for herself, family, and friends. A human resource administrator might refinish furniture pieces and sell them at weekend antique fairs.[10] By moonlighting you retain the security of a regular salary while you supplement your income, learn a new business, and test new career options.

- *Educate yourself.* Before you go out on your own, select a business to learn about. Scan the Yellow Pages and trade journals for future competitors. If possible, visit various establishments and through observation see what you can learn about their strengths and weaknesses.[11] Read books, magazines, and newsletters, and attend seminars targeted to entrepreneurs. Useful magazines include *Inc., Entrepreneur, Black Enterprise*, and *Hispanic Business.* Join relevant trade associations. There is an association for almost every kind of business: apartment owners and managers, bridal consultants, quilters, professional picture framers, translators—you name it.[12]

PROVIDING SERVICES FOR OTHERS

Government Agencies

Certain services in our society are provided by units of our local, state, and federal government. Regulation of industries for our health and safety, defense of the nation against enemies, protection from criminals and punishment for crimes, free education for children, mail delivery, and the building and maintaining of highways and bridges are just a few examples of these public services.

There are over 21 million jobs in government settings. Nearly one in seven civilian employees works for the government.[13] Examples of organizations at various levels of government include the National Park Service, the CIA, state driver licensing bureaus, county sheriffs' offices, and city landmarks preservation commissions. An overview of typical government services is provided in Table 8.2.

Salaries of government workers are paid out of tax revenues. Starting salaries are usually good, but salaries at the top (i.e., over $100,000) do not rival those in profit-oriented settings. For example, many business executives make more than the $390,000 earned annually by the president of the United States.[14]

Government employment is typically characterized by comprehensive benefits plans, including pension, health care, and vacation time. However, job security, once an attraction of work in the government, is disappearing. At the national level, Washington is cutting federal programs. Government jobs at the state, county, and city levels are also subject to government cost-cutting measures, known as RIF (reductions in force). Still, openings occur at all levels, every day, due to retirements and people leaving government service.

Government organizations are bureaucracies. Career paths and promotional practices are clearly outlined in a formally defined hierarchy. Job responsibilities are carefully spelled out at each level. Often, to obtain an entry-level job, you must follow a prescribed application procedure and score well on an examination.

Don't be discouraged by the formal hiring procedures, or assume that you must relocate to get a government job. Investigate further. Many myths abound. For example, only 13 percent of jobs with the federal government are in the Washington, D. C., area.[15]

Chen Zhang, the accounting major, is leaning toward government service. He must conduct more specific research because a wide variety of government agencies employ accountants.

Types of Public Service	Examples of Services	TABLE 8.2
Administration and regulatory services	Protecting the environment; promoting highway safety, including driver's license regulation; enforcing customs regulations; handling consumer complaints	*Types and examples of public service.*
Defense	Defending the country: both military and civilian roles in the army, navy, air force, marines, and coast guard	
Education	Teaching children in elementary and secondary schools; setting standards in city boards of education; measuring performance in state and federal departments of education	
Labor affairs	Preventing child labor; administering occupational safety and health programs; gathering statistical information on the state of the economy	
Justice	Running the court system	
Mail services	Delivering mail and packages	
Parks and recreation	Maintaining national, state, and city parks	
Protective services	Protecting against crime (e.g., FBI, highway patrols, sheriff offices, police)	
Public health	Preventing lead poisoning; administering immunization programs; providing sanitation services; running hospitals; maintaining AIDS hot lines	
Public transportation	Building and maintaining roads, highways, and bridges; running city bus services	
Social services, rehabilitation, correction	Administering programs such as Meals-on-Wheels; ensuring child welfare; managing Social Security; providing shelter for the homeless; offering substance-abuse programs; managing prisons	
Urban development	Promoting housing development at the federal, state, and local levels	

Source: Ronald H. Fredrickson, *Career Information* (Upper Saddle River, NJ: Prentice Hall, 1982, p. 112). Adapted with permission.

Nonprofit Organizations

The purpose of nonprofit organizations is generally to further an idea or cause. There are over 1 million nonprofit organizations in the United States dedicated to such diverse goals as improving education, health, housing, parks, and neighborhoods; supporting cultural institutions and events; representing special interests; and advocating for or against a wide variety of issues.

Types of nonprofit organizations include art museums, libraries, historical societies, foundations, charities, patriotic societies, industry trade groups, labor organizations, and religious groups.[16] Examples of specific nonprofit organizations are the Jaycees, the United Farm Workers of America, the

Sierra Club, Disabled American Veterans, and the Gay Men's Health Crisis Center. It is the smallest of our four work settings, employing about 10 million people.[17]

The attraction of working for nonprofit organizations is the opportunity to champion passionately held beliefs. You link your efforts to an organizational mission that you believe will make the world better in some way.

Most nonprofit organizations depend on charitable donations, grants, endowments, or funding from members. Starting salaries are typically lower than in the other work settings that we discussed, although midlevel and top positions in well-established organizations provide their occupants with a comfortable middle-class lifestyle. Benefits packages typically are not as generous as those in government. Reliance on donations or grants means that the existence of those organizations without solid funding may be shaky, providing little job security.

Organizations that advance business-related interests may offer more lucrative careers, especially in large cities such as Washington, New York, Chicago, or Los Angeles. These include the Chamber of Commerce, the Better Business Bureau, industrial trade organizations, professional societies, and farm and agricultural organizations.[18]

Nonprofit organizations are often small, so their structure and operating procedures are usually less bureaucratic than government agencies. Job openings are generally filled informally through personal contacts. Internships and volunteer experience are other avenues that can lead to employment. Robert, the history major, is attracted to community service. He has decided to look for nonprofit organizations that specialize in urban development, especially housing for the poor.

Two unique types of opportunities in the nonprofit world are careers in fund-raising and lobbying. Fund-raising is crucial to the growth and success of most nonprofit organizations. Lobbyists represent special-interest groups and industry associations to government officials and provide information related to pending legislation and regulations.[19]

REFINING DECISIONS ABOUT WORK SETTINGS

You have now had an opportunity to examine four basic career directions: (1) working in a particular industry, (2) working for yourself, (3) working for the government, and (4) working in a nonprofit organization. Use Activities 8.1, 8.2, and 10.2 to guide your search for additional information and to help you assess career opportunities. Using these activities, you can make balanced decisions about the kind of work setting that you find most appealing.

Although these activities get you off to a great start, you must generally continue to refine your career direction still further. Courtney, Naomi, and Jason, who are examining specific industries, need to make additional refinements. Targeting the chemical or the photographic equipment and supply industry is just too broad. They also need to target the kinds of tasks that they would perform on the job. Could marketing, information services, or human resources hold attractive career possibilities for them?

ORGANIZATIONAL SPECIALTIES: ANOTHER WAY TO MOLD A CAREER

Eight Key Organizational Specialties

In complex organizations, people often specialize. Their jobs consist of one type of organizational activity, such as marketing, human resources, or finance and control. Each of these organizational activities plays a unique role in helping an enterprise to achieve its mission.

A useful way to refine your career direction is to specialize in one of these types of organizational activity. Over time your jobs will build your expertise within that one function. The most popular organizational specialties are described in Table 8.3.

In small businesses there is no need for organizational specialists. Typically, the owner does almost everything. For example, in a neighborhood laundromat, the owner usually oversees the entire operation, making sure that the washers and dryers are operating, customers are served, and money is collected. In addition, the owner keeps the books, hires any relief staff, buys the computer, and creates the advertisement for the local paper.

When an organization is large, activities such as creating ads and keeping the books are allocated to separate departments. For example, Kellogg's sells its cereal brands worldwide. One person could not possibly handle all its advertising. General Mills has thousands of employees, too many for one person to do all the hiring. In these companies, whole departments of employees specialize in one type of organizational work.

TABLE 8.3

Eight key organizational specialties.

Marketing specialists are engaged in developing, pricing, advertising, and promoting an organization's products and services. In addition, they decide where to distribute products so that customers can make their purchases conveniently. Marketing includes product planning, market research, advertising, promotion, and product distribution channels.

The importance of marketing specialists can be seen when two companies compete to get you to buy a product such as athletic shoes. First, the design of the shoes must be appealing. That underscores the role of product planning. Second, their cost must be affordable for college students. That's pricing. Third, you must be persuaded that these are the best shoes for the performance you want. That's what advertising and promotion are all about. Finally, you must be able to find them in places where you shop, such as your favorite mall. That's product distribution. The company that has the best marketing specialists is more likely to get your money.

Human resources (HR) specialists help organizations handle employee-related matters. HR specialists are in charge of the procedures used to hire, train, promote, and evaluate employees. They develop job descriptions and recommend salaries and benefits for each job category. They develop policies to comply with government regulations, promote job safety, and eliminate discrimination. HR specialists are involved with forecasting the need for employees as an organization grows or downsizes. They help determine how the organization structures its jobs, whether along departmental, functional, or product lines. Other names of this function include personnel, personnel administration, and industrial and labor relations.

(continued)

TABLE 8.3

Eight key organizational specialties, continued.

Sales specialists help organizations persuade potential customers to purchase their products or services. Many students reject sales because they are familiar with only low-level sales positions in retail stores or have a stereotype that sales is all smooth talking and high pressure. Every profit-oriented company needs salespeople and provides them with the training to understand and sell their products. Jet engine makers, surgical equipment suppliers, speedboat manufacturers, ballpoint pen makers, and college textbook publishers all depend on salespeople to present their products and services to customers. Salespeople are typically responsible for customers in a geographic area. Salespeople often increase their income by increasing sales in their territory. Manufacturers' representatives are independent sales agents who may represent several product lines for different companies. In addition, sales administration, customer support for technical information, and supervising national accounts are other roles within the sales function.

Public relations (PR) or communication, specialists help an organization communicate with its employees, its stockholders, the government, and the public. They handle press and media coverage. They may design and produce an annual report, put out an employee newsletter, or serve as an organization's media spokesperson during a crisis, such as product tampering or an industrial accident.

Administrative services specialists provide the support services to maintain an organization. Activities include buying facilities, buying and leasing office space for an organization (i.e., facilities management), providing security, arranging for cleaning and maintenance services, purchasing supplies, and providing secretarial and clerical services.

Information systems specialists are engaged in running an organization's computer systems. They are responsible for operating and maintaining the necessary hardware and software and selecting and upgrading the computer equipment. This organizational specialty is also known as MIS (management information systems) or IT (information technology).

Finance and control specialists help an organization manage its money. Activities in this specialty include preparing and analyzing financial reports, investing and borrowing for the company, budgeting, and preparing balance sheets. This specialty includes accounting and financial planning.

Operations specialists oversee the activities necessary to create products and services. These activities include product development, planning for production, and operations control. Research and development specialists create or refine products. Planning for production includes deciding how to produce the product or service and how best to use the facilities and resources. Operations control includes purchasing, inventory control, scheduling, and quality control.

Choosing an Organizational Specialty

Selecting an organizational specialty is an even more important decision than selecting a college major. You invest a year or two of study taking coursework in your major, but you will probably spend many years of your working life building know-how in an organizational specialty. Naturally, you'll want to invest your time learning an organizational specialty that you find attractive and that provides the practical payoff you want. Gradually, your organizational specialty will come to play a larger role in defining your career path than your education does, so you must select it with care.

Some organizational specialists may move more easily than others among profit-oriented, government, or nonprofit settings. The following broad generalizations serve as a general guide:

- Administration, finance, human resources, information services, and public relations specialists are found in profit-oriented industries, government, and nonprofit organizations.

- Operations specialists are used most heavily in business, although the government and nonprofit organizations may also use them to increase productivity and enhance quality. Research and development specialists are found primarily in profit-oriented companies and government research centers, such as the National Institutes of Health.

- Marketing specialists are found primarily in business, although there are some exceptions. In nonprofit organizations, marketing specialists may be called *development* specialists, and they focus on obtaining funding for projects and services. In government settings, there are few marketing jobs. Exceptions include military recruitment and the U. S. Postal Service, which competes with profit-oriented parcel delivery services.

- Sales specialists are also found primarily in business. They may or may not be important to nonprofit organizations. Ticket sales for performance organizations may be crucial, while sales of books from trade associations are likely to be incidental. There are relatively few sales specialists in government because its funding comes primarily from taxes, not sales.

Liberal arts and nontechnically trained graduates usually find it easier to enter specialties such as marketing, sales, human resources, public relations, and administrative services. They learn about these specialties on the job. Specialties and subspecialties such as research and development, finance and control, legal functions, strategic and corporate planning, and computer information services usually require specialized college coursework.

Courtney, the sociology major, is intrigued by the work of marketing specialists, while Naomi has begun to do research on human resources and public relations careers. Jason was attracted to sales. He began to look at the photographic equipment and supply industry more closely and to think about sales, particularly sales of products that require technical knowledge and support. Still, he needed to weigh the advantages and disadvantages of this career direction against those of working in a law firm.

Is Management an Organizational Specialty?

Management is "the science and art of running an organization."[20] Managers are responsible for supervising people, overseeing projects, and allocating money to reach the organization's goals. Once the organization has several employees, there is usually a manager. If an organization is large, there are various levels of management. Executives, the title often given to high-ranking managers, have the power to make decisions that will influence the future of an organization.

You can major in management in college to prepare for management responsibilities someday. In fact, however, management is *not* an organizational specialty. The typical route to becoming a manager is to gain experience in an organizational specialty and move up through the ranks. Once, many organizations had management trainee programs for college grads, but such programs have all but disappeared. Today, you have to prove yourself in the lower ranks before you can progress to the responsibilities of a manager.

LEARNING THE VOCABULARY OF WORK SETTINGS

A difficult aspect of making the transition from school to work is the need to educate yourself about various work settings. Your general lack of familiarity with various work settings and the different ways that they are described can lead to confusion and upset. You have had years of familiarity with the structure and the vocabulary of school settings—grade levels, GPAs, majors. Now, you are confronted with a new vocabulary—the equipment leasing industry, operations research, distributorships and franchises, manufacturers' representatives, facilities management, and so forth. Such concepts can seem daunting to the newcomer.

Moreover, while you were in school, you could find a lot of classmates who were following the same track that you were on. As you move into the job market, you are on your own. The only solution is an individualized program of research. Take some time to learn about the opportunities in the world that you are about to enter. It will serve you like a good map. You will be better able to select destinations that are interesting to you, and you will see the best way to get there. Without such a map, you may wander around, hoping that the trip will turn out well. Before you start to pound the pavement or fax your resume off to a prospective employer, spend some time gathering information.

WHERE STUDENTS GET STUCK, AND WHAT TO DO IF IT HAPPENS TO YOU

My First Job Commits Me Forever

Some students are so insistent that their first job be a perfect fit that they are afraid to make a commitment to any possibility. One way to get over this fear is to think about your first postcollege job as a two-year commitment. During this period, give it your best efforts. The career development tips in the third section of the book will help you make the most of your experience. At the end of two years, evaluate your career situation; if it is not working out, look for other possibilities.

ASAP INFORMATION SEARCHES AND BALANCED CAREER DECISIONS

Your information needs are unique. Depending on your educational choices and prior work history, the decisions that you face and the information searches that you need to conduct will differ from those of your classmates.

Some students, especially those with occupation-specific majors and relevant job experience and internships, are very focused and knowledgeable about work settings. Other students, especially liberal arts students who have not yet confronted the practical aspects of their career decisions, are almost totally unfamiliar with their options.

Here's a good rule of thumb. The more general your knowledge base is or the more undecided you are, the more information searches you need to conduct about opportunities in various work settings. Use Activity 8.1 to investigate specific industries, and Activity 10.2 to investigate specific government agencies or nonprofit organizations. Use Activity 8.2, Starting Your Own Business, to stimulate your thinking about self-employment. This research will help you to make a balanced decision, using your head and listening to your heart.

KEY POINTS

1. As you set your career direction, it is helpful to examine different types of work settings. Your choice of work setting will influence your career satisfaction, lifestyle, and economic prospects.

2. You can work in profit-oriented settings (i.e., work for a business firm or be self-employed) or in not-for-profit settings (i.e., work for government agencies or in nonprofit organizations).

3. About 80 percent of workers are employed in the profit-oriented business world. The business setting is so large that it is divided into industries.

4. Industries are groups of companies that produce similar products or provide similar services. Your career thrives when the industry in which you work is rich in opportunity.

5. About 8 percent of workers are self-employed. Increasing numbers of people, especially women and minorities, are starting their own businesses. Advantages include being in charge, trying out your own ideas, and setting your own lifestyle. Disadvantages include the high failure rate of new businesses, the potential for loss of job challenge, and difficulty in obtaining capital for start-up or expansion purposes.

6. Popular business areas for self-employment are personal, business, and health services; real estate, insurance, and finance; and wholesale and retail establishments. These types of businesses comprise about 75 percent of U. S. small businesses.

7. The mission of the government is to provide public services at the national, state, and local levels. These services, funded by tax revenue, include delivering mail, running city bus systems, providing foster care, and administering flood relief programs. One in seven civilian employees works for the government.

8. The nonprofit setting is composed of organizations whose purpose is to further an idea or a cause. Most nonprofit organizations depend on charitable donations, grants, endowments, or funding from members.

9. Choosing an organizational specialty, such as human resources or marketing, may be another useful way to set your career direction.

10. Organizational specialists have job responsibilities associated with particular organizational functions. The eight key organizational specialties are the following:

Marketing	Administration
Sales	Information systems
Human resources	Finance and control
Public relations and communications	Operations

11. You invest a year or two of study taking coursework in your major, but you will probably spend many years of your working life building know-how in an organizational specialty. Gradually, your organizational specialty will play a larger role in defining your career path than your education does, so you must select it with care.

12. A difficult aspect of making the transition from school to work is the need to educate yourself about various work settings in order to make intelligent, informed decisions.

13. One way that students get stuck is believing that their first job commits them forever to a particular career direction.

14. The more general your knowledge base or the more undecided you are, the more information you will need about various work settings.

ACTIVITY 8.1   **INDUSTRY PROFILE**

OVERVIEW

In this activity your main purpose is to *gather information* about a specific industry. You can use this profile in several ways: (1) to help you solve your career dilemma; (2) to assist you in setting your career direction; and (3) to help you prepare for job interviews.

If you need more room, or if you are instructed to do so, type your answers separately.

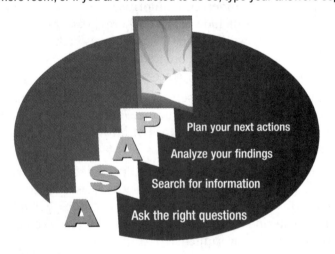

- **P** Plan your next actions
- **A** Analyze your findings
- **S** Search for information
- **A** Ask the right questions

STEP 1 ASK THE RIGHT QUESTIONS

Step 1.1 Industry Overview

The list of industries below is taken from a U. S. Department of Labor *Career Guide to Industries.* The *Career Guide* discusses more than 42 industries, accounting for over 7 out of every 10 wage and salary jobs in 1998.

Scan the list and circle all the industries you are curious about. Take some time to get familiar with the list so that you won't overlook possibilities just because you are unacquainted with the names and classifications of industries.

FARMING, MINING, AND CONSTRUCTION

Agricultural Production

Agricultural Services

Construction

Mining and Quarrying

Oil and Gas Extraction

MANUFACTURING

Aerospace Manufacturing

Apparel and Other Textile Products

Chemicals Manufacturing, Except Drugs

Drug Manufacturing

Electronic Equipment Manufacturing

Food Processing

Motor Vehicle Equipment Manufacturing

Printing and Publishing

Steel Manufacturing

Textile Mill Products

TRANSPORTATION, COMMUNICATION, AND PUBLIC UTILITIES

Air Transportation

Cable and Other Pay Television Services

Public Utilities

Radio and Television Broadcasting

Telecommunications

Trucking and Warehousing

WHOLESALE AND RETAIL TRADE

Department, Clothing, and Accessory Stores

Eating and Drinking Establishments

Grocery Stores

Motor Vehicle Dealers

Wholesale Trade

FINANCE AND INSURANCE

Banking

Insurance

Securities and Commodities

SERVICES

Advertising

Amusement and Recreation Services

Child-Care Services

Computer and Data Processing

Educational Services

Health Services

Hotels and Other Lodging Places

Management and Public Relations Services

Motion Picture Production and Distribution

Personnel Supply Services

Social Services, Except Child Care

GOVERNMENT

Federal Government, Excluding the Postal Service

State and Local Government, Excluding Education and Hospitals

Step 1.2 Industry Selection

What industries, industry, or industry segment are you researching?

_____

_____

_____

Step 1.3 Selection of Questions

Below are 10 questions, arranged in three categories:

- A. The nature of the industry
- B. Career opportunities
- C. Outlook for the future

These questions will guide your research. Be sure to cover at least some of the questions in every category. Using all questions will provide a well-rounded profile.

Some questions have background explanations to clarify their significance.

INDUSTRY PROFILE QUESTIONS

A. The Nature of the Industry

1. What are the product(s) or service(s) of this industry? What kind of value does the product or service add to our society?

   Begin your research by getting an understanding of the industry's products or services. You may find that an industry, such as the computer industry, is so large that a reference guide divides it into segments. For instance, *Standard and Poor's Industry Surveys* divides the computer industry into seven segments: (a) software, (b) storage, (c) desktops, (d) laptops (mobile), (e) client-server technology (enterprise), (f) networks, and (g) computer services. Now you need to decide whether to continue your research on just one segment or continue to look at the industry as a whole. One tactic is to get an industry overview and then select one or two segments for an in-depth look.

2. Who uses these products or services?

    You will want to know about the industry's customers: who they are, how many there are, and whether they are increasing or decreasing. A strong and growing demand means that opportunities in this industry may be increasing.

    Describe the customers (e.g., other businesses, consumers, or both). For example, although businesses and consumers both use laptop computers, the networking segment of the computer industry serves businesses.

3. How many people want to buy the product or service? What is the estimated demand? What is the size of this industry?

4. How would you characterize the typical working conditions of this industry?

    Production may be quiet or noisy, seasonal or steady, relatively safe or dangerous, employ large numbers of college-educated workers, have many part-timers, and so on.

B. Career Opportunities

5. What kinds of companies are found in this industry? Is this industry dominated by large, midsize, or small companies, or by single proprietorships?

6. Comment on where the industry is located—within the United States or world-wide. Focusing on where you live (or want to live), list at least three companies in this industry.

7. How does the pay in this industry compare with that in other industries?

    Industry standards influence pay levels, so that there are compensation differences by industry. For example, *The American Almanac of Jobs and Salaries* (2000–2001 ed.) notes that the average salaries in purchasing were:

    $62,200 for the chemical industry

    $54,900 for the construction industry

    $53,800 for the printing and publishing industry

C. Outlook for the Future

8. What is the impact of technology on this industry?

    Is the industry experiencing stormy times because of technology and innovation? Technological innovation affects all industries. When an industry is undergoing drastic changes in technology, employment opportunities may change rapidly and radically. Employment patterns change, increasing opportunities for some kinds of jobs while eliminating others.

9. Is this a growing industry? What is the direction of the demand for the products or services (i.e., increasing, decreasing, stagnant, or no growth)?

    As an example, the demand for cellular phones is rapidly increasing, while the demand for typewriters has plummeted since the introduction of personal computers.

10. What do experts predict is the future for this industry?

Step 1.4   Personal Concerns

Write down any additional questions related to your specific career dilemma or career concerns.

_____

_____

_____

_____

_____

Step 1.5   Sources of Information

- Government Sources

  The *Career Guide to Industries:* **www.bls.gov/blshome.htm** provides information on available careers in the industries listed above. Each entry includes the nature of the industry, working conditions, employment, occupations in the industry, training and advancement, earnings and benefits, employment outlook, and lists of organizations that can provide additional information.

  The U. S. Department of Commerce, the Department of Labor, the International Trade Administration, and the Bureau of the Census publish additional up-to-date industry data.

  State and local Chambers of Commerce and state economic development offices are additional sources of information.

- Electronic Databases

  InfoTrac: Business and Company Resource Center

  Dialog@CARL: Business & Industry

  Lexus–Nexus: Business

  Wilson Business Abstracts

  Your library probably subscribes to these databases so you won't have to pay any fee to use them. Ask your librarian for help. Often the articles can be E-mailed to you.

- Industry Associations and Publications

  Check to see if the industry has an industry association and whether it publishes any magazines, newsletters, or journals. If you are not sure about the names of relevant industry associations, check the *Encyclopedia of Associations* (Gale Research) or browse Internet sites such as the Internet Public Library's **(www.ipl.org)** Reference Section, which contains "Associations on the Net."

- Web Sites

  Wetfeet.com: www.wetfeet.com

  Hoover's Online (Industry Snapshot): www.hoovers.com

- Business Periodicals

  Articles profiling industries often appear in major newspapers such as the *Wall Street Journal,* and in business magazines such as *Business Week's* annual "Industry Outlook."

Cite the Web sites, electronic databases, and print sources that you consult. If you interview industry insiders, give the names (and, if appropriate, the titles) of the people you talk with. Use at least two sources of information.

STEP 2   SEARCH FOR INFORMATION

Information Summary

Search for information from the sources you selected and answer the questions from Step 1. Take notes on separate paper.

You can summarize the information for your industry profile in one of two ways: You may list each question you researched and the information you found, or you may summarize the major points.

Your summary should include the nature of the industry, the career opportunities, and the outlook for the future.

STEP 3   ANALYZE YOUR FINDINGS

Step 3.1   Comparison of Advantages and Disadvantages

List the advantages and disadvantages of working in this industry.

Hints and Reminders

In the Advantages column, identify the specific aspects of the industry that you like (e.g., size, working conditions, outlook for the future, kinds of companies). In the Disadvantages column, identify the specific aspects of the industry that you dislike.

Remember to listen to your heart.

- Identify which interests and values might be a good fit with this industry (advantage) *or* poor fit (disadvantage).

- If you like, admire, and feel you want to be identified with the kind of people you would work with every day, put this in the "Advantages" column. If you prefer not to associate with such people, put this reason in the "Disadvantages" column.

- Consider your dreams and preferred lifestyle. Does this industry put you on a path that will help you fulfill your life goals?

Also remember to use your head.

- Assess whether the economic rewards you would receive in an entry-level position in this industry are adequate (advantage) *or* insufficient for your needs (disadvantage).

- Assess whether this industry seems to offer the opportunity to increase your skills (advantage) *or* not (disadvantage).

- Describe the skills and personal qualities that will be assets in this industry (advantage) *or* underutilized in this industry (disadvantage).

Advantages +	Disadvantages −

Step 3.2 Tentative Decision

In view of your list of advantages and disadvantages, are you seriously considering working in this industry? Identify the advantage(s) and disadvantage(s) that most heavily influenced your decision.

STEP 4 PLAN YOUR NEXT ACTIONS

Step 4.1 Learning Summary

What did you learn that will be useful to you in the future? How is this industry profile useful in terms of solving your career dilemma?

Step 4.2 Next Steps

What's next?

ACTIVITY 8.2   STARTING YOUR OWN BUSINESS

OVERVIEW

Starting a business may entail significant risks, yet it has the potential to provide significant psychological and economic rewards. The purpose of this activity is to stimulate your thinking about the kinds of knowledge, skills, experience, and personal qualities that would be useful in starting a business. You will identify current resources and outline your need for further information.

TASK 1 MY BUSINESS IDEAS

What kind of business(es) am I interested in starting? To what industry does each belong?

_____

_____

_____

What are my reasons for wanting to start a business?

_____

_____

_____

TASK 2 MY PERSONAL ASSETS AND NEED FOR DEVELOPMENT

What personal characteristics will help me succeed in my own business? What personal qualities will I have to develop further?

_____

_____

_____

_____

What skills do I have that will help me succeed in my own business? What skills will I have to develop further?

_____

_____

_____

_____

TASK 3 RESOURCE IDENTIFICATION

What kinds of jobs and work experience will help me prepare for starting my own business?

_____

_____

_____

What kinds of coursework, seminars, books, magazines, newsletters, or conferences might be helpful?

_____

_____

_____

What kinds of professional associations and support groups (e.g., National Association of Women Business Owners or the International Franchise Association) might be of help?

_____

_____

_____

What federal, state, and local government agencies might provide help?

_____

_____

_____

Are franchises, licenses, or distributorships an attractive option for the kind of business that I want to start? Why or why not?

_____

_____

_____

What other resources are available to help me (e.g., financial resources such as savings or inheritance, expert advice or free labor from friends and family)?

TASK 4 NEXT STEPS

What further research would it be helpful to conduct?

_____

_____

_____

What are my next steps?

_____

_____

_____

CHAPTER 9

Finding a Job

Never give up.
Never, never give up.
—Winston Churchill

JOB SEARCH SKILLS

Developing good job search skills will boost your career. These skills are best developed during your college years. The more skilled you become, the better your chances are of landing a career-building position after you graduate.

In this chapter you will learn how to get your foot in the employer's door. You will see how to tap into the job market, clarify your job objective and information needs, and compose a resume. The next chapter teaches you how to profile a company, conduct interviews, evaluate job offers, and start a new job on the right foot.

These chapters will acquaint you with the key elements of a job search. Essential information will be summarized in tables for easy reference. An activity is provided that will help to guide you in developing your resume.

Most students realize, though, that they will need to dip into reference books to get additional information to address their individual needs. For example, some will need to master the writing of cover letters and other correspondence. Others will want additional guidance on how to select a temporary agency or make direct contact with employers. References are provided to guide your search for further information.

JOB HUNTING WHILE IN COLLEGE

You may not have considered looking for a job until you are very near graduation. Many students believe that their college degree is a virtual guarantee of a good job (after a quick, painless job search). In fact, however, because there are more college graduates than ever before, a college degree no longer guarantees a satisfying or high-paying job.

A related problem is underemployment. You may be offered a job that will not use your talents, thus wasting your hard-earned education.[1] The reality is that you are facing stiff competition for the best jobs. What can and should you do while you are still in college?

Use the Placement Office and Career Services

You should start by visiting your on-campus career services center. Your best strategy, according to Dr. Patricia Imbimbo, Director of the Career Development Center at Baruch College, is to make your first visit to the placement office during your first year in college.

Regular visits throughout your college career will allow you to get to know the staff and to learn about and take advantage of workshops and events that will increase your readiness for a job search. For example, you may decide to sign up for a resume-writing workshop.

Placement offices usually have free information about this year's job market. Pick up a copy of such sources as *Managing Your Career* or *The Black Collegian*. *Job Choices* publishes specialized editions for business and science and engineering majors, two-year college students, and four-year college students.

In your final year of college, the most intense period of your job search, you will want to visit the placement office often. You'll find a list of job openings, which are updated continually. In addition, you can sign up for on-campus interviews. Many recruiters visit in the fall semester, and some add campus visits to the schedule at the last minute—compelling reasons to begin early and to stop by the placement office regularly.

Your college may also hold job fairs and organize job search clubs. There may be an active alumni association or network that informs students about job opportunities in alumni's companies.

Participate in Internship Programs

College co-op, fieldwork, and internship programs are another valuable resource. Participation in an internship program is beneficial in several ways: it provides a structure in which to build your job search skills during your college years; you develop resume-writing and interviewing skills; you can explore various career options that help you refine your job objectives; and you gain access to employers in your field. An internship or fieldwork builds your resume and makes you more competitive in the job market.

Employers often hire their former interns, so participation in such programs is a source of job leads. So popular are internship experiences with employers that many feel it would be difficult to get hired without one.[2] In addition, college advisors in experienced-based learning programs often have leads for full-time positions because of their extensive company contacts.

Network

Most job openings are never advertised. According to most surveys, about a third of job seekers learn of unadvertised openings through someone they know—a classmate, a cousin, or a friend of their mother's.[3] Networking is a job search method in which you deliberately take the time to inform others that you are looking for a job. You provide them with details about your background and skills, and outline your job objectives.

When you network, include everyone on campus who might be able to help. Your professors are a source of job leads, especially in industry-related majors such as hotel management and occupationally specific majors such as architecture. They can refer you to professional societies, conferences, and trade magazines that advertise job openings. They may also have contacts in the field. Part-time, adjunct professors who are employed in the field are also a potential source of leads.

In addition to your college community, your network consists of family, friends, neighbors, past and current employers, and coworkers. Don't overlook members of your religious community or those who provide professional services, such as your dentist. Provide them with copies of your resume. Although they might not personally know of a position in your career field, they could refer you to someone who does. The more contacts you develop, the more unadvertised openings you are likely to hear about.

Networking is an important way to advance your career. Getting your foot in the door is just one way that members of your career network can help you. Chapter 13 is devoted to the benefits and process of networking. Be sure to review that chapter as you begin your job search.

JOB HUNTING AFTER GRADUATION

Contact Your Network

As a graduate, you should stay in touch with your college's placement office and continue to network with members of your college community. Expand your networking efforts. In many industries, such as advertising, biotechnology, consulting, fashion, film, television, law, medicine, public accounting, and public relations, networking is especially important, because coveted job openings are rarely advertised.[4]

Make Direct Contact with Employers

Another powerful way to uncover job openings is to get in touch directly with employers you are interested in. Over a third of job seekers get their positions this way.[5]

One reason this method is so much more effective than using employment agencies or answering classified ads is that jobs are concentrated in smaller companies. Over 50 percent of the work force is employed by small businesses.[6] Small companies advertise job openings less frequently and use less formal hiring procedures than large organizations.

Effective direct contact with employers does not mean just faxing or mailing off your resume to hundreds of companies. It requires that you identify potential employers and develop a script for calling and visiting them directly. Many books, such as *Knock 'Em Dead*, *The PIE Method for Career Success*, and *The Very Quick Job Search*, coach you on techniques for direct contact with employers.

Use Internet Job Boards and Company Web Sites

The Internet is emerging as a rich resource for learning about job openings. There are estimated to be more than 30,000 electronic job boards worldwide where you can learn about job openings and post your resume.[7] Table 9.1 provides a list of the most popular online sites for job seekers. In addition, more and more companies are posting their job openings on a career section of their Web sites.

New technology is increasing the efficiency of these sites. One trend is toward more interaction with job seekers. For example, some sites will notify job seekers when an opening occurs that matches their skills and interests. Sprint, Qwest, Eli Lilly, General Instruments, and NationJob.com use this approach.[8] Other sites, such as CareerBuilder.com, combine the results of searching several job boards into one list. Job boards that specialize by profession (e.g., Hospitalityonline.com, Engineerjobs.com, Accounting.com) and by categories of job seekers (e.g., Collegegrad.com) are beginning to provide more focused information about job openings.

Use of job boards and company Web sites to connect job seekers with employers is increasing. Employers like to use the World Wide Web because it is less expensive than using newspaper ads.[9] Job seekers like the Internet because they can search any day or time.

Although online job searches are becoming more common, a recent survey by Yankelovich Partners found that only one job seeker in ten found a job

TABLE 9.1	**Name of Job Board**	**Web Address**
Popular Internet job boards.[10, 11]	America's Job Bank	www.ajb.dni.us
	Best Jobs USA	www.bestjobsusa.com
	CareerBuilder	www.careerbuilder.com
	Careermag.com	www.careermag.com
	College Grad Job Hunter	www.collegegrad.com
	Cool Works	www.coolworks.com
	FlipDog.com	www.flipdog.com
	HotJobs	www.hotjobs.com
	JobDirect	www.jobdirect.com
	JobsOnline	www.jobsonline.com
	Monster.com	www.monster.com
	NationJob Network	www.nationjob.com
	National Teacher Recruitment Clearinghouse	www.recruitingteachers.org

online.[12] The same survey noted that more than 50 percent of job seekers complained that their online efforts "seldom or never" resulted in an interview for a job that matched their qualifications. Dick Bolles, author of *What Color Is Your Parachute?*, believes that, at the present time, technical types have the most luck using the Internet for job leads.[13] He pegs their success rate at two in ten. Recruiters suggest that you can increase your chances for success by targeting your search and identifying a few companies that you want to work for rather than posting your resume at many sites.[14]

If you choose to apply online, protect your privacy. Read the job board's confidentiality and privacy policies. Does the job board allow you to store your resume and apply only for specific openings? Can you selectively block some companies from viewing your resume? For how long will your resume be posted? Two additional tips: (1) Don't post your resume on newsgroups, because it may be widely copied and you lose control of its distribution, and (2) get a separate E-mail address to use during your job search.[15]

Respond to Classified Ads

Traditional sources of job leads are classified ads and job fairs advertised in your local newspapers. A survey by the Society for Human Resource Management found that the Sunday classified ads are still one of the most effective ways in which people find jobs.[16]

Check Out Employment Agencies

Another resource, though limited in its effectiveness, is a private employment agency. These account for about 5 percent of job leads.[17] Agencies often specialize in groups of positions, such as financial management or administrative support. When the employer pays the fee, using an agency doesn't cost you anything. If you agree to pay a fee, it may cost up to 15 to 25 percent of your first year's salary. Don't sign anything unless the fee arrangements are perfectly clear.

If you decide to use an employment agency as one way of uncovering job leads, use only a well-established company. Make sure that the agency is a member of the National Association of Personnel Consultants and that your contact is a Certified Personnel Consultant or Certified International Personnel Consultant. Another recommendation is to use well-established national and franchised firms.[18]

State employment agencies offer free services. It doesn't hurt to visit your local state employment office as part of your job hunt efforts, especially if you are able to see the same staff person each time. The office's computerized job bank is updated daily.

Try Temping

Another way to discover key employers in your area is to work for temporary service firms. These firms should be members of the American Staffing Association (**www.natss.org**) or National Association of Personnel Services (**www.napsweb.org**).

An experienced temp worker notes that temps gain work experience, build skills, earn money, network, and uncover full-time job opportunities.[19] If you are reluctant to commit to a company until some personal matters are resolved or if you want the flexibility to leave on short notice, this option may be especially attractive.

ACTIVE METHODS ARE BEST

Table 9.2 summarizes the ways to uncover job leads that are discussed in the preceding section. The most effective methods for uncovering job leads in college are active. They require action on your part: talking with people in your network, visiting the placement office, and participating in an internship program. They entail advance planning and a commitment of time and energy. As a graduate, active methods win out, too; this means spending your time making direct contact with potential employers, responding to specific ads, and working as a temp.

Passive job search techniques are less effective. Don't rely on placing your resume on an Internet job board in case there is an opening that matches your qualifications. Don't bet that an employment agency will be able to do a successful job hunt for you.

A survey of students in the prestigious Harvard M.B.A. program revealed that they averaged 150 to 175 hours of job hunting activity while still in school. They reported spending ten hours each week during the three-month period from January to March. This peak commitment is the equivalent of carrying two extra courses.[20]

If you begin your job search while still in college, you might have a good job offer in hand on the day you graduate. What could be more gratifying than negotiating your start date with an employer and planning your graduation celebration at the same time?

TABLE 9.2	**College Resources**
Uncovering job leads.	Career services & placement offices
	Professors
	Contacts from experiential learning programs (e.g., internships, co-ops, fieldwork, community service)
	Alumni groups
	Network Resources
	Friends
	Family
	Employers and coworkers, past and present
	Classmates
	Community members
	Internet mailing lists and newsgroups
	Additional Resources
	Direct contact with employers
	Internet job boards
	Company Web sites
	Job fairs
	Newspaper ads
	Professional societies: newsletters, conferences, trade magazines
	Employment agencies
	Temporary agencies

CLARIFY YOUR JOB SEARCH OBJECTIVES AND INFORMATION NEEDS

Set Your Job Search Goals

Once you begin actively searching for a job, you need to take some time to set your job search objectives. What kind of outcome would be personally satisfying and practical? Having a personal goal is a motivator. It's easier to put your full energy behind a job search when you are committed to attaining a specific objective.

Another reason for setting an objective is to narrow your search. Doing so allows you to concentrate your efforts and avoid wasting time pursuing unsuitable positions. Finally, a job objective makes it easier for other people to let you know about appropriate job leads.

Your job objective reflects your unique situation and may be unlike those of your classmates. Table 9.3 identifies nine typical types of job seekers, their search goals, and examples of how they express their objectives. As you review this table, identify which of these types of job seekers you resemble most.

TABLE 9.3 *Types of job seekers.*

Type of Job Seeker	Goal	Examples of Students' Job Search Goals
The Target Shooter	A specific position in a specific work setting	I want a position in the FBI. I want a position as a city elementary school teacher. I want to work in San Francisco in the commercial lending department of a bank.
The Mission Fulfiller	A position in a particular career field	I want to work in the environmental protection area. One possibility is a position in quality control in private industry. Another is lobbying for a nonprofit agency that serves as a watchdog for various environmental issues. Another is a position in a local, state, or national government agency that enforces environmental protection laws.
The Fit Finder	The best fit in a specific geographic location, industry, organizational specialty, or company	I want to work in Denver. I want to work for a brand-name product in marketing. I want to work in telecommunications in Portland, Oregon. I want to work in human resources in Philadelphia.
The Toehold Grabber	A position in a glamour industry, specialty, or company	I want to work for MTV. I want to work in films. I want to work in sports marketing.
The Field Explorer	To gain experience in a specific work environment	I want to work in a hospital. I want to work in a classroom setting. I want to work in a lab. I want to work for a law firm.
The Skill Builder	To develop or improve particular skills (e.g., computer software, graphic design, or writing)	I want to work in the art department of a magazine. I want to work on a community newspaper.
The Lifestyle Seeker	A position that permits a certain lifestyle	I want to be able to work overseas. I want time to pursue my painting lessons. I want plenty of part-time opportunities.
The Graduate School Positioner	A position that will build credentials for entry to a specific graduate school program	I want a position in the business world that will make me more attractive to a graduate school admissions committee in an M.B.A. program. I want to work in a hospital setting to gain exposure to the work of physicians' assistants.
The Adventurer	To explore several different possibilities simultaneously	I am exploring positions in high-tech start-up companies and Fortune 500 research and development departments.

Job seekers of many types begin their search with objectives that define some limits. The Toehold Grabber wants work in a glamour area such as the music business and will consider a broad range of positions to break into the field. The Fit Finder might identify a specific geographical location such as Boston and initiate a broad search of industries within that location.

Several factors account for the differences in types of job objectives. A job objective will reflect the importance of a career in your life. For some, striving for a specific career goal is paramount; they are the Target Shooters. Lifestyle Seekers place less emphasis on the work and more on a particular kind of life situation, such as working outdoors. Any job that they accept must support their preferred lifestyle.

Students define their career direction at different rates and in different ways. Some students are best at deciding what they want in action, by trying out several options. The objective of this kind of search is a position that will allow further career exploration. These types of job seekers are the Field Explorer, Skill Builder, and Adventurer.

Finally, job search goals tend to reflect the amount of specificity in your college major. Typically, the more occupationally specific or industry-related your major is, the more focused are your job search goals.

ACTIVITY 9.1   YOUR JOB SEARCH TYPE

Review Table 9.3. What type of job seeker are you? Give the reasons that you selected this type. (If you see yourself as a combination of job seeker types, list all that apply and give the reasons for choosing each one.)

_____

_____

_____

_____

_____

_____

_____

Describe your job search objectives.

_____

_____

Search for Information:
Matching Job Titles with Your Objectives

Once you have identified your objective, you may still be in the dark about what to do next. What's missing is an understanding of the kinds of jobs that will meet your criteria. For example, a Mission Fulfiller, like Andrew, who wants to work in the environmental field, must gather information about entry-level job duties in environmentally related industries, government agencies, and nonprofit organizations.

One wrinkle in this type of research is that job titles vary in different companies and industries. Your research must go beyond a search for a job title. You must become aware of the ten to fifteen job tasks and the responsibilities associated with typical entry-level jobs.[21] When you focus on job tasks and responsibilities, you can recognize similar jobs, even if they have different titles.

Articulating your job objective is useful because it helps you see what information you require as you launch your job search. You must learn enough about the job market to identify job titles and responsibilities that match your qualifications and objectives.

For example, one Fit Finder, Deborah, wants to work in the cosmetics industry. She must discover specific types of job responsibilities that are reasonable matches with her skills in sales and marketing (her preferred organizational specialties). She must locate companies that offer these kinds of positions in the Southeast, which is where she wants to live. Such research about job opportunities is a significant element of a good job search.

COMPOSING A RESUME

Your resume is one of your most important job search tools. In this section you will learn how to write a resume that shows off your skills and grabs the employer's attention.

Employers use resumes to identify applicants whom they wish to interview. As they screen resumes, they toss out those from applicants who don't appear to have the skills that they want. Studies show that employers spend less than a minute reading the average resume. To avoid being screened out, your resume must convince the employer that you have the skills to do the job. Since your resume has less than a minute of the employer's time, it must be short, easy to read, and to the point.

The Resume: Your One-Page Advertisement

Think of your resume as a one-page advertisement. In this advertisement you seek to persuade the employer that you are the ideal candidate for the position.[22] The resume provides an overview of your skills and summarizes your experience and education. Its goal is to convince the employer that what you have done in the past makes you a highly qualified candidate who is worth interviewing.

The resume does not tell the whole story of your life or even necessarily list all the jobs that you have ever held. You select the information that will best persuade the employer. Not only is your resume often your first introduction to an employer; it is also typically used to remind an employer of your skills after an interview. Therefore, it is crucial to highlight your strengths.

One more thing about your advertisement: never lie. Your personal reputation is one of your most important assets. Don't put your integrity and ethics in question by including false information in your resume.

I once had a co-op student—let's call her Brenda—who had the skills to meet the requirements of a much-sought-after position. It was a prestigious company, the starting salary was excellent, and there was a commitment to make a permanent job offer if the co-op internship went well. Brenda passed her interview and employment tests easily. She needed the job desperately and was thrilled to get the offer.

However, she had been secretly ashamed of her employment history. Unfortunately, she never discussed her fears with me. Instead, she made up an employment entry for her resume and extended the length of two others by a few months.

When the company's human resources department couldn't verify Brenda's employment, she was let go just two days into her dream job. She was devastated. Ironically, the company was sorry, too, because they liked her and valued her skills. She was more than qualified even without the false work experience. The company rule was clear: honesty is imperative. They reason that if you are not honest in your application you may not be trustworthy on the job. Other career counselors tell of resume lies coming to light years later, with employees being fired even after several promotions when a lie is discovered.

Brenda fixed her resume and she did get another co-op position, but it was not the plum she could have enjoyed.

Resume Format and Appearance

The chronological resume is the most popular format. It presents your work experience starting with your most recent position and proceeding backward. This format is used in the sample shown in Figure 9.1 and in Activity 9.3, Your Resume. Even if you end up with a different format, the tips in the activity will help you with the preliminary organization of your resume.

Standard Resume Categories

If you have never prepared a resume or you have relatively little work experience, your best bet is to begin by following these standard resume practices. Custom dictates that certain information be included in a resume. Table 9.4 describes standard categories found on resumes: a heading, education, experience, and skills.

After you provide this information, you have lots of freedom to decide what additional information would enhance your "advertisement." Table 9.4 also describes three optional categories: a career objective, or summary and extracurricular activities. You may choose among these optional categories according to their power to show off your skills.

Look at Mark Brown's resume in Figure 9.1. It shows the customary style and appearance of a chronological resume. For example, you have already learned that one such customary practice is to limit a resume to one page until you have considerable career-related work experience. Other customs pertaining to resume style and appearance are summarized in Table 9.5.

Personal data that are irrelevant to your ability to perform a job should be excluded. Omit personal data such as age, gender, ethnicity, marital status,

MARK BROWN

342 Los Gatos Boulevard, Apt. 3A   562-555-1212
Del Mar, California 92922   mark_brown1492@collegesite.com

EDUCATION   San Diego State College
San Diego, California
Major: Psychology B.A. Expected June 200X

Relevant coursework General Psychology, Group Dynamics, Social Psychology, Psychology of Motivation, Interviewing Techniques, Oral Communication, English Composition, Calculus 1, and Introduction to Business

Achievements: G.P.A. 3.7/4.0

EXPERIENCE   DON'S SERVICE STATION, La Jolla, CA   *06/0X–present*
Manager
Serve customers and resolve complaints; supervise three people; sell merchandise and operate cash register; order and take inventory on supplies.

BAYSIDE SECURITY SERVICES, San Francisco, CA   *01/0X–06/0X*
Security Guard (Part-time)
Screened and logged incoming visitors, maintained secure entrance and exits, monitored security system, apprehended shoplifters, and performed investigative work.

INTERNATIONAL HIGH SCHOOL, San Francisco, CA   *09/0X–12/0X*
Math Tutor (Volunteer)
Tutored students in Algebra, Geometry, and Logic. Graded papers, checked homework, and gave make-up exams for instructors. Worked with individual students and small groups. Assisted classroom teacher.

SKILLS   Applications: Word, PowerPoint, Excel

SELECTION OF INFORMATION

- The essential categories are the Heading, Education, Experience, and Skills. Optional sections are omitted to avoid clutter.
- Job descriptions begin with action verbs.
- This resume emphasizes interpersonal and communication skills.

TABLE 9.4	**Essential Categories**	
Essential and optional resume categories.	HEADING	Your name, mailing address, and other contact information such as telephone, cell phone, fax, and E-mail address.
	EDUCATION	Your college work and any other special training. Include relevant coursework, achievements, and awards.
	EXPERIENCE	Any activity, usually work experience, that may help convince an employer to hire you. Examples include full-time paid employment, part-time and temporary positions, internships, work-study assignments, self-employment, work in a family business, and military and community service.
	SKILLS	Highlight skills that are most important for the position, and add skills that are not obvious from your work experience or coursework (e.g., foreign language skills, keyboarding skills).
	Optional Categories	
	CAREER OBJECTIVE	A description of the kind of work you are seeking.
	QUALIFICATION SUMMARY	An overview of your qualifications. It is used instead of a career objective, especially when the job seeker has relevant work experience.
	ACTIVITIES	Highlights of extracurricular and nonwork activities that add to your qualifications. Professional certifications, professional affiliations, publications, community service, and unusual hobbies are included here.

health, and country of origin from a resume. Also, never send a picture with your resume.

Your goal is to convince an employer to interview you and eventually make a job offer. The information in your resume should be selected and emphasized with this goal in mind. For example, in the health care, education, and customer service fields, you might highlight your people skills, as Mark Brown did in the sample resume. For technical positions, you might emphasize your computer and math abilities or special training. For the business world, you might feature your work experience and knowledge of a particular organizational specialty. In creative areas, you would feature your artistic achievements and skills.

Producing Your Resume

Your resume is written in a series of drafts. In your first draft, focus on the information content. In your second draft, work on an attractive presentation. In your third draft, polish your resume based on feedback from others.

While working on the first draft, examine sample resumes for your major and career objective. There are many resume books geared to every type of

Resume Style	TABLE 9.5
Job descriptions begin with action verbs (e.g., *serve, resolve, supervise, order, maintain, tutor, check*). "I" is understood as the subject of each sentence and is omitted. The articles *the, a,* and *an* are omitted.	*Customary resume style and appearance.*

Resume Appearance
One-inch margins frame the resume. Lots of white space gives a clutter-free, businesslike impression. Various typefaces, boldface, and underlining are used in moderation to highlight strong points.

job hunter, from the inexperienced college student to the mature career changer. Your college placement office is often an excellent resource for getting help with your resume.

Once you have a first draft, get feedback from several people and use their comments to revise it. Consider asking your counselor, your professors, people in the field, your boss, your family, and friends. Your final step is to polish, polish, polish.

THE TECHNOLOGY TRANSITION IN SENDING, STORING, AND MANAGING RESUMES

Advances in technology and increased workloads are changing the way companies process your resume. Gone are the days when a personnel clerk received your resume by mail, did a quick evaluation of your qualifications, and either passed it along or filed it.

Increasingly, employers want you to send your resume by E-mail or to apply on-line at their company Web site. Over a third of human resources professionals prefer to receive resumes by E-mail.[23] They may also get your resume by advertising their openings though an Internet job board, such as Monster.com.

No matter how employers get your resume, even if you mail it in, more and more companies now scan resumes into a database. According to a survey of human resources professionals, about 25 percent of companies, mostly the larger ones, use resume databases.[24] And database services help many smaller companies by maintaining resume databases for them.

Surveys of employers also reveal wide differences in their preferences for how they want you to send your resume and how they process it once they receive it.[25] These differences reflect the fact that the technology is in transition and is still too expensive for some smaller employers. No one standard practice has yet emerged. This changing state of affairs means that you must have three versions of your resume ready when you begin your job search: (1) an interview version, (2) a scannable version, and (3) an E-mail or plain-text version.

The Interview Resume

The "interview resume" is the one that you take to any job interview, because it is an attractively formatted one-page advertisement of your skills. You will also give this version to members of your network and use it in information interviews.

Tables 9.4 and 9.5 outline the resume categories and appearance guidelines for your interview resume. Activity 9.3, Your Resume, will guide you in creating a chronological interview resume using your favorite word-processing program.

As you will soon see, your interview resume is the foundation for both your scannable and plain-text resumes. These two versions of your resume are created by making modifications to your interview resume.

The Scannable Resume

The Internet Riley Guide suggests that you make a copy of your interview resume and save it under the name "scanres.doc."[26] This will help you identify this version as scannable.

Scannable resumes must include key words. Key words are nouns and noun phrases that reflect your education, experience, competencies, and personal qualities. Examples of key words include degrees, job titles, skills, and personality attributes, such as the following: *B.S, A.A., health care, market research, teacher, guest services, law enforcement, accounts payable, Excel, Spanish, Mandarin, detail-minded, team player, 50 w.p.m.*

Key words are important to include in the scannable resume because they are the terms that the company's computer program uses to search its resume database. The resumes that have the greatest number of key-word matches with the job requirements are ranked the highest. These candidates are then most likely to be called for an interview.

To increase your chances of being selected for an interview, electronic resume expert Rebecca Smith (**www.eresumes.com**) suggests that your resume contain 25 to 35 key words relating to your qualifications for your ideal job.[27] Key-word summaries are usually placed immediately following the resume heading.

To find key words, Smith suggests several resources. Check the *Occupational Outlook Handbook* (**http://stats.bls.gov/ocohome.htm**) for the key words associated with specific occupations. Use nouns and phrases from the job descriptions posted on the prospective employer's Web site and from related newspaper ads. Consult trade journals and magazines for occupational and industry jargon. Smith's Web site provides sample key words for a variety of occupations.

In addition to including key words in your scannable resume, you must change its appearance. The appearance changes are necessary to ensure that your resume is scanned accurately into resume databases and can be retrieved appropriately for openings that suit your skills and interests.

The best scannable resumes have a plain vanilla appearance. They avoid all the special formatting features that word-processing programs offer. Typical causes of scanning errors include scanner technology limitations and incompatibility between your computer system and word-processing program and those used by the company where you are applying. Table 9.6 offers tips for eliminating scanning and retrieval problems.

TABLE 9.6

Tips for creating a scannable resume.[28,29]

- Use a laser-quality printer and 8-1/2" x 11" white paper.

- Print on one side only.

- Use a standard typeface, such as Helvetica, Arial, Times, Univers, Courier, or Palatino.

- Use a 12-point font for the text, 14 points for headings, and 16 points for your name.

- All text should be in one column; do not center type or use tabs.

- Place your name on the top line of each page. Use separate lines for each phone, fax, and E-mail address.

- Do not use bold typeface, underlining, shading, or italics. Instead, use capital letters and white space to identify and separate items.

- Do not use bullet points, graphics, or rule lines. Eliminate the # sign, boxes, or any special characters or symbols that your word-processing program offers, because the scanner may not recognize them properly.

- Send an unfolded original hard copy, never a photocopy.

The Plain-Text Resume

The third, plain-text version of your resume is suitable for E-mail transmission and for submission directly on-line through company Web sites. Use your scannable resume to create the plain-text version. Name this version "resume.txt" and save it to text only (also called ASCII text).[30] If you don't know how to save your file in this format, ask a college lab technician or a knowledgeable friend for help.

The plain-text resume is in a file format that can be read by all computer systems. Many companies prefer the plain-text resume format for several reasons: (1) They save time by not having to open and print attachments; (2) they avoid the risks of virus infections associated with attachments; and (3) they avoid the difficulties caused by computer program incompatibilities.

You send your plain-text resume in the body of an E-mail or cut and paste it into an E-form on the company Web site. Typically, this is the fastest way to get your resume into the right hands and should be used whenever a company offers it as an option. An example of a plain-text resume and formatting tips are given in Figure 9.2.

When you E-mail your plain-text resume, use the subject line to provide a specific job title or reference to a particular ad. Begin with a cover letter in the body of the E-mail. Your plain-text resume follows the cover letter.

Shifting Employers' Requirements for Resume Submission

The technology for sending, storing, and managing resumes is evolving rapidly. Check Internet sites, such as the Riley Guide: Resumes and Cover Letters (**www.rileyguide.com**), Rebecca Smith's eResumes & Resources (**www.eresumes.com**), or The Damn Good Resume (**www.damngood.com**) to get up-to-the-minute suggestions for preparing and sending your resume electronically.

Your best bet is to check the employer's preferences each time you want to send your resume. Always follow these instructions to the letter. If you have prepared the three versions of your resume, you will be ready to use whichever method the employer favors.

FIGURE 9.2   *Plain-text resume.*

Put your name at the top on its own line.

Use separate lines for each phone number and E-mail address.

Keywords make your resume easier to find in a database.

Capital letters emphasize headings. Avoid **bold,** *italics,* and underlining.

Asterisks and plus signs replace bullets.

OTHER TIPS

Set margins to 0 and 65. Align (justify) all material at left. Single column only.

Use the space bar to align. Avoid tabs.

End each line with a hard carriage return. (Press the Enter key.)

Use a standard-width typeface such as Courier.

E-mail a copy to yourself as a final check.

Save as text-only document or as ASCII text.

Source: Adapted from Olivia Crosby, "Résumés, Applications, and Cover Letters, *Occupational Outlook Quarterly,* 43, No. 2 (Summer 1999): 11.

CHRISTINE TECHIE
1078 Campus Drive
College Town, MN 41224
(454) 555-5555
Techie@somewhere.com

KEYWORD SUMMARY
BS COMPUTER SCIENCE, 200X, C++, Visual Basic, Assembly, FORTRAN, TUTOR, HTML, XML, CAD, Oracle, MS Office, Adobe Illustrator, IBM 360/370, Windows NT, TCP/IP, UNIX

EDUCATION
Bachelor of Science, Computer Science, 200X
Large State University, College Town, Large State
Minor: Mathematics G.P.A.: 3.0/4.0

RELATED COURSES
Database Design, Compiler Design, System Architecture,
Operating System, Data Structures, Calculus 1, 2, 3

COMPUTER SKILLS
System: IBM 360/370, Windows NT, and UNIX
Software: CAD, Oracle, Adobe Illustrator, and MS Office
Languages: C/C++, Visual Basic, Assembly, FORTRAN, TUTOR, HTML, XML

EXPERIENCE
Support Desk, Large State University, 0X–0X
* Maintained computer systems in campus lab
* Installed applications and performed troubleshooting
* Instructed students on applications and system

Programmer (Intern), Generic Company, 0X–0X
* Wrote instructional programs using TUTOR language
* Corrected errors in prewritten programs using C++
* Altered existing program to fit users' needs

Data Entry Clerk, ABC Sales, Summers XX, XX, XX
* Updated inventory and sales data

COMMUNICATION SKILLS
Served as Vice President of Computer Science Society
Received A's in technical writing and speech classes

++ Willing to relocate ++

OTHER JOB SEARCH TOOLS

The Cover Letter

The cover letter is used to introduce your resume when you are mailing it to a potential employer. Figure 9.3 provides general guidelines for writing a cover letter.

Sample cover letter.   **FIGURE 9.3**

Guadalupe Reyes
2115 Spring Avenue, Apt. 3B
City, CA 90911
(545) 555-5555
G_Reyes17766@somewhere.com

December 5, 200X

Brian Carson
Director of Human Resources
Highrise Hotel
City, CA 90901

Dear Mr. Carson:

The assistant manager position you advertised in today's Hamlet Gazette greatly interests me. The Highrise Hotels have always served as landmarks for me when I travel, and I would like to contribute to their continued growth. I have enclosed my resume for your review.

In May, I will be graduating from Large State University with a bachelor's degree in business. While in school, I developed strong organizational and customer service skills. As a dormitory assistant, I organized events, led meetings, and assisted students. As Treasurer of the Business Society, I maintained the budget and presented budget reports. My summer internships also required extensive interaction with the public. I believe these experiences have prepared me for your assistant manager position.

I would appreciate the opportunity to discuss my qualifications more fully in an interview. I will call you next week to follow up.

Sincerely,

Guadalupe Reyes

Guadalupe Reyes

Enclosure

Address letters to a specific individual if possible

State position applied for and where you found the opening listed

Sell yourself

Request an interview

Sign letter

Enclose your resume

Source: Adapted from Olivia Crosby, "Résumés, Applications, and Cover Letters," *Occupational Outlook Quarterly,* 43, No. 2 (Summer 1999): 13.

TABLE 9.7

Job reference tips.

Select three to five people for references. The best references are those who can speak about your performance. They are your current and former employers and your college professors. If you lack such contacts, use character references such as your pastor or rabbi and friends who are respected members of the community.

Select reliable people. Choose people who are easy to reach, who can write or speak well of you, and who will follow up promptly.

Ask permission first. Never use someone as a reference unless you ask permission first. Provide your references with a copy of your resume. Talk about your career goals. This helps them to support you in obtaining a position.

Get all relevant contact information. List name, title, business address with ZIP code, E-mail address, and phone and fax numbers. A business card usually has this information.

Carry a typed reference list to all interviews. You may need your reference list to complete job applications.

Building a Reference List

Every employer will ask you for references. Don't wait until you are seeking job offers to think about this requirement. Begin building your reference list in college. Some guidelines for obtaining references are given in Table 9.7.

ACTIVITY 9.2   STARTING A REFERENCE FILE

List five people who might serve as potential references. Indicate your reason or reasons for including each person on your list.

1. _____

   Reason for selection _____

   _____

2. _____

   Reason for selection _____

   _____

3. _____

   Reason for selection _____

   _____

4. _____

   Reason for selection _____

   _____

5. _____

Reason for selection _____

_____

TIPS TO DECREASE JOB SEARCH STRESS

A job search is often accompanied by strong emotions. Most job seekers experience times when they are anxious, scared, uncertain, discouraged, and lacking in confidence. If you don't recognize and manage your emotions, they can drag on your job search efforts and slow you down. There are two major sources of negative emotions: the pressure to succeed and the need to structure the search by yourself.

The economic pressure to earn money for food, clothing, and shelter is a significant source of stress. Added to this practical pressure is social pressure. Our society's approval depends on having a job, and out-of-work people are devalued. You may also feel a sense of internal pressure to succeed, to prove yourself, and to make it in the working world. For your own self-esteem, you need a job.

Merely understanding that you are under pressure can help to relieve it. Talking with a close friend, a fellow job seeker, or a counselor is another way to restore your emotional equilibrium. Recognize that a job search is a big challenge, one in which success provides significant rewards, economic independence, and status in the community.

Most experts advise that looking for a job should be a full-time job. You should set up a schedule, keep a contact log book, and develop a system for finding and following up on job leads. Reading books on job search may provide you with ideas on structuring your search. Organizing a daily routine can reduce your anxiety.

Many students are juggling home, work, and school responsibilities. The thought of adding a job search may feel overwhelming. Still, you have now learned the advantages of freeing some energy to get to work on this task. While you are searching for a job, you may have to reset your priorities and let some other activities go. Another strategy is to ask friends and family members to pitch in to relieve you of some of your current responsibilities.

WHERE STUDENTS GET STUCK, AND WHAT TO DO IF IT HAPPENS TO YOU

Poor and Uneven Educational or Work History

Prospective employers look for clues that you have the skills and abilities to do the job well. They get those clues from your educational background and prior job experience. Many students believe that their past mistakes or an uneven educational or work history will work against them in the job market. The key lesson is to market your strengths so that the overall impression an employer gets of you is positive.

Consult with other people, especially those professionals on campus who help students with their resumes. They will work with you to highlight your strong points and downplay your weaknesses.

The world is filled with successful people who either began their education and careers late in life or turned their lives around. In the interesting publication *Profiles in Success*,[31] nearly 300 former students from colleges as diverse as Yavapai College in Arizona to Norwalk Community College in Connecticut, from Chemeketa Community College in Oregon to Williamsburg Technical College in South Carolina, chronicle their stories. Many of these students transformed their lives and overcame difficult circumstances: from living as a high school dropout who fed livestock in exchange for free rent, to earning a living as a ceramic engineering technologist; from overcoming substance abuse to becoming a counselor; from working as a motel maid while supporting four children as a single mother to working as a registered nurse—to cite just a few. All these people are successful in the work world because they were able to focus themselves and other people on their assets.

Seek expert advice about how to handle a specific situation. For example, if your overall grades are poor, you might list your average in your major ("GPA Major: 3.5") or your average with an explanation ("GPA 2.6—worked 35-hour weeks during academic semester"). You may decide to omit your GPA and address the issue in an interview. You may find it easier to talk about flunking out of premed in your first year if you can show how this event turned out to be a wake-up call to start getting serious about your career goals. Experienced resume reviewers, like placement personnel, can help you work out the best solution for your particular situation.

KEY POINTS

1. Develop your job search skills during your college years. While in college, visit your placement office regularly, participate in college internship programs, and develop your network.

2. After you graduate, continue to network, get in touch with employers directly, respond to classified ads, surf the Internet, check out employment agencies, and try temporary work. All are sources of job leads.

3. As you begin your active job search, set your job search goals. Clarify what kind of outcome would be practical and pleasing.

4. The nine basic types of job seekers are

The Target Shooter	The Skill Builder
The Mission Fulfiller	The Lifestyle Seeker
The Fit Finder	The Graduate School Positioner
The Toehold Grabber	The Adventurer
The Field Explorer	

5. Through a variety of information searches, you need to learn enough about the job market to identify job titles and responsibilities that match your qualifications with your objectives.

6. A resume is a one-page advertisement of your skills.

7. Create a resume through a series of drafts. Work on the content and the format until you can print an error-free copy.

8. You'll need three versions of your resume: (1) The interview resume is an attractively formatted version used in interviews. (2) The scannable resume is a plain vanilla version of your interview resume. Specific word-processing codes and symbols, such as bold type, underlining, and italics, are eliminated from it so that it can be scanned accurately into a resume database. Key words are added so that it will be retrieved for openings appropriate for your skills and experience. (3) The plain-text resume is created in a ASCII or plain-text format so that it can be sent in the body of an E-mail or used in E-forms to apply for openings on company Web sites.

9. Other job search tools include the cover letter and the list of references.

10. Tips for decreasing job search stress include talking with others; resetting your priorities to make time for looking for a job; and setting up a daily schedule so that you don't waste time.

11. Where students often get stuck in resume writing is in knowing how to present uneven or mediocre educational and work history. Emphasizing your strengths is the key. Experts on resume writing can often suggest ways of downplaying your weaknesses.

YOUR RESUME

ACTIVITY **9.3**

OVERVIEW

In this activity you will create a chronological resume. In this type of resume your work experience is listed in reverse order. You start with your current or most recent job and then work backward. First, you assemble and organize the information that you might want to include. Second, you select from this information the most relevant items and you work on the appearance of your resume. Finally, you polish your resume until it presents your qualifications effectively.

The instructions guide you step by step. If you already have a resume, use this process to revise and update it.

TASK 1 ASSEMBLE THE INFORMATION THAT YOU NEED

An employer expects to see certain information on a resume. Other types of information may add to your presentation.

The essential sections of a resume are

- Heading
- Education
- Experience
- Skills

Optional sections include

- A career objective
- Qualification Summary
- Extracurricular activities

Study the sample resumes that follow. Note the sequence in which information is presented, and get a picture in your mind of how your finished resume might look on the page.

We will discuss the essential and optional sections in the order in which they typically appear on the resume. Read the instructions for each section and fill in the information on the blanks provided.

As you assemble information to include, do not rule out anything. After you have a complete picture, you can select the most relevant information later, when you have a specific employer in mind.

FIGURE 9.4   *Sample resume.*

ALICIA CARRERAS
2971 21 Street, NW Apt. 13B
Gainesville, Florida 32104
352-555-1212 (cell)
acarreras2204@collegexpres.com

EDUCATION   Santa Fe Community College
Gainesville, Florida
Major: Liberal Arts
Completed 36 credits.

Relevant Courses:
Oral Communication, English Composition 1 & 2, Group Dynamics

EXPERIENCE   THE GAP—Gainesville, FL
Salesperson (part-time)   05/xx–present
- Help customers in busy retail store.
- Take cash and checks, and process credit card transactions.
- Close register and balance daily intake.
- Maintain stock and inventory.

Achievement:
Employee of the Month, 11/xx

ABC FINANCIAL SERVICE CORPORATION—Jacksonville, FL
Receptionist   03/xx–04/xx
- Greeted visitors from diverse cultural backgrounds.
- Answered phones, took messages, and scheduled appointments for investment bankers.
- Typed correspondence and reports.
- Maintained security log.

WINN DIXIE SUPERMARKET—Orlando, FL
Cashier (Part-time)   09/xx–02/xx
- Promoted to head cashier (02/xx).
- Trained new employees.
- Rang up sales, packed merchandise, closed out register.

SKILLS   Fluent in Spanish
MS Office: Word, Excel, PowerPoint, Access

ALLISON SMITH

123-23 95th Road, Apt. 13B
Flushing, NY 11212

718–555–1212
asmith@xprs.com

OBJECTIVE   Rehabilitation Services

EDUCATION   LAGUARDIA COMMUNITY COLLEGE
Long Island City, NY
A.A.S. Major: Physical Therapist Assistant
Completed 36 credits.

Coursework
- Introduction to Physical Therapy
- Biology 1 & 2
- Introduction to Aging
- Oral Communication

EXPERIENCE
02/xx–present   Macy's Department Store — New York, NY
Sales Associate

Assist customers in selection of merchandise. Take cash and checks, and process credit card transactions. Operate cash register and balance daily intake.

03/xx–01/xx   CBQ Home Nursing Service — Flushing, NY
Receptionist

Greeted and directed visitors. Answered phones and took messages. Typed correspondence and reports. Entered insurance data into computer.

09/xx–02/xx   HB Home Health Care — Brooklyn, NY
Home Attendant (Part-time)

Assisted homebound seniors with activities of daily living. Monitored medication intake. Provided companionship and support.

SKILLS   Word, Type 45 w.p.m.
Patient, good listener

Heading

The first step is easy. Identify yourself and provide information about how you can be reached by mail and phone.

Line 1 YOUR NAME

Use the form of your name that you prefer. If your name is Walworth Standford but you prefer Wally Standford, use Wally Standford on the resume. However, avoid using nicknames that do not have a professional ring.

Lines 2 and 3 Your mailing address

Lines 4 and 5 Your telephone numbers (home, cell, and business) with the area code

Line 6 Your E-mail address

If you have a fax number or use a pager, include those numbers. A potential employer likes to be able to contact you quickly and reliably. If you use a message machine during your job search, make sure that the message announcement is businesslike. Eliminate any musical background.

HEADING

1. _____Brian Town_____
   YOUR NAME (use capital letters to help it stand out)

2. _____2937_____
   Street address (include apartment number, if applicable)

3. _____
   City, state, ZIP code

4. _____
   Area code and phone number (home)

5. _____
   Area code and phone number (business or cell phone)

6. _____
   E-mail address

Career Interest and/or Objective

Provide a brief statement of your career interests. List a career field, industry, or job function area. Avoid long sentences and the words *entry level*.

Examples:

CAREER INTEREST	Elementary Education
CAREER OBJECTIVE	Marketing and Advertising

CAREER INTEREST

_____

Education

List your most recent education first. Under the main heading "Education" you may include several subheadings, including "Achievements," "Selected Coursework," and "Activities."

> Line 1 College name and its location
>
> Line 2 Type of degree, program of study, or major, and date (the month and year) that your degree was awarded or the number of credits that you have completed so far

Typical community college degrees are Associate in Arts (**A.A.**), Associate in Science (**A.S.**), and Associate in Applied Science (**A.A.S.**). Degree types in four-year colleges include Bachelor of Arts (**B.A.**), Bachelor of Science (**B.S.**), and Bachelor of Business Administration (**B.B.A.**). Check your college catalog to see which degree is awarded to students with your major.

Subheading: Achievements

Highlight relevant academic achievements (for example, Dean's List, cumulative GPA above 3.0/4.0), awards and scholarships. List articles, poems, or other writing that appeared in the school newspaper or other publications. Indicate any special research projects or presentations. If you have not had an outstanding academic record, omit this section.

Subheading: Selected Coursework

List the most advanced courses in your major; your highest-level math, English, or communication skills courses; and technical skills courses such as accounting or word-processing courses. List first the courses related to your major or career objective and courses in which you received good grades.

Subheading: Activities

List your extracurricular school activities, including clubs, school newspaper, and leadership positions. Seek to impress the potential employer by presenting evidence of leadership, broad interests, and career-related skills. For example, getting elected to a school office suggests an ability to run a successful campaign. Playing on a sports team suggests that you can work with others toward a common goal.

EDUCATION

1. _____

   Name of college   City, state (no zip code)

2. _____

   Type of degree   Program of study   Graduation date (month/year)
                                                  or credits completed

Achievements

■ _____

■ _____

■ _____

■ _____

Selected Courses

- _____
- _____
- _____
- _____
- _____

Other Colleges and Advanced Training

As you assemble information for your resume, include any other college or advanced training. For now, don't worry if your record there was not the best. You can decide later whether to include this section in a final draft. Highlight only the most important information, such as relevant coursework, achievements, and activities.

1. _____

   Name of college   City, state (no ZIP code)

2. _____

   Type of degree   Program of study   Graduation date (month/year)
                                                   or credits completed

Coursework, achievements, activities

- _____
- _____
- _____

High School

List your high school if you have very little to put in the "Experience" section. Also list your high school if you obtained special skills or had special achievements or experiences that an employer might consider relevant. Highlight relevant coursework, achievements, and activities.

1. _____

   Name of high school   City, state (no ZIP code)

2. _____

   Graduation date (month/year)

Coursework, achievements, activities

- _____
- _____
- _____

Experience

List your most recent experience first and work backward. Include paid full-time employment, part-time and temporary positions, internships, work–study assignments, self-employment, work in a family business, odd jobs, and military and community service.

If you are an immigrant or foreign student, you may include your work experience in your country of origin. If you have work permits or valid visas or have become a citizen, include this information at the bottom of the resume. For instance, you can add "U. S. Resident Alien, valid Green Card. Qualified for immediate employment."

Form of Entries in Experience Section

Line 1
- Company name
- Location (city and state; no ZIP code)

Line 2
- Job title (Indicate part-time, volunteer, or intern status if applicable)
- Dates of employment, using month and year: 09/02–10/03

Line 3
- Description of responsibilities and accomplishments: List first the responsibilities that you want to highlight. For example, *if* you are seeking a position dealing with people, list first your activities with people (e.g., sell, answer phones, provide information). List data-oriented activities (e.g., keyboarding, filing, and balancing a cash drawer) later.

Begin each description with an active verb such as those listed below. Be sure to use the present tense for a current position and past tense for positions that you held in the past (e.g., "made," "recorded," "balanced," "produced").

SAMPLE ACTION VERBS

administer	create	handle	pioneer	sell
analyze	cut	implement	place	serve
arrange	design	improve	plan	set up
assist	direct	install	post	solicit
balance	distribute	invent	prepare	solve
build	edit	keep	price	supervise
calculate	enter	lead	purchase	take
check	establish	maintain	record	teach
collect	expand	make	reorganize	type
compose	file	manage	research	utilize
compute	fill out	operate	resolve	verify
conduct	follow up	order	ring up	
contact	generate	organize	schedule	

Sample Job Descriptions

In the following sample job descriptions, different formats and devices are used to emphasize certain features of the description. Capital letters, underlining, bold type, font size, and bullets are used to set off your experience in an attractive manner. Experiment a bit and then select *one* format that fits your needs the best. Then stick to that format for every experience entry. A consistent format makes your resume easier for potential employers to read. Other job descriptions are provided in the sample resumes.

METROBANK

Richmond, Virginia

Legal Affairs Department: Co-op intern
- Provided clerical support services for corporate legal staff (65 attorneys).
- Answered phones, sent faxes, operated copy machines, filed.
- Updated computer records of legal documents.

New York City Department of Housing, Preservation and Development
New York City, New York
<u>ENGINEERING INTERN</u>
Developed technical drawings, wrote specifications, made engineering calculations (mechanical and electrical), and inspected premises for construction and alteration of structures.

<u>Heynda Japanese Inn</u>, Hatagun, Kochi (Japan)
Assistant to the Manager (family-owned inn)
- Coordinated and supervised private parties.
- Greeted and assisted English-speaking patrons.
- Purchased linens, bedding, and dining room items.

<u>St. Mary's Catholic Church</u>, Seattle, WA
Administrative Assistant (volunteer, part-time)
- Produced weekly church bulletin, gathering and verifying information from parishioners and designing the layout.
- Answered telephones, performed clerical work.

Santa Fe Community College
Gainesville, FL
<u>Library clerk</u> (work–study)
Checked out books and other library materials. Assisted students in using on-line computer catalog of library materials. Reshelved books.

Big Pops International, Kew Gardens, NY
Owner
- Market lollipops throughout Borough of Queens at block parties, street fairs, private children's parties, etc.
- Earned $1,500 (net) 20xx, $2,500 (net) 20xx.
- Supervise staff of three in making lollipop batches as needed.

<u>Parent Teacher Association, John F. Kennedy Elementary School</u>, Chicago, IL
Treasurer
- Collected and disbursed funds
- Maintained bank records
- Presented treasurer's report at monthly meetings

Achievement:
- Fundraising coordinator. Headed drive that raised $10,000 for library books. Convinced 10 local merchants to donate computer equipment and software.

FORMAT
Describe each experience, beginning with your most recent one. Begin each description with an active verb. Use additional sheets if necessary.

EXPERIENCE

1. _____

    Name of company   City, state (no ZIP code)

2. _____

    Position title   From month/year to month/year

■ _____

    Active verb (description of responsibility)

■ _____

    Active verb (description of responsibility)

■ _____

    Active verb (description of responsibility)

■ _____

    Active verb (description of responsibility)

1. _____

    Name of company   City, state (no ZIP code)

2. _____

    Position title   From month/year to month/year

■ _____

    Active verb (description of responsibility)

■ _____

    Active verb (description of responsibility)

■ _____

    Active verb (description of responsibility)

■ _____

    Active verb (description of responsibility)

1. _____

    Name of company   City, state (no ZIP code)

2. _____

    Position title   From month/year to month/year

■ _____

    Active verb (description of responsibility)

- _____

  Active verb (description of responsibility)

- _____

  Active verb (description of responsibility)

- _____

  Active verb (description of responsibility)

Activities

List community service, nonschool activities, and unusual and relevant travel under this heading. Include an item if it establishes your skills and experience or provides some human interest that might help your resume to stand out. Exclude general items such as watching TV, listening to music, and reading, because these hobbies don't set you apart in any way.

Evaluate the relevance of the entry to your employment goal. For example, if you want a position in travel and tourism, "Travel in South America and Europe" is relevant to include. If you want a position in a creative field, your position in a rock group and interest in composing music are relevant. If you want to work in a highly competitive field, "Marathon Runner" is relevant.

Activities

_____

_____

_____

_____

Skills

- Exclude vague statements such as "Good interpersonal skills." Instead, let your education, work experience, or activities provide evidence of good communication skills (e.g., Coursework: Voice & Diction; Work experience: Customer service; Activities: Club secretary).

- List your language and computer skills.

  Proficient in Spanish

  Fluent in Mandarin Chinese, conversant in Urdu

  Applications: Word, Excel, type 45 w.p.m.

- Add any relevant technical skills.

  Bookkeeping, C++, HTML

Skills

_____

_____

_____

_____

Not Included on a Resume

Some items are not included on a resume.

PERSONAL DATA	IRRELEVANT DATA
Your age	Street addresses of companies
Your marital status	Reasons for leaving past jobs
Your ethnicity	Names and addresses of references
Your health status	Salary requirements
Your country of origin	

TASK 2 MAKE YOUR RESUME ATTRACTIVE

Enter the information that you have assembled in Task 1 into your computer. It is now time to select the most important material and concentrate on layout.

Your resume should be one page long with one-inch margins all around. Consider two pages only if you have a great deal of relevant experience in the field in which you are searching for a position.

The following suggestions will help you place your resume on one page and make it attractive. After you input your resume, compare its layout with the samples in the preceding Overview section. You may wish to look at other resume-writing guides to get ideas on how to lay out your resume on one page.

1. Highlight your name in the heading by typing it in bold, capital letters or by centering it.

2. Use bold and capitalize the major headings, such as **EDUCATION** and **EXPERIENCE.**

3. Use fonts, italics, capitalization, or underlining to highlight important information. Do not use script or italic type too often, because they are more difficult to read and are seen as less businesslike than roman type.

4. Avoid abbreviations such as "intro" for "introduction" and "psych" for "psychology."

5. Avoid end-of-line hyphenation, because it does not look neat and takes longer to read.

6. The most important consideration in your layout is consistency of presentation. Whatever format you use for your job descriptions, be consistent and use the same format for all the entries.

7. Print on high-quality white bond paper, using a laser-quality printer.

Suggestions for lengthening your resume:

- If you have very little experience, add the **Objective** section.
- List your high school in the Education section.
- Triple space between sections.
- Use formats with vertical lists like those in the sample resume of Alicia Carreras.

Suggestions for shortening your resume:

- Cut job descriptions to the most important items. You may have to eliminate some descriptions of past jobs that are irrelevant.
- Use horizontal lists for job descriptions like those in the sample resume of Allison Smith.

- Reduce the spacing between sections.
- Avoid making the font too small in order to fit your resume onto one page, as that makes it difficult to read. It is usually better to omit irrelevant information.

TASK 3 GET FEEDBACK FROM OTHERS, REVISE, AND POLISH

The contents and the appearance of your resume must work together to show off your qualifications. Ask for feedback from your professors, friends, family, fellow students, and coworkers. Then revise and polish your resume.

Save your basic resume on a disk. Add items as you gain experience or obtain further education. Make a disk copy and tailor your basic resume for specific positions as the need arises.

Use the following guidelines to check the quality of your resume. You should be able to put a check mark in each box.

Resume Checklist

☐ There are NO errors of fact, spelling, or grammar.

☐ The layout is consistent throughout. All job descriptions are presented in the same format.

☐ Your resume is an effective presentation of your skills and interests related to the type of position that you want.

☐ Other people have no further suggestions for revision.

☐ You have a sense of pride in the presentation.

CHAPTER 10

Making a Job Choice

You never get a second
chance to make a first
impression.
—Unknown

INTERVIEW PREPARATION

Getting a job offer is tough. Added to that stress is the pressure of deciding "Is this job right for me?" Beginning a new job has some pitfalls, too. How can you avoid costly early career mistakes? This chapter takes on these issues. It covers interview etiquette, evaluating a job offer, and getting started on the right foot. It begins with the interview.

The process of meeting with prospective employers varies widely. Sometimes you will have several interviews before an organization makes a decision, and other times you will be offered a position in your first interview. You may begin the process with a quick screening interview. This screening can take place over the telephone, with an on-campus interviewer, or even on videotape. If you do well, you will be invited for a more in-depth second interview. Often you are asked to return again to meet with higher-ups before they make a decision about whether to extend a job offer.

Interview formats differ, too. You may be placed in a group and questioned along with other candidates. You may face a panel of interviewers all alone. Sometimes you are asked to share a meal with company representatives or to meet in unconventional places such as an airport or a hotel lobby. Of course, there is the traditional format, a one-on-one encounter at the job site.

Wherever and however you are interviewed, you need to be prepared. It's during the interview that you really persuade the employer to extend a job offer.

The job interview is also a special opportunity for you to learn the particulars: What would your responsibilities be? Who would be your boss? What is the physical environment like? What are the possibilities for advancement? You have many specifics to uncover.

Research the Organization

Begin your preparation by searching for information about the organization. If an interview comes up at the last minute, at the very least, check out their Internet Web page. You'll feel more secure during the interview because you won't be scrambling to understand what the organization does. It will be easier to grasp the additional information the interviewer provides. You'll learn more details about the job.

Research may give you a competitive edge over other candidates. Your effort shows the interviewer that you care enough about this job to do some detective work. It also demonstrates that you know how to prepare for challenges by doing your homework.

Research takes some of the sweat out of the interview. When you are knowledgeable about the organization's products or services and aware of its challenges, you are better positioned to convince the interviewer that you are the best candidate.

Your own research empowers you to make an independent judgment about the organization. The information an interviewer provides is biased, naturally, because she or he will emphasize the positive. It's up to you to get the full picture. Organizations of all sizes and descriptions can have fatal flaws: an unfavorable reputation, out-of-date technology, smarter competitors.

A cautionary note is in order. Searching for detailed information about an organization can be a bit frustrating. Unlike the wealth of information that is readily available for a college profile, data on some aspects of an organization may be unavailable. This is especially true when a company is privately owned and relatively small.

The easiest way to gather information about an organization is to visit its Web page. It will tell you about the product(s) the company makes or the service(s) it provides. You will typically find information about its mission and values. If it is a public company that issues stock, you can also get information about its financial performance. The organization's Web page, like a college's home page, is always positive and accentuates its best features.

Talking with someone who works for the organization, or reading recent newspaper or magazine articles about the organization may provide a more balanced picture. You will find detailed guidelines for gathering information about an organization, with appropriate questions for profit-oriented companies, nonprofit institutions, and government agencies, in Activity 10.2.

Have a Dress Rehearsal

The interview ritual is uncomfortable. It requires you to talk about yourself to a stranger, stressing one favorable point after another. It's not every day that you are asked "What are your greatest strengths?" and "Why do you think you would be successful in this position?" Answers to such questions don't just roll off the tongue. Rehearsal sessions before the interview will help you to deliver winning answers. A good performance is imperative. Your ability to handle a job will be judged by how well you do during the interview.

Interview questions are usually open-ended. For example, the most frequently asked interview question is "Tell me about yourself." This type of question cannot be answered with a "Yes" or "No." Open-ended questions unnerve many candidates because they don't know where to begin or what to include. Some unprepared candidates are so nervous that they say too little; others talk on and on. Enlightened candidates have already formulated their answer before the interview. They will also have practiced its delivery aloud.

Activity 10.3, Interview Preparation, is dedicated to getting you ready to perform well in an interview. It familiarizes you with standard topics and recommends ways to respond. It provides guidelines for distinguishing between legal and illegal questions. Also included is a list of questions to guide your search for details about the position.

Some students who have held many jobs are puzzled by this discussion. They have never encountered a question like "What is your most rewarding college experience?" Nor has an interviewer ever asked "What would your references say about you?" The reason you will get these questions now is that the positions you seek as a college graduate entail more responsibility. Your competition is stiffer. The employer is choosier.

There are several pointers to keep in mind while answering. You will find them in Table 10.1. They underscore the need to be upbeat about your qualifications, focusing on how your skills and experience are relevant to the requirements of the job.

TABLE 10.1	
Interview response guidelines.	Be positive. Highlight your qualifications.
	Be specific. Give examples of your strong points.
	Show an interest in the job and organization.
	Never complain about former employers and coworkers.

INTERVIEW ETIQUETTE

Dress the Part

Dress professionally for your interview. Know the standards in the industry and, if possible, for the company. Dress more conservatively than you might dress for work in that organization. You may need to purchase an appropriate interview outfit when your job search heats up. Anticipate the need to put some money aside for this purpose.

Bring the Necessary Information

Bring the information and materials listed in Table 10.2 to the interview. Many people obtain a standard job application form and fill it out to ensure that they have essential data. Some interviewees are in constant readiness for interviews because they have created a career portfolio that includes copies of degrees, transcripts and relevant course syllabi, a philosophy of work or a mission statement, samples of past work, copies of awards and other forms of recognition, and copies of recommendation letters and notes of appreciation. They select items from their portfolio that demonstrate relevant knowledge, skills, and experience to bring to the interview.[1]

Allow extra travel time beyond what the interviewer estimates. Even when you arrive at the location, sometimes it is difficult to find the right floor and office. You can waste time wandering in the wrong direction. Some people make a practice run before the interview to get to know the route and to time the trip. Arriving early allows you time to compose yourself.

TABLE 10.2

Your interview kit.

The name, title, and phone number of the interviewer: You may need to clarify the directions en route. You can also become familiar with the interviewer's name in advance.

Directions: You'll need a complete organization address and some suggestions on the best route to travel from your home. If you did not get them when the interview was set up, a secretary or receptionist will provide them. Another strategy to obtain directions is to use a map program on the Web, such as mapquest.com. A good road map may also be helpful if you are driving.

Your company research notes

Two or three copies of your resume: There may be more than one person interviewing you. The interviewer may have misplaced his or her copy of your resume.

Job application information:

Social Security number

Employment history: Names, addresses, and phone numbers of current and former employers; supervisors' names and titles; dates of employment.

Education history: Names and addresses of educational institutions from high school on; dates of attendance. If you have a GED, you need to have the month and year it was awarded.

Military history: If applicable.

Your typed reference list: This separate list consists of the names, titles, business addresses, phone and fax numbers, and E-mail addresses of the people that you plan to use as references.

Paper and erasable ballpoint pen: You may want to take notes or need to fill out a job application.

CASE 10.1   *"I Ran into Traffic"*

An interview tale from our college internship program illustrates how important being on time is to an employer. One of our international students—let's call him Subryan—was after a coveted, paid bank internship. He was highly competent and rightly confident that he would get the job.

The internship coordinator got a call from the company. "We didn't interview him. He showed up late." This bank takes no excuses and makes no exceptions. This policy is extreme, and the bank loses a few qualified candidates like Subryan, but they're not worried. Plenty of excellent students clamor for their jobs.

The bank executives reason that if you can't manage to get to an interview on time, allowing for mishaps, your planning skills are not up to their standard. It was a painful lesson, but it's not a mistake that Subryan will make twice.

If you arrive very early and are certain you have located the correct office, wait until five or ten minutes before your scheduled appointment before you go in. Spend the time in the waiting room looking at any company material or reviewing your research notes. Arriving too early can exert subtle pressure on the interviewer that he or she may resent. The interviewer may be running late, so waiting is not unusual. Allow plenty of time for your interview and be courteous to everyone you meet.

Send a Thank-You Note

After the interview, no matter whether you want the job or not, write a brief note. Thank the interviewer for the opportunity to meet with him or her. If you want the job, express your interest in it. Remind the interviewer of your strengths for it. (See Figure 10.1.)

DEALING WITH CIRCUMSTANCES OUT OF YOUR CONTROL

You may run up against interview situations you are powerless to change. The interviewer could have a bad day and take it out on you. The job might go to the boss's brother-in-law, even if you are more qualified. Whether there are many openings or only a few depends on the job market and the state of the economy.

Many people react strongly to this lack of total control. Some become increasingly passive. Some can't get moving because they are panicked. Still others complain bitterly. All these negative emotions demoralize their spirit, and their job search activities decrease day by day.

In truth, the more difficult the conditions are, the greater the number of actions you need to take. The focus of your attention must steadfastly remain on the elements that *are* in your control: producing a resume, mastering interviewing skills, and searching out job leads with diligence. These actions do make the difference between successful and unsuccessful job candidates, especially in a poor job market.

Catlin Ryan
15 Spring Road
Hamlet, LA 41112
555-555-5555
C_Ryan@somewhere.com

August 25, 200X

Ms. Susan Carson
Director of Child Development
Hamlet Child Development Center
Hamlet, LS 41112

Dear Ms. Carson:

Thank you for the opportunity to interview with you yesterday afternoon. I am very interested in the child-care position you described.

My child development classes, college internships, and recent volunteer work as a storybook reader at the community center have prepared me well for a preschool teaching position. I am especially interested in the field trip program you mentioned. I would welcome the opportunity to contribute to that effort.

I enjoyed meeting you and your staff and look forward to hearing from you soon. If I can provide any additional information, please call me at (555) 555-555. Thank you again for your time and consideration.

Sincerely,

Catlin Ryan

Catlin Ryan

Include the person's title

Thank the interviewer

Mention the position you were interviewed for

Highlight your qualifications

REMINDER

Ask somene to proofread the letter before you send it.

Send within two days of the interview.

E-mail only if you have been exchanging E-mail prior to the interview.

Use solid white, off-white, or gray stationery.

Express interest in the job

Place your phone number near the end

Sign your first and last name

Source: Adapted from Olivia Crosby, "Employment Interviewing: Seizing the Opportunity and the Job," *Occupational Outlook Quarterly*, No. 2 (Summer 2000): 2.

COPING WITH REJECTION

Another unpleasant reality of job interviews is that rejection is a common experience. This prospect unsettles most people. Our self-esteem is threatened when we try our best, only to be turned down.

When this happens, stand back and analyze the reasons why you didn't get the job. Do you need to redirect your job search toward more promising targets? Should you polish your interviewing skills further? Was there a poor fit between you and the organization? Were you a victim of events out of your control? If there is something that you can fix, get on with it. If not, give yourself a pep talk or seek out a supportive friend to cheer you up, and then continue looking.

Remember, if you turn down a job offer, do it graciously. Organizations don't like to be rejected either. You want to leave the door open in case you decide to reapply one day.

THE JOB OFFER

Sometimes a condition of employment is that the new employee must test negatively for drugs. Drug tests are required most frequently in large companies or for jobs that require the handling of dangerous materials.

Drug Tests[2]

The drug test is generally used to detect the presence of amphetamines (speed), opiates (heroin, codeine, morphine), phencyclidines (PCP or angel dust), cocaine (including crack), and cannabis (marijuana and hashish). Marijuana is the most frequently found substance in drug tests; it can stay in your system for several weeks.

Prior to the test, you will be asked to complete a form that asks about medications that you are taking. To be on the safe side, list all medications you have taken within the past few weeks. This includes over-the-counter medications, such as aspirin, cold medications, and vitamins, as well as prescription drugs. Bring a list of these medications to the drug test. In addition, some cautious people advise you to drink plenty of fluids before testing and to avoid drinking gin or eating food containing poppy seeds.

Most drug tests require that you provide a urine sample. Be sure that the sample is labeled correctly and completely with your name and phone number.

Drug tests are not perfect. Mistakes, called *false positives*, can identify someone as a user of illegal substances. If you have tested positive and you believe the results are wrong, ask to have an additional test of another type. Most companies are aware that drug-testing labs can make errors. Often they will automatically follow up any positive result with a more thorough test to verify that it is correct.

Salary Negotiations

Salary negotiation is one aspect of the interview process that fascinates and terrifies most people. Timing is key. Until a formal job offer is made, avoid talking about salary. Don't bring it up in an interview. Once you have a firm offer, observe the three R rules given next. They will help you to negotiate the best offer.

The Research Rule

Begin by finding out the typical pay for the position. This is the only way to negotiate realistically. It is easier than you think to find out about salaries offered to college graduates.

Your college's placement office is a good place to start. They know the typical starting salaries for students in different disciplines. Check out the job postings in your field. You will also find magazines for college job seekers. Look for the *Job Choices* series or the *Black Collegian*, magazines that publish salary data and are given to students at no cost.

You can research salaries in fields that interest you on the Internet, too. Table 10.3 provides a list of sites where you can locate salary data.

The *American Almanac of Jobs and Salaries* provides a variety of entry-level salary figures for various jobs in easy-to-find form. Another good source is the *Occupational Outlook Handbook*. This government reference is found in book form and on-line (see Table 10.3). Its salary data are updated every two years.

Use entry-level data. Average or median salaries lump experienced and inexperienced workers together, making the dollar figures too high to be of use. If you are offered health insurance, paid vacation time, and other benefits, keep in mind that the typical benefit package is worth an additional 20 to 30 percent above the salary base.

Adjust your figures on the basis of your location. Urban pay scales are usually higher than rural ones. Most Internet salary sites have "salary wizards" that provide salary data by job title and geographic location. You can compare salaries for the same job title in different locations, too. This feature is especially helpful if you are planning to relocate after graduation.

If you are using published data several years old, adjust the salary figure for inflation. For each additional year since the data were issued, you can reasonably add 5 percent.

You must also create a budget to see how much money you will need to survive. Without an idea of your living expenses, you won't be able to gauge the adequacy of a salary offer.

The Range Rule

When asked what salary you have in mind, never name just one amount, but instead give a salary range. The range is two figures. The low figure reflects the bottom end of what you will accept, while the top figure represents your ideal salary.

Make sure that the range that you give is supported by your research. If the employer's range is fair, be prepared to give the reasons why you deserve a salary at the high end of his range.

The Respect Rule

Always conduct your salary negotiations in a respectful, friendly tone. You don't want to provoke a confrontation or threaten the interviewer. If the salary offered is nonnegotiable, other items to consider include a salary review in two to four months, a change in the start date, reimbursement for relocation expenses, or other benefit items.

Respect your own skills and qualities, too. Ask for an offer letter confirming the job responsibilities, the location, the pay, and the start date in writing. Request a few days to think over the offer. It will give you time to weigh its advantages and disadvantages. That's what we'll turn to next: how to analyze the job offer.

TABLE 10.3	
Salary data on the Internet.	**CareerJournal: www.careerjournal.com** The *Wall Street Journal* site provides salary information for a wide variety of occupations, especially in business. **JobStar California: www.jobstar.org/tools/salary/sal-surv.htm** This California Public Library site is the most frequently cited for the best links to salary surveys. **JobWeb: www.jobweb.com** The National Association of Colleges and Employers publishes the results of its quarterly survey of starting salaries for four-year college graduates by college major. **Occupational Outlook Handbook: http://stats.bls.gov/ocohome.htm** The Department of Labor updates its salary information every two years. Look in the Rewards and Benefits section for the occupations that interest you. **The Riley Guide: www.dbm.com/jobguide/salguides.htm** This reliable mega-site has links to U. S. Government wage surveys and general salary surveys, and covers related topics, such as evaluating salary data and devising negotiation strategies. **Salary.com: www.salary.com** This site boasts an easy-to-use salary wizard that allows you to get salary data relevant to specific geographic locations. **WorkingWoman.com: www.wwn.com** *Working Woman* magazine publishes an annual salary survey. It discusses salary issues relevant to women. **Note:** Web sites are frequently reorganized. You may experience difficulties using the exact Web address for some of the sites listed above. As an alternative, do a key word search to locate the site (e.g., The Riley Guide, JobStar) and then drill down into the site for the salary information.

ASSESSMENT OF CAREER POTENTIAL

Before you decide whether to accept a particular job offer, you need to examine its long-term effects on your career. You need to take a hard look at whether the position is likely to provide a solid platform of experience and skills from which to launch further career moves. You can't assume, for example, that the bigger the company, the better the job will be.[3] The career advantages and disadvantages of positions in large and small companies will be considered first.

You also need to be aware of the telltale signs of a dead-end job. A full assessment of a position's career potential will help you make a wiser choice. You'll learn the best questions to ask before you say "Yes" to a job offer.

A Large Company or a Small One?

Formerly, a large corporation was the best guarantee of a secure and well-paid future, but global competition and downsizing have changed all that. Today, excellent opportunities can be found in companies of all sizes. In fact, fewer than 13 percent of Americans are employed by companies with more than a thousand employees.[4]

Nevertheless, many college students still equate career opportunities with companies that have household, brand-name recognition. In reality, most jobs are in small and midsize companies.

If you went to a large school, you may know how hard it is to stand out, form personal relationships with key professors, or be selected for special opportunities. It's the same story working for a large company. It is easy to get overlooked and undervalued. In a small company, the atmosphere is informal, your work is noticed by top management, and the pace is fast.[5]

The best part of working for a small company is the opportunity to gain experience quickly. You are often assigned to important projects early. Career exploration is easier, too, because job descriptions are less rigid. You may find your niche by getting to try types of work you hadn't considered or even known about in college.

There are downsides to working for small companies. They are often understaffed. You need to be versatile and willing to pitch in when the crunch comes. One trade-off for that invaluable job experience is a lower salary. Salary offers are often 10 to 20 percent less than from large companies, and benefits such as relocation expenses or company day-care facilities are fewer.

The choice of a company to work for must be made with care. Think about companies as "elephants," "gazelles," or "mice."[6] Elephants are the huge and slow-growing companies, offering some opportunities. Mice are the millions of mom-and-pop businesses that will remain small and offer limited opportunities for advancement to outsiders. Target the gazelles, the vibrant, growing companies that are typically small or midsize. As the company grows, your job responsibilities and financial rewards are likely to grow, too. If your company goes public, you may share in the wealth. The Microsoft millionaires are legendary examples of this phenomenon.

You have to dig a bit to find the gazelles. They do not usually recruit on campus. There are several ways you can identify fast-growing, successful businesses. Read magazines such as *Fast Company* or consult annual listings of fast-growing, successful companies such as *Inc.* magazine's *500* or *Forbes's* "200 Best Small Companies in America."

Avoiding Dead-End Jobs

You get an education so that you will not wind up in a dead-end position. Yet, in a major study of college students one year after graduation, one in four students believed that they were in this predicament.[7] How can you avoid this fate?

The job's career potential is a very important factor to consider in any job offer. You'll want to make sure that you are on a career path that leads to more challenge, responsibility, rewards, and satisfaction in the future.

The practical questions in Table 10.4 have a much broader focus than mere promotion. You'll see that they address the prospects for learning new skills and gaining important knowledge. They help you evaluate whether you

TABLE 10.4

Questions to ask yourself about a job's career potential.

What kind of training will I receive? Are there established training programs? Does this position allow me to learn from the best people in the field?

Will I have a variety of challenging assignments? (For more on the importance of challenging assignments, see Chapter 12.)

What opportunities will I have to work with more senior people?

What opportunities will I have to network with people in other fields within the organization?

How much exposure will I have to clients? To professionals in other organizations?

With the knowledge and skills that I gain in this position, can I move among profit-oriented, government, and nonprofit work settings? Move among industries? Move among companies? Start my own business someday?

Will this position increase and improve my portable skills?

Will this position help me achieve my career goals?

will be able to transfer your experience to other settings. These issues are crucial in today's job world, where your advancement is linked more to what you can do than to where you have worked.

In making this assessment, you are also considering the degree of correspondence between this experience and the goals that you have set for yourself. You are contemplating the job's effect on your career direction.

Once you have analyzed a job offer for its potential and made your decision, accept or reject it in writing. If you are accepting a verbal offer, your letter should outline your understanding of the terms of employment, including the position title, start date, salary, benefits, and any agreements about reviews or promotions. If you decline, be sure to affirm your appreciation of the offer. Also be sure to let your references and other contacts know that you have found a position and thank them again for their help.

TAKE CHARGE OF YOUR OWN JOB ORIENTATION

Starting a new job or an internship means plunging into a new environment. What makes your transition more difficult is that few organizations do an excellent job of orientation and training. You may be the sole newcomer in the unit. The group may be busy and assume that you'll just catch on. The worst thing that you can do is to take a passive, waiting attitude. Unless the company has a formal training program, it is up to you to take charge of getting your own job orientation.

Most important, schedule at least one meeting with your boss to discuss his or her expectations of you. Trust is essential before you will be allowed to make a significant contribution and have your ideas accepted. The relationship with your boss is key. You must learn to support your boss. When you help your boss succeed, you succeed. You must strike a balance between pestering your boss and getting the information and resources that you need to complete your work. You must understand all you can about his or her goals and priorities. You must also prove that you are dependable and honest. Bosses don't like surprises. They don't want to learn about your problems or your ideas for making improvements from other people first.

Make sure you understand your job responsibilities. Learn all you can about the organization and its policies. Ask for an organizational chart; if there is none, scan the company phone book. Read the available manuals and company publications. Ask questions.

Gradually extend your knowledge of the organization beyond your job description and your department. Your general fund of knowledge and broader understanding are useful in seeing the big picture and in solving problems, so they add value to an enterprise. They also make you a more valued employee.

Broaden your knowledge of what your organization's strategy is, how it is designed to accomplish its mission, and how well it is doing. This is the kind of knowledge that you might seek if you were thinking of career advancement in this organization. Employ this tactic, even if you are only on a part-time exploratory internship. By doing this, you not only add to your knowledge, but you also sharpen your research skills.

Keep the list of relevant questions from Activity 10.2, the Organization Profile, at your desk or workstation. At first, review them each week and, as time goes on, each month. See how much you can increase your knowledge about these topics.

As part of your self-directed orientation program, learn the names and titles of coworkers. Find out what they are responsible for. Over time, notice who has power in various areas.

If you were introduced briefly during the interview or on the first day, you may have to repeat your introduction to your coworkers. Let them know your job title and identify your boss.

Get to know your coworkers in informal settings, too. Sharing lunch or coffee breaks is a good icebreaker. Take advantage of opportunities to join athletic teams, participate in charity fund-raising activities, attend a holiday party, or go on company picnics or outings. These social events cement working relationships.

Your main purpose is to establish smooth working relationships. Be sure to behave with proper dignity. You cannot let your hair down as if you were with old friends and family. Eventually, most people do develop lasting friendships at work. Allow some time for this to happen.

Polish your group skills, too. In school, individual achievement counts. In the workplace you are expected to be a team player. Many organizational tasks are accomplished in groups. Almost every complex endeavor—such as health care delivery, customer service, or software development—requires the coordinated efforts of many people. Establishing relationships at work is so important for your career success that Chapter 13 is devoted to this topic.

WHERE STUDENTS GET STUCK, AND WHAT TO DO IF IT HAPPENS TO YOU

From ages 18 to 30, the average person changes jobs more than seven times. Only 20 percent have three jobs or fewer during those years. Although college-educated workers have more stable job patterns than less educated employees, job change is not unexpected. People make mistakes and test their choices in real life.[8]

Failure to use a balanced decision-making style is a common mistake. Six months into her first job, Christine E-mailed her former college roommate: "I'm so bored by my job. I don't really fit in. Everyone else here likes minute details, but I just want a job with more contact with other people. But where else can I get this salary? I have to make the payments on my new car and condo." At about the same time Ron was E-mailing his fraternity brother: "I can't really make it on my salary. The industry is in a big downturn. There won't be any salary increases for a while, especially since we lost the big contract with the government. I don't know whether I should stick it out or what."

Both Christine and Ron have gotten stuck. Christine didn't listen to her heart. The big salary lured her into work that didn't fit her personality. To make matters worse, she had made expensive purchases right away. A better strategy would have been to wait before making financial commitments that would make it hard for her to leave her job. Ron was so impressed by his boss in the interview that he overlooked practical factors such as the economic condition of the company and the industry. He is having difficulty coming to grips with the realization that he is on the brink of getting laid off. Both need to reinstitute a job search.

As you recall from Chapter 6, the balanced decision-making style involves listening to your heart and using your head in making your career decisions.

TABLE 10.5	**Fit with Your Personality, Values, and Interests**
Listening to your heart.	In listening to your heart, you are considering your feelings. You are looking at whether the organization and its people are compatible with your personality, values, and interests.

- What would I do every day? Am I attracted to the job tasks?
- What does the organization stand for? How does it treat its employees? Do its values fit mine?
- What kind of people would I work with (e.g., Holland or Campbell type)? As I look at their goals, ethics, expertise, and lifestyle, would I be proud to associate with them?
- What is the supervisory style of my boss?
- What is the general quality of management?
- How much interaction and what kind of interaction is there among coworkers (e.g., meetings, lots of phone calls, memos, E-mail)?
- What is the predominant interpersonal style (e.g., formal, structured, and hierarchical; casual, friendly, and supportive; competitive)?
- What are the working conditions (e.g., office space, location, furnishings and equipment, dress code)?
- How would I spend my time (e.g., typical working hours per week, deadline and seasonal pressures, travel requirements, flextime and telecommuting options)?
- Where is the position located and how does it fit with my lifestyle and commute?

Economic Rewards and Financial Security	TABLE 10.6
In using your head, you analyze the job offer in terms of your financial requirements. You also assess the economic health of the organization.	*Using your head.*

- What are the salary and benefits? Are they enough to live on?
- What kind of salary increases can I expect with a good performance?
- What is the financial soundness of the organization and, if relevant, the industry (e.g., healthy, growing, competitive, shaky)?
- What is the outlook for this organization?

You have become accustomed to analyzing any career options in these terms. Tables 10.5 and 10.6 provide you with detailed lists of questions to ask yourself as you ponder a job offer. These questions are much more extensive than those in Step 3 of Activity 10.2, the Organizational Profile, where your goal is a more general look-see.

Making Trade-Offs: It's Not Always Easy to Decide

No job offer is perfect. You must make trade-offs, giving up some things that you want in order to obtain other things. As you read Case 10.2, put yourself in Hallie's shoes.

Hallie's Job Offer Dilemma — CASE 10.2

Hallie, 24, a women's studies major, was determined to get a social service position helping women. She also wanted to leave her parents' home and live on her own. First, she researched the salaries for entry-level social service positions for applicants who had a bachelor's degree. In her area, the salary range for such jobs was between $25,600 and $34,900. Second, she prepared a personal budget for the expenses of living on her own and concluded that she needed to earn at least $28,000 to $29,000. This gave her two vital pieces of information: She knew her projected living expenses and the salary range for entry-level counseling positions.

Hallie was offered a job in an agency that worked with victims of domestic abuse. She would make $27,800 with excellent benefits. However, the commuting costs were very high, $2000 per year. She had not included high commuting costs in her budget. In addition, the commute took two hours a day. During the interview she learned that the agency was in the midst of a reorganization and was becoming more cost conscious.

On the plus side, when Hallie met the woman who would supervise her, she felt an immediate rapport. The supervisor told her about the extensive training program, an aspect of the job that Hallie found attractive.

One option was to take the job with the admired agency and live at home. The other was to keep looking for a position that would enable her to reach both of her goals. Should Hallie take this job?

ACTIVITY 10.1   HALLIE'S OFFER: WOULD YOU ADVISE HER TO ACCEPT?

List the advantages of the offer.

1. _____

2. _____

3. _____

List the disadvantages of the offer.

1. _____

2. _____

3. _____

What would you advise?

_____

_____

_____

It is a difficult call, and reasonable people could disagree over the decision. Hallie took the job, despite the disadvantages, because she felt that the experience was just what she was looking for. Unfortunately for Hallie, during the reorganization her supervisor was promoted and the training program was cut. Eventually, the negatives began to weigh more heavily with her. Within a year she was thinking about going to graduate school.

Hallie's story illustrates both the difficulties of making trade-offs and the unknown elements about a job that inevitably emerge once you have accepted a position. The fact that the future is unknown doesn't make the analysis any less worthwhile. Ron and Christine might have chosen more wisely if they had been more thoughtful up front.

The understanding and the skills that you gain from this chapter will be valuable for as long as you work. If you grow dissatisfied with your position, you'll need job search skills to find a better one. Moreover, external forces, like those affecting Ron's situation, may push you back into the job market. The next chapter addresses the larger trends in the workplace and helps you examine the different kinds of paths your career might follow.

KEY POINTS

1. Search for information about the organization before your interview. You'll feel more secure, and this will enable you to perform better. It will impress the interviewer, too, giving you a competitive edge.

2. To cope with interview pressure, rehearse beforehand. Be upbeat about your qualifications, focusing on the relevance of your skills and experience to the requirements of the job.

3. Good interview etiquette includes dressing appropriately and having immaculate grooming, bringing relevant data to the interview, arriving early, and sending a thank-you note afterward.

4. Circumstances out of your control, such as a poor job market, affect your job search. The psychological challenge involves overcoming rejection, a normal part of the process. Be analytical about any improvements that you might make to your job search skills. Be philosophical about events that are out of your control. Stay action oriented, redoubling your efforts in the face of difficulties.

5. Your job offer may require that you test negative for illegal drugs.

6. Always negotiate your salary *after* you receive a firm job offer. Better negotiators follow three rules:

   a. Before you begin to negotiate, research the typical salary range for the type of responsibilities that you would be undertaking.

   b. When asked, give a salary range, never just one amount.

   c. Carry on your negotiations in a respectful, courteous tone.

7. Large companies generally offer greater prestige, more structured orientation and training programs, higher salaries, and better benefit programs than smaller organizations. The downside is that you are a little fish in a big pond. Your responsibilities may be limited. The climate is frequently bureaucratic and formal.

8. Small companies generally are faster paced and more informal and give you a shot at significant responsibility earlier in your career. You have contact and visibility with senior people. If you succeed, your job responsibilities will grow as the organization grows.

9. Getting off on the right foot means taking the initiative for your own orientation and training. Form smooth working relationships with your boss and colleagues. Learn all you can about the organization.

10. Students make poor decisions about job offers if they fail to listen to their hearts or to use their heads in a balanced way.

11. No job offer is perfect. You will have to weigh the trade-offs. After you take the job, conditions can change in a way that leads you to decide to look for a new position. Remember that, in the beginning of a career, job change is more frequent.

ORGANIZATION PROFILE   ACTIVITY **10.2**

OVERVIEW

In this activity your main purpose is to *gather information* about an organization. Select a profit-oriented company, a nonprofit institution, or a federal, state, or local government agency. You will find questions in three categories to guide your research: (1) nature of the organization, (2) career opportunities, and (3) outlook for the future.

You can use this profile in several ways:

- To evaluate an organization's attractiveness as an employer
- To uncover employment opportunities and job leads
- To prepare for a job interview
- To decide whether to accept an employment offer

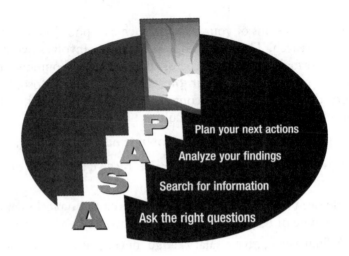

If you need more room, or if you are instructed to do so, type your answers separately.

STEP 1 ASK THE RIGHT QUESTIONS

Step 1.1 Selecting an Organization

Your first task is to select an organization and identify whether it is a profit-oriented, a nonprofit, or a government organization. If relevant, you may even select specific types of positions to research within one of these organizations. For example, you may decide to research teaching positions in a local school district or accounting positions in a specific profit-oriented company.

Give the name of the organization and identify whether it is a profit-oriented company, a nonprofit institution, or a government agency.

_____

_____

Step 1.2 Selection of Questions

The questions that you ask depend on the kind of organization that you selected. The following questions will guide your research of a profit-oriented company. The set of questions for a government agency and for a nonprofit institution are found at the end of the activity. Use the appropriate question set for the kind of organization that you have chosen to profile. Once you select your questions, go on to Step 1.3.

PROFIT-ORIENTED COMPANY PROFILE QUESTIONS

Some questions have explanations to clarify their significance for a company profile.

A. NATURE OF THE COMPANY

1. Describe the company.
   Brief history
   Industry membership
   Ownership (e.g., public, private, employee-owned, foreign-owned, or American-owned)
   Geographic scope (i.e., local, regional, national, or international)
   Headquarters location
   Number of employees

2. What are the product(s) and/or service(s) of this company? If the company is multi-industry or multibusiness, you may want to concentrate your research on just one industry, business, division, or subsidiary.

3. Describe this company's customers (e.g., other businesses, consumers, or both).

4. Who are the major competitors?

5. If you visit the company, pay attention to visual cues, such as size and style of offices, to obtain data on the working conditions and atmosphere. Describe the facilities. Are they safe, pleasant, attractive, and clean?

6. What is the dress code for employees in your area (e.g., formal, casual, uniforms)?

7. What kind of working hours are typical for someone in your area?

8. Does the company have policies and benefits that would make your life better or easier (e.g., day-care facilities, flextime, telecommuting)?

B. CAREER OPPORTUNITIES

9. What kind of background (i.e., education and experience) is preferred for the positions that you are interested in?

10. Are there opportunities for advancement? Does the company prefer to promote from within or hire from the outside?

11. How do the pay and benefits compare with those of other companies in this industry?

12. Identify other kinds of rewards: bonuses, profit sharing, stock options, tuition reimbursement, and the like.

13. What are the signs that this company might be a great place to work?

14. What is the hiring process?

C. OUTLOOK FOR THE FUTURE

15. What is the future outlook for this company?

16. How would you describe the financial soundness of this company?

    Financial health questions are often difficult to answer unless you have a business background. Consider this section optional unless your instructor asks you tackle this topic in your research.

    Listed next are a number of ways to assess the financial health of a company. A pattern of increases typically indicates economic growth and health, while a pattern of decreases indicates a shrinking company and economic decline.

    Several indicators should be used to assess economic health.

- Sales and sales trends over the past five to ten years
- Revenues and revenue trends over the past five to ten years
- New products and services introduced in the past five years
- Employee hiring or downsizing in the past five years
- Expansion or closing of facilities (e.g., plants, stores)
- Mergers, joint ventures, and acquisitions that increase or decrease the ability to compete
- Beating competitors or losing to competitors

- Rankings by *Fortune* or *Forbes* as leaders or losers
- Favorable or unfavorable articles in the press
- Stock prices (for companies whose stock trades publicly)

Step 1.3   Interview Questions

No matter what type of organization you selected, if you are able to interview a current employee, use these optional questions.

FIRSTHAND KNOWLEDGE OF THE ORGANIZATION FROM SOMEONE WHO WORKS THERE

1. How did you go about getting your position?
2. What is the best thing about your position? What is the worst thing?
3. What surprised you about working in this position?
4. What advice would you give me about seeking a position?
5. If you were starting over, would you go into this field? Why or why not?

Step 1.4   Your Personal Concerns

Write down any additional questions related to your specific career dilemma or career concerns.

_____

_____

_____

Step 1.5   Sources of Information

Some possibilities are as follows:

- Checking the organization's Web page.
- Finding company profiles on the Internet by doing a key word search. The following sites specialize in organizational information. Some sites, such as Hoover's Online, offer both free information and fee-based information on a subscription basis. Often college libraries subscribe to this kind of database so you won't have to pay. Otherwise, use the free information.

    Action Without Borders: www.idealist.org (nonprofit organizations)

    Lycos Companies Online: www.companiesonline.com

    JobWeb: www.jobweb.com (employer search)

    Hoover's Online: www.hoovers.com

    The Riley Guide: www.dbm.com/jobguide/employer.html

    WetFeet.com: www.wetfeet.com

    Vault: www.vault.com

- Doing an electronic database search, searching local and national newspaper and magazine articles published within the past two years. Ask your librarian to help you. Often these articles can be E-mailed to you.

    Some popular electronic databases are:

    InfoTrac: Business and Company Resource Center

    Dialog@CARL: Business and Industry; Company Information

Lexus–Nexus: Business

Wilson Business Abstracts

- Interviewing knowledgeable people
- Visiting the organization
- Consulting print sources, such as *Good Works: A Guide to Careers in Social Change* and *Adam's Job Bank Series (published for individual cities and states across the country)*

Cite the books, magazines, database resources, and Web sites that you consulted. If you conducted interviews, give the names (and, if appropriate, titles) of the people you talked with. Use at least two sources of information.

STEP 2   SEARCH FOR INFORMATION

Search for information from the sources that you selected and answer the questions from Step 1. Take notes on separate paper.

You can summarize the information for your organizational profile in one of two ways. You can list each question that you researched and the information that you found, or you may prefer to summarize the major points.

STEP 3   ANALYZE YOUR FINDINGS

Step 3.1   Comparison of Advantages and Disadvantages

List the advantages and disadvantages of working for this organization.

Hints and Reminders

In the Advantages column, list those specific organizational qualities (e.g., size, outlook for the future, reputation) that you like. In the Disadvantages column, list those specific qualities that you dislike.

Remember to listen to your heart.

- Identify which interests and values might be a good fit with this organization's mission and purpose (advantage) or a poor fit (disadvantage). For example, creating advertising campaigns is a good fit for someone with Creating or Artistic interests (advantage) and a poor fit for someone with Producing or Realistic interests (disadvantage). Working for a small entrepreneurial company is a good fit for someone who values "variety" and a poor fit for someone who values "security."

- If you like, admire, and feel you want to be identified with the kind of people you would work with every day, put this in the Advantages column. If you prefer not to associate with such people, put this reason in the Disadvantages column.

- Ask yourself if this organization would be a good match or a poor match for your dreams and lifestyle.

- Table 10.5, Listening to your heart, may also help you analyze the advantages and disadvantages of working for this organization.

Also remember to use your head.

- Assess whether the economic rewards you would receive in an entry-level position in this organization are adequate (advantage) or insufficient for your needs (disadvantage).

- Assess whether or not the organization seems to offer the opportunity to increase your skills.

- Assess whether or not the organization seems to offer the opportunity for advancement.

- Describe the skills and personal qualities that would be assets (advantage) or underutilized in this organization (disadvantage).

- Table 10.6, Using your head, may also help you identify the advantages and disadvantages of working for this organization.

Advantages +	Disadvantages −

Step 3.2 Tentative Decision

If you received a job offer, would you like to work for this organization? Identify the advantage(s) and disadvantage(s) that most heavily influenced your decision.

_____

_____

_____

STEP 4 PLAN YOUR NEXT ACTIONS

Step 4.1 Learning Summary

What did you learn about this organization that may help you in the future?

_____

_____

_____

Step 4.2 Next Steps

What's next?

_____

_____

_____

IF YOU SELECTED A **GOVERNMENT AGENCY** TO PROFILE, USE THE FOLLOWING QUESTIONS.

GOVERNMENT AGENCY PROFILE QUESTIONS

There are 17 questions arranged in three categories:

A. Nature of the government agency

B. Career opportunities

C. Outlook for the future

A. NATURE OF THE GOVERNMENT AGENCY

1. Describe the government unit.

    Agency scope: city, county, region, state, or national

    Location(s)

    Number of employees

2. What is its mission (e.g., provide transportation, maintain beaches, or track weather patterns)?

3. Who is served by this government unit (e.g., elementary school children, city residents, seniors, or all members of the community)?

B. CAREER OPPORTUNITIES

4. What types of entry-level jobs are available?

5. Salaries: What does an entry-level worker earn? What is the salary range of people after they have acquired some job experience? What are the top salaries?

6. What employee benefits, such as paid vacation time, sick leave, pension, and health insurance, are typical?

7. What advancement opportunities exist? What factors influence advancement?

Each government agency has its own personnel system and engages in different hiring practices. Questions 8 through 10 help you to learn about the ones used in the agency that you are researching.

8. How are openings advertised?

9. Who does the hiring? When is hiring done (e.g., at the beginning of the school year or when a new class of recruits is formed)?

10. What are the specifics of the hiring process?

    What are the degree requirements (associate's, bachelor's, master's, or other advanced degrees)?

    What examinations, if any, are required? How often are they given? How can you prepare for these examinations? What score is necessary to have a good chance of being hired?

    Are psychological tests, drug tests, or fingerprinting necessary for this position?

    Are there any physical requirements that must be met (e.g., passing a color vision test)?

11. What is the standard application form called? Where can I obtain this form?

12. What are the best ways to get selected for an interview?

13. What kind of informal hiring system will help me to learn of openings, prepare for interviews, and provide strong recommendations on my behalf?

14. What kinds of people tend to do well? What qualities are important (e.g., patience, attention to detail, ability to work under stress, or ability to negotiate)?

15. What coursework, work experience, or skills (e.g., languages) would give me a competitive advantage?

C. OUTLOOK FOR THE FUTURE

16. What is the outlook for the future?

17. Are job opportunities increasing or decreasing? What are the reasons for predicting an increase or decrease?

IF YOU SELECTED A **NONPROFIT ORGANIZATION** TO PROFILE, USE THE FOLLOWING QUESTIONS.

NONPROFIT ORGANIZATION QUESTIONS

There are 16 questions, arranged in three categories:

A. Nature of the nonprofit organization

B. Career opportunities

C. Outlook for the future

Some questions are accompanied by explanations of their significance.

A. NATURE OF THE NONPROFIT

1. Describe the organization:

   Brief history

   Geographical scope (local, regional, national, or international)

   Number of employees or number of regular volunteers

   Size of annual budget

2. What is the mission of this organization?

3. Who is served by this enterprise (e.g., AIDS patients, history buffs, a religious community, or a political group)?

4. What are its methods of operation (e.g., community organizing, lobbying, research, public education, or litigation)?

5. What are the signs that the organization is fulfilling its mission?

Questions 6 through 9 concern the working conditions.

6. If you visit the organization, pay attention to visual cues such as size and style of offices to provide data on the working conditions and atmosphere. Describe the facilities. Are they safe, clean, pleasant, and attractive?

7. What is the dress code for employees in your area (e.g., formal, casual, or uniforms)?

8. What kind of hours are typical for someone in your area?

9. Does the organization have policies and benefits that would make your life better or easier (e.g., day-care facilities, flextime, or telecommuting)?

B. CAREER OPPORTUNITIES

10. What kind of background (i.e., education and experience) is preferred for the positions that I am interested in? What kinds of people tend to do well?

11. How does this organization go about hiring (e.g., job openings often filled by former interns or volunteers)?

12. Are there opportunities for advancement?

13. How do the pay and benefits compare with those offered by other nonprofits in this area?

14. What are the signs that this organization might be a great place to work?

C. OUTLOOK FOR THE FUTURE

15. What is the outlook for the future?

16. How would you describe the financial health of this organization?

    Financial health questions are often difficult to answer unless you have a business background. Consider this section optional unless your instructor asks you tackle this topic in your research.

    Financial health is a fundamental requirement for success. If the organization does not have a solid financial base, it may have difficulty fulfilling its mission, no matter how worthwhile the cause.

Listed next are a number of ways to assess the financial health of a nonprofit. Several indicators should be used to assess economic health.

- Endowment size: Some organizations have been given substantial sums of money. They invest this money and use the investment gains to fund the organization. Check to see if the organization has an endowment and find out what size it is.

- Fund-raising goals and success in the past five years

- Methods of raising money: grants from the government or private foundations, ticket sales, book sales, sales of products (e.g., cookies, candy, or greeting cards)

- Number of paid employees

- Favorable or unfavorable articles about the organization in the press

- Percentage of the organization's money used for administrative expenses, such as salaries for executives, office space, and travel. More reputable organizations seek to keep administrative costs low.

INTERVIEW PREPARATION   ACTIVITY **10.3**

OVERVIEW

The purpose of this activity is to prepare you for job interviews. You will be introduced to standard interview questions and learn how to frame an effective response. A general guideline to distinguish legal and illegal questions is provided, along with some options for dealing with inappropriate questions. A job candidate's list of questions for the interviewer will sort through various issues that you will want to clarify during the interview. The activity ends with practice tips and advice.

STANDARD INTERVIEW QUESTIONS

This activity provides 35 typical interview questions. Similar questions are grouped together and pointers are given on how to approach these types of questions.

THE MOST FREQUENTLY ASKED QUESTION: "TELL ME ABOUT YOURSELF."

1. Many interviews begin with this open-ended question. It is your opportunity to convince the employer that you have the skills and interests to succeed in the job.

Points to Consider

- You will be expected to provide a one- to two-minute summary of your education and work history, which has led you to apply for this position.

- Emphasize your strengths as they relate to the position in question.

- You might begin by restating the most job-relevant aspects of your education and experience that appear on your resume. Highlight pertinent accomplishments and honors.

- Portray yourself as someone highly qualified for the job. For example, you might stress your excellent educational background and add some personal traits that highlight your strengths. While one person might stress "motivation," a second person might stress "reliability," and a third person might spotlight his or her "ability to be flexible." It is helpful to have an example to back up your assertion.

- In some cultures and families, talking about yourself and your strengths is simply not considered polite. If you come from such a background, you may have to struggle harder to present yourself in a strongly positive way.

- If you stumble, mumble, or seem surprised by this question, the initial interview impression is that you are unprepared, disorganized, and lacking in knowledge and confidence. Many employers will conclude that if you aren't prepared for the interview you won't be prepared on the job.

Outline some major points that you might want to include in your answer.

_____

_____

_____

_____

DEFINE YOUR STRENGTHS

Questions 2 through 12 probe your ability to relate your background and skills to the job requirements. They ask you to define your strengths.

2. Describe one of your greatest strengths.
3. What two or three accomplishments have given you the most satisfaction? Why?
4. What qualifications do you have that will make you successful in this company? In the field?
5. How would a former coworker or professor who knows you well describe you?
6. What would your references say about you?
7. What courses have you taken that will be helpful to you in this position?
8. What courses did you enjoy the most? The least? Why?

9. What is your grade-point average at college?

10. What were (are) your duties in your most recent position?

11. What did you enjoy *most* and *least* about your last position?

12. Why do you feel that you'll be successful in this position?

Points to Consider

- Have a clear picture of the job so that you can relate your strengths to the job requirements.

- Give examples of your strengths and skills that expand the job descriptions found on your resume.

- Mention more than one strength.

- If you are light on work experience, highlight your recent academic experience.

- If your grades were less than wonderful, highlight your combination of work and education or your personal qualities.

- Be positive. Don't put yourself down when asked about your strengths.

Example

"As I understand this position, it requires the ability to listen. In my job as a server, I had to listen carefully to record the details of orders. No one wants to get whole-wheat toast when she or he has ordered rye. Regular customers asked to be seated in my section because they knew I could listen accurately. Furthermore, this position requires that I work under pressure. On a busy Saturday night when we were short on staff, I had to function under time pressure. I know what it means to perform in a team to deliver high-quality service."

Now jot down some notes about your strengths.

DEFINE YOUR SHORTCOMINGS

Questions 13 through 15 probe your shortcomings.

13. What are your weaknesses?

14. What have you learned from your mistakes?

15. Describe a major problem that you have encountered. How did you deal with it?

Points to Consider

- Be brief about your shortcomings. Name one, not several.

- Make sure the weakness that you choose to mention is only a minor consideration in getting the job. For example, if the job requires precise work, don't cite lack of attention to detail.

- Select a weakness that might be a normal part of development, such as shyness as a teenager.

- Lack of experience may be an obvious weakness. You can acknowledge this fact briefly and then go on to emphasize the strengths that you would bring to the position.

- Use this question as an opportunity to dispel doubts that might be in the interviewer's mind. For example, if English is not your first language and you speak with an accent, acknowledge it. Add any information that seems relevant. Note, for example, that it has not interfered with past job performance or that you are actively working on your English oral communication skills by taking communication courses. Remind the interviewer that your bilingual ability is an asset.
- If possible, select a weakness that you have overcome.

Example

The student quoted next was interviewing for a human services position.

"I can be too soft-hearted. I had a friend who used to take long breaks to talk with her boyfriend and I used to cover for her. It got so I resented it, and finally I realized that no one can do the job for two people. I went to her privately and told her that I would no longer cover for her every day. She would have to do her part. She was upset at first, but now she understands. I realize now that I waited too long to take action."

Now outline one of your weaknesses and how you might describe it in an interview.

_____

_____

_____

_____

MOTIVATION AND GOALS

Questions 16 through 28 test your motivation, maturity, self-awareness, and long-term goals.

16. Why are you interested in this position?
17. What are your short-term and long-term career goals? How does this job fit your overall plans?
18. Where do you see yourself in five years?
19. Which is more important to you, the money or the type of job?
20. In what previous work experience have you been most interested? Why?
21. What do you think this company can offer you?
22. Why did you select your college? Your major field of study?
23. What college subjects did you like best? Least? Why?
24. Describe your most rewarding college experience.
25. If you could do your college education again, what would you do differently?
26. Do you have plans for further education?
27. What two or three things are most important to you in your job?
28. Define success. According to your definition of success, have you been successful so far?

Points to Consider

- Relate your goals to the position. Show how the position will give you an opportunity to contribute your knowledge, utilize your skills, and so forth.
- You can be vague in talking about the future. "Since the future is uncertain, I am focused on getting a position such as the one you offer and doing my best." If you

cite a position, make sure that it is a reasonable goal. This means that you must know the typical career progression in your area. A wild answer such as "president of the company" displays ignorance of the work world, not ambition.

- Be positive about your college experience, but show that you learned from mistakes. For example, poor grades might be the result of a lack of time management skills. Saying "If I had college to do over, I would master time management skills sooner" shows that you have analyzed your experience and attempted to learn from it.

- Your worst school subjects should not be crucial to the job you are applying for. Your best subject should not be a frivolous elective.

- Know what you value. Your values help you establish your definition of success. For example, you might say "I value the opportunity to solve problems" or "I really gain great satisfaction in helping people."

Now outline your version of success and some core values.

_____

_____

_____

_____

FIT WITH COMPANY

Questions 29 through 35 are about your fit with the company. Everyone wants to feel comfortable around his or her coworkers. Your ability to work with others, particularly on a team, is crucial. Your potential employers will also probe to understand your willingness to be supervised and, if necessary, corrected.

29. What is your opinion of your present boss and coworkers?
30. Describe a problem with a former supervisor and how you dealt with it.
31. In what kind of work environment are you most comfortable?
32. What experience have you had working in a team?
33. Why do you want to leave your current job?
34. How well do you work under pressure?
35. Is overtime, job-related travel, or working on weekends a problem?

Points to Consider

- Always be positive, even if you currently have the world's worst boss and coworkers. Never badmouth or blame others in an interview.

- Any problems that you describe should be in the past and resolved.

- Stress your ability to work with all kinds of people. Have some examples ready.

- Acceptable reasons for leaving a job might include the following: you want more challenge or opportunity for advancement in your field; you want to avoid such a lengthy commute; you feel that your skills and contributions are undervalued in your current position; you believe the company where you are seeking a job offers more opportunities.

- Before you answer questions about work outside typical hours, make sure that you know how extensive such overtime, travel, or weekend work is. If you have a problem, state it honestly. There is no sense in taking a job if you can't (or don't want to) work under certain conditions. At the same time, be positive about your willingness to go the extra mile in a special situation.

- When you talk about activities outside work that might show job-related skills, keep details of family and religion out of it. Although it may be an honest answer, don't stress passive activities such as TV watching. Mention active pursuits such as coaching a Little League team, or community service. Another approach is to stress that you have been working and going to school and have little leisure time.

Select one question from 29 through 35 and outline a suitable answer to it.

ONE OTHER TYPE OF QUESTION YOU MIGHT ENCOUNTER: BEHAVIORAL QUESTIONS

The interviewer might give you a case situation, usually drawn from situations that you will face on the job, and you will have to think through your answer. These kinds of questions ask you to apply your knowledge to typical job problems.

Points to Consider

- Don't be afraid to ask for clarification if you don't understand the question.
- In your response, show that you understand the important elements in the problem.

ILLEGAL INTERVIEW QUESTIONS

Various laws are designed to protect you from employment discrimination. You should not be asked questions about your age, race, sex, color, national origin, citizenship, health, religion, military discharge, or arrest record unless the employer shows that the question relates to your qualifications to perform essential job functions.

"Are you married? How old are you? Do you have any disabilities? Do you plan to have children? Does your religion allow you to work on Saturdays? Where were you born?" are not job-relevant, and an employer should not ask you such questions. Legal questions are job related.

Employers can ask questions about personal matters that would directly bear on your ability to perform the job in question. For instance, although employers cannot ask if you are a U. S. citizen, they can ask "Are you authorized to work in the United States?" They can ask about your availability to work overtime if the job requires it. "This job requires overtime several months of the year. Would you be able and willing to work overtime as necessary?" does address job performance requirements. Although you cannot be asked about your arrest record, it may be pertinent and legal for an employer to know if you have ever been convicted of a crime.[9]

An interview often begins with informal, social chitchat. Inexperienced interviewers may bring up inappropriate topics. Steer the conversation to more neutral topics such as the weather and sports teams. Avoid bringing the topics of family, religion, gender, or ethnicity into your interview responses unless your response addresses a job-related issue. Otherwise, these topics may make the interviewer uncomfortable.

You may find that you are asked a question that you believe is illegal. You must make a judgment about what action to take. Your action will probably depend on whether you believe the interviewer is practicing discrimination or is ignorant about illegal interview questions. Here are a few of your options.

1. Answer the question anyway, knowing that an "incorrect" response may eliminate you from consideration.

2. Respond to the concern behind the question. Many times employers are not trained in interviewing skills and their questions are not intended to discriminate. For instance, you might reply to a question about your family that you have family commitments but have always made arrangements to make sure that you keep your work commitments. Stress the separation of your business life from your family, social, or religious life outside work.

3. Ask the interviewer in a courteous tone to clarify the relevance of the question to the job responsibilities. For instance, "Can you help me to understand how this is related to the position that we are discussing?" This approach might be construed as challenging the interviewer and may cost you the opportunity for a job. However, the job interviewer may rephrase the question so that you can see why it is appropriate.

4. Decide whether to initiate follow-up action after the interview. If you have been asked questions that you believe were not job related and were intended to discriminate, make a written note of them soon after you finish your interview. You may decide to contact the Equal Employment Opportunity Commission. Unfortunately, this approach will take time and energy away from your job search. Or you might ask a relevant employer watchdog association for advice. Another option is to write to the company president or the chairman of the board about your experience, providing relevant details.[10]

JOB CANDIDATE QUESTIONS FOR THE INTERVIEWER

An interviewer will expect you to ask some questions about the job and the company.

1. What are the major day-to-day responsibilities of this position?

2. What would the first assignment or project be?

3. What are typical working hours? Where is the job located? What are the travel requirements, if any?

4. What type of training is required? How long is the training?

5. How is performance measured in this job? Are there regular performance reviews?

6. What qualities will a successful candidate have?

7. To whom would I report? Will I have the opportunity to meet her and other people in the department?

8. What is the supervisor's management style?

9. What is the next career step from this position?

10. How would you describe the work environment or culture of this organization?

11. Why is this position open?

12. Why did the last person leave this job?

13. How has the job changed in the past three years?

14. How many people have held this job in the past three years?

15. What are the major challenges that this department and company are facing?

16. What is the timetable for filling the position?

17. When will I know your decision?

DO NOT ASK ANY QUESTIONS ABOUT SALARY OR BENEFITS UNTIL YOU HAVE A JOB OFFER.

PRACTICE TIPS

Research on the company, the position, and, if possible, the interviewer's job and background will provide you with the knowledge to tailor your answers to the needs of the employer.

Write out responses to the most difficult questions, especially "Tell me about yourself." Each answer should have a concrete example, a little story that illustrates the point that you are making. Once you have organized your thoughts, you can concentrate on your delivery.

You can practice alone or with others. If you're alone, consider using a tape recorder. Listen to the results and find ways to improve your responses. Stand in front of a mirror so that you can check your nonverbal behavior. You can practice with a friend or family member. If possible, videotape your practice session. In this way, you have the opportunity to get feedback on your verbal and nonverbal behavior.

Expect some discomfort when practicing. This is normal. The words may not flow out the way you want. This too is normal. Don't let that stop you from practicing. Remember: if you are uncomfortable in the privacy of your home or with friends, you are likely to be more so in an actual interview situation. With practice, you will have the opportunity to sharpen your responses and lessen the discomfort. Practicing can dramatically improve your interview performance.

NONVERBAL BEHAVIOR

- Shake hands firmly and address the interviewer by name.
- Sit straight; don't slouch.
- Make frequent eye contact, but don't stare.
- Smile when appropriate.

VERBAL BEHAVIOR

- Use standard English.
- Project a consistent voice tone, one that is neither too loud nor too soft.
- If it is genuine, express interest in the position. Always thank the interviewer by name when you leave.

PART III

Make Your Experience Count

CHAPTER 11

How to Take Charge of Your Career

Economists tell us that with today's market shifts, college graduates can expect to work at 12–15 jobs in at least three different fields.
—Deborah Stead

11

TAKING CHARGE OF YOUR CAREER: A MULTIDISCIPLINARY PERSPECTIVE

The transition from school to work is one of the biggest changes you will face in life. Sociologists predict that you will experience what they call "reality shock." In this chapter you'll find out what they mean by reality shock, and how to cope with it. Psychologists underscore the importance of your personal transition as you leave the college classroom and enter the workplace. They see your career as developing in stages and describe how this transition marks the beginning of the "establishment stage." You will learn all about the establishment stage and the tasks associated with it.

Economists foresee a workplace in continual upheaval. You'll learn why the workplace is changing so rapidly and which habits and skills you should cultivate to thrive in this turbulent environment. Humanists concern themselves with the role that your values play in guiding your choices amid so much change. You will see how the boundaries between home and work life are blurring, and examine what this means for your lifestyle. You'll also examine various meanings of "career advancement." Although career advancement is typically associated with power, recognition, and money, many alternative possibilities exist. This chapter offers you a chance to clarify your values and refine your personal definition of "career advancement."

All these perspectives will help you understand that succeeding in the workplace today is not a matter of climbing a career ladder on which the steps are predictable. Unlike school, where you advanced in a structured series of grades from elementary through high school and then on to college, the workplace offers more paths to choose from and more uncertainties about the outcomes. This chapter will help you prepare yourself to take charge of these choices and to cope with the uncertainty. We begin with a phenomenon that surprises many students: "reality shock."

SOCIOLOGISTS CAUTION YOU ABOUT "REALITY SHOCK"

If you are like most students, you are excited about the prospects of starting your career. You set out with high hopes, eager to conquer the job world. These wonderful feelings often evaporate quickly. After the honeymoon period, students wonder if they made the right move, because their first job or internship is not living up to their expectations.

Sociologists call this "reality shock"—a period of disillusionment that inevitably follows the emotional high of starting a new job.[1] Some call it the "joining-up blues." As one student put it, "Everyone was busy with their own work. They ignored me. I was at the bottom of the heap." You may wonder why this happens and what you can do to overcome it.

During your interview, the organization showed you its best side. No person or organization is perfect, however, and as you get to know the organization better you may feel betrayed. You begin to see flaws not apparent to outsiders.

What is happening is that unconsciously, you have built up some unrealistic expectations based on college life. On campus your professors (bosses) change frequently, and you are free from day-to-day supervision. You are guaranteed a variety of challenges because each semester you have a new set of courses. Through your papers and exams, you get regular feedback on your performance. Promotions are frequent, often annual events. By the time you get your bachelor's degree, you'll have had 16 promotions since kindergarten!

It's a real jolt to find yourself at the bottom of the heap all over again when you start your first job. The reality is that entry-level positions often lack glamour and decision-making power.

As a novice, you're expected to "pay your dues." Often this means that your initial assignments are the group's least attractive tasks. Often they are below your capability. You may wonder why you went to college if all you're given to do are menial tasks.

New management trainees at Enterprise Rent-a-Car begin at the rental counter.[2] William D. Lucy, 25, a marketing major with a minor in management, graduated from Southwest Missouri State University. He acknowledges, "I did not go to college thinking I wanted to rent cars." Another management hopeful at Enterprise, Julie Schenk, graduated from the University of Dayton in communications management. She was surprised to learn that she had to wash cars on occasion. Still, both will have the chance to apply for promotion within a year, once they have "paid their dues."

At the Dayton Hudson Corporation in Minneapolis, new grads may start their careers the way Rachel Gunderson did. A journalism major with a marketing and business minor, she graduated from the University of Wisconsin at Madison. Her initial duties as a merchandising analyst are to order potting soil for 750 Target stores. If she is successful, she may be promoted to buyer within five years and her salary will increase by 65 to 100 percent. By the way, she faced stiff competition to get that job. Dayton Hudson hires only one out of 20 students who apply.

Recognize that you, too, will go through a transition period. You no longer belong to the world of college students, yet you have not been fully accepted as a working professional. In the words of Dr. Ed Holton of Louisiana State University, you must practice the "art of being new."[3] Part of being new is excelling at the tasks you are given. Menial tasks are common, especially in the glamour fields.

The "grunt work" that newcomers are typically asked to do may include stuffing envelopes, updating files, photocopying, getting coffee, and running errands. Alex Ruttenburg's summer job as a production assistant on a Robert Redford film included plenty of grunt work, but in return, he got an inside look at how a film is made. After graduating from Middlebury College, he used his contacts to get a job at Redford's production company in Los Angeles—doing slightly higher-level grunt work. After three years of paying dues, he was offered the job of assisting the director on the set.[4]

One rule that helps: No matter how severe your reality shock is, never respond with, "I'm too busy" or "It's not my job." Over time, if you feel overloaded or taken advantage of, schedule an appointment with your boss and discuss the situation.

Before you can make a real contribution, you must learn the organization's jargon, its communication patterns, the norms and values, and which behaviors it rewards and which ones are taboo. Dip into Chapter 12, "How to Learn from Internships, College Jobs, and Extracurricular Activities." It describes several strategies for extracting the maximum career benefits from any internship or job.

PSYCHOLOGISTS SEE YOU AS MOVING GRADUALLY INTO A NEW CAREER STAGE

Now let's turn to a psychological transition that accompanies the start of your career—a change in career stage. This idea comes from the work of Donald Super, a pioneering vocational psychologist. He and his associates found that a career develops in stages, each marked by a different set of developmental tasks.[5] A brief picture of the five career stages with their associated tasks is found in Table 11.1.

Launching Your Career: The Exploration and Establishment Stages Overlap

The typical college student is in the *exploration stage*. The tasks of the exploration stage are to clarify interests and values, identify strengths, and make an initial, tentative occupational choice.

The exploration stage is followed by the *establishment stage*. The tasks of the establishment stage are to commit more fully to one's career choice and begin to make one's mark in that field. Those are the tasks you undertake once you enter the work world.

Career Stage	Tasks	**TABLE 11.1**
Growth Stage (birth–age 14)	Form a clear self-concept, a picture of who you are as a person.	*Career stages.*
Exploration Stage (age 15–24)	Make initial tentative choices by narrowing options through self-assessment, coursework, tryouts, early work experience.	
Establishment Stage (age 25–44)	Make a commitment to a career field and make your mark in it.	
Maintenance Stage (age 45–64)	Hold on to your place in the work world.	
Disengagement (age 65 and over)	Prepare for retirement; leave the work world.	

Source: Roger A. Myers, "Super's Developmental Stages, Tasks, and Coping Behaviors," unpublished table, Teachers College, Columbia University, n.d. Adapted with permission.

As you move from school to work, you are straddling the exploration and establishment stages. Your exploration and decision making do not end when you finish school—far from it. It is crucial to try out in real life the tentative commitment you made in school. These early years of your career are a period of trial and experimentation as you test your choices in the workplace. Some students find their career choices confirmed. Others need to make minor readjustments. Still others must change directions radically in order to find success and satisfaction. You must continue the process of exploration in order to see what kinds of shifts you must make in your career direction in the early years of your career.

However, as you begin your career, you face new tasks. You begin to establish yourself in the workplace. You need to build skills by taking on challenging work assignments. You need to learn how to solve on-the-job problems and develop career networks. These are tasks of the early establishment stage, and they are described in more detail in Chapters 12 and 13.

You may be familiar with some of these tasks and may have already begun to address them if you have held jobs while in school. Be aware, however, that these tasks take on a new urgency and importance as your identity shifts from student to worker. Whatever sharp turns you take in your career direction and whatever shifts you make in your industry, occupation, or employer, be mindful that your career life has begun. In order to move ahead, you need to begin to address seriously the career tasks of the establishment stage.

New theoretical formulations[6] emphasize that you typically go through these stages more than once. As opportunities shift, you may go through repeated minicyles of new growth, re-exploration, re-establishment, and disengagement throughout your career. For example, you may return to school in midlife to explore new career options, which will require you to undergo the process of establishment in a new occupation or a new industry. Later, you may disengage from that area to restart the process of exploration and establishment in yet a third area.

Figure 11.1 depicts this cyclical movement through the various career stages. Notice that the maintenance stage, in which the task is holding on to

FIGURE 11.1

Career stages may be repeated several times over your career.

your place, is missing from this diagram. After you complete Activity 11.1, we'll examine the predictions of economists and futurists, so you'll understand why the maintenance stage is disappearing from many people's working lives and why changes of career direction are becoming more common.

ACTIVITY 11.1　YOUR CAREER STAGE AND TASKS

1. What career stage are you in now? Please explain the reasons for your selection.

_____

_____

2. What career tasks are next for you?

_____

_____

_____

_____

ECONOMISTS STRESS THE WIDESPREAD IMPACT OF HIGH TECHNOLOGY AND THE GLOBAL MARKETPLACE

Now let's look at the major transformations taking place in the workplace. It's important to recognize the magnitude and pace of these changes. They are leading to many new opportunities and are increasing your options. However, these changes also present more risks because career paths are no longer clear-cut. Some occupations, industries, and companies will become obsolete. Others will undergo a metamorphosis, requiring you to obtain additional skills and knowledge. In order to survive in this turbulent environment, you must engage in three activities: (1) gathering information about workplace developments through research; (2) building skills through ongoing, self-directed learning; and (3) developing teamwork skills. We'll discuss the need for each of these practices in turn.

Make It a Habit to Stay Informed About New Developments in the Workplace

Sweeping Changes in the Workplace

When mass production of the automobile made the horse and buggy obsolete, it sparked a radical transformation of many industries, companies, and occupations. Most carriage makers and blacksmiths went out of business; tire factories were built; and gas stations sprang up. Right now, powerful technological innovations are causing an upheaval of industries and companies even more profound and widespread than those the automobile brought about. These innovations include the Internet; portable communication devices; and advances in biotechnology, agriculture, robotics, and nanotechnology. Let's begin with the Internet.

The Internet is linking companies and industries into one global marketplace, spawning what is known as e-commerce. With an Internet site a business can attract customers from any country on the planet. Global exchanges, E-bays for specific industries, are being created.[7] In construction, for example, an auction site called metalsite.com has been created to allow organizations to buy and sell steel.[8] Auction sites for chemicals, plastics, rubber, cement, and insurance are also in the works. By 2004 between 30 and 40 percent of businesses will use these exchanges to buy and sell their products and services. Using these exchanges, U. S. national and regional companies will find it easier to become global businesses selling to customers worldwide. However, these Internet exchanges will also provide foreign companies with easier access to U. S. customers, so competition will become fiercer.

Small local businesses, such as dog grooming, landscaping, and dentistry, may not be globalized, but for most companies or industries, the imperative is "e or be eaten."[9] A midwestern china manufacturer learned about the power of the Internet the hard way. Founded in the 1920s, it sold dinnerware to diners, office cafeterias, and hospitals within a 100-mile radius of its factory. Then one day, a major customer found a cheaper European supplier on the Internet. Soon, other customers switched to the European supplier, too. The customer base that had provided jobs for the U. S. china factory for seven decades was gone within a few months.[10] The china factory did not have a strategy to respond to the global marketplace and lost out.

The Internet is changing the not-for-profit world, too, as individuals and groups utilize the power of the Internet to organize on a global scale. For example, Jody Williams was awarded a Nobel Peace Prize for spearheading a campaign for an international ban on landmines.[11] She was able to overcome opposition from powerful countries by organizing 1,000 different human-rights and arms-control groups on six continents—using only E-mail and the Internet.

Even the fight against poverty is being affected by the Internet. The practice of lending individuals (often women) from $100 to $1,000 to start a business has proven to be a powerful way to overcome poverty. The money buys such things as a bicycle to get produce to market, a cell phone to start a village phone service, or beauty supplies to start a neighborhood salon. PlaNet Finance, founded by a French banker, is linking 7,000 separate microlending organizations into one worldwide network. As a network they are working on a tracking device like a FedEx system, to keep track of loans and repayments. PlaNet will help keep the cost of banking services down and make more loan funds available for the poor.[12]

The Internet is not the only technology changing industries and occupations. Other powerful technologies are creating new products to solve long-standing problems. For example, biotechnology has helped to create a strain of rice that could help prevent blindness in developing nations because it facilitates the formation of vitamin A.[13] Precision farming uses satellite data beamed to tractors to monitor planting, watering, and fertilizing—yard by yard.[14] It has resulted in increased crop yields, lower costs, and decreased use of pesticides and fertilizers. Fish farming is expected to emerge as an important industry.[15] In manufacturing, robotic devices are infiltrating the factory floor. A Lexus factory in Japan produces 300 sedans a day using 66 human beings and 310 robots.[16] Such automated factories will become commonplace in the next decade. Nanotechnologies, providing engineering breakthroughs on the level of individual atoms and molecules, are revolutionizing product designs.[17]

The pace of change has picked up, too. In 1990 few people had heard of the Internet or had an E-mail address. In a decade the Internet became a global post office, shopping center, research library, and university.[18] It took radio 30 years to reach an audience of 50 million. It took television 13 years. It took the Internet a mere four years.[19]

Historians call the movement of people off farms and into factories the Industrial Revolution because its impact on society was so far-reaching. John Chambers, president of Cisco Systems (makers of Internet connecting devices) believes that the Internet will have a similarly momentous impact on our lives. While the Industrial Revolution took 100 years to unfold, Chambers predicts that the Internet Revolution will take just seven.[20] No wonder Cisco's first major advertising campaign featured the tag line, "Are you ready?"

The ability of companies and employees to predict the future is difficult because the workplace is changing so dramatically and rapidly. For instance, early research by an automobile company predicted that people might buy used cars over the Internet, but would shop at the showroom for new ones. Yet that's not what has happened. At least 50 percent of new cars are preselected using the Internet. The car dealership, an extremely profitable small business, is being redefined.[21]

Another example of unexpected business opportunity created by the Internet is found in the publishing industry. Although by 2007 experts believe that most books will be published on-line,[22] no one predicted that Amazon.com would become a global bookstore that would ship printed books.[23]

What's next? We know that people are booking their airline flights, buying their holiday gifts, shopping for mortgage rates, and going to school on-line. We can predict that these changes will transform the work of travel agents, retail store managers, bankers, and university professors. Yet the shape of this transformation is not yet clear.

No matter what the industry or occupation, technological change is transforming the workplace. The result of all these changes is that college students today are the first to face so many choices and so much uncertainty.

Monitor Workplace Changes Continually

To understand what threats and opportunities exist in the workplace because of the rapid pace of technological innovation, you must stay informed. You need to monitor changes in your occupation, industry, and organization. This knowledge is one key to your career survival.

Teaching yourself about the workplace requires you to read widely. The rapid pace of change means that you cannot undertake these searches merely every now and again. You must always be on the lookout for signs of change. Make your searches an ongoing activity throughout your work life. To be unprepared for a job loss or to miss an emerging career opportunity can damage your career.

Become "Learning Obsessed"

In the Global Marketplace You'll Need World-Class Skills

Companies are scouring the globe for the best talent, and the Internet has made the search easy. They advertise opportunities on their Web sites or on job boards such as Monster.com. Your competition could come from anywhere in the world. Since the labor market is global, your skills need to be world-class.

Many companies are moving accounting, customer services, and programming functions to countries that have large numbers of English-speaking educated workers, in particular India, Pakistan, the Philippines, and South Africa. America Online has customer service reps in Manila answer questions about E-mail for U. S. customers. GE Capital has Indian phone operators calling people in California about credit card payments. An American HMO uses a firm in Delhi to transcribe doctors' dictation.[24] If you are in accounting, customer service, or computer programming, take note: you have global competition for jobs.

Another change that is increasing your competition is the use of telecommuting. By 2010, 80 percent of employees will perform at least some of their work at home or in some location other than the company's offices.[25] The practice helps companies hire and retain talented employees. When employees don't have to live within commuting distance of company headquarters, the company has a wider pool of potential employees to choose from.

Even basketball, that all-American sport, has internationalized its talent search. The number of international players drafted into the NBA increased fourfold in the 1990s.[26]

Keep Adding To and Improving Your Skills

When your competition steps it up a notch, you need to keep pace. You must continually develop your ability to use information in written and numerical forms. You must develop the reading skills to obtain and interpret complex information, the writing skills to share information with others, and the ability to use information to solve complicated problems. These brain skills, along with people skills, provide a kind of "mobile security."[27]

By seeking to increase your skills, you will be able to adapt to emerging organizational opportunities. This strategy will prepare you to survive in the changing workplace. Although a specific job position won't be guaranteed, having an abundance of updated skills will ensure that you will be attractive to many employers. The more attractive your skills, the more opportunities and choices you will have.

Competing successfully means becoming a self-directed, lifelong learner. You must be what *Fast Company* calls "learning obsessed."[28] Put another way, in today's workplace we have shifted from earning a living to "learning a living."[29]

Build Your Teamwork Skills

Companies Are Throwing Out Their Organizational Charts

Companies, like workers, are scrambling to survive amid this rapid, sweeping change. They need to respond quickly to these new market conditions. They value flexibility in terms of structure and location. Companies or parts of companies are being bought, sold, and moved around the world. Mergers, acquisitions, buy-outs, and joint ventures are frequent. Temporary alliances and partnerships are being formed to strengthen companies' competitive strength for particular products or services. Significantly greater numbers of workers than ever before are on temporary assignments. Use of part-timers, freelancers, consultants, and contract workers has increased.

Bureaucracies and hierarchies are disappearing. Job titles with fixed responsibilities are also vanishing. You will see this trend particularly in smaller and newer companies. Their fanciful job titles—such as Chief Learning Officer and Customer Evangelist,[30] Director of First Impressions, Animation Skeptic,[31] and Chief Acceleration Officer[32]—poke fun at older, more formal and rigid organizational structures. But even well-established companies are becoming more team oriented and less hierarchical. Consider Kimberly-Clark, makers of Kleenex and Huggies. In a description of their culture you find:

> At Kimberly-Clark people do not stand on rank. Thought, contribution and teamwork are valued over job titles and status. Therefore, all Kimberly-Clark people throughout the world operate on a first-name basis with one another. We see ourselves as members of a global team, all with something important to contribute.[33]

Companies, Large and Small, Expect You to Be an Effective Team Player

More work is now organized by project and accomplished through teamwork. As projects change, so do your coworkers. Some team members may be full-time company employees; others may be on board only for a specific project. The team members may not even be in the same location. Using technology, companies can create virtual teams. As early as 1997, IBM was using a worldwide team with members in Beijing, Seattle, Latvia, Belarus, and India to work on the same software project around the clock.[34]

If you look at the job openings section of any company's Web page, you will see that companies emphasize the importance of teamwork. For example, the Philosophy and Values statement of Genentech, a biotech drug company based in San Francisco, includes this assertion: "We understand the value of working in teams and bringing perspectives and expertise to the achievement of our objectives."[35] The ability to work in a team is clearly an important factor in succeeding in today's workplace.

Your ability to cooperate with others will be tested in this environment. You must work at becoming a good team member, doing your share of the work according to the deadline agreed on by the team. When you are in group meetings, you must learn to speak up and to listen effectively. Since your team members may come from different backgrounds and countries, you must become sensitive to cultural differences and learn to work effectively with a diverse set of colleagues.

HUMANISTS ALERT YOU TO A NEW CHALLENGE: THE PERPETUAL WORKDAY

The global workplace is changing the boundaries of the workday. With employees and functions scattered around the globe, the workday no longer starts at 9 A.M. and ends at 5 P.M. This trend has been called the "rise of the 24/7 worker."[36] Stock markets in Tokyo and London need to be monitored even if it is the middle of the night. Are you working for a company doing business in Colombia, Vietnam, Bangladesh, or Italy? Conference calls are scheduled to include participants from different time zones; important faxes arrive at all hours. In the round-the-clock, round-the-world workplace, weekends cease to be meaningful. The workweek no longer has a distinguishable beginning or end.

Wireless communication devices including Palm Pilots, cellular telephones, and two-way pagers are also changing the workplace. You can access the Internet from a device you put in your pocket or purse. Estimates are that one billion portable Internet connections will be used in 2005, and three billion by 2010.[37] These portable devices will make it easier to be in touch with coworkers and customers anywhere, anytime.

Set a Boundary Between Your Work Life and Personal Life

High technology and the global marketplace are blurring the boundaries between the work life and the personal life of many workers. On the positive side, the new working arrangements offer more flexibility. Working from home makes it easier to take a break and attend a child's soccer game or run a personal errand. You work not by the clock, but to meet specific project goals. With flextime, you gain the freedom to decide when to put in the hours and when to take time off. You might work on Saturday and Sunday and go surfing (or do some other leisure activity) on Wednesday and Thursday.

On the negative side, your employer gains more access into your life. Many employees are now routinely on call. They answer E-mail from home, take their laptop to the beach, and have their cell phone handy during their child's birthday party. You may have to be available at odd hours to communicate with coworkers in different time zones, or work long hours over a weekend to meet a project deadline. In Europe and Latin America the traditional two-hour lunch break is disappearing. Many American managers complain that getting two weeks off for a vacation is impossible, given their heavy workloads. Long weekends spaced throughout the year have become more common forms of vacation.

The consequence of these new technologies is that the boundary between your work and personal life is not set for you. You must work harder to maintain your priorities and get your work done. You must not let work consume too much of your personal life or get so distracted by personal matters that you let project goals slip.

Is the Dot-Com Life for You?

One possibility that intrigues many college students is working for a dot-com, an Internet start-up company. You have heard the stories about young millionaires with custom suits and custom cars. Or you have been frightened by the news of sudden layoffs and paper wealth that evaporated overnight. Are you attracted to the intense, focused work atmosphere? The ability to create something new? The high-risk, high-reward atmosphere?

Activity 11.2, Am I Ready to Be a Dot-Commer?, is a self-assessment of your readiness to join the dot-com world. It is based on research done by *Fast Company* magazine.[38] You'll find an example of a dot-commer accompanying each item. Many of these people started their own Internet companies while still attending college. Their attitude is summed up in a saying by Will Rogers: "Why not go out on a limb? That's where the fruit is."

Following the checklist is Activity 11.3, Dot-com Winners and Losers. It invites you to explore the fates of several promising start-ups. Looking at the Web sites of successful start-up companies will give you additional insights into the dot-com culture.

ACTIVITY 11.2   AM I READY TO BE A DOT-COMMER?

Below are nine questions about your aptitude for work in the dot-com culture, each accompanied by a real-life example. If you believe that the answer to a question is yes, place a check in the box next to that item. The more boxes you check, the more likely you are to be a successful and happy dot-commer.

☐ *Would you start or join a company because you are more interested in the mission of the company than in the money you might earn?*

Greg Tseng founded Flyingchickens.com when he discovered that he could get his textbooks cheaper on-line than in the college bookstore. His company eventually merged with Limespot, a Web portal for college students founded by another college student. Tseng eventually hopes to head a technology company that has as much impact on the future of technology as Intel.[39]

☐ *When you work for a company, are you completely dedicated to your own, your team's, and your company's success?*

Phillips Merrick's software firm was on the verge of bankruptcy with only $31 left in the budget. He persisted using a then-new data standard, XML, to develop business-to-business software. His dedication paid off handsomely. When the firm went public three years later, he earned $700 million.[40]

☐ *Are you willing to put in long hours—all-nighters, Saturdays, Sundays, whatever it takes—to get the job done?*

Founder of CollegiateMall.com, Jeffrey Gut, age 21, began his company while in college. He says, "I love what I'm doing, and I'd love to keep doing it." However, he also realizes that he has made some sacrifices. He observes that when his room-mates are partying the night away, he is holed up in his dorm room working on his computer.[41]

☐ *Can you make quick decisions, even if you have incomplete information?*

Tracy Pettengill, cofounder of 4Charity.com, found, "You have to get used to the idea that some days you'll make good decisions, and other days you won't. . . . You train yourself to think fast if you want to survive."[42]

☐ *Are you able to prioritize and stay focused on the most important objectives?*

Kartik Ramakrishnan, vice president of business development for Quiq Inc., receives about 100 E-mails each day. Of the 6,466 E-mail messages in his inbox, 2,189 are unread.[43]

☐ *Do you like to operate without an organizational chart or established procedures?*

Russell Reynolds Associates, a recruiting firm, found that the best dot-commers weren't stuck on job titles and responsibilities. Successful dot-com executives are willing to work in the warehouse if it that's what it takes to get the job done.[44]

☐ *Can you improvise in the face of changing conditions?*

Within a year of joining UBUBU.com, Josh Keller led the company to change its fundamental business model from business-to-consumer (B2C) to business-to-business (B2B).[45]

☐ *Do you like to do things you have never done before in an atmosphere of high risk and high reward?*

President of E-Bay, Meg Whitman is fighting big, powerful competitors, such as Amazon.com, Yahoo!, and Lycos, who want to put her company out of business. She's masterminding E-Bay's efforts to expand.[46]

☐ *Are you willing to risk working for an Internet company that is likely to fail, because you believe that you will walk away a winner in terms of learning?*

Marc Benioff left a lucrative position at Oracle to start Salesforce.com, taking on a well-established competitor. His attitude toward failure? "Even if Salesforce.com doesn't work out, I can try it again. I have that sort of confidence in myself."[47]

Based on the number of "yes" responses, do you believe that you would be happy and successful as a dot-commer? Why or why not?

_____

_____

_____

_____

ACTIVITY 11.3   DOT-COM WINNERS AND LOSERS

Every year since 1993, *Fortune* magazine has devoted an annual cover story to its new "cool companies." Some, like Netscape, Cisco, CNET, DoubleClick, Qwest, and VeriSign, made it big. Others were acquired. Many, though, didn't make it. The companies below are taken from the Fortune 2000 list.[48]

JamCracker: software portal for midsize companies   **www.jamcracker.com**

Zing: a photo-sharing site   **www.zing.com**

AvantGo: software for viewing Web pages on wireless   **www.avantgo.com**

NeoPoint: smart phones   **www.neopoint.com**

Resonate: Internet management software   **www.resonate.com**

Quantum: Web site for live advice   **www.keen.com**

Digital Paper: digital document transmission   **www.digitalpaper.com**

iBeam: streaming video and audio via satellite   **www.ibeam.com**

1. Select three of these companies and check their Web sites. Have any survived?

_____

_____

_____

2. Go the Web site of at least one company that is succeeding. Read its mission statement and the overview of the company. Check out their job offerings. Are there signs that the company is an innovative, fast-paced, informal, and team-oriented place to work?

_____

_____

_____

_____

_____

3. Would you like to work for this company? Why or why not?

_____

_____

_____

_____

Whether you want to work for a dot-com or not, when you have so many career options, you need to decide what "advancement" means to you. Your personal definition will help guide the decisions you make about your career options. We will consider this issue next.

WHERE STUDENTS GET STUCK, AND WHAT TO DO IF IT HAPPENS TO YOU

Deciding What Advancement Means to You

It is difficult to escape the powerful influence of our cultural definitions of success, advancement, and the importance of work. In U. S. culture we are reminded every day that work is important. It is seen as a principal source of an individual's dignity. People who don't work are often perceived as not worthy of respect. Full-time homemakers, for example, struggle with feelings of devaluation because they are not earning money. People who are laid off often become depressed because they have lost status in the eyes of others and themselves.

Our culture also emphasizes progress. It is good to move up on the job, to increase your earnings, to be promoted to a higher rank, and to take on more responsibility. These are signs of success. The idea of career advancement is powerfully associated with being successful in our society.

We are validated when we meet society's expectations. We are accorded prestige, status, recognition, and influence if we succeed in advancing at work. However, career decisions and behavior are not driven solely by cultural messages. Definitions of advancement show great diversity, and you have the freedom to define the term for yourself.

You'll find that people have different opinions about whether the overriding goal of work should be economic gain or psychological fulfillment. You might choose to emphasize the fulfillment of your economic needs and see yourself as advancing when you increase your earnings. Or you might choose to emphasize your psychological needs and see yourself as advancing when your work becomes more challenging, creative, or responsible. Another choice might be to emphasize a sense of belonging and see yourself as advancing when you join a group of coworkers who are compatible, supportive, and encouraging.

There are some people who reject the prevailing cultural notions about work and advancement and downplay individual fulfillment. They commit their energy to causes other than work. Case 11.1, describing the career of Sister Wendy, is just one example of such a career.

Sister Wendy[49]   **CASE 11.1**

While many people in the United States have never heard of her, Sister Wendy is a beloved celebrity in Britain. For the past several years she has been the star of several popular BBC-TV series on fine art, including "Sister Wendy's Odyssey" and "The Story of Painting."

The center of Sister Wendy's existence is not her work as a TV commentator or as a book author (15 so far). Now in her late sixties, she has been a nun since the age of 16. After teaching in South Africa for 15 years, she was given permission to pursue a life of solitude and deliberate poverty and moved to Great Britain. She spends seven hours of her day in prayer. An epileptic, her health is frail. She lives primarily on 1 1/2 pints of milk a day. Her home is a trailer so cold that she goes to bed bundled in head coverings, sweaters, and three pairs of bed socks. She has not been inside a movie theater since 1946. For 25 years she read art books borrowed from a local library.

She was discovered by chance on her annual trip to an art gallery when a local TV crew that was filming someone else overheard her remarks and asked to film her as well. The TV series have given her a chance to see her favorite art in person for the first time, but she gives her TV salary to the religious order that supports her. Her TV contract stipulates that she must be taken to Mass once a day. For Sister Wendy, the idea of career advancement is alien to her life of religious devotion.

There are many less dramatic examples than Sister Wendy. Some people decide to center their lives on their families. They work to earn a living, not to forge a career. They also reject the idea that work and advancement should be central to their lives.

As you establish your career, it is your responsibility to come to your own personal definition of career advancement. It is useful to think about whether the career path you are choosing is in accord with your personal definition of advancement.

In the course of defining advancement, you will come to terms with your own values and the degree to which they correspond with cultural expectations. It means looking again at your economic and psychological needs and deciding what trade-offs you are willing to make.

Your personal definition of advancement may be in accord with cultural expectations: You simply want fame and fortune. Other definitions emphasize psychological fulfillment. If you were to say, "I am doing better," what would you mean? Are you referring to economic gain, psychological satisfaction, or society's approval?

The worst thing you can do is to accept or reject the cultural definition of success without serious reflection. Struggling with your own definition may not be easy, but if you don't face up to this challenge, you risk your personal satisfaction.

ACTIVITY 11.4   A PERSONAL DEFINITION OF ADVANCEMENT

1. Listed below are thirteen typical indicators of advancement. Rank them 1 through 13 in order of your preference, with 1 the highest priority and 13 the lowest.

_____ Be recognized by others as an expert in my field

_____ Make more money than the average person in my field

_____ Make more money than the average person in the United States

_____ Build a highly profitable business from scratch

_____ Get promoted repeatedly to higher positions with increasing authority and responsibility for others' work

_____ Work with the best people in my field

_____ Be awarded the best sales territory and customers

_____ Be in demand by industry leaders for challenging projects

_____ Be able to set my own hours of work, to come and go according to a work schedule that I set

_____ Work in plush, fancy surroundings (e.g., office with a view, original art, wood paneling)

_____ Have a full-time position with benefits such as health insurance and paid vacations in a well-respected firm

_____ Be able to travel and dine on a company expense account

_____ Be my own boss

2. Are there any indicators of advancement that you would like to add to the list above?

_____

_____

_____

_____

_____

3. Will the career paths available in your field allow you to obtain the signs of advancement that you ranked highest? Explain.

_____

_____

_____

_____

_____

KEY POINTS

1. The transition from school to work is one of the biggest changes you will face in life. You are undergoing an identity transition from student to worker at a time when the workplace is undergoing sweeping changes. You will find that you have more options about your career direction than ever before, but less certainty about which ones hold the most promise for the future.

2. In any new job or internship, the honeymoon is typically followed by reality shock. You may become discouraged because you are at the bottom of the heap. College students often have more challenge, autonomy, and independence than entry-level workers. In addition, during the interview process the company presented an idealized image of itself. You may find that your initial tasks do not have the level of responsibility you imagined.

3. Before an organization accepts you completely, you must pay your dues. Even if your initial tasks are menial, excel in everything you do without complaining. Once you have learned the ropes, you will move beyond such "grunt work."

4. As you launch your career, you straddle two career stages. You are still in the exploration stage, testing your career direction in the work world. At the same time, you enter the establishment stage, where you will gradually feel pressure to commit more fully to a specific career choice and begin to make your mark.

5. Technological innovation is causing sweeping change in the workplace. The Internet and the global marketplace are transforming companies and industries. One result is rapid shifts in career opportunities. Some innovations will be threats to your career, while others will open up new opportunities.

6. Make it a habit to stay informed about developments in the workplace so that you can understand emerging threats and opportunities.

7. You will need world-class skills to compete successfully in the global marketplace. Become "learning obsessed." Commit yourself to ongoing skill development so that you can stay competitive.

8. Company structures are changing so that they can respond rapidly to changing market conditions. One important change is that jobs no longer have a fixed set of duties. More work is done in teams, so you need to be flexible and build your teamwork skills.

9. The workday never ends officially when you work for a company competing in the global marketplace. The technology has made it possible to work anywhere, anytime, so the workday is now known as "24/7/365." In this kind of work environment you must set the boundary between your work life and home life.

10. A start-up dot-com culture is typically fast-paced, innovative, informal, and team oriented. Its high-risk, high-rewards lifestyle may or may not be for you.

11. You must decide what career advancement means to you. It is useful to think about whether the career path you've chosen is in accord with your personal definition of advancement.

The world has gotten smaller; competition has gotten more intense; choices have become more plentiful.

—Alan Murray

ACTIVITY 11.5   CAREER ADVICE ON-LINE

OVERVIEW

The purpose of this activity is to give you some experience using on-line resources to help you manage your career. You now know that in the establishment stage of your career you must learn how to make your mark on the job. What are the best techniques to get your contributions recognized? Stand out as a team member? Ask for a raise? Put yourself in line for a promotion or important project? Often you can find some answers on-line. In the chapter's section on workplace transformation you

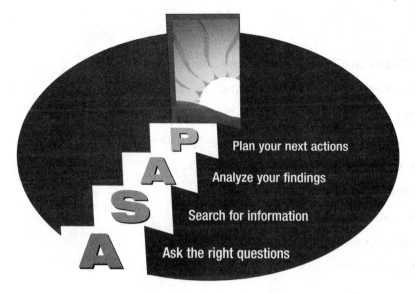

learned how quickly the work world is changing. Obtaining information about work-place trends will allow you to spot emerging opportunities and avoid threats to your career success.

You can use career advice for everyday problems at work, too. You can learn how to handle new or difficult situations, such as dining out with colleagues, juggling home and work commitments, attending professional conferences for the first time, dress-ing professionally on casual workdays, and coping with office politics. You can even find advice on very serious matters, such as sexual harassment and discrimination in the workplace.

Use the questions below to guide your research and report-writing. If you need more room, or if you are instructed to do so, type your answers separately.

STEP 1 ASK THE RIGHT QUESTIONS

Step 1.1 Information Sources

In the table on the following page you will find some excellent Web sites that will help you navigate today's workplace. Some of the listed sites are the on-line versions of well-known print newspapers and magazines. At the home page look for a channel or section called "career" or "work." Other sites have been created solely for Web users. Remember, addresses change so frequently on the Web that you may find a key-word search as effective as using the listed Web address.

STEP 2 SEARCH FOR INFORMATION

Step 2.1 Select an Article at an Internet Site

Select something to read and provide the proper and complete citation for your informa-tion source.

_____

_____

_____

_____

TABLE 11.2	
Career advice Web sites.	**Black Enterprise** (Click on Careers): **www.blackenterprise.com.**
	Business Week (Click on Careers): **www.businessweek.com**
	CollegeJournal (from the *Wall Street Journal*): **www.collegejournal.com**
	ComputerWorld (Click on Careers): **www.computerworld.com**
	Entrepreneur: www.entrepreneurmag.com
	Fast Company: www.fastcompany.com
	Forbes: www.forbes.com/magazines/
	Fortune: www.fortune.com
	HispanicOnline.com (Click on Career Center): **www.hispaniconline.com**
	Inc: www.inc.com/incmagazine
	JobWeb (Click on Resources): **www.Jobweb.com**
	New Work News: www.newwork.com
	Occupational Outlook Quarterly: www.bls.gov/opub/ooq/ooqhome.htm
	Saludos Web: www.saludos.com
	SuperOnda (Click on Career): **www.superonda.com**
	The Black Collegian Online: www.black-collegian.com
	Women.com (Click on Career): **www.women.com**
	Working Woman (Click on Career, Small Business, Work/Life Balance): **www.working woman.com**
	U. S. News Online (Click on Work): **www.usnews.com/usnews/home.htm**

Step 2.2 Provide the Reasons for Your Selection

Why are you seeking information about this particular topic right now?

_____

_____

Step 2.3 Reading Summary

Summarize the main points in your own words.

_____

_____

_____

_____

_____

_____

_____

STEP 3 ANALYZE YOUR FINDINGS

Recommendation to Others

Would you recommend the reading to other students? Why or why not? Give reasons for your recommendation.

STEP 4 PLAN YOUR NEXT ACTIONS

Step 4.1 Learning Summary

What did you learn from this reading that will help you in the future? Be specific and explain fully.

Step 4.2 Next Steps

List any topics that were covered briefly in the article you read that you want to research in greater depth.

What sources of information do you plan to consult to get further information?

CHAPTER 12

How to Learn from Internships, College Jobs, and Extracurricular Activities

Don't wait until
your ship comes in.
Swim for it.
—Anonymous

12

VALUE LEARNING OUTSIDE THE CLASSROOM

For 31-year-old billionaire Jerry Yang, some of the pivotal events of his college education happened outside the classroom. Although you may not know Yang by name, if you've searched the Internet, you know Yahoo!, the search engine he designed with his partner, David Filo. We will examine Yang's college experience more closely because it illustrates the importance of utilizing out-of-classroom experiences, even on-campus work-study jobs, to get a leg up on your career.[1]

Jerry Yang did not come from privileged beginnings. He lost his father when he was two. Raised by a single mother, he came to the United States from Taiwan at age 10 knowing one word, *shoe*.

Yang was smart and worked hard. When it came to choosing colleges, he had some wonderful choices: UC Berkeley, Cal Tech, and Stanford. He was offered better scholarships elsewhere, but he chose to go to Stanford because he did not have to pick a major his first year. Although he was leaning strongly toward electrical engineering and eventually majored in it, he wanted to explore other possibilities before making a commitment.

Yang had to work part-time to pay for college. One of those jobs was in the college library, shelving books. It sounds boring, but there he learned that librarians organize books into categories in a systematic way, called the Dewey Decimal System, and use that system to locate books easily. Later on, in late 1993, when the World Wide Web was just beginning, he noticed that using the Web was difficult because no one had categorized Web sites. Along with his partner, he began to design software that would group sites into categories such as "Recreation & Sports," "Health," and "Entertainment." Yahoo! became one of the first systems that enabled people to find the information they were looking for on the Internet in the same way they might in a library.

A second influential nonclassroom experience for Yang was his participation in a study-abroad program in Japan. There he cemented a friendship with Filo, his Yahoo! cofounder, who hailed from Louisiana. He got to know Srinija Srinivasan, who was born in India and grew up in Kansas. She was studying artificial intelligence and information organization and would later become Yahoo!'s editor-in-chief. He met his future wife, Akiko, there, too. Born of Japanese parents, she had grown up in Costa Rica.

By the time Yang was in graduate school, "Jerry's Guide to the World Wide Web," as Yahoo! was first called, was using too much of Stanford's computer space, so he and his partner moved it off campus and began to set up their business. In less than a decade they built a portal that is now visited by more than 100 million people a month. They took Yahoo! international, too, beginning—where else?—in Japan. It is now the number one portal in that country.

Yang's story demonstrates the essential points made in this chapter: Get a variety of experiences, and strive to learn something from every experience you have. Notes business writer Brent Schlender in *Fortune* magazine, "Indeed, if Jerry has a hallmark, it's that he gleans something useful from just about everything he does."[2]

Seek a Variety of Non–Coursework Experiences

If you want your college education to pay bigger career dividends, include some variety in your college experience. In addition to part-time work and study abroad, you might consider such other nonclassroom activities as sports, clubs, student government associations, honors courses, summer programs, cooperative education, volunteer community service, research projects, and service learning.

Think of your college education as a pie chart in which each type of experience is given a percentage reflecting the value it adds to your college education. Some students have a narrow view of college experience. They equate the value of college solely with courses in their major. They don't even notice other sources of potential learning. If they drew a pie chart of their college experience, their major would cover 100 percent of it. Activity 12.1 shows two hypothetical pie charts, one for Jerry Yang based on his life story and another for a student named Michaela. Yang's chart includes major coursework (30 percent), general coursework (20 percent), study abroad (30 percent), part-time library job (15 percent), and research projects (5 percent). Michaela divided her college experience into six parts: general coursework (20 percent), major coursework (20 percent), internships (20 percent), community service (20 percent), part-time job (10 percent), and club membership (10 percent). You can fill in the blank circle to create your own pie chart. Label each section and assign a percentage reflecting its value to your total education.

ACTIVITY 12.1   YOUR COLLEGE EXPERIENCE CHART

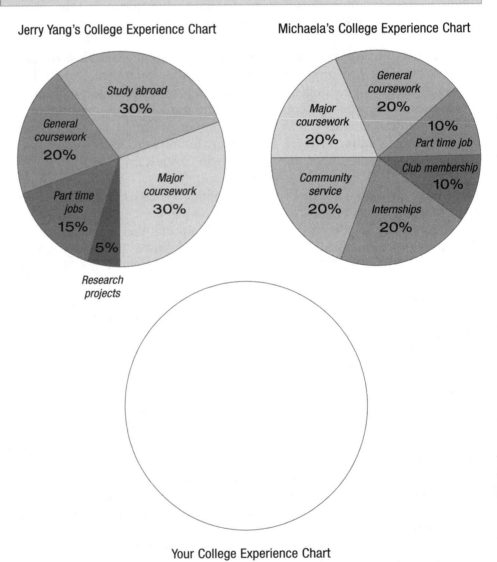

Jerry Yang's College Experience Chart

Michaela's College Experience Chart

Your College Experience Chart

To see the impact that nonclassroom experiences can have, consider a recent study of community service. This research found that five years after college, volunteer work in college, including in-service learning programs, is associated with having a greater sense of empowerment, attending graduate school, earning higher degrees, socializing with persons from culturally diverse groups, and possessing good preparation for work.[3]

Club memberships, especially leadership positions, provide valuable experience, too. For example, some years ago I was leading a daylong workshop on leadership for the community college honor society, Phi Theta Kappa. There I met a student officer from a Midwestern college; let's call her Taylor. The honor society sponsored Taylor's trip to the West Coast. She had never had any money to travel, so for her the chance to visit Seattle and Vancouver was exciting. One of the experiences that she found most memorable was "my first sight of the ocean." But it was more than a sightseeing trip; Taylor also had the chance to participate in a week of leadership training with fellow honor students from around the country.

Internships Link School and Work

One of the most valuable nonclassroom experiences is the internship. Sometimes these programs are called experiential education, work-based learning, cooperative education, or fieldwork. The goals of an internship are to test career choices, build career skills, and apply classroom coursework to real-world problems. Internships are resume builders. You can gain the experience that many employers demand. They give you a foot in the door, allowing you to establish professional contacts.

College internship programs vary in scope and structure. Some are small programs, and internships carry no course credit. Some colleges maintain a list of internships or hold an internship fair; the student must do the work of getting in touch with prospective employers. Other colleges have big programs. These colleges actively develop internships related to student majors, provide resume-writing and interviewing support, and award academic credit for the experience.

Pay and hours vary, too. Some internships are well paid for highly qualified, technically trained students. Others, especially in the arts, education, social services, and entertainment fields, typically provide no pay at all or a small stipend for expenses. Whereas some employers require a full-time semester or summer commitment, others will sponsor interns for a day or two a week for a total of 100 or 200 hours over a year.

The Popularity of Internships Continues to Increase

The most recent survey by the National Association of Colleges and Employers shows that by graduation, more than 80 percent of college students have had an internship or cooperative education experience.[4] Vault.com's Internship Survey showed that internship participation has risen 13 percent in just three years. It also found that 69 percent of students have had two or more internships.[5,6]

Employers like internships because they have been proven an effective way to recruit new employees. Students are realizing that in today's competitive job market, internships may be the best way to test career goals in the real world and to get an inside track for that dream job.

Adam Dawes's case illustrates how internships can help. Adam wanted to work as an independent film producer. He found two internships with production companies: one volunteer, the other paying a stipend. These internships showed him that filmmaking was not for him. He refocused his career goals and decided that a more interesting and smarter move for him would be to combine his visual arts training with multimedia computing. He sought out new internships to test this goal. It took him a year and several internships, but finally an internship led to a full-time job with benefits, doing exactly what he wanted in high-tech multimedia.[7]

Check the internship offerings at your college and then go on-line and see what you can find. This search may open you up to possibilities you had not imagined.

ACTIVITY 12.2   SEARCHING FOR INTERNSHIPS ON THE INTERNET

Check the Riley Guide, **www.dbm.com/jobguide.** Go to the "A-Z Index," click on "I," and scroll down until you find "Internships, Fellowships, and Work Exchange Programs." Then choose a link that is relevant to your interests. Another possibility is the Princeton Review, **www.review.com.** Check the career home page and click on Internships. Two other Web sites are Rising Star Internships, **www.rsinternships.com,** and InternshipPrograms.com, **http://internshipswetfeet.com.** Your college career services office may also list internships, so check its home page.

Describe two internships you found interesting.

_____

_____

_____

_____

_____

_____

_____

Three Sources of Career-Building Lessons

A variety of experiences is important, but the quality of the experience counts, too. Not all experiences provide equal value. Certainly you could guess that such passive activities as watching TV don't generally belong on your college experience chart, no matter how much time you spend watching TV or how much you enjoy particular programs.

If you take the trouble to go on an internship, however, you want to make sure it is truly enriching. The Center for Creative Leadership (CCL),[8] an internationally recognized nonprofit research and training organization, also wondered about what makes a particular work experience truly valuable. They were especially interested in the kinds of experiences that mold successful executives. They asked top executives what events had been significant in helping them reach the top spots in their companies. They analyzed more than 1,000 stories told by business leaders and found that most learning had come from three types of events:

- challenging assignments
- encounters with key people
- coping with hardships[9]

As you will see in the sections that follow, these three types of events are important for everyone, not just for executives, because they improve the odds that career-building learning will occur. We will look at each kind of experience in turn, pointing out its notable characteristics and discussing how you can learn from it.

CHALLENGING ASSIGNMENTS

In the CCL research, both men and women managers describe challenging assignments as the most powerful way to learn new skills.[10] These executives described challenges such as supervising for the first time, starting a new business, and serving on an important project task force. They built their management expertise and became more self-confident.

Expand Your "Comfort Zone"

You don't have to be headed toward the executive suite to take on challenging assignments. All challenging assignments have one feature in common: they force you to go outside your *comfort zone.*[11] Your comfort zone consists of skills you have already mastered. Once you learn to use a computer mouse, for example, you don't have to spend much time or energy thinking about how to work it. Using the mouse is a task inside your comfort zone because you know how to work it. There is only one problem with operating solely in your comfort zone: your learning is at a standstill.

In contrast, when you operate outside your comfort zone, you are doing something you are not used to doing. You are facing a challenge; to meet it, you must learn something new. For Carin on her journalism internship (see Case 12.1), preparing her first story was a significant challenge that required her to operate outside her comfort zone. For a bilingual student interning in a hospital emergency room, interpreting for a doctor during a medical crisis is a challenge. These interns are engaged in doing real-world tasks that take them outside their comfort zone.

My Journalism Internship   **CASE 12.1**

My internship was with *Greenline,* a community newspaper. I wanted to learn aspects of journalism I would not necessarily be exposed to in the classroom. I also thought it was time to build a resume that would help me attain a career as a journalist.

At *Greenline* my primary responsibility was to assist the editor [Tina Filiato] with the monthly publication of the newspaper. Some of my responsibilities included writing stories, proofreading, editing, and creating ads. I also helped around the office: whoever needed extra hands with mail campaigns and the sort.

My very first interview was scary; I did not know what to say or do. I asked my first question and things went well, although I was a bit hesitant. It took me about a week to put my first story together. It was printed in the April issue of *Greenline*—just like that. I felt at the time that Tina had more faith in me than me. I finally saw my work in print and from then on started to believe that this was not an unattainable dream.

After my first interview, I reflected on how I could improve my interviewing skills. . . . I learned with each interview how to deal with different people and their attitudes—often quite defensive. Tina is an excellent role model. I watch and listen to her interact with others. She is always friendly and manages to get her point across. For the June issue, Tina put my story on the front page.

I am writing more than ever and have the freedom to incorporate a little of me in each story. I have noticed that my style of writing has already changed and is improving with each story.

I was unsure and somewhat pessimistic before I started interning. My co-op counselor, Paul Saladino, however, told me that "what you get out of the internship experience is really what you put into it." He was right. With everything I did, from filing to writing stories, I made sure I let my work represent who I was: an ambitious, hard-working, and conscientious person. . . . I have always loved to write, but working with the newspaper has made me see a career in journalism as something I can really pursue.

—Carin D.

Consider the following scenario. Suppose that you had to learn a new computer program for an important project with tight deadlines. Here you are operating outside your comfort zone. You are learning on the run, acquiring new knowledge and increasing your skills.

Now imagine that you have faced this challenge, learned the software program, and met the project deadline. Just imagine the difference in the size of your comfort zone. What was once outside your comfort zone—using the new software program—is now part of your set of skills, like using the mouse. An expanded comfort zone means that you have new skills and new knowledge.

Understandably, people are often reluctant to leave their comfort zones. Outside your comfort zone, your feelings are likely to be intense and wide-ranging. You may feel excitement mixed with anxiety as you struggle to learn and get the job done simultaneously. In working on her first interview with a news source, Carin was scared and hesitant. In truth, it's seldom easy to operate outside your comfort zone. Your performance level may dip, and that's an unpleasant feeling. The temporary discomfort is well worth it, though, because as you learn, you gain the satisfaction and the self-confidence that come with mastery of new skills.

Take the Initiative: Go After Challenging Assignments

Ask for challenging assignments. Volunteer for tough duties; don't depend on your boss to give them to you. The good news about organizations today is that challenges are plentiful.

Taking the initiative can make you a star. Lucent Technology (formerly Bell Labs) is considered one of the best research and development centers in the United States, full of top-notch scientists and engineers. Even among such talented professionals, though, some stand out from the rest. A study found that these stars took the initiative in seeking challenges. They didn't wait for tough assignments to be handed to them.[12] Be a star—step up and ask.

ENCOUNTERS WITH KEY PEOPLE

Role Models and Observational Learning

For the CCL project, successful executives told many stories about their encounters with key people. These encounters were highly influential learning events. This finding might have been predicted, because the powerful boost that key people can give to the career of a junior associate is widely understood. Chapter 13, How to Develop Your Career Network, underscores the central role that others play in your career success. In that chapter you will learn about the many ways a strong network of mutual support and help is beneficial.

What we will focus on here is observational learning. Executives who rose to the top kept their eyes open and learned by watching others. You can, too.

You have already had a lot of practice in observational learning. It is the kind of learning that all children use spontaneously to prepare for adult roles. Children mimic what they see their family members and those around them do.

Psychologists who have studied how we learn through observation have found that you do not have to use your learning about a role right away.[13] You can learn through observation today and not use the learning until much later, whenever an appropriate situation arises.

Observational learning provides information that cannot be found in a textbook. Want to be an entrepreneur, hotel manager, architect, you name it? Go observe someone performing that role. A good role model will provide a standard of excellence toward which you can strive. You can observe competent key people handling real problems on the job, every day.

By watching role models at work, you can get a head start on becoming a professional yourself, because they give you a pattern to follow. Seeing a real lawyer, systems analyst, or pediatrician in action helps you understand the true demands of that particular role. The "reality check" that such observation provides is extremely important, given that media portrayals of professional roles are often distorted or glamorized.

Observe Others, Especially Your Boss

Children's observational learning is largely unconscious. Children tend to observe those closest to them, imitating the behavior of poor role models as well as good ones.

In contrast, the kind of observational learning advocated here is conscious. Make your observations in the workplace an intentional act of learning. Observe people whom you respect, whether it is for their technical knowledge, their interpersonal skills, or their ability to handle the politics of organizational life.

Although Unkyoung was primarily focused on learning new software packages, she took advantage of her internship to watch a skillful communicator in action (see Case 12.2).

CASE 12.2   *A Window on Excellence*

Unkyoung worked as a college intern designing brochures for a small computer company. You can see by her description of the company's salesperson, James K., that she also used her internship to observe how real business situations were effectively handled.

"He has excellent communication skills and always gives a good impression to others. He knows how to handle difficult situations like customers who are not in a good mood or not interested in any products. [He] sits near me. . . . When he talks to customers, he is always polite and generous. Even if the other person is not in a good mood, he has an ability to change the other person's feeling."

—Unkyoung L.

The CCL researchers found that the one person you are most likely to learn from is your boss.[14] One thing that surprised the researchers was that all types of bosses—good bosses, bad bosses, and flawed bosses—turned out to be important teachers.

Those who learned from their bosses had one trait in common: they believed that you can learn from anyone. Your observations can point the way to the behavior and attitudes you want to cultivate or avoid. Carin did significant learning by observing her boss on her journalism internship, described earlier. Activity 12.4, Understanding Your Boss's Style, will help you learn from your boss, whether he or she is good, bad, or flawed.

COPING WITH HARDSHIPS

It's How You Respond to Hardship that Counts

The successful executives interviewed by the CCL researchers told story after story of hardship. The executives had experienced terrible times and they recalled feeling all alone at such times. Their hardships included their own mistakes and failures, such as waiting too long to act, making the wrong decision, or not taking the other person's perspective into account. Traumatic events happened: getting stuck in the wrong job, being demoted, getting fired.

The poem "Don't Be Afraid to Fail" (page 308) is a reminder that everyone makes mistakes and fails at times. It also illustrates the fact that many very successful people experienced spectacular failure at some point and recovered. How did they do it?

To answer this question, *Fortune* magazine interviewed more than 200 people, including leadership experts, coaches, and executives, to learn more about the people who recover from hardship. In a cover story, "So You Fail, Now Bounce Back!" *Fortune* dubbed these people Rebounders.[15] The article's conclusions were similar to those reached by the CCL researchers who studied the hardships of successful executives.

First, rebounders know that they can't control everything that happens in life, but they can control their response to what happens. As a teenager, Arthur Blank, a cofounder of Home Depot, was in a gang and saw one close friend stabbed and another shot to death. His partner, Bernie Marcus, was a poor Russian immigrant's son. Both were fired from a now-defunct home improvement center chain, Handy Dan, on the same day, because of personality differences with the boss. How did they react? They founded Home Depot and built it into a chain of hardware stores with revenues in the billions.

Second, rebounders react with flexibility. Many people who have the ability to rebound from failure experienced tough times while growing up. They learned to adapt. In a crisis, they know how to roll with the punches. A highly successful AT&T executive grew up with an alcoholic father and took nine years to get his college degree. Less than a month after he started his first job, the company went bankrupt. While he was trying to turn around two other companies, they were sold. Now he is in a top position with a powerful company. Everything did not always go smoothly for him, but he succeeded because he learned to be flexible.

Third, rebounders don't play the "blame game." They look inward to see what mistakes they made so that they can learn from them. Even when the executives in the CCL study were not at fault when problems arose, they asked themselves, "Could I have done something different?" Hardships became valuable experiences when executives took the time to look at themselves and to decide what was important in their lives and careers.

Turn Mistakes into a Learning Experience

The process of transforming hardship begins with the recognition that hardships are a part of life. The CCL researchers found that successful executives accept that life isn't always fair. During a bad period, the executives respond with fortitude and patience, and take the long view.

When they come up against failure, rebounders react with positive thinking. They are likely to describe even a big mistake as a "false start" or a "stumble." They retain an underlying sense of optimism and faith in themselves, no matter how bad things get. Although basketball great Michael Jordan was cut from his freshman high school team, he didn't let this initial setback kill his passion for basketball.[16] Successful entrepreneurs average nine failures for every success.[17] They just keep at it. Harry Saal, the founder of a highly successful Silicon Valley software diagnostic systems company, found it easier to raise money from venture capitalists because he had failed a few times. "People say, 'Oh, he went bankrupt on that first venture? I bet he learned something from that, so I'll bankroll him again.'"[18]

Get Back in the Ring

Consider what happened to the lion tamer Graham Thomas Chipperfield. His 500-pound lioness Sheba mauled him so badly that he needed 80 stitches. But Chipperfield didn't blame Sheba. Upon reflection, Chipperfield realized that his near-fatal mistake had been to run into the cage to break up a fight between lions. Since lions regard their trainers as other lions, Sheba had thought that Chipperfield wanted to fight, too.

Chipperfield admitted that the mauling was his fault because he hadn't considered the lion's perspective. However, he did not dwell on his mistake. Although the doctors advised him to rest for two months, he was back with his lions nine days after his injury. Had he waited, he believed, he would never have returned. He understood that making a mistake and reflecting on what happened does not mean wasting time putting yourself down. If you make a mistake, the best response is to confront your shortcomings, see what you can learn, and get back into action.[19]

TAKE CHARGE OF THE LEARNING PROCESS

We have already discussed in Chapter 11 the importance of becoming a self-directed, lifelong learner. Self-directed learners are like Jerry Yang, Yahoo!'s founder: They can extract value even from experiences as mundane as shelving books in the library. Here we look at the practices that successful self-directed learners utilize in the workplace. Unlike challenging assignments, where you learn by plunging into the thick of the action, these practices require you to step back from your experience. It is akin to half-time in that you take a break to examine the game from all angles and make corrections in your game plan.

Call Regular Time-Outs for Reflection

We lead such busy lives and juggle so many responsibilities that we can rush from one thing to another without ever looking back and trying to understand what we have just gone through. Yet stopping on a regular basis and reflecting on your career is a powerful habit to cultivate. Although he is now in his nineties, Peter Drucker, author of 31 books, is still sought after as a business consultant. He says that one of the most important reasons he has been so productive and successful is his practice of setting aside time for reflection. He had the good fortune to learn this habit from a boss when he was just 22 and a journalist at a daily newspaper.[20] Each week his boss would discuss his work. Before the Christmas and summer holidays, the boss would conduct a more extensive review for the entire work team that lasted a day and a half. The review always followed the same format. First, says Drucker, the boss would start with the things the team had done well. Then, he would note areas where they had tried hard and those areas where they had not tried hard enough. Finally, he would give a thorough critique of things that had been done badly. A week later, the boss requested from each team member a written plan for work and learning that covered the next six months. Drucker remembers those sessions with pleasure because they were such a rich source of learning. Later on, after he left the newspaper, he began to conduct a similar review of his own work and make a plan for future learning.

The key element is to put in place a mechanism, like a referee's whistle, that will signal you to take a time-out for reflection. At City University's LaGuardia Community College in New York, students are required to take a seminar while on their internships and, after each internship, to write a self-evaluation essay. Both the group seminars and the individual essays are designed to help students cultivate the habit of reflection. Carin's essay (Case

12.1) is typical. She looked back and traced her development over the course of her internship. In this case, she focused on how she was able to move outside her comfort zone with her boss's support. Activity 12.3, Lessons of Experience, will help you examine the challenges, key people, and hardships in your current internship or work experience.

One popular method for stepping back from the action is the practice of keeping a journal. If you keep one already, include events from your work or community service to deepen your understanding. To start a journal, use the same structure of key events and lessons that was used in the CCL research. Describe three events during the selected time period. For each event, answer two questions: (1) What makes it significant? and (2) What did you learn from it? Make weekly, monthly, or quarterly entries. Your diary of critical incidents will help you cull important lessons from your work experience.

Another possibility, if you like to talk things through, is to review your workplace experiences with a friend, a mentor, or a family member—someone who will listen to you. Here is what Shannon, a student intern, said about the time she spent talking with a colleague: "I discussed my career last night with John for about an hour and a half. Although we always talk to each other, we have never had this kind of discussion. He has gone through school transferring, job hunting, career changes, and made many important decisions. . . . I learned a lot from this informal interview. . . . It was very helpful for me."

Use a Multi-Lens Perspective to Examine Your Experience

In a complex world filled with confusing events, syndicated columnist Thomas Friedman argues, the only way to make sense of your experience is to look at the world through a multi-lens perspective. Jerry Yang developed a multi-lens perspective. You may recall that he came from Taiwan, married a woman of Japanese parentage who grew up in Costa Rica, and became close to a diverse set of people. He has surrounded himself with cultural viewpoints other than his own. An advantage of such a multicultural environment is that the people in Yang's inner circle are more likely to challenge him to think differently and more deeply about an issue because their experience and knowledge differ from his. In college Yang also resisted a narrow focus on engineering, opting instead to include study abroad as part of his program. His broader knowledge base gives him the intellectual flexibility to examine an event from many angles, thus leading to a more comprehensive understanding of the issues. *Futurist* magazine notes that many colleges are starting master's programs in liberal arts for technically trained workers such as accountants, engineers, and systems analysts, because a broad knowledge of many areas is necessary to adapt to today's fast-changing workplace.[21] At a recent career seminar, a 26-year-old political fund-raising consultant who has her own business shared her personal technique for developing a multi-lens perspective. She reads a quality newspaper every day. She includes not just the topics that she typically is drawn to, but three articles that she would not normally read. Over the years this simple technique will broaden her view of the world and give her a multi-lens perspective.[22]

Get Feedback on Your Strengths and Developmental Needs

In school, you get regular feedback in the form of grades. However, in the workplace, few are as lucky as Peter Drucker, whose boss took the time for regular feedback. How will you know how you are doing? Often you have to ask.

Here are some tips on how to get feedback. Think of one or two people whom you trust and who have had the opportunity to observe your work. Schedule a private meeting, even if only a short one. Before the meeting, let the person know that you would like some feedback on your performance for the purpose of your career development. You may be surprised at what he or she tells you. Even if you hold a less than challenging job to support yourself in school, your work style will be apparent to others.

It's not always easy to hear feedback, either positive or negative, so take notes during a feedback session. Ask your respondents for examples to help you understand their points. During a feedback session, don't defend yourself or blame others. Just write down what they say and think it over. At the end, thank them.

The CCL researchers were told about an executive who finally had to be removed from her job because she denied all the feedback she received. "'There is nothing wrong with me,' was her stance; 'The rest of the world is all messed up.'"[23] Contrast this case with that of another high-level manager who was almost fired. Her management style intimidated those around her, especially those people she supervised. In a training program she listened to feedback from others, even though it was painful. As a result, she realized that she needed to change her leadership style and become more approachable. Now she is a more effective manager. When you hear feedback about your shortcomings, especially when it comes from several sources you trust, it's important to listen—and learn.

Create a Development Plan to Build Your Skills

A powerful tool for directing your own career learning (rather than leaving it to chance) is a *development plan*. A development plan outlines your learning objectives and identifies the kinds of activities that will help you achieve them. This tool ensures that you will continually build your skills. Peter Drucker's editor required one every six months. Making such a career plan is typical for high-level executives, but you don't have to be at the top of an organization to use this tool. An editor of financial newsletters decided as her development plan to learn one new skill every year. One year she tackled public speaking; another year, the Internet and popular computer software. She has learned about financial derivatives and explored how to get a book published. These skills were acquired without formal education, and they saved her when the real estate company where she had been working suddenly went bankrupt. Her new skills have allowed her to change careers and have opened many doors for her. She now has more choices and more income security.[24]

A typical development plan begins with a self-assessment, in which you identify your strengths and shortcomings. Then, you select one or more developmental targets. For example, say you want to work more effectively with a difficult boss. Your self-assessment process may have revealed a tendency to operate too independently, so your development plan would include giving your boss more frequent updates on your work. Your development plan might also include readings from magazine articles or Internet sites, observation of a coworker who is more effective at dealing with your boss, or a chat with someone outside of work—maybe even a former boss—on how to manage your boss better.

If you are looking for developmental targets, go back to Activity 3.4, Your Portable Skills Profile, and select an item or two that you want to work on. It could be becoming a better listener, learning to speak up in meetings, or getting to work on time. You may need to practice patience, check your work more carefully, or become more assertive.

A good development plan is specific. A goal like "becoming a better worker" is too general and won't lead to an increase in skills. All good plans share the same elements: clear goals, a list of actions to reach the goals, and a timetable for review. Activity 12.5 provides you with a worksheet to outline a development plan.

Increasingly, people are turning to someone who will act as their career coach. Career coaches help you formulate development goals and brainstorm ways to reach them, keep you on track, and help you when you get stuck. There is even a new class of professionals who specialize in providing this type of career support. In college, you might look to a counselor, internship advisor, or professor to be your career coach.

CELEBRATE YOUR SUCCESS

Hardships and failure are painful experiences, but it may surprise you to learn that it is not uncommon to have mixed feelings when you succeed. While you feel happy and triumphant, at the same time you may experience feelings of emptiness, sadness, or loss. A significant accomplishment at work—overcoming a challenge or receiving a promotion—may bring thoughts that you are fooling others and are unworthy of this success. Psychologists have called these feelings the "success blues."[25] Another name for these feelings is the "Alexander syndrome," after Alexander the Great, who fell into a depression when, at last, he had conquered all the known world.

If you find yourself having these unexpected feelings, you can do several things: (1) Acknowledge your mixed-up feelings. Talk with an understanding friend. (2) Celebrate your success in a small way. You might splurge on a dinner out, buy a keepsake to remind you of the occasion, or take a day off. Spend time with those who will be impressed with your achievement and will rejoice in your success. (3) Give yourself some time to adjust to your new status. After this adjustment period, you can think more clearly about new goals and challenges.

WHERE STUDENTS GET STUCK, AND WHAT TO DO IF IT HAPPENS TO YOU

You must guard against drawing sweeping conclusions from one bad experience, more commonly known as "throwing out the baby with the bath water." A common situation will illustrate this point. Fiona wanted to work in the computer field. On her first internship she had to work alone and felt isolated most of the time. She announced to her internship advisor that she had decided to pursue another choice, elementary school teaching. She did not explore whether other companies or positions would offer her more contact with people or use more teamwork, which would suit her preferred working style. Nor did she explore fields that combine working in the computer field with teaching, such as conducting computer training courses. Her advisor encouraged her to try another internship in the computer field that used her people skills before she made such a drastic switch.

KEY POINTS

1. Seek a variety of nonclassroom experiences as part of your college education so that you can build different kinds of skills and knowledge.

2. Internships link school and work, providing opportunities to test career choices, build new skills, and apply what you learned in school to real-life situations.

3. Center for Creative Leadership researchers found that successful executives learned the most from the following three types of events:
   - challenging assignments
   - encounters with key people
   - coping with hardships

4. Challenging assignments are tasks that force you to operate outside your comfort zone and to learn something new.

5. Observe key people at work. Good role models will show you how to deal effectively with a variety of real-life situations in the workplace. By observing a bad or flawed role model, you can decide how not to behave and avoid costly career mistakes.

6. To learn from hardships, strive to learn from your mistakes (so you won't repeat them), but don't dwell on them. Get on with your career and your life.

DON'T BE AFRAID TO FAIL

You've failed many times, although you may not remember. You fell down the first time you tried to walk. You almost drowned the first time you tried to swim, didn't you? Did you hit the ball the first time you swung a bat? Heavy hitters, the ones who hit the most home runs, also strike out a lot. R. H. Macy failed seven times before his store in New York caught on. English novelist John Creasey got 753 rejection slips before he published 564 books. Babe Ruth struck out 1,330 times, but he also hit 714 home runs. Don't worry about failure. Worry about the chances you miss When you don't even try.

© 1986 United Technologies Corporation. Used with permission.

7. To take charge of the learning process: call regular time-outs for reflection, get feedback on your strengths and limitations, and draft a development plan.

8. Use a multi-lens perspective, looking at your experience from different angles. It will enrich your learning.

9. When you succeed, you may experience feelings both of happiness and of loss or emptiness. Acknowledge your mixed feelings. In some modest way, celebrate your triumph. Take time to adjust to your success.

10. If you have one bad work experience, don't overreact; analyze its causes. Drawing sweeping conclusions may cause you to change directions unnecessarily.

LESSONS OF EXPERIENCE   ACTIVITY **12.3**

OVERVIEW

In this activity you will analyze your internship or work experience. You will reflect on events at work and describe what you have learned from them. The purpose of this activity is to teach you *how to learn* from your work experience.

Analyzing your work experience is a technique that you can use throughout your working life. Such analysis increases your awareness of your on-the-job career development. Reflection about your past experience is often the starting point for setting new learning objectives.

You will recall that the Center for Creative Leadership's researchers studied the key work experiences of successful executives. Their results suggest that four actions are particularly effective in furthering your career development on the job.

1. Seek challenging assignments.
2. Observe key people and let them teach you.
3. Cope with hardships.
4. Get feedback and know your strengths and areas for improvement.

In this activity, you will use this framework to examine your own work experience.

In you need more room or are instructed to do so, type answers separately.

TASK 1 DESCRIBE AND ANALYZE A CHALLENGING ASSIGNMENT

A challenging assignment is one that involves tackling something new or difficult. Challenging assignments take place outside your "comfort zone" and, when completed, build a sense of mastery.

Describe a challenging assignment that you have done well.

_____

_____

_____

_____

_____

Trace your feelings from the beginning to the end of this challenge.

_____

_____

_____

_____

What did you learn from this experience?

_____

_____

_____

_____

TASK 2   OBSERVE KEY PEOPLE

Identify people at work whom you admire. Then specify the ways that you would wish to be like them. You might want to acquire the same knowledge or the same kinds of job assignments. You might want to develop skills or personal qualities that they exhibit. Observe these people as often as possible and imagine yourself being like them someday.

Think of two people at work whom you admire. For each person, provide the following information.

a. Give the person's name, title, and a brief job description.

b. Why did you select this person? What specific knowledge, kinds of job assignments, skills, or personal qualities do you admire?

c. Describe a situation that you observed that involved this person and taught you something that you will find helpful in the future.

PERSON #1 Name: _____

_____

_____

_____

_____

PERSON #2 Name: _____

_____

_____

_____

_____

TASK 3   DESCRIBE A HARDSHIP AT WORK AND HOW YOU COPED WITH IT

Hardships are trying situations with which you must cope and in which you feel all alone. These ordeals may be the result of your mistakes. They may also be caused by someone or something else.

Describe a hardship from your work experience.

_____

_____

_____

_____

How did you cope during this period?

_____

_____

_____

_____

What did you learn from it?

_____

_____

_____

_____

Some students feel that they have not endured any hardships on their present jobs. If this is true for you, use an example from a previous internship or job. Confer with your instructor if you still have difficulty identifying a difficult situation, setback, or mistake.

TASK 4 GET FEEDBACK ON YOUR STRENGTHS AND AREAS FOR IMPROVEMENT

Feedback helps you to see yourself as others see you. *Self-assessment* is a way of giving feedback to yourself. Both are powerful techniques to identify your strengths and the areas in which you need improvement, such as your ability to work in groups, solve problems, or manage your time.

According to the feedback that you have received from other people, describe the primary reasons for your success to date.

_____

_____

_____

_____

From your own self-assessment, describe the primary reasons for your success to date.

_____

_____

_____

_____

According to the feedback that you have received from other people, describe an important area in which you need to improve your skills or performance.

_____

_____

_____

_____

From your own self-assessment, describe an important area in which you need to improve your skills or performance.

_____

_____

_____

_____

ACTIVITY 12.4   UNDERSTANDING YOUR BOSS'S STYLE[26]

OVERVIEW

In this activity you will find some questions to guide your observation of your boss. Once you understand your boss's style, you can usually think of ways to interact with her or him more effectively.

TASK 1

Answer the following questions about your boss's style.

1. What are your boss's strengths?

_____

_____

_____

_____

2. What are your boss's blind spots?

_____

_____

_____

_____

3. How does your boss like to get and give information (e.g., face-to-face, reports, memos, E-mail, phone calls)?

_____

_____

_____

4. What is your boss's style of interacting with others (e.g., one-on-one, team meetings, brainstorming sessions, touching base informally, formal meetings with set agendas)?

_____

_____

_____

5. What will get you into trouble with your boss? What does this reveal about your boss's values and priorities?

_____

_____

_____

TASK 2

What can you learn from your boss that can make you more effective?

_____

_____

_____

_____

TASK 3

Once you understand your boss's style, you can often develop a more effective working relationship. On the basis of your assessment of your boss's style, describe some ways to work more effectively with your boss.

_____

_____

_____

_____

A DEVELOPMENT PLAN WORKSHEET   ACTIVITY 12.5

OVERVIEW

The purpose of a development plan is to outline your learning objectives and the kinds of activities that will help you achieve them. The best development plans have clear goals, a list of actions to reach those goals, and a timetable for tracking your progress. Use the guide below and outline your development plan. Complete the following using a separate sheet of paper.

TASK 1 ANSWER SELF-ASSESSMENT GUIDE QUESTIONS

What skills do I want to learn (e.g., a specific computer software application)? What qualities and habits do I want to cultivate (e.g., patience, time management)? What are some weaknesses that I want to improve (e.g., speaking up in a group, researching on the Internet)?

_____

_____

_____

_____

_____

_____

You may recognize the need to develop certain skills and habits from your own analysis of your strengths and development needs. Feedback from others may also point out important development needs.

TASK 2 SET A GOAL

Identify a specific goal from the list above.

_____

TASK 3 LIST ACTIONS

List the actions you will take to achieve your goal.

Remember the value of challenging assignments and of observing key people in developing skills and competencies. Another technique is to find a partner and learn together. You may also want read more about developing this skill or competency. There are many good books and articles on how to listen better, deal with conflict, think critically, etc. Biographies and autobiographies also show you how others have mastered a wide variety of skills, from delivering superior customer service to persisting despite obstacles.

_____

_____

_____

_____

_____

TASK 4 ESTABLISH A TIMETABLE AND MONITORING

Select a date for completion and put this in your calendar. Also identify two or three intermediate points to monitor your progress and adjust your actions, if necessary. It is especially valuable if you can get feedback from others on your progress at these monitoring points. Put these monitoring points in your calendar.

_____

_____

CHAPTER 13

How to Develop Your Career Network

Very few people ever make it alone. We all need someone to lead the way, to show us the ropes, to tell us the norms, to encourage, support, and make it a little easier for us. Who are these people who will do that and where do we find them?
—Natasha Josefowitz, *Paths to Power*

CAREER NETWORKS

A fundamental way to advance your career is to build a career network. Its purpose is to help you do your job better. A network supports your efforts to be successful. The assistance provided by a career network is rich and varied. Network members provide information, instruction, and vital information. They are there when you need emotional support and honest feedback. They open doors to career opportunities.

A career network operates on the same principle as a computer network. The key element is linkages. When computer experts link individual computers into a computer network, they ease communication and exchanges between computers. Each computer in the network becomes more powerful and effective. Career networks operate the same way. When you network with others, communication and exchanges increase. You (and the people you link with) become more powerful and effective. A career network provides benefits for all its members.

People began career networking when they started to understand the power of the *old-boy network*. The old-boy network is the name given to an informal association of privileged men. These men are linked because they have attended the same prestigious colleges, belong to the same country clubs and churches, and live in the same exclusive neighborhoods. Members of the old-boy network share information and resources, and they provide each other with mutual support. The result is that members of the old-boy network have greater career opportunities and chances for success. Other groups have realized that they too need to link up to form career networks, share information and resources, and offer support.

In this chapter you will see the value of a large and diverse network. You will see the many ways that your network can help. A section is devoted to the erroneous beliefs and misguided attitudes that inhibit networking activity. You will identify your network members and be introduced to methods that can increase the size of your network. You will learn about the networking opportunities offered by professional associations. Advice will be offered so that you can avoid the typical ways in which students get stuck when trying to network.

SEVEN WAYS THAT YOUR CAREER NETWORK WORKS FOR YOU

In this section we will examine seven specific ways in which career network members provide help. In her career book *Paths to Power*, Natasha Josefowitz used popular expressions involving parts of the body to describe three of these ways. In her words, network members can be a "brain to pick," a "shoulder to cry on," and a "kick in the pants."[1] In this spirit, we have looked at other sources on networking and have come up with four additional ways in which network members help: a "foot in the door," a "nose for the truth," a "hand to guide you," and an "ear to the ground." You can see that network help is multifaceted. Let's look at each area of helpfulness in more detail.

1. *A Brain to Pick.* A brain to pick is an expert, someone who provides problem-solving help and information. This person can give you advice and suggestions. Remember the old saying, "Two heads are better than one."

2. *A Hand to Guide You.* A hand to guide you is a teacher, someone who helps you learn new skills or new job tasks. Your guiding hand could be your supervisor, a talented coworker, a professor, or even a fellow student.

3. *An Ear to the Ground.* Certain people in organizations have an ear to the ground. They seem to be in the know. They know what projects will be canceled or funded and why, who will be promoted, and what might happen next that could affect your working life. They are not gossips or rumormongers. Instead, their information helps you anticipate and understand organizational decisions. These people are found at all organizational levels, from the copy and mail room to the president's office. They may share vital information that is crucial to your success *if* you can be discreet and *if* you reciprocate with factual information when you can.

4. *A Shoulder to Cry On.* A shoulder to cry on is someone who provides support to help you get through a hard time. These people are often drawn from your circle of family and friends.

CASE 13.1   *It Helps to Have a Hand to Guide You*

Jon, a recent graduate, tells how he benefited from the example of a fellow student.

"I was used to 'getting by' with very little work. Then, I became friends with Bob, who studied every day and cared about getting excellent grades. I began to study with him. Gradually, I began to care about getting top grades, too.

"Well, I won a scholarship worth over $30,000 a year because I had excellent grades. Bob, who taught me to study every day, made a significant contribution to my winning this scholarship. By the way, Bob is a winner, too. He also got a big scholarship."

5. *A Kick in the Pants.* You need a kick in the pants from someone when you need to be challenged to get into action, manage your time better, or structure a task. Such people help you when your motivation is low. Select these people carefully so that they don't undermine your confidence.

6. *A Nose for the Truth.* A nose for the truth is someone who acts as an appraiser and helps you to honestly answer the question "How am I doing?" An appraiser helps you to gauge your strengths, showing you where and how you need to improve. Select someone whose judgment you trust. Find someone who can be candid with you without putting you down.

7. *A Foot in the Door.* A foot in the door is someone who provides you with access to career opportunities. A foot in the door is that special person who looks out for your well-being. This person speaks up for you, takes your side, and sees that you get challenging job assignments. Sometimes this type of person is referred to as a godmother or godfather. This person can be your boss, an influential member of your organization, a professor, internship advisor, or placement director.

CASE 13.2   *Out of a Job*

"I NEED A FOOT IN THE DOOR"

Unfortunately, the beginning of Stephanie's story is all too common today. She lost her job due to a company downsizing. Everyone in the New Jersey branch where she worked was laid off with a week's notice. She was very upset about losing her job, because, although the commute was long, the job enabled her to have her own place and pay her tuition. How was she going to pay her bills now, and buy textbooks?

Used to taking care of herself, Stephanie immediately began job hunting and visited an employment agency, but was discouraged by impersonal treatment. In thinking about what to do next, she remembered learning about career networks in her career seminar. She decided to tap her career network for job leads. She began to ask her managers if they knew of any job opportunities. One of her managers recommended her to his friend. In less than two weeks she had a new job within walking distance of her college. Furthermore, she increased her annual salary by $3,000.

Stephanie noted that the employment agency couldn't match the efficiency of her network. The employment agency did not know her skills and experience as well as someone who was a member of her network. Her manager was pleased to help her and his friend link up. Her short job search and better job were the result of the help that she got from her manager.

OVERCOMING THE INTERNAL OBSTACLES TO NETWORKING

Some students have attitudes and beliefs that inhibit their networking activity. These attitudes are internal obstacles to networking. In "Why Networking Isn't Sleazy,"[2] Richard Fein, a college placement director, outlines several attitudes and beliefs that prevent students from building a career network. He wants to dispel these self-defeating attitudes toward networking.

"I'm Not the Insincere Type!"

Some students are repelled by the notion that they should cultivate relationships deliberately to increase the size and diversity of their network. Students describe this *deliberate* relationship-building as sleazy and political, especially if the relationship is with someone higher up in the organization. This attitude presumes that you can get your job done in isolation and that you will never need others to help you. In fact, taking the initiative to establish a productive working relationship (which may differ from a friendship) is not insincere. It is efficient and effective. Remember, it is hard to ask for and get cooperation from a stranger.

"It's Not Part of My Job to Network!"

This attitude assumes that your job consists of a narrow set of well-defined and isolated tasks. This way of working is old-fashioned. Now you must know whom to contact and be able to count on their help to solve the problems associated with your job responsibilities.

"I Hate to Ask for Favors!"

Some students dislike the idea of networking because they are uncomfortable asking for help. They are shy. They feel embarrassed. These students say that they hate to put someone else out or intrude on someone's time and goodwill. What these students overlook is that networks are mutually beneficial. The person who does you a favor today may need one from you tomorrow.

"I'm Not the Power-Hungry Type!"

This attitude is often displayed by those who like to help others, such as teachers, social workers, and drug counselors. They believe that since they are not interested in obtaining power and influence for themselves, there is no need to network. What they overlook is that when they have a strong network they are often able to use it to increase services for the people that they want to help. When you increase your power and influence, you can use that power to advance the causes, ideas, and programs that you believe are important.

EXAMINE YOUR CAREER NETWORK

Career networks thrive on mutually beneficial relationships. Count someone as a network member if you are confident that he or she would be willing and able to provide at least one of the kinds of help just outlined. For the most part, you should be able to provide that person with at least one kind of help in return. Although network members are frequently friends, mutual benefit is what defines the career network relationship. There is one exception to this rule. Sometimes people in your network who extend their help have dedicated their careers to helping others. They don't expect you to return the favor. Your counselor or co-op advisor is an example of this kind of person. Remember, too, that it is typical that early in your career you may receive more help than you can provide. Later, you will have the opportunity to help others.

Strive for Many Linkages

A strong career network has many linkages. The more people that you link up with, the stronger your network will be. Don't overlook *anyone* who might provide assistance in becoming more effective on the job or in reaching your career goals. There is no one correct number of network members, but the greater the number, the more likely you are to get the help you need.

Draw Members from Every Arena of Your Life

Create your personal career network of people from all arenas of your life. Members of your career network may be drawn from your family and friends. You may also include members of neighborhood and community groups to which you belong, such as religious groups, parent groups, volunteer service groups, or hobby or sports groups. Don't forget service professionals such as your dentist or your barber. Remember to include your spouse's friends or the parents of your children's friends.

Since you are creating a career network, pay special attention to including members from your workplace (current and former) and your college. From your college, consider including fellow students, graduates, counselors, and faculty members. Strive to include members from all these arenas. Don't be discouraged if one arena seems to offer few networking opportunities. Make up for it with strength in other areas.

Create your personal network chart after you study the sample chart in Table 13.1. This sample includes about a quarter of the members of Laurie Crowne's career network. Laurie lists her network members, her relationship with each, and the kinds of help that are exchanged. Figure 13.1 reminds you of the variety of help that you can get and give within a network. In the sample in Table 13.1, the mutually beneficial relationships are clear. The one exception is the professor. One goal of the college faculty is to provide you with career help.

Create your own career network chart. Strive to list at least 35 people. The easiest way to think about potential network members is to review the four principal sources: your family and friends, your community, your college, and your workplace. Test whether they truly belong in your network by showing the type of help that they can provide you and the kind of help that you can provide them in return.

Network Member	Ways You Get Help	Ways You Might Give Help	TABLE 13.1
Family			*A portion of the network chart for Laurie Crowne.*
Carol Crowne (sister)	Shoulder to Cry On, Kick in the Pants	Brain to Pick	
Dennis Gallagher (cousin)	Brain to Pick, Kick in the Pants, Hand to Guide You	Brain to Pick	
Community			
Megan Taylor (PTA)	Foot in the Door	Hand to Guide You	
Gabrielle Mazique (church member)	Shoulder to Cry On	Shoulder to Cry On, Kick in the Pants, Hand to Guide You	
College			
Keith Kirkland (student)	Nose for the Truth	Shoulder to Cry On	
Renée White (professor)	Nose for the Truth, Hand to Guide You		
Internship Site, Workplace, Former Jobs			
Kathleen Ryan (administrative assistant)	Ear to the Ground	Ear to the Ground	
Lili Han (former coworker)	Kick in the Pants, Nose for the Truth	Hand to Guide You	
Sabrina Howard (boss's boss)	Foot in the Door	Ear to the Ground	

FIGURE 13.1

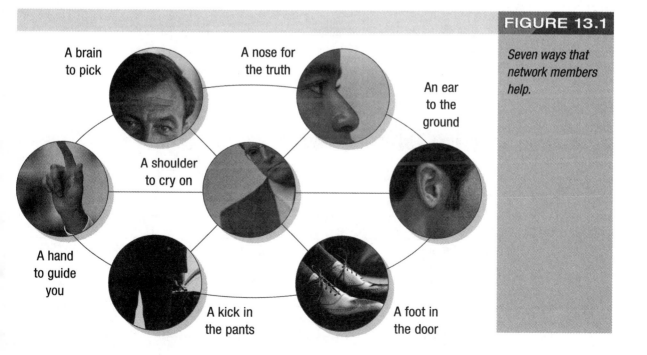

Seven ways that network members help.

ACTIVITY 13.1   YOUR NETWORK CHART

Network Member	Ways You Get Help	Ways You Might Give Help
Family		
Community		
College		
Internship Site, Workplace, Former Jobs		

PROFESSIONAL ASSOCIATIONS: A KEY NETWORKING OPPORTUNITY

Professional associations are formal groups of individuals engaged in similar work or who share career interests. Their purpose is to advance the concerns of their members. Virtually every professional group has a professional association. Some examples are the American Speech–Language–Hearing Association, the National Restaurant Association, the American Society of Landscape Architects, and the American Bar Association.

Networking is one of the primary reasons that such groups exist. They provide opportunities for their members to get to know one another through conventions and meetings. They recognize the accomplishments of their members and often encourage new members. They publicize job openings in their field. Frequently, they encourage student membership by lowering the annual dues, sponsoring special social hours and panels for students, and offering awards and scholarships to recognize student accomplishments.

An easy way to locate the professional association most closely related to your career interests is to consult the *Occupational Outlook Handbook*. Another valuable print reference is the *Encyclopedia of Associations*.

Some groups, especially if their members are typically underrepresented in a particular workplace, provide special sources of support and knowledge (serving as a foot in the door, a nose for the truth, a shoulder to cry on). The Society for Advancement of Chicanos and Native Americans in Science is one such group. These groups seek to cut down on the isolation that their members sometimes feel at work. These groups are especially helpful if your family and community cannot help you with your career. You may want to join one of these formal networking groups to increase your networking possibilities.

Suppose that you want to start your own business. It is an increasingly popular option, especially for women (who are five times more likely to start their own company than men). Yet, up to half of new businesses fail within five years. Before you take the plunge, use the resources of the National Association of Women Business Owners. They offer brains to pick and hands to guide you.

Table 13.2 will help you utilize the Web for networking purposes. You will find Web sites for professional organizations, support group and chatroom sites, and address-finding tools for locating people and organizations.

Networking Pays Off in a Job Search   CASE 13.3

When the author interviewed Jose, he was about to start a great new job. He had five offers to choose from! He credited networking as an important source of job offers and job support. Jose joined the Society of Hispanic Professional Engineers (SHPE) as a college student. He started going to their conferences. One immediate gain was "seeing Spanish engineers working in the real world throughout the country."

He remained active in SHPE, even though his first two jobs after graduation were obtained through his college's career services office. After he completed his master's degree at night in solid-state mechanical engineering, SHPE was the source of one of his five job leads.

Jose's goal is to start his own engineering consulting firm with his friends within five years. You can be sure that SHPE will be an important source for talent in his new company. And his networking skills will be invaluable as he seeks clients for his new business.

TABLE 13.2	Guides to Professional Organizations
Web resources for networking.	These three sites provide links to professional associations. **American Society of Association Executives:** www.asaenet.org **Yahoo!** (Business & Economy>Organizations>Professional): **www.yahoo.com** **Internet Public Library** (Reference>Associations on the Net): **www.ipl.org**
	Additional Resources and Support
	America's Career InfoNet (Career Resource Library): **www.acinet.org** Provides resource links for disabled workers; ethnic groups; military; older workers; self-employed workers, homebased workers, and telecommuters; veterans; and women.
	The Riley Guide (Resources for Women, Minorities, and Other Affinity Groups and Audiences): **www.dbm.com/jobguide/** Provides links to a wide variety of groups, including those for gay workers and Native Americans.
	The Job Hunters Bible (Contacts): **www.jobhuntersbible.com** The "contacts" section of the Job Hunter's Bible provides links to chat-room message boards, newsgroups, and mailing lists, as well as telephone directories and E-mail address-finding tools.
	JobStar California (Hidden Jobs): **www.jobstar.org** Provides sources for electronic networking and tips for becoming an effective networker.

ACTIVITY 13.2   PROFESSIONAL ASSOCIATION MEMBERSHIP

Convinced about the value of networking? Then become aware of your professional network opportunities. List the professional associations that you might benefit from joining, along with their mailing, E-mail, and Internet addresses and their telephone and fax numbers.

PROFESSIONAL ASSOCIATIONS

_____

_____

_____

_____

_____

_____

_____

_____

_____

_____

WHERE STUDENTS GET STUCK, AND WHAT TO DO IF IT HAPPENS TO YOU

Your Career Network Lacks Diversity

A healthy network is not restricted. When your criterion for inclusion in your network is too narrow, you needlessly limit the effectiveness and power of your network. Sometimes people are unaware that they have restricted their network. One way that people restrict their networks is to associate only with people who work at the same level of the organization (i.e., all peers). Another way is to associate only with those who share a common characteristic (e.g., all women, all college students, or all members of one occupation). Sometimes people limit their network to people who come from one source (all family members). Reach out to all types of people for your network.

Always Receiving, Never Giving

Networking is a two-way street. When you always ask for help but never reciprocate, your network will fall apart. People stop wanting to help you. Leanne, for example, always had an "emergency." At work she would go to one coworker and then another, asking them to cover for her while she made a phone call, take her shift because she had some errand to run, or trade days off so that she could study for her "killer" exam. Yet, as her coworkers soon discovered, Leanne always had some excuse when it came to returning the favor. One by one her coworkers turned a deaf ear to her requests. Leanne never caught on. She just wondered why her "friends" had turned against her and would no longer help her out.

Relationships require maintenance on an ongoing basis. Stay in regular touch with the people in your career network. Typical ways to stay in touch include telephoning periodically, sending greeting cards, and going out for lunch together. Basic manners are essential. When someone helps you, remember to say thank you.

One way to think about whether you are doing the necessary work to maintain a healthy network is to imagine that you have a "favor bank." Naturally, you want to maintain a big balance in your account. This means making regular deposits into the favor bank. Offering help and sharing information are two important ways that you can build up a substantial balance in your favor bank. Sometimes this means doing things that are not exactly a part of your job description (e.g., running an errand or staying late to meet a deadline). Without making deposits in the favor bank, you can't make withdrawals when you have a need.

KEY POINTS

1. A fundamental way to advance your career is to build a career network. A network supports your efforts to be successful. It will help you to do your job better. Career networks are sources of advice, instruction, and vital information. Network members can provide emotional support and honest feedback. They open doors to career opportunities.

2. The assistance provided by a career network is rich and varied. Seven principal ways in which people in your network offer help can be characterized as follows:

A brain to pick	A kick in the pants
A hand to guide you	A nose for the truth
An ear to the ground	A foot in the door
A shoulder to cry on	

3. Negative attitudes and misunderstandings about networks are internal obstacles that lead some college students to avoid networking.

4. A career network is a mutually beneficial relationship. You give as well as receive help from your career network.

5. You create a strong network by linking up with as many people as you can. Your career network is made up of people from all arenas of your life: family, friends, community, college, and workplace.

6. Professional associations provide key networking opportunities, since that is one of their main reasons for existing. Student membership enhances your career advancement.

7. Make your network as diverse as possible, and stay in contact with your network members on a regular basis.

CASE 13.4 *A Career Discussion with a Valued Network Member*

I discussed my career with John. He and I are in the same career area, which is the legal field.

John is working in a prestigious entertainment law firm. . . . John has foresight for his career. Although he is now in a good position, he always thinks about the future. . . . He prepares himself in law school. . . . Since he has an M.B.A. degree with a major in International Marketing, he wants to combine his law degree and M.B.A. degree by getting a position in an international law firm.

I asked John to give me suggestions about what majors will be good for me. John's suggestion and my idea are the same: English. I need to improve my language and writing skills first because these are my weaknesses.

John is the most important person in my career network, and I will keep getting suggestions from him and other network members because this is very helpful for me.

—Shannon C.

ACTIVITY 13.3 CAREER INFORMATION INTERVIEW

OVERVIEW

In this activity you will meet with a knowledgeable person in your career network to discuss your career. Your main purpose is to *gather information* from someone established in a career similar to the one that you hope to pursue. This interview will help you to (1) solve your career dilemma, (2) set your career direction, and (3) practice holding effective discussions.

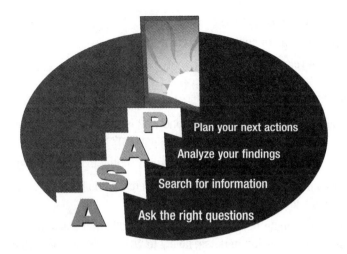

If you need more room, or if you are instructed to do so, type your answers separately.

STEP 1   ASK THE RIGHT QUESTIONS

Step 1.1   Selection of Interview Questions

To conduct a career information interview, you will need to prepare a list of questions. You were introduced to these questions in Chapter 4. They are repeated here for your convenience.

Check the types of career information that are particularly important to you.

☐ Nature of the work

☐ Entry requirements

☐ Rewards and benefits

☐ Outlook for the future

☐ Firsthand knowledge about the career from the person being interviewed

CAREER DISCUSSION QUESTIONS

The following 33 questions are grouped according to these five types of information. Be sure that you cover each type of career information by asking at least one question in each area.

Circle at least 10 questions that you want to ask during your career information interview.

NATURE OF THE WORK

1. What kind of work is done in this field (e.g., types of tasks, responsibilities, assignments, projects)?
2. What kinds of people do you work with?
3. How much of the work is with data? With people? With things?
4. Do you work indoors, sitting, or standing? Do you work outdoors? Do you travel?
5. What kinds of pressures are felt by a person working in this field?
6. What are the working conditions? Could they affect my health and safety?
7. How flexible are the work hours in this field? Does it involve long hours, shift work, overtime, weekends?

8. Who are the major employers?

9. What are the areas of concentration in this field?

10. What are the related occupations?

ENTRY REQUIREMENTS

11. What education is required for someone who is entering this field (associate's, bachelor's, master's, or other advanced degrees)?

12. What college majors do you suggest as good routes to enter this field?

13. How competitive are the entrance requirements to the educational programs in this field? Are they available in this area?

14. What kinds of people tend to do well in this field? What skills and qualities are important (e.g., attention to detail, ability to work under stress, negotiating skill)?

REWARDS AND BENEFITS

15. What does a typical worker earn in this field?

16. What is the salary range of people in this field after they have job experience?

17. Are employee benefits, such as paid vacation, sick leave, pension, and health insurance, typical in this occupation?

18. Is there an opportunity to learn new skills?

19. Will my work be recognized by my coworkers?

20. Do people in this field work independently? Are they closely supervised? Do they work in teams?

21. How is technology changing this field?

22. What is the job market for this field in this area?

OUTLOOK FOR THE FUTURE

23. Are job opportunities increasing or decreasing in this area? Could you explain the reasons for the change?

24. Is there much competition in this area for jobs in this field? What are the reasons for this?

25. What factors influence advancement in this field?

26. Can you describe a sequence of jobs that would lead to increased responsibility and earning power in this field?

27. Can I develop skills that I could transfer to another field?

FIRSTHAND KNOWLEDGE ABOUT THE CAREER FROM THE PERSON BEING INTERVIEWED

28. Can you describe your typical workday?

29. What made you decide to become a(n) . . . and why do you stick with it?

30. What do you like best about your job? What do you like least?

31. Do you have a specialty in your particular field? If so, what is your specialty?

32. What was the sequence of training that you received in preparing for your job?

33. What kinds of work experience were helpful in preparing you to work in your field?

Step 1.2 Your Personal Concerns

Write down additional questions directly related to your specific career dilemma.

Step 1.3 Identify People to Interview

List three people whom you might like to interview for your career information interview. If you are on an internship or working in a field that interests you, at least one person should come from your internship or place of work. What are the reasons for each selection?

Step 1.4 Make an Interview Appointment

Arrange to meet with one of the people listed above. Be sure that you set up a long enough appointment to get through all your questions. If possible, get a business card.

If you feel shy about requesting an interview, utilize the suggestions given in Activity 5.4, the College Information Interview, Step 1.4.

Record the person's name, job title, and organization. Note the date and time of the interview.

STEP 2 SEARCH FOR INFORMATION

Information Summary

Conduct your career information interview and take notes on separate paper.

You can summarize the information you gathered in one of two ways. You can list each question that you asked and the interviewee's response, or you may prefer to summarize the major points. Ideally, your summary should include the nature of the work, entry requirements, rewards and benefits, outlook for the future, and the perspective of the person interviewed.

STEP 3 ANALYZE YOUR FINDINGS

Step 3.1 Comparison of Advantages and Disadvantages

List the advantages and disadvantages of one career option you discussed.

Hints and Reminders

In the Advantages column, list the specific occupational aspects (e.g., nature of the work, entry requirements, rewards and benefits, outlook for the future) that you like. In the Disadvantages column, list those specific aspects that you dislike.

Remember to listen to your heart.

- Identify which interests and values might be a good fit with this occupation (advantage) or a poor fit (disadvantage). For example, teaching is generally a good fit for someone with Helping or Social interests and a poor fit for someone with Enterprising or Influencing interests. A vice president of a bank is a good fit for someone who values "prestige" and a poor fit for someone who values "aesthetics."

- If you like, admire, and feel you want to be identified with the kind of people you would work with every day, put this in the Advantages column. If you would prefer not to associate with them, put this reason in the Disadvantages column.

- Consider your dream and preferred lifestyle. Does this occupation or career field put you on a path that will help you fulfill your life goals?

Also remember to use your head.

- Assess whether the economic rewards you would receive in this occupation are adequate (advantage) or insufficient for your needs (disadvantage).

- Describe the skills and personal qualities that would be assets (advantage) or underutilized in this occupation (disadvantage).

Advantages +	Disadvantages −

Step 3.2 Tentative Decision

In view of your list of advantages and disadvantages, are you considering this occupation seriously? Identify the advantage(s) or disadvantage(s) that most heavily influenced your decision.

_____

_____

_____

STEP 4 PLAN YOUR NEXT ACTIONS

Step 4.1 Learning Summary

How is the interview information useful to you in terms of solving your career dilemma?

_____

_____

_____

_____

What did you learn from this interview that will help you in the future?

_____

_____

_____

_____

Step 4.2 Plan to Gather Additional Information

Identify at least one additional person from your network to interview in the future. Give the name of the person, his or her occupation or career path, and your reasons for selecting this person.

_____

_____

_____

_____

CHAPTER 14

Reflections

Choose to be optimistic.
—The Dalai Lama

CONGRATULATIONS

What you have gained in knowledge, skill, and understanding from this book will serve you long after you have finished college and solved your current career dilemma. In this final section we will highlight the differences between an untutored approach to career planning and the kinds of actions and attitudes you have learned in reading this book and completing its activities.

Look over Table 14.1, a comparison between an untutored approach to career planning and the *Turning Points* career advancement guide. Then complete the short self-assessment activity that follows. We hope that you see yourself as very committed to ongoing career management.

REAFFIRMING YOUR COMMITMENT TO ONGOING CAREER MANAGEMENT

| TABLE 14.1 | *A comparison between an untutored approach to career planning and the* Turning Points *career advancement guide.* |

ATTITUDES AND ACTIONS	UNTUTORED APPROACH TO CAREER PLANNING	*TURNING POINTS* CAREER ADVANCEMENT GUIDE
Attention to Career Issues	Occasional attention to career progress; typically reactive and crisis oriented	Ongoing attention to career progress; proactive; uses periodic checks to review career progress
Approach to Dilemmas	Haphazard; approaches issues through trial and error	Systematic; gets a clear and specific picture of issues; assesses need for information; relies on self-assessment and research
Sources of Information	Relies on few sources	Seeks out many sources of information
Research Plan	Lacks a systematic approach to research; easily becomes disorganized, confused, or overwhelmed	Uses four-step ASAP method to conduct a systematic search for information and to analyze the findings
Picture of Self	Lopsided or incomplete; tends to focus only on best points or shortcomings	Complete; considers values, personality, interests, and skills in making choices
Knowledge of Work World and Occupations	Incomplete, sketchy	Focuses on four key dimensions: nature of the work, entry requirements, rewards and benefits, and outlook for the future

(continued)

ATTITUDES AND ACTIONS	UNTUTORED APPROACH TO CAREER PLANNING	*TURNING POINTS* CAREER ADVANCEMENT GUIDE
Knowledge of Educational Options	Incomplete, sketchy	Focuses on four key dimensions: nature of the program or training; entry requirements; student profile and facilities; and cost and financial aid
Education Decisions	Unclear about the link between one's college major and various career possibilities; lacks knowledge of degree options; selects a major without considering interests, skills, or values	Understands the differences among occupationally oriented majors, graduate school readiness majors, and multipotential majors; investigates the relationship between major and various career options; selects a major that fits his or her interests, skills, and values and career direction
Decision Making	Uses no consistent guidelines to evaluate alternatives	Employs a balanced style; listens to heart and uses head to evaluate career options
Time Orientation	Present-oriented	Present- and future-oriented; spends time looking ahead at upcoming opportunities and threats
Job Search	Lacks knowledge about different types of work settings; doesn't research companies prior to interviews; overlooks some important job search methods, such as networking; uses one standard resume; doesn't practice interviewing skills	Aware of differences among for-profit, government, and nonprofit settings; researches organizations prior to interviews; uses active job search methods; tailors resume to specific position; practices interviewing skills
Transformation of the Workplace	Unaware of the forces changing the workplace	Continuously monitors changes in the workplace
Attitude Toward Learning	Believes that finishing a degree program will complete his or her education	Understands that learning is a lifelong endeavor; strives to become a self-directed learner
Learning from Experience	Sees learning as taking place in limited contexts, such as in school or a training program; doesn't reflect on experience; doesn't seek feedback and denies negative feedback	Takes initiative to learn from every situation; knows the value of challenging assignments, observing key people, and coping with hardships; takes charge of the learning process; uses a multi-lens perspective to examine experience; seeks feedback and listens to positive and negative feedback carefully; creates a career development plan
Networking	Goes it alone; tries to be self-sufficient	Builds a strong network of mutual help and support; values interdependence and collaboration

ACTIVITY 14.1   **REAFFIRMING YOUR COMMITMENT TO ONGOING CAREER MANAGEMENT**

This activity summarizes the major career-planning and decision-making techniques presented in *Turning Points.* Take a moment to reflect on your commitment to using them to advance your career.

For each item below, circle the number from 1 to 5 that best represents your level of commitment to utilizing the technique in the future. If the technique was not covered in your reading or in your class, circle "NA" for "not applicable."

5	=	Very committed
4	=	Committed
3	=	Somewhat committed
2	=	Slightly committed
1	=	Not at all committed
NA	=	Not applicable

Level of Commitment

	Low				High	NA

1. Paying ongoing attention to my career progress — 1 2 3 4 5 NA

2. Defining my career dilemmas clearly and specifically — 1 2 3 4 5 NA

3. When solving my career dilemmas, seeking out many sources of information — 1 2 3 4 5 NA

4. Using the four-step ASAP method to conduct a systematic search for information — 1 2 3 4 5 NA

5. Considering my values, personality, interests, and skills in making career choices — 1 2 3 4 5 NA

6. When conducting my career research, focusing on the nature of the work, the entry requirements, the rewards and benefits, and the outlook for the future — 1 2 3 4 5 NA

7. When investigating educational options, researching the courses and training provided, the entry requirements, the facilities, and possible ways to pay for whichever program I choose — 1 2 3 4 5 NA

8. Using a balanced career decision-making style, listening to my heart and using my head — 1 2 3 4 5 NA

9. When searching for a job, conducting research about the organization prior to the interview, preparing a targeted resume, and practicing my interviewing skills — 1 2 3 4 5 NA

10. Continuously monitoring changes in the workplace by reading, getting involved in professional organizations, and networking — 1 2 3 4 5 NA

11. Striving to increase my skills throughout my career — 1 2 3 4 5 NA

12. Learning on the job by taking on challenging assignments, observing key people, reflecting on my experience, and planning for my career development — 1 2 3 4 5 NA

13. Taking charge of the learning process, using regular time-outs for reflection and using a multi-lens perspective to examine my experience   1   2   3   4   5   NA

14. Seeking feedback on my performance as well as my strengths and development needs   1   2   3   4   5   NA

15. Continuing to build a strong network of mutual help and support   1   2   3   4   5   NA

CAREER ADVANCEMENT

What's ahead—how many dilemmas? . . . decisions? . . . career fields? Whatever your future holds, you are going forward with an increased understanding about career planning, which you have derived from this book. Your know-how will provide a measure of confidence that you can make the right trade-offs—ones that fit your life situation and foster your personal development.

Hold on to your dreams and let them guide you as your career unfolds. As José Ortega y Gasset observed some years ago, "Life is a series of collisions with the future; it is not a sum of what we have been but what we yearn to be."

ACTIVITY 14.2 Summary Essay

disk & paper copy attached

Endnotes

CHAPTER 1

1. Garth Pitnam, "Dilemmatic Constructions of Career in the Career Counseling Interview," *Career Development Quarterly*, 48, No. 4 (March 2000): 226–236.

2. Gina Imperato, "Fetch a Good Job at This Site," *Fast Company*, October 2000, 352.

CHAPTER 2

1. Roger Myers, "Maintaining Professional Growth" unpublished exercise, Teachers College, Columbia University, 1990. Adapted with permission.

2. Maya Angelou, "The Divining Ms. Morrison," *Working Woman*, August 1989, Advertisement, Sara Lee Corporation.

3. John Holland, "Exploring Careers with a Typology," *American Psychologist*, 51, No. 4 (April 1996): 397–406.

4. Adapted in part from Roger Myers, "Maintaining Professional Growth" (unpublished exercise) and the Center for Creative Leadership, Leadership Development Program's Supplemental Biographic Inventory.

5. Adapted from Charles Handy, *The Age of Unreason* (Boston: Harvard Business School Press, 1990), 78–79.

CHAPTER 3

1. Deborah Betsworth and Nadya Fouad, "Vocational Interests: A Look at the Past 70 Years and a Glance at the Future," *The Career Development Quarterly*, 46, No. 1 (September 1997): 23–47.

2. " . . . I have concluded that the answer to the question, 'How many ways are there to make a living?' is, essentially, seven, or combinations thereof." David Campbell, "Inklings," *Issues and Observations*, 12, No. 3 (1992): 9.

3. Activity adapted from David P. Campbell, "Inklings," *Issues and Observations*, 12, No. 3 (1992): 9–10. The activity is similar to the well known "party" activity in which students gather in different areas according to their Holland personality types and discuss common career interests and hobbies.

4. Kristina Shelley, "The Development of the O*NET," *Occupational Outlook Quarterly*, 42, No. 1 (Spring 2000): 22–28. This article outlines the O*NET framework. The O*NET database will replace the *Dictionary of Occupational Titles (DOT)*, the resource book that used to identify the tasks of more than 20,000 occupations. The *DOT* was revised periodically for more than 60 years, but in the 1990s the U. S. government realized that the *DOT* was outmoded. It reflected an industrial economy and the predominance of blue-collar workers. The O*NET database reflects the need for multiskilled workers and is more flexible and easier to update than the *DOT*. I expect that in the near future there will be many ways to use the O*NET materials for career planning.

5. "Employers Look for Civility," *Occupational Outlook Quarterly*, 44, No. 2 (Summer 2000): 22.

6. Jean Britton Leslie and Diane Reinhold, "New Research Uncovers Shifts in How Successful Leaders Lead," *Leadership in Action*, 20, No. 2 (September 2000): 11–13.

7. The development of this skill appraisal exercise has been influenced by a number of managerial feedback instruments including Personnel Decisions' Management Skills Profile and PROFILER™; the Center for Creative Leadership's Benchmarks®, Skillscope®, and Reflections; Campbell's Leadership Index™ and the Campbell Interest and Skill Survey™; and Michael Lombardo and Robert Eichinger's

LEADERSHIP ARCHITECT®. In addition, I drew on the presentation to the Metropolitan New York Association for Applied Psychology by Elaine D. Pulakos of Personnel Decisions Research Institute Inc., "Defining Adaptability in the Workplace and Selecting an Adaptive Workforce," on October 5, 1999. The activity is designed to help college students conduct a self-assessment of their portable skills. I have devised my own skills clusters and item arrangement.

8. This activity is adapted with permission from an unpublished exercise by Judy Bieber of LaGuardia Community College, CUNY, Long Island City, NY.

CHAPTER 4

1. U. S. Department of Labor. *Occupational Outlook Handbook*, 2000–2001 ed. (Washington, D. C.: U. S. Government Printing Office) and Office of Personnel Management 2001 General Schedule, www.opm.gov/oca/01tables/GSannual/html/2001.gs.htm, accessed March 5, 2001.

2. "Charting the Projections: 1998–2008," *Occupational Outlook Quarterly*, 43, No. 4 (Winter 1999–2000): 2–24.

3. Chad Fleetwood and Kristina Shelley, "The Outlook for College Graduates, 1998–2008: A Balancing Act," *Occupational Outlook Quarterly*, 44, No. 3 (Fall 2000): 2–9.

CHAPTER 5

1. This idea is based on Robert Kegan, *In Over Our Heads: The Mental Demands of Modern Life* (Cambridge, MA: Harvard University Press, 1994). "I would say this: people grow best where they continuously experience an ingenious blend of support and challenge; the rest is commentary. Environments that are weighted too heavily in the direction of challenge without adequate support are toxic; they promote defensiveness and constriction. Those weighted too heavily toward support without adequate challenge are ultimately boring; they promote devitalization . . . the balance of support and challenge leads to vital engagement" (p. 42).

2. Daniel Goleman, *Emotional Intelligence* (New York: Bantam Books, 1995).

CHAPTER 6

1. Donald Super, Mark Savickas, and Charles Super, "The Life-span, Life-space Approach to Careers." In Duane Brown, Linda Brooks, and Associates (eds.), *Career Choice and Development*, 3rd ed. (San Francisco: Jossey–Bass, 1996), pp. 121–178.

2. Adapted from the Johari Window concept developed by Joe Luft and Harry Ingham. Joseph Luft, *Group Processes: An Introduction to Group Dynamics*, 2nd ed. (Palo Alto, CA: National Press Books, 1970).

3. Daniel Levinson, "A Conception of Adult Development," *American Psychologist*, 41, No. 1 (January 1986): 3–13. He writes, "The Entry Life Structure for Early Adulthood (22 to 28) is the time for building and maintaining an initial mode of adult living" (p. 7). This time frame corresponds roughly to the late exploration and early establishment stages in Super's maxicycle of life stages. Of course, as noted in Super, Savickas, and Super, "The Life-span, Life-space Approach to Careers," there are minicycles of new growth, reexploration, and reestablishment each time that a person decides or is forced by external circumstance to change career directions.

CHAPTER 7

1. David Francis, "What You Learn at College Counts More Than Where," *Christian Science Monitor*, April 8, 1993, p. 7.

2. Data on general estimates of major change were difficult to locate. These estimates are based on two recent studies and their reviews of earlier literature: (a) Gary Kramer, H. Bruce Higley, and Danny Olsen, "Changes in Academic Major among Undergraduate Students," *Colleges and Universities*, 69, No. 2 (Winter 1994): 88–98. In their study at Brigham Young University, on average only 15 percent never changed their major. (b) ERIC ED382 068 Microfiche, "Factors Affecting Undergraduate Student Persistence and Time to Degree in Illinois Public Universities," May 2, 1995. In this study of 1993–94 graduates, 73 percent made changes. However, there was a great deal of variation between student groups, with the approximately one-third who attended a single university changing far less frequently than the two-thirds who attended multiple institutions.

3. Linda Sax, Alexander Astin, William Korn, and Kathryn Mahoney, *The American Freshman: National Norms for Fall 1998* (Los Angeles: Higher Education Research Institute, University of California, Los Angeles, December 1998).

4. Kramer, Higley, and Olsen, "Changes in Academic Major among Undergraduate Students," p. 93.

5. ERIC Document ED382 068, "Factors Affecting Undergraduate Student Persistence and Time to Degree in Illinois Public Universities," May 2, 1995.

6. I relied on descriptions of training and educational requirements in the *Occupational Outlook Handbook* and other Department of Labor publications including the *Occupational Outlook Quarterly* articles cited in this chapter.

7. *Undergraduate Bulletin 1998/00*, Baruch College, City University of New York, p. 12.

8. Susan Dodge, "The Hottest College Majors," *Chicago Sun–Times*, January 15, 2001.

9. Chad Fleetwood and Kristina Shelley, "The Outlook for College Graduates, 1998–2008: A Balancing Act," *Occupational Outlook Quarterly*, 44, No. 3 (Fall 2000): 2–9.

10. Arthur Chickering and Linda Reisser, *Education and Identity*, 2nd ed. (San Francisco: Jossey–Bass, 1993), pp. 344–348.

11. Ernest Pascarella and Patrick Terenzini, *How College Affects Students* (San Francisco: Jossey–Bass, 1991), p. 111.

12. Darrel Patrick Wash, "A New Way to Classify Occupations by Education and Training," *Occupational Outlook Quarterly*, 39, No. 4 (Winter 1995–96): 28–40.

13. Alexander Astin, *What Matters in College?* (San Francisco: Jossey–Bass, 1993), p. 264.

14. Paula Knepper, "A Descriptive Summary of 1992–93 Bachelor's Degree Recipients: One Year Later," *NCES 96158*, U. S. Department of Education, National Center for Education Statistics (August 1996): 81.

15. *Emory University 1999–2001* Catalog, Atlanta, GA, p. 59.

16. Paul Lermack, *How to Get into the Right Law School*, 2nd ed. (Lincolnwood, IL: VGM Career Horizons, 1996), p. 16.

17. Keith Russell Ablow, *Medical School: Getting in, Staying in, and Staying Human*, rev. ed. (New York: St. Martin's Press, 1990).

18. Knepper, "A Descriptive Summary of 1992–93 Bachelor's Degree Recipients," p. 59.

19. Daniel Hecker, "Earnings of College Graduates, 1993," *Monthly Labor Review*, 118, No. 12 (December 1995): 3–17.

20. Daniel Hecker, "Earnings and Major Field of Study of College Graduates," *Occupational Outlook Quarterly*, 40, No. 2, p. 16.

21. Ibid., pp. 10–21.

22. Sax, Astin, Korn, and Mahoney, *The American Freshman*, p. 28.

23. Hecker, "Earnings and Major Field of Study of College Graduates," p. 13.

24. Hecker, "Earnings of College Graduates, 1993," p. 4.

25. E. T. Pascarella and P. T. Terenzini, "How College Makes a Difference: A Summary," in Frances Stage, Guadalupe Anaya, John Bean, Don Hossler, and George Kuh (eds.), *College Students: The Evolving Nature of Research* (Needham Heights, MA: Simon & Schuster Custom Publishing, 1996), p. 247.

26. Pascarella and Terenzini, *How College Affects Students*, pp. 114–115, and Pascarella and Terenzini, "How College Makes a Difference: A Summary," p. 254.

27. Hecker, "Earnings and Major Field of Study of College Graduates," pp. 10–21.

28. Hecker, "Earnings of College Graduates, 1993," pp. 3–17, and Hecker, "Earnings and Major Field of Study of College Graduates," pp. 10–21.

29. U. S. Department of Labor. *Occupational Outlook Handbook*, 2000–2001, www.bls.gov/oco/ocos030.htm, accessed April 19, 2001.

30. Margo Kaufman, "College Majors Often Prove Minor," *New York Times*, April 4, 1993, Section 4A, Education Life, p. 21.

31. Yun Jong Moh, "Leaving College: One ET Graduate's Struggle to Redefine Success," *Beyond Exploring Transfer*, Vassar College, 1996, Poughkeepsie, NY, 1, No. 1.

32. Elizabeth Ann Koberg, "Students Talk about Choosing a Major," *The College Board Guide to 150 Popular College Majors* (New York: The College Board, 1992), p. 21.

33. Candace Jones and Robert DeFillippi, "Back to the Future in Film: Combining Industry and Self-knowledge to Meet the Career Challenges of the 21st Century," *Executive*, 10, No. 4 (November 1996): 91.

34. Derek Bok, *The Cost of Talent* (New York: The Free Press, 1993), p. 230.

35. David G. Myers, "The Funds, Friends, and Faith of Happy People," *American Psychologist*, 55, No. 1 (January 2000): 56–67.

CHAPTER 8

1. Marni Davis, "Profiting from a Nonprofit Career," *Tools for Life*, 1, No. 2 (Spring 1997): 10.

2. "Charting the Projections: 1998–2008," *Occupational Outlook Quarterly*, 43, No. 4 (Winter 1999–2000): 27.

3. Ricky Griffin and Ronald Ebert, *Business*, 4th ed. (Englewood Cliffs, NJ: Prentice Hall, 1996), p. 228.

4. Coutland L. Bovée and John V. Thill, *Business in Action*, (Upper Saddle River, NJ: Prentice Hall, 2001), p. 82.

5. William Pride, Robert Hughes, and Jack Kapoor, *Business*, 5th ed. (Boston: Houghton Mifflin, 1996), p. 144.

6. Griffin and Ebert, *Business*, p. 230.

7. Pride, Hughes, and Kapoor, *Business*, p. 156.

8. Lyle Maul and Dianne Mayfield, *The Entrepreneur's Road Map to Business Success*, rev. ed. (Alexandria, VA: Saxtons River Publications, 1992), pp. 63–64.

9. Ibid., p. 41.

10. Phillip Holland, *How to Start a Business without Quitting Your Job* (Berkeley, CA: Ten Speed Press, 1992).

11. Ibid.

12. Coralee Smith Kern and Tammara Hoffman Wolfgram, *How to Run Your Own Home Business* (Lincolnwood, IL: VGM Career Horizons, 1996).

13. Ronald Krannich and Caryl Rae Krannich, *The Directory of Federal Jobs and Employers* (Woodbridge, VA: Impact Publications, 1996), p. v.

14. Office of Personnel Management 2001 General Schedule, www.opm.gov/oca/01tables/GSannual/html/2001.gs.htm, accessed March 5, 2001, and "Presidential Pay and Compensation," About.com U. S. Gov Info/Resources, http:// usgovinfo.miningco.com/newsissues/usgovinfo/library/weekly/aa011600a.htm, accessed April 20, 2001.

15. Ronald Krannich and Caryl Rae Krannich, *The Complete Guide to Public Employment*, 2nd ed. (Woodbridge, VA: Impact Publications, 1990), p. 51.

16. Although many health care organizations, such as hospitals and nursing homes, are often nonprofit, they are not discussed as a nonprofit setting since their salaries and career opportunities are typically competitive with those of similar organizations in the for-profit sector.

17. Davis, "Profiting from a Nonprofit Career," p. 10.

18. Adrian Paradis, *Nonprofit Organization Careers* (Lincolnwood, IL: VGM Career Horizons, 1994).

19. Ibid., pp. 14–16, 133–146.

20. *Undergraduate Bulletin 1998/00*, Baruch College, City University of New York, p. 33.

CHAPTER 9

1. Chad Fleetwood and Kristina Shelley, "The Outlook for College Graduates, 1998–2008: A Balancing Act," *Occupational Outlook Quarterly*, 44, No. 3 (Fall 2000): 3–9. There are an average of 1.31 million college students competing for 1.12 million college-level jobs. Each year more than 90,000 college graduates enter positions that do not require the skills learned in a bachelor's degree program.

2. Emma Taylor, "The New Rung on the Corporate Ladder," *Tools for Life*, 1, No. 2 (Spring 1997): 17–19.

3. J. Michael Farr, *The Very Quick Job Search*, 2nd ed. (Indianapolis, IN: JIST Works, 1996), 14.

4. Candace Jones and Robert DeFillippi, "Back to the Future in Film: Combining Industry and Self-knowledge to Meet the Career Challenges of the 21st Century," *Executive*, 10, No. 4 (November 1996): 90.

5. Farr, *The Very Quick Job Search*, 2nd ed., 14.

6. Small Business Association Web site, http://smallbusinesssuccess.sba.gov/stats.html, accessed March 1, 2001.

7. Alan B. Krueger, "Economic Scene," *New York Times*, July 20, 2000, p. C2.

8. Annie Fisher, "Enjoy Being Unemployed? Keep Job Hunting Online," *Fortune*, January 22, 2001, p. 197.

9. Krueger, "Economic Scene," p. C2.

10. "Top Career Sites in September 2000 According to Unique Visitors," http://us.mediametrix.com/img/charts/us_top10_career_009750.gif, accessed March 8, 2001.

11. "Top-Ranked Job Sites," 100 Hot Web Rankings, www.100hot.com/directory/business/jobs.html, accessed March 8, 2001.

12. Anne Fisher, "Enjoy Being Unemployed? Keep Job Hunting Online," p. 197.

13. Dick Bolles, "The Fairy Godmother Report on Résumé Sites," JobHuntersBible.com www.job huntersbible.com/resumes/fgmresumes.shtml, accessed March 1, 2001.

14. Annie Fisher, "Enjoy Being Unemployed? Keep Job Hunting Online," p. 197.

15. Joyce Lain Kennedy, *Resumes for Dummies*, 3rd ed. (Foster City, CA: IDG Books Worldwide, 2000), pp. 176, 181–182.

16. Susan J. Marks, "Chuck Those Classified: Web Catches Up as Source for Jobs," MicroTimes. com, Issue 215, December 12, 2000, www.micro times.com/215/hrmarks215p.html, accessed February 24, 2001.

17. Farr, *The Very Quick Job Search*, 2nd ed., 14.

18. Martin Yate, *Knock 'Em Dead* (Holbrook, MA: Bob Adams, 1993), pp. 38–40.

19. Rick Melchionno, "The Changing Temporary Workforce: Managerial, Professional, and Technical Workers in the Personnel Supply Services Industry," *Occupational Outlook Quarterly*, 43, No. 1 (Spring 1999): 24–32.

20. James Clawson, John Kotter, Victor Faux, and Charles McArthur, *Self-Assessment and Career Development*, 3rd ed. (Englewood Cliffs, NJ: Prentice Hall, 1992), p. 240.

21. Daniel Porot, *The PIE Method for Career Success* (Indianapolis, IN: JIST Works, 1996), p. 46.

22. Donald Asher, *From College to Career* (Berkeley, CA: Ten Speed Press, 1992).

23. Kennedy, *Resumes for Dummies*, 3rd ed., p. 11.

24. Ibid., p. 14.

25. Ibid., p. 11.

26. "Preparing Your Resume for the Internet and Posting It Online," The Riley Guide: Resumes & Cover Letters, www.dbm.com/jobguide, accessed February 14, 2001.

27. Rebecca Smith, "Keyword Summaries," Rebecca Smith's eResumes & Resources www.eresumes. com/tut_keyres_examples.html, accessed February 17, 2001.

28. Joyce Lain Kennedy, *Resumes for Dummies*, 3rd ed., pp. 142–147.

29. Yana Parker, "Guide for a Scanner-Friendly Resume," TheDamnGoodResume, www.damn-good.com/jobseekers/ScanGuide.html, accessed February 14, 2001.

30. "Preparing Your Resume for the Internet and Posting It Online," The Riley Guide: Resumes & Cover Letters, www.dbm.com/jobguide, accessed February 14, 2001.

31. Robert Bahruth and Phillip Venditti (eds.), *Profiles in Success* (Washington, DC: American Association of Community and Junior Colleges, 1990).

CHAPTER 10

1. Fran Steigerwald, "Portfolio Development: Documenting the Adventure," *Counseling Today*, November 1997, 30.

2. This section draws from information found in Martin Yate, *Knock 'Em Dead* (Holbrook, MA: Adams Media, 2001). Most interview books overlook this topic, and his discussion is thorough. It provides details omitted here for reasons of space.

3. See discussions in Peter Drucker, *Managing for the Future* (New York: Truman Talley Books, 1992), pp. 257–262, 275–279; and Charles Handy, *The Age of Unreason* (Cambridge, MA: Harvard Business School Press, 1990).

4. Ricky Griffen and Ronald Ebert, *Business*, 4th ed. (Englewood Cliffs, NJ: Prentice Hall, 1996), p. 219.

5. The advantages and disadvantages are adapted from Kevin Collins, "When It Pays to Be a Big Fish In a Small Pond," *Managing Your Career*, Spring 1990, 28, 29, 32.

6. Lee Smith, "Landing That First Job," *Fortune*, May 16, 1994, 58–60.

7. Paula Knepper, "A Descriptive Summary of 1992–93 Bachelor's Degree Recipients: One Year Later," *NCES 96158*, U. S. Department of Education, National Center for Education Statistics, August 1996, 65.

8. "Employment Relationships in a Changing Economy," *Report on the American Workforce* (Washington, DC: U. S. Government Printing Office, 1995), 19–21.

9. Rochelle Kaplan, "Handling Illegal Questions," *Planning Job Choices: 1998—Minorities Edition* (Bethlehem, PA: National Association of Colleges and Employers, 1997), E61–62, and David Kirby, "There Are Questions You Shouldn't Answer," *New York Times*, Section: Working, January 30, 2001.

10. William Scott, "Sex and the Job Interview," *National Employment Business Weekly*, February 21, 1982 (Princeton, NJ: Dow Jones Reprint Service, 1982).

CHAPTER 11

1. John Van Maanen, "Breaking In: Socialization to Work." In Robert Dubin (ed.), *Handbook of Work, Organization and Society* (Chicago: Rand McNally College Publishing, 1976), pp. 67–129.

2. The cases of William Lucy, Julie Schenk, and Rachel Gunderson were adapted from Robyn Meredith, "For This We Sent You to College," *New York Times*, Money & Business, Section 3, Sunday, June 8, 1997, 1, 10–11.

3. Ed Holton, "The Critical First Year on the Job," *Planning Job Choices: 1999, Diversity Edition* (Bethlehem, PA: National Association of Colleges and Employers, 1998), pp. 80–81, 84, 86.

4. The Alex Ruttenberg case is adapted from "The 1997 Career Survival Guide," *Tools for Life*, 2, No. 1 (Fall 1997): 12.

5. Donald Super, Reuben Starishevsky, Norman Matlin, and Jean Pierre Jordaan, *Career Development: Self-concept Theory* (New York: College Entrance Examination Board, 1963).

6. Donald Super, Mark Savickas, and Charles Super, "The Life-Span, Life-Space Approach to Careers." In Duane Brown, Linda Brooks and Associates (eds.), *Career Choice and Development*, 3rd ed. (San Francisco: Jossey–Bass, 1996), pp. 121–178.

7. Thomas L. Friedman, *The Lexus and the Olive Tree* (New York, NY: Anchor Books, 2000), pp. 203, 387.

8. Eryn Brown, "Is the Internet Stronger Than Steel?" Special Report: The B2B Boom, *Fortune*, May 15, 2000, 148–176.

9. Friedman, *The Lexus and the Olive Tree*, p. 73.

10. Peter F. Drucker, "Beyond the Information Revolution," *The Atlantic Monthly* (on-line version in three parts: www.theatlantic.com/issues/99oct/9910drucker.htm), October 1999, accessed September 1, 2000.

11. Friedman, *The Lexus and the Olive Tree*, p. 14.

12. Friedman, *The Lexus and the Olive Tree*, pp. 210–211.

13. William E. Halal, "The Top 10 Emerging Technologies," *The Futurist*, 34, No. 4 (July–August 2000): 1–10.

14. Ibid., p. 4.

15. Peter F. Drucker, "Beyond the Information Revolution," *The Atlantic Monthly* (on-line version: www.theatlantic.com/issues/99oct/9910drucker.htm), October 1999, accessed September 1, 2000.

16. Friedman, *The Lexus and the Olive Tree*, p. 30.

17. Bill Joy, "Why the Future Doesn't Need Us," *Wired*, 8, No. 4 (April 2000): pp. 238–262.

18. Friedman, *The Lexus and the Olive Tree*, p. 141.

19. Dan Pryor and Nancy Pryor, "Snippets . . . ," *Speedbumps*, August 1999, p. 2.

20. Friedman, *The Lexus and the Olive Tree*, p. 140.

21. Peter F. Drucker, "Beyond the Information Revolution," *The Atlantic Monthly* (on-line version: www.theatlantic.com/issues/99oct/9910drucker.htm), October 1999, accessed September 1, 2000: Part 2, p. 4.

22. Ibid.

23. Halal, "The Top 10 Emerging Technologies," p. 6.

24. Friedman, *The Lexus and the Olive Tree*, p. 52.

25. Halal, "The Top 10 Emerging Technologies," p. 6.

26. Friedman, *The Lexus and the Olive Tree*, p. 311.

27. Peter F. Drucker, *Managing for the Future* (New York: Truman Talley Books, 1992), p. 5.

28. Anna Muoio, "Should I Go .Com?" *Fast Company*, July 2000, p. 170.

29. Friedman, *The Lexus and the Olive Tree*, p. 447.

30. Lucy McCauley, "Learning 101," *Fast Company*, October 2000, p. 114.

31. John Kador, *Internet Jobs!* (New York: McGraw Hill, 2000), p. 110.

32. Christine Canabou, "Job Titles of the Future," *Fast Company*, August 2000, 60.

33. Kimberly-Clark, The Culture, k-c people, www.kc-careers.com/culture.htm, accessed October 22, 2000.

34. Friedman, *The Lexus and the Olive Tree*, pp. 133–134.

35. Genentech, Inc., Philosophy and Values, www.gene.com/careers/culture/philosophy.html., accessed December 29, 2000.

36. John Challenger, "24 Trends Reshaping the Workplace," *The Futurist*, 34, No. 5 (September–October 2000): 35–41.

37. Friedman, *The Lexus and the Olive Tree*, p. 356.

38. Muoio, "Should I Go .Com?" pp. 164–172.

39. Amy Harmon, "When That Corner Office Is Also a Dorm Room," *The New York Times*, Money & Business Section 3, Sunday, October 20, 2000: 1, 12–14.

40. Kathy Rebello (ed.), "Up-and-Comers," *Business Week*, May 15, 2000, EB78.

41. Harmon, "When That Corner Office Is Also a Dorm Room," pp. 1, 13, 14.

42. Christine Canabou, "Tracey Pettengill," *Fast Company*, www.fastcompany.com/feature/speed/pettengill.html, accessed October 10, 2000.

43. Christine Canabou, "Kartik Ramakrishnan," *Fast Company*, www.fastcompany.com/feature/speed/ramakrishnan.html, accessed October 10, 2000.

44. Muoio, "Should I Go .Com?" p. 170.

45. Feliciano Garcia, "It's Great to Be Part of a Dot-Com. Really," *Fortune*, January 8, 2001, 188.

46. Jim Kerstetter, "The E.Biz 25: Empire Builders," *Business Week*, May 15, 2001, EB30.

47. Jay Greene, "Movers & Shakers: Marc Benioff: Taking on a King of the Software Mountain," Businessweek Online: Business Week ebiz, February 16, 2000, www.businessweek.com:/ebiz/0002/em0216.htm, accessed December 31, 2000.

48. Julie Creswell, Christine Y. Chen, Melanie Warner, Cora Daniels, Mark Gimein, and Erin Kelly, "Cool Companies," *Fortune*, Vol. 142, No. 1, June 26, 2000, 98–124.

49. Profile based on an article by Marshall Sella, "You Have a Cold Heart, Degas!" *The New York Times Magazine*, January 26, 1997, 22–25.

CHAPTER 12

1. Brent Schlender, "How a Virtuoso Plays the Web," *Fortune*, March 6, 2000, pp. F-79–F-83.

2. Ibid., F-82.

3. Alexander W. Astin, Linda J. Sax, and Juan Avalos, "Long-Term Effects of Volunteerism During the Undergraduate Years," *The Review of Higher Education*, 22, No. 2 (Winter 1999): 187–202.

4. Joyce Crane, "No Lazy Days of Summer for College Students," MSN Careers, http://content.careers.msn.com/Communities/college/0005_nolazydays.asp, accessed August 19, 2000.

5. "86% of College Students Doings Internships: New Survey Results Underscore Growing Popularity of Internships," *Business Wire*, Lexis–Nexis Academic Universe, May 9, 2000, accessed August 19, 2000.

6. "How Common Are Internships These Days?" Yahoo! Careers, http://careers.yahoo.com/employment/vault/story.html?s=n/emp/vault/internships/3.html, accessed September 17, 2000.

7. Louis Richman, "A Generation X-er's Fuzzy Career Path," *Fortune*, April 17, 1995, p. 166.

8. The Center for Creative Leadership (CCL) has three U. S. branches (located in Greensboro, NC, Colorado Springs, CO, and San Diego, CA); overseas offices in Brussels, Belgium, and Singapore; and a network of associates world-wide. Its mission is to develop effective leaders. This section of the chapter is based on CCL's groundbreaking research on learning from experience and on its approaches to teaching high-level executives about this topic.

9. Bernie Ghiselin, "Images," *Issues & Observations*, 7, No. 3 (Summer 1987): 8–10.

10. Ellen Van Velsor and Martha Hughes, *Gender Differences in the Development of Managers: How Women Managers Learn from Experience*, Technical Report No. 145 (Greensboro, NC: Center for Creative Leadership, 1990), p. 14.

11. The notion of a "comfort zone" has been used in the Center for Creative Leadership's Leadership Development Program unit "Enhancing the Learning Process."

12. Robert Kelley and Janet Caplan, "How Bell Labs Creates Star Performers," *Harvard Business Review*, July–August 1993, pp. 128–139.

13. J. Richard Hackman, "Group Influences on Individuals in Organizations." In *Handbook of Industrial and Organizational Psychology*, 2nd ed., Vol. 3, Marvin Dunnette and Leaetta Hough, eds. (Palo Alto, CA: Davies–Black, 1992), p. 226.

14. Morgan McCall Jr., Michael Lombardo, and Ann Morrison, *The Lessons of Experience*, (Lexington, MA: Lexington Books, 1988), pp. 67–85, and Van Velsor and Hughes, *Gender Difference in the Development of Managers*, pp. 24–29. The authors note that relationships with good, bad, and flawed bosses varied in length. Some were very brief; seldom did they last more than a few years. The researchers make it clear that they found very little to support the notion that executives need a long-term mentoring relationship with a special boss to become successful.

15. Patricia Sellers, "So You Fail. Now Bounce Back!" *Fortune*, May 1, 1995, 49–66. Sellers coins the term "Rebounders" and illustrates her article with numerous stories. Several of the examples in this section are from this article: the Home Depot founders, the AT&T executive, Graham Thomas Chipperfield, and the American Express executive.

16. Dan Pryor and Nancy Pryor, "Snippets . . . ," *Speedbumps*, November 1996, p. 2.

17. Charles Handy, *The Age of Unreason* (Boston: Harvard Business School Press, 1990), p. 69.

18. Thomas L. Friedman, *The Lexus and the Olive Tree* (New York: Anchor Books, 2000), p. 370.

19. Bernie Ghiselin, "Images," p. 9.

20. Peter F. Drucker, "My Life as a Knowledge Worker," *Inc.*, February 1997, 76–82.

21. Roger E. Herman, "The Case for Liberal Arts," *The Futurist*, July–August 2000, 16–17.

22. Daedre Levine, oral communication, "Career Spectrum: Careers for Liberal Arts Students Panel," LaGuardia Community College, New York, NY, April 13, 2000.

23. Ann Morrison, Randall White, Ellen Van Velsor, and the Center for Creative Leadership, *Breaking the Glass Ceiling* (Reading, MA: Addison–Wesley, 1987), p. 37.

24. Mary Ludwig, "Skill by Skill, Year by Year," *New York Times*, Section 3, Money & Business, June 30, 1996, p. 9.

25. This section draws on Harry Levinson, *Career Mastery* (San Francisco: Berrett–Koehler, 1992), pp. 26–29.

26. Jack Gabarro and John Kotter, "Managing Your Boss," *Harvard Business Review*, May–June 1993, 150–157.

CHAPTER 13

1. Natasha Josefowitz, *Paths to Power* (Reading, MA: Addison–Wesley, 1980), p. 93.

2. Richard Fein, "Why Networking Isn't Sleazy," *Managing Your Career—The College Edition of the National Employment Business Weekly*, Fall 1994, 27–28.

Index